Hiking
Pennsylvania

by

Rhonda and George Ostertag

FALCON®

HELENA, MONTANA

⒜FALCON GUIDE ®

Falcon® Publishing is continually expanding its list of recreation guidebooks. All books include detailed descriptions, accurate maps, and all the information necessary for enjoyable trips. You can order extra copies of this book and get information and prices for other Falcon guidebooks by writing Falcon, P.O. Box 1718, Helena, MT 59624 or calling toll free 1-800-582-2665. Also, please ask for a free copy of our current catalog. Visit our web site at http://www.falconguide.com

© 1998 by Falcon® Publishing Co., Inc., Helena, Montana
A division of Landmark Guidebooks, Inc.

10   9   8   7   6   5   4   3   2   1

Falcon and FalconGuide are registered trademarks of Falcon Publishing Co., Inc.

Printed in the United States of America.

All photos by George Ostertag.
Cover photo by authors.

Library of Congress Cataloging-in-Publication Data
    Ostertag, Rhonda, 1957-
        Hiking Pennsylvania / by Rhonda and George Ostertag.
            p.   cm.
        ISBN 1-56044-592-0 (pbk.)
            1. Hiking—Pennsylvania—Guidebooks. 2. Trails—Pennsylvania—
        Guidebooks. 3. Pennsylvania—Guidebooks.   I. Ostertag, George,
            1957-   .   II. Title.
        GV199.42.P4078   1998
        917.4804'43—dc21   97-28394
                                                                        CIP

♻ Text pages printed on recycled paper.

CAUTION

Outdoor recreational activities are by their very nature potentially hazardous. All participants in such activities must assume the responsibility for their own actions and safety. The information contained in this guidebook cannot replace sound judgment and good decision-making skills, which help reduce risk exposure, nor does the scope of this book allow for disclosure of all the potential hazards and risks involved in such activities.

Learn as much as possible about the outdoor recreational activities in which you participate, prepare for the unexpected, and be cautious. The reward will be a safer and more enjoyable experience.

Contents

Acknowledgments

We would like to acknowledge the trail associations and individual volunteers who help blaze and maintain the trails, the preservationists who work to save Pennsylvania's prized natural areas, and the landowners who have allowed the state trail system to grow. Most especially, we would like to salute the staffs of Pennsylvania's public agencies for their dedication to trails and their cooperation. They have been helpful every step of the way from research to review, and we thank them. We would also like to thank the people we met along the way who volunteered their ideas or faces for the book, and we would like to thank our east- and west-coast base camps for freeing us to do our work.

—Rhonda and George Ostertag

Overview Map

A. Lake Erie Region
B. Allegheny National Forest Region
C. Pocono Mountains Region
D. Valleys of the Susquehanna Region
E. Pittsburgh Region
F. Laurel Highlands Region
G. Hershey Dutch Region
H. Philadelphia Region

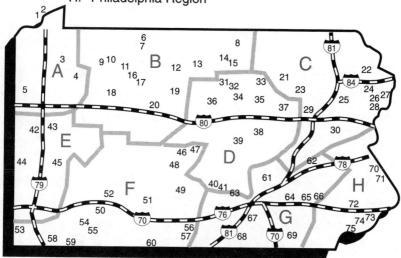

Map Legend

Interstate	(955)	Wetland	
U.S. Highway	(101)	Campground	
State or County Road	(222)	Picnic Area	
Paved Road		Trail Shelter	
Gravel Road		Bridge	
Unimproved Road		Building	
Trailhead/Parking	(P)	Cemetery	
Described Trail		Mine/Quarry	
Alternate Trail		Viewpoint	
Brook		Point of Interest	
River		Powerline	
Pier		Lookout Tower	
Body of Water			
Dam		Railroad	
Summit	2,477ft.	Scale	0 0.5 1 Miles
Waterfall		Spring	
Forest Road	7745	Boat Launch	

Introduction

The Commonwealth of Pennsylvania rolls out like an intriguing canvas, with thousands of miles of trails leading the way to discovery. Hikes range from short nature walks to lengthy rail trails to challenging mountain treks. Travel Penn's Woods and become immersed in its geologic, cultural, and natural tales.

This guidebook samples the gamut of hiking opportunities found across the state. Here, find a collection of nature walks, day hikes, and backpack trips to challenge, excite, and engage you. The described trails explore many of the state's premier parks, forests, mountains, runs, swamps, and private reserves and sanctuaries.

Hikers travel past sparkling waterfalls and outcrop mazes, stand humbled by old-growth forests of white pine and eastern hemlock, traverse broad mountain summits, dip through valley floors, and walk in the footsteps of Native Americans, colonial soldiers, and the blue and the gray of the Civil War. Seasonally, hike in a shower of colored leaves or a profusion of rhododendron and mountain laurel blooms. White-tailed deer seemingly lurk around each bend, while each fall, kettles of broad-winged hawks turn hikers' eyes skyward. Although some of this outdoor treasury is well-known, great expanses remain little tapped.

Pennsylvania boasts a first-rate network of trails, committed management by its public agencies, and ardent groups of volunteers. For the most part, visitors will find the trails highly accessible and well-designed, allowing passage without destroying the natural terrain and habitat. So lace on your boots and see what Pennsylvania really has to offer.

WEATHER

Overall, Pennsylvania offers 3-season hiking. Winter hikes generally require you to strap on snowshoes or don cross-country skis. Spring and fall offer a preferred mix of mild temperatures and low humidity. Summers can bring extremes in both categories, as well as dramatic afternoon thunder-and-lightning storms. Come prepared for changeable weather, regardless of season.

Like much of the East, Pennsylvania can have a tormenting mosquito season. Carry insect repellent on spring and summer hikes, especially in the wet lowlands.

TERRAIN

From the Delaware Water Gap to the lowlands of Lake Erie and from the Allegheny Mountains to the arched Appalachian Mountains of the Valley and Ridge Province, Pennsylvania presents a varied tapestry. Much of the state is clad with hardwood forests, with rivers, creeks, and runs carving deep valleys through the mountain plateaus. The state flower—the mountain laurel, was aptly chosen, occurring across much of the state.

Amid Penn's Woods, naturally occurring vistas are treasured finds. Outcrops of flagstone, sandstone, shale, quartz, and schist invite exploration. A migrating peninsula; a wildflower prairie harkening to those of the Midwest; swamps, potholes, and glacial lakes; abandoned fields and thickets; and a tidal freshwater marsh complement woods travel.

The historic presence of iron ore, oil, and coal did much to shape the development and present-day look of the state. The indiscriminate, sweeping harvest of trees for making charcoal to fuel the iron furnaces—the pyramids of the Pennsylvania landscape—brought about the demise of native conifer forests and the rise of hardwoods.

LAND OWNERSHIP

While this book concentrates primarily on public land offerings, some trails do cross or occur on individual, company, or trust-held private lands. Hikers assume full responsibility for their own well-being when they cross onto these lands; they also consent to heed posted rules. Keep to the trail, leave gates as they were found, and police your own actions as well as those of less considerate hikers who may have passed before you. "Pack it in, pack it out."

The text will indicate if and where a trail traverses private land. Occasionally though, land ownership changes or a landowner may withdraw the privilege of thru-trail travel; respect such closures. Privately operated resorts or reserves may charge fees or suggest donations.

Trails traveling state or federally managed lands constitute the core of this book. Of the state-operated properties, *State Parks* typically include developed recreation areas and visitor amenities, with networks of fine nature and hiking trails and often ties or spurs to the long-distance trails traversing the state. The day use is presently free.

Within state parks, overnight camping is restricted to designated, fee campgrounds; trail camping is prohibited. At Oil Creek and Laurel Ridge state parks, where trail shelters are provided, hikers find first-rate lodging in the wild; well worth the modest maintenance fee charged.

The *State Forests* account for large blocks of open space, where visitors enjoy multiple-use recreation amid the natural and planted woods. Typically, the developed facilities are more rustic. Trail camping is generally allowed; secure permits from the district headquarters. At *State Forest Wild Areas* and *State Forest Natural Areas*, different rules may apply to camping and travel; inquire before visiting.

The *State Game Lands* primarily promote and sustain waterfowl and wildlife populations, and strive to make hunting, fishing, bird watching, and hiking compatible recreations. Trail camping is prohibited in these areas, except along the Appalachian Trail. Learn and heed the restrictions that apply to the privilege.

2

Ancient sycamore, Mill Grove–Audubon Wildlife Sanctuary.

TRAIL MARKINGS

Some manner of trail blazing: paint, diamond, or disk markers and/or junction signs typically guide hikers along these routes. Often a double-blazing pattern warns of a change in direction, with the top blaze offset to the right or left to indicate the direction of turn.

As the intervals between blazes can vary greatly, familiarize yourself with the blazing frequency. An uncommonly long lapse between blazes may indicate that you have strayed off course. Autumn hikers need to be especially alert, as leaves conceal the tracked path. Cairns and stakes are other methods of marking a route.

Several fine long-distance routes crisscross the state, including the Appalachian Trail, the North Country Trail, the Laurel Highlands Hiking Trail, the Mid State Trail, and the Susquehannock and Tuscarora trails.

THE VOLUNTEER COMPONENT

Devoted, energetic individual volunteers and established hiking organizations such as the Keystone Trails Association, the regional Appalachian Trail clubs, and other trail-specific clubs keep the Pennsylvania trail system maintained, promoted, and growing. Hikers should support these groups through membership and through the purchase of their maps and printed materials. Typically, maps produced and sold by volunteer organizations hold the most current information on the lay of the trail, land ownerships, shelters, facilities, and obstacles.

Hikers likewise owe thanks to private landowners who allow long-distance trails to cross their lands. Such trails would slip from existence without their cooperation.

HOW TO USE THIS GUIDE

We have structured this book to aid in the trail selection process. First, we have grouped the trails according to eight commonly accepted geographical regions to ease page-flipping comparisons of the trails. Second, a trail summary presents a quick measure of each trail's overall interest. Information bullets identify the trail, its general location, special features, length, elevation change, difficulty, maps, special concerns, and season. At the end of each summary, you will find detailed directions. For contact information, turn to Appendix D for the complete address and phone number of each named source.

"The hike" component of the text describes the progress of the trail, drawing attention to special features and alerting readers to obstacles and potentially confusing junctions. Mentions of habitat changes, seasonal surprises, sidelights, and discoveries flesh-out the tour descriptions. Where appropriate, we have mentioned flaws and disappointments.

The maps within the text are not intended to replace the more detailed agency maps, road maps, state atlases, and/or topographic maps, but they do indicate the lay of the trail and its attractions, helping readers visualize a tour.

AN EXPLANATION OF SUMMARY TABLE TERMS

Distance measures for the trails represent pedometer readings. Backpacking excursions—sometimes dictated by distance, sometimes by attraction—are left to the hiker's judgment and the rules of the appropriate managing agency, landowner, or private trust.

The subjective classification of "easy," "moderate," or "strenuous" takes into consideration overall distance, elevation change (the difference between elevation extremes), cumulative elevation (how rolling a trail is), trail surface, obstacles, ease of following, and its relative difficulty to the other hikes in the book.

We deliberately excluded estimated hiking times, as personal health and physical condition, party size, the interest of the trail, weather, and a trail's condition, can all influence time on the trail. Gain a sense of your personal capabilities and hiking style and judge for yourself the time. Consider the distance, the elevation change, the difficulty rating, and what you glean from the text.

Customize the hikes to fit your needs; you need not continue just because a description does, nor must you stop where it stops. Interlocking loops, side trails, and alternative destinations await you.

GLOSSARY

Car-shuttle hikes. Typically, these are linear routes which allow for a drop-off and pick-up arrangement or for the spotting of a second vehicle at the trail's end, for one-way travel.

Corduroy. This side-by-side alignment of logs, boards, or branches provides dry passage over soggy trail segments or delicate meadow sites.

Forest lanes. These routes typically are narrower than a road, yet wider than a trail, serving both foot and horse travelers.

Jeep trails. These 2-track routes typically serve foot and horse travelers. Most are no longer drivable.

Service roads. These routes hold minimal traffic, allowing official vehicles only.

Woods roads. These dirt, grass, or rocky roads or faint road depressions represent old logging, mining, or farm routes that through time have fallen into disuse. Reclaimed for trails, most are closed to vehicle travel, although some may allow snowmobile or mountain bike use. We have attempted to alert readers when vehicle use may occur and when it is illegal.

OUTDOOR PRIMER

Whether wilderness trekking is a revitalizing experience or an ordeal depends largely on preparation. Nature does not come without some inherent risks and discomforts, but learning to anticipate and mitigate these clears the path to great outdoor fun.

PREPARATION

Ten Essentials. Outdoor experts have assembled a list of "Ten Essentials"—the cornerstone to safe backcountry travel. The essentials are (1) extra food, (2) extra clothing, (3) sunglasses, (4) knife, (5) candle or chemical fuel to ignite wet wood, (6) dry matches, (7) first-aid kit and manual, (8) flashlight with bulb and batteries, (9) maps for the trip, and (10) compass.

Dress. The amount and the types of clothing worn and carried on a hike depend on the length of the outing, the weather conditions, and your personal comfort. Layering is key to comfort; select items that can serve more than one purpose. A long-sleeve shirt may be layered for warmth, lends sun protection, hinders mosquitos, and protects against ticks. A lightweight raincoat may double as a windbreaker. Choose wool for cold, wet, or changeable weather conditions; it retains heat even when wet. Choose cotton for dry summer days. For their weight, hats are invaluable for shielding eyes, face, and top of the head and for preserving body heat.

Footgear. While sneakers may be passable for nature walks, for long hikes and uneven terrain, wear boots for comfort and protection. Sock layering, with a light undersock worn next to the foot and a second wool sock worn atop, helps prevent rubbing, cushions the sole, and allows for the absorption of perspiration. Avoid socks with a large cotton content, as they are cold when wet and slow to dry.

Food. Pack plenty as hiking demands a lot of energy and pack foods that will not spoil, bruise, or break apart in the pack. Maximize the energy value for the weight, particularly when backpacking. Food fends off fatigue, a major contributor to accidents on the trail.

Equipment. The quantity and variety depend on the length and nature of the hike and on the season (Appendix A offers a checklist of commonly carried items), but a good pack for transporting the gear is essential. A day pack with padded straps, a reinforced bottom, and side pockets for water bottles works for most short outings. For overnight outings, select a backpack that has a good frame and balance and supports the weight without taxing hips, shoulders, or neck.

As backpacks represent a major investment, newcomers should first try renting a backpack. One cannot evaluate a pack in the store with only a few sandbags for weight. A trail test delivers a better comfort reading, plus it demonstrates how well the unit packs with one's personal gear. Most good backpacking stores with a rental program will allow the charge of one rental to be applied to the purchase price of a new pack; ask the manager.

Map and Compass. All hikers should become familiar with maps and know how to read them in conjunction with a compass. Maps provide an orientation to an area, suggest alternative routes, and aid in the planning and preparation for the journey.

Become familiar with the United States Geological Survey (USGS) topographic maps. While most of the quads for Pennsylvania are too dated to show the lay of the trail, they still provide information about the steepness and flatness of the terrain, whether a site is treed or open, waterways, and the works of human hands. The USGS offers two sizes: the 7.5-minute and 15-minute series.

Remember that true north does not equal magnetic north. For Pennsylvania the declination is between 9 and 12 degrees west. Search the map border for the exact declination.

TAKING TO THE TRAILS

Pacing yourself. Adopt a steady, comfortable hiking rhythm, take in the surroundings, and schedule short rests at regular intervals to guard against exhaustion.

Crossing streams. Cross at the widest part of a watercourse, where the current is slower and the water more shallow. Sandy bottoms suggest a barefoot crossing; fast, cold waters and rocky bottoms require the surer footing of boots.

Shed socks before mounting a boot-clad wade, that way once across, you will have a dry sock layer to help protect and warm your feet in the wet boots; wool socks show their thermal value. The discomfort of hiking in wet boots is minor compared to the alternative dunking. For frequent stream crossings or for hiking streambeds, lightweight sneakers earn their portage.

Hiking cross-country. For safe cross-country travel, you must have good map and compass skills, good survival skills, and good common sense. Steep terrain, heavy brush, and downfalls physically and mentally tax hikers, increasing the potential for injury. This of all hiking should not be attempted alone. Even know-how and preparation cannot fully overcome the unpredictability of nature and human fallibility.

Hiking with children. For young children, choose simple destinations and do not insist on reaching any particular site. Allow for the difference in attention span and energy level. Enjoy the passing, and share and encourage children's natural curiosity, but come prepared for sun, mosquitos, and poison ivy. Discuss what to do should you become separated. Be sure your child knows to "hug a tree," not wander, and even small ones should carry essential items: a sweater, water jug, and food.

A WILDERNESS ETHIC

Trails. Keep to the path. Shortcutting, skirting puddles, and walking two abreast, all contribute to erosion and the degradation of trails. Report any damage.

Permits and Registration. In a few areas, land agencies issue trail or camp permits to help monitor and manage the trails and minimize overuse. Check under the heading of "special concerns" in the trail summary. To protect the integrity of the wild, keep your party size small.

Be sure to use the trailhead registers, as the gathered information helps secure funding for trail maintenance, improvements, and expansion.

Pets. Owners should strictly adhere to posted rules for pets. Controlling your animal on a leash is not just a courtesy reserved for times when other hikers are present; it is a responsibility to protect the wildlife and groundcover at all times.

Camping. No-trace camping should be everyone's goal. Select an established campsite and do not alter the ground cover, bring in logs for benches, bang nails into trees, or dig drainage channels around the tent. The clues that a hiker passed this way should be minimal.

Where no established campsite exists, select a site at least 200 feet from the water and well removed from any trail or road. Avoid delicate meadow environments, and do not degrade lakeshore, waterfall, overlook, or other prized sites with a camp.

Reduce comforts (as opposed to necessities). Carry a backpacker's stove for cooking; when a campfire is unavoidable, keep it small. Snags and live trees should never be cut.

Sanitation. For human waste disposal, select a site well away from the trail and at least 300 feet from any water body. There dig a cat hole 8 inches deep in which to bury the waste. This biologically active layer of soil holds organisms that can quickly decompose organic matter. If the ground prohibits digging a hole of the specified size, dig as deep as possible and cover well with gravel, sticks, and leaves.

Use tissue sparingly, carrying a zip-locked plastic bag for packing out soiled tissue. Burying results in the tissue becoming nest-building material for rodents or unsightly garbage scattered by salt-seeking deer.

Litter. "Pack it in, pack it out." This includes aluminum foil, cans, orange peels, peanut shells, cigarette butts, and disposable diapers. For nature to reclaim an orange peel it takes 6 months, a filter-tip cigarette butt 10 to 12 years. Disposable diapers have become an incredible nuisance and a contaminant in the wild. Burying is not a solution.

Washing. Washing of self or dishes should be done well away from the lake or stream. Carry wash water to a rocky site and use biodegradable suds sparingly.

SAFETY

Water. Water is the preferred refreshment; carry a safe quantity from home on all excursions, as wilderness sources dry up or may become fouled. Know that caffeine and alcohol are diuretics which dehydrate and weaken.

When taken from wilderness sources, drinking water and any water used to wash foods or eating utensils should be treated. *Giardia lamblia*, a waterborne protozoan causing stomach and intestinal discomfort, finds a home in even the most remote, clear streams. Water purification systems that remove both debris and harmful organisms offer the most convenient solution. But as these filters come in varying degrees of sophistication, make certain the selected system strains out harmful organisms. The traditional method of bringing the water to a full boil for at least 5 minutes still works. Iodine tablets offer less protection and no protection against *Giardia* and are not considered safe for pregnant women.

Getting Lost. Prior to departure, notify a responsible party of your intended destination, route, and time of return. Then keep to it and notify them upon your return.

If lost, sit down and try to think calmly. No immediate danger exists, as long as you have packed properly and followed the notification procedure. If hiking with a group, stay together. Short outward searches for the trail, returning to an agreed-upon, marked location if unsuccessful, are generally considered safe. If near a watercourse, following it downstream will typically lead you to a place of habitation or a roadway, where help may be sought. Aimless wandering is a mistake.

Blowing a whistle or making loud noises in sets of three may summon help. If you are lost late in the day, prepare for night by finding a means to stay warm and dry. Unless one has good cross-country navigational skills, your efforts are best spent conserving energy. Aid rescuers by staying put and hanging out bright-colored clothing as a signal.

Hypothermia. This dramatic cooling of the body occurs when heat loss surpasses bodyheat generation. Cold, wet, and windy weather command respect. Attending to the Ten Essentials, eating properly, avoiding fatigue, and being alert to the symptoms of sluggishness, clumsiness, and incoherence among party members remain the best protection. Should a party member display such symptoms, stop and get that member dry and warm. Dry clothing, shared body heat, and hot fluids all help.

Heat Exhaustion. Strenuous exercise combined with summer sun can lead to heat exhaustion, an over-taxation of the body's heat regulatory system. Wearing a hat, drinking plenty of water, eating properly (including salty snacks), and avoiding fatigue are safeguards.

Poison ivy and poison sumac. The best way to avoid contact with these and other skin irritating plants is to learn what they look like and in what environments they grow. Consult a good plant identification book. Vaccines and creams are beginning to come on the market, but science has yet to conquer these irritating plant oils. If you suspect you have come in contact with one of these plants, rinse off the affected area as soon as possible and avoid scratching, as it spreads the oils.

Ticks, stings, and bites. Again the best defense is knowledge. Learn about the habits and habitats of snakes, bees, wasps, ticks, and other "menaces" of the wild and how to deal with the injuries they may cause. Also become aware of any personal allergies and sensitivities you or a party member might have.

Lyme disease, transmitted by the tiny deer tick, has become a serious concern in the East, but it need not deter you from the outdoors. Hikers come into contact with these ticks amid grasses and shrubs; the ticks do not drop from trees. Wear light-colored long pants and long-sleeved shirts, and keep your layers tucked into one another. This will help you identify any ticks and keep them on the outside of your garments. While hiking, make frequent checks for the unwanted hitchhiker. When at home, shower and search skin surfaces thoroughly and launder hiking clothing directly.

Should a tick become lodged in the skin, remove it by drawing evenly on the body, disinfect the site with alcohol, and monitor over the next few weeks. Look for a red bull's-eye swelling at the site of the bite; also be alert to inexplicable muscle pain and tiredness. Consult a physician immediately should any symptoms occur.

Bears. The black bears in the East represent more nuisance than threat. Use common sense; do not store food near camp, and especially not in the tent. If clothes pick up cooking smells, suspend them, along with the food, from an isolated overhanging branch well away from camp. Sweet-smelling creams or lotions should be avoided.

Hunting. While most public lands open to hunters do not prohibit hiking during the hunting season, and few have any record of conflict, we would still advise fall hikers to point their boots toward lands and trails where hunting is not allowed. If you hike where hunting occurs, wear bright orange clothing and keep to the trail.

Trailhead Precautions. Hiker's unattended vehicles are vulnerable to break-ins, but the following steps can minimize the risk:

Whenever possible, park away from the trailhead at a nearby campground or other facility.

Do not leave valuables. Place keys and wallet in a button-secured pocket or secure pack compartment where they will not be disturbed until your return.

Stash everything in the trunk, and be sure any exposed item has no value.

Be suspicious of loiterers and do not volunteer the details of your outing.

Also, be cautious about the information you supply at the trailhead register. Withhold information such as your license plate number until you are safely back at the trailhead.

Backcountry travel includes unavoidable risks that every traveler assumes and must be aware of and respect. The fact that a trail or an area is described in this book is not a representation that it will be safe for you. While this book attempts to alert users to safe methods and warns of potential dangers, it is limited. Time, nature, use, and abuse can quickly alter the face of a trail. Let independent judgment and common sense be your guide.

For more detailed information about outdoor preparedness, consult a good instructional book or enroll in a class on outdoor etiquette, procedure, and safety. Even the outdoor veteran can benefit from a refresher.

Lake Erie Region

While the trails are few in number, this region of Pennsylvania boasts a richness of features. Here, hikers travel a migrating isle; overlook the waters of Lake Erie; relive Commodore Perry's heroic naval battle that won the United States control over the Great Lakes; discover the birth of the petroleum industry; and explore creeks, canals, wetlands, and woods. Wildlife watchers seldom walk away disappointed.

Lake Erie and the petroleum boom of the late 1800s gave rise to the region's towns, making the port city of Erie the third largest city in the state. For the most part, you will find the terrain mild and the flavor rural. Many of the region's creeks fan into marshes.

1 Presque Isle State Park, Beach Hike

OVERVIEW

This 3,200-acre state park protects a 7-mile-long peninsula jutting into Lake Erie. The curving finger of land represents a treasure trove of discovery. Within its 2-mile breadth, discover six biological habitats, ranging from open sand shore to climax forest, and discover a moving isle. In the past century, the actions of wind, wave, and current have brought about an eastward migration of nearly half a mile. The isle holds National Park Service recognition as a National Natural Landmark and is recognized as one of the ten best birding sites in the United States.

General description:	This hike travels along the bathing beaches and natural sands of Presque Isle's western shore, overlooking Lake Erie.
General location:	3 miles northwest of Erie.
Special attractions:	Uninterrupted sandy strand, the beauty and power of Lake Erie, the abutting dune habitat, wildlife sightings, weather-watching, clues to migration, fishing, and the state's only surf swimming.
Length:	Beach Hike, 5.5 miles one-way.
Elevation:	The hike is flat.
Difficulty:	Moderate, due to leg-working sands.
Maps:	State park brochure.
Special concerns:	North of Beach 10, be alert for the posted Special Management Area. From April 1 through November 30, the tip of the spit is closed to the public to

Presque Isle State Park, Beach Hike

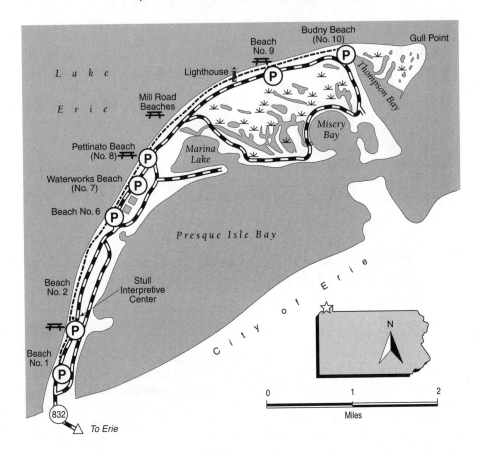

protect critical habitat for nesting and migrating shorebirds; heed closure. In places, lake and wind erosion may steal the narrow strand.

Season and hours: Year-round, with winter treks reserved for the hardy and snowshoe clad. Sunrise to sunset. Swimming restricted to guarded beaches: 10 a.m. to 8 p.m. from Memorial Day weekend to Labor Day, unless otherwise posted.

For information: Presque Isle State Park.

Finding the trailhead: Where Interstate 79 ends in the city of Erie, take exit 44B and go west on Pennsylvania 5, following signs. In 1.5 miles, turn north on PA 832/Peninsula Drive. Enter the park in 1.2 miles, reach the interpretive center in 2 miles, and reach the park office in 3.3 miles. Marked beach accesses branch left off the divided park road.

Beach near Gull Point, Presque Isle State Park.

The hike: On a south-to-north tour, begin at Beach 1 and turn north; the state beach also stretches south about 0.25 mile before reaching private homes. With swimming restricted to the immediate area of the lifeguard stations, hikers find much of the broad strand wide open for hiking.

Vegetated with cottonwood, locust, beachgrass, honeysuckle, and wild grape, low dunes or mild ridges abut the beach. Gravelly sands then stretch to the lapping waters of Lake Erie, meeting it with a downward dip. The lingering tracks from the patrol vehicles steal from the pattern of the sand. Away from the bathing beaches, drift logs and sticks strew the strand, while loose sands work the calf muscles.

Beach 1 marks the start of regularly spaced white-rock breakers, forming a dashed line 100 feet off shore. Together with some subsurface metal grates, the breakers are intended to slow migration and halt the loss of the isle's west-facing beaches. A scalloped shore results.

Travel the sunset beach, enjoying an ocean-like horizon. Songbirds, shore-birds, rabbit, deer, skunk, and raccoon may offer fleeting companionship. Off-season and cool cloudy days promise less bustle, as do sunrise treks.

At 0.8 mile, an electricity generating windmill towers above the upper edge of the beach, signaling the site of Stull Interpretive Center. Near it find a covered picnic shelter, a native plant garden, and the start of the 0.2-mile **Self-Guided Interpretive Trail** that travels north along the dune before looping back to the center. Signposts explain the process of succession and identify plant species. Beware of poison ivy amid the cottonwood-shrub habitat.

To the north find a longer stretch of unsupervised shoreline, with seed-lings pushing up through the beach sands. At 2 miles, reach Beach 6. Where the beach narrows, the abutting bank becomes more pronounced. Breaches in the dune ease passage between shore and the developed beach facilities.

North of the lifeguard headquarters (Beach 7), pass a boardwalk and ramp that allows wheelchair users lake access for swimming, viewing, and pic-nicking. Enormous cottonwoods command notice. Winds transform the face of the beach, launch breakers, present a choppier inland sea, and energize the treetops. The sand grows finer, losing some of its cobble.

Pass below Presque Isle Lighthouse, now a private residence semi-hid-den in the cottonwoods. The still active beacon recalls the past. A treed point and small jetty feature likewise mark the site. Northeast of the light-house, locate the **Sidewalk Trail**, spanning the breadth of the isle. Histori-cally, the lightkeeper used this path to access his boat on Misery Bay.

The buffer between beach and roadway broadens, as hikers pass into an ecological reservation. North of Beach 9, encounter a more exciting, un-tamed beach, with rolling, irregular shoreline, migrating sand, invading young trees, and more extensive beachgrass. The tops of pines and cottonwoods overlook the beachward dune.

Where the terrain again flattens and opens up, find Sunset Point. Beach 10/Budny Beach then follows, for a temporary, although abrupt, interrup-tion to the natural tour. Hikers may proceed along the northeast curving isle as far as beach real estate or the Special Management Area restrictions allow.

For hikers with limited time, the shore between Beaches 9 and 10 encapsulates the story of the isle's migration and the human attempt to control nature. Here view both natural and recreational strands.

2 Presque Isle State Park, Inland and Bay Trails

OVERVIEW

This state park encompasses a 7-mile-long Lake Erie spit, with unique environments and a tendency for walking. In the past century, the isle has migrated eastward nearly half a mile. Recognized as a national natural landmark, the isle captivates with its beach and bay shores, dune and woods habitats, and its history.

In the 1813 Battle of Lake Erie, six of the nine ships in Commodore Perry's fleet were constructed on Presque Isle from native materials. After the battle, the fleet moored at Misery Bay. Battle casualties and those who died during the winter of 1813–1814 were laid to rest in what is now known as Graveyard Pond.

General description:	Explore up to 18 miles of trail through bay shore, inland ponds, reclaimed dunes, woodlands, and wetlands, and visit chapters from Presque Isle's past. The selected hikes represent the range of offerings.
General location:	3 miles northwest of Erie.
Special attractions:	More than 300 bird species, with peak migration witnessed May 10 through May 25 and again in September; spring and summer wildflowers; habitat diversity; fishing; surf swimming; Perry's Monument.
Length:	Presque Isle Multi-purpose Trail, 5.8 miles one-way; Gull Point Trail, 2.5-mile loop (including spur to Thompson Bay); Sidewalk Trail, 2.5 miles round trip; Dead Pond Trail, 4 miles round trip.
Elevation:	Trails are virtually flat at an elevation of 580 feet.
Difficulty:	Presque Isle Multi-purpose Trail and Sidewalk Trail, both easy; Gull Point and Dead Pond trails, both easy to moderate, depending on amount of standing water.
Maps:	State park brochure.
Special concerns:	Heed posted special management area closure April 1 through November 30; this closure of the eastern tip of the spit protects critical habitat for nesting and migrating shorebirds. No collecting, no pets. Amid inland wetlands, standing water can turn back hikers.

Carry insect repellent and take necessary precautions against ticks.

Season and hours: Year-round, with winter snowshoe and cross-country ski travel; sunrise to sunset.

For information: Presque Isle State Park.

Finding the trailhead: Where Interstate 79 ends in Erie, take exit 44B and go west on Pennsylvania 5, following signs. In 1.5 miles, turn north on PA 832/Peninsula Drive. Enter the park in 1.2 miles, reach the interpretive center in 2 miles, and reach the park office in 3.3 miles. Find marked beach and trail accesses off park roads.

The hikes: The paved **Presque Isle Multi-purpose Trail** parallels the isle's eastern and southern shores, overlooking Presque Isle Bay and thrice crossing park roads. Despite the trail's roadway proximity, naturalists find surprisingly good bird and wildlife watching, as well as modest habitat diversity. Share the bustling family-oriented corridor with cyclists, babystrollers, rollerskaters, and joggers. In winter strap on cross-country skis.

Locate the trail's start east of the park entrance sign, its terminus at Perry's Monument on Misery Bay. Multiple developed parking sites allow travelers to vary starts and stops, customizing tour length. With 0.1-mile increments counted off and convenient access to restrooms, picnic tables, and benches, the trail serves both the exercise-conscious and the casual stroller. Find off-season and midweek touring more tranquil.

Birding on Dead Pond Trail, Presque Isle State Park.

Presque Isle State Park, Inland and Bay Trails

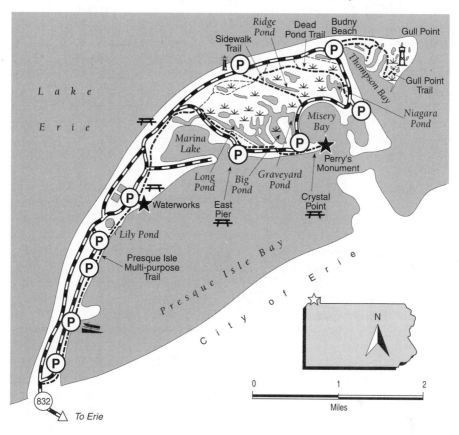

Views include Presque Isle Bay, the Erie Bayfront, the curved profile of Presque Isle itself, wetlands, lily-capped inland ponds, and the watery neck between Marina Lake and Long Pond. Cottonwood, locust, alder, willow, and dogwood intermittently shade the route. In places, honeysuckle, wild grape, maple-leaf viburnum, Virginia creeper, and poison ivy knit a tanglewood. Look for sunfish, snapping turtle, cardinal, oriole, killdeer, heron, woodpecker, and rabbit. A few interpretive signs dot the tour.

North past the Waterworks (2.8 miles), the trail drifts farther from the bay. Beyond the 1st Marina Drive crossing (3.9 miles), silver and red maples join the other shade-givers. At 5 miles, the trail crosses back to the bay shore for the final leg to Perry's Monument—an attractive stone-block tower and water fountain. Its metal crown rivals the treetops.

Gull Point Trail leaves from the east end of Budny Beach (Beach 10), traveling a relatively new addition to the migrating spit—Gull Point, with its 319 acres of rare plants and animals. In 1903 Presque Isle ended at Budny

Beach. The trail particularly appeals to birders. Sixty-seven acres at the eastern tip of Gull Point have been set aside as a special management area to protect critical shorebird habitat.

The mowed or sandy path threads between vine-entangled concentrations of bayberry, honeysuckle, dogwood, and willow. Watch out for poison ivy. Cottonwoods sit back from immediate aisle; birch sometimes grow trailside. Beyond the tight corridor, spy wetlands of cattail and phragmites (plumed reeds).

At 0.3 mile reach a fork, with a sign indicating left for Gull Point. To the right find a 0.4-mile, round-trip detour to similarly vegetated Thompson Bay peninsula. The path ends on the shore below an osprey nesting platform, with a cross-bay view of a beaver lodge; avoid this trail during nesting season.

En route to Gull Point, pass an unmarked connecting spur heading left in 250 feet. This spur quickly meets up with a parallel return route. Proceed straight, still pursuing the attractive wooden signs to Gull Point. More freshwater pond/marsh habitat characterizes this part of the trail.

At the 0.5-mile junction reach a wooden-rail barrier and view of a large open-water pond. Here an arrow points hikers right to reach the observation platform. The left fork holds a loop return to the trailhead, touring amid dunegrass and bayberry, but reserving Lake Erie views until the second half of its 0.6-mile distance.

Postpone the loop, bearing right to reach the observation platform. Ahead find a troublesome wet spot, aggravated by the tide. Planks and high ground generally allow for evasion, but sometimes soaked feet are unavoidable. Sightings along Gull Point may include a turtle burying its eggs (stay back); deer tracks in the loose sand; and monarch butterflies on milkweed. Beach pea, daisy, cinquefoil, yarrow, and fleabane sprinkle the sand with color.

By 0.8 mile overlook Thompson Bay, where splashing fish and the noses of submerged turtles may draw attention. The observation platform rises to the left. Bypass the regularly spaced postings for the special management area, reaching the single-story platform (1 mile).

Views pan the cove curvature; a point frequented by Canada geese and gulls; the textured plain with its standing water, phragmites, young cottonwoods, beach scrub, and open sand; and the industrial skyline of Erie. Return as you came, or make a loop.

A sign marks the start of the **Sidewalk Trail**, which heads southeast across the peninsula to Misery Bay. Find it east of Presque Isle Lighthouse (now a private residence) and 0.4 mile west of Beach 9. This historic trail provided the isle's lightkeeper convenient access between the beacon and his boat. The present thin concrete walk (poured in 1925) replaced the original boardwalk.

The straight-arrow trail cuts a visually stunning line. Pass red and silver maples, cottonwoods, black cherry trees, and oaks. Baneberry, wild grape, honeysuckle, and poison ivy edge the trimmed corridor. At a multiple junction in 0.1 mile, find artistic wooden signs pointing out side-trail options:

Mallard Family, Presque Isle State Park.

the **Fox Trail** angles back to the right, the **Marsh Trail** heads due right, and **Dead Pond Trail** journeys left. Continue on the Sidewalk Trail.

Wetlands next border the tour, with sensitive fern and arrowhead growing in their midst. Here bramble and bayberry form the trail's shoulder. Young trees and silver snags open the cathedral. At 0.5 mile glimpse a matted water seasonally colored with yellow spatterdock blooms; elsewhere view open-water. This linear wetland is Ridge Pond. Red-winged blackbird, turtle, frog, heron, fox, or raccoon may share the area.

At 0.8 mile, look for a beaver-cut log in the marsh and a weathered beaver lodge across the way. A low ridge then builds to the right before the trail exits at Thompson Drive east of Graveyard Pond (1.25 miles). Closing views are of Misery Bay; return the way you came.

For **Dead Pond Trail**, retrace the first 0.1 mile of the Sidewalk Trail and bear left, traveling a trimmed track beneath a mostly maple canopy. Expanses of bayberry-grassland and stands of full-grown sassafras add variety. Soggy pockets can mar travel, at times turning back hikers. Here highbush blueberry finds favorable growing conditions. Birds fill the air with muscial notes and chatter.

Connector trails branch left to the park road, beginning at 0.5 mile; keep right. A vernal wetland often claims the **A-Trail** (the first of the connector trails). Mixed woods follow, with shrubs measuring shoulder to head high. Loose sands hint at the inland isle's dune past. At 0.7 mile pass a stand of pine and tamarack, busy with squirrel and towhee.

Approaching the mile mark, ankle- to shin-deep waters may turn back hikers. When passable, continue bearing right. Again the trail overlooks an open bayberry-grassland, with distant pines off to the left. Birders proclaim that the isle rivals Point Pelee National Park in Canada for springtime sightings of warblers, flycatchers, rails, and shorebirds.

As the forest again builds, climb a 6-foot-high ridge to the right. Spurs top it for views of Niagara Pond. At 1.9 miles, a spur heads left for Thompson Circle; bear right to complete the trail. Views now include an open cattail marsh. The main trail ends at Thompson Drive north of Beach 11.

3 Erie National Wildlife Refuge

OVERVIEW

Two isolated land parcels, the Sugar Lake Division and the less intensively-controlled Seneca Division, make up this 8,777-acre national wildlife refuge named for an extinct lake tribe of Indians—the Eries. Wetlands, ponds, creeks, meadows, upland woods, cropland, and grassland contribute to the refuge mosaic. Naturalists encounter a diverse roster of amphibians, reptiles, birds, fish, and mammals. The three selected hikes explore the Sugar Lake Division. For hikers still in the mood to wander, a fourth trail tours the Seneca parcel.

General description:	3 trails and a short spur to an observation blind present the habitat diversity, welcoming wildlife and nature discovery.
General location:	35 miles south of Erie. Sugar Lake Division: 10 miles east of Meadville on the outskirts of the village of Guys Mills; Seneca Division, 10 miles to its north.
Special attractions:	2,500 acres of wetland; waterfowl migrations (March to early April; September to November); nesting wood ducks; screech owls, bald eagles, and osprey; observation blind; a beaver-pond boardwalk; fox dens.
Length:	Deer Run Trail, 3-mile loop; Observation Blind Spur, 0.3-mile round trip; Tsuga Nature Trail, 1.6-mile loop, with option to shorten; Beaver Run Trail, 1.1 miles round trip.
Elevation:	Trails show minimal elevation change.
Difficulty:	All easy.
Maps:	Erie Refuge and Tsuga Nature Trail brochures.
Special concerns:	Expect wet conditions in spring; carry insect repellent. Winter visitors may cross-country ski or snowshoe the Tsuga Nature Trail and Deer Run Trail.

Erie National Wildlife Refuge

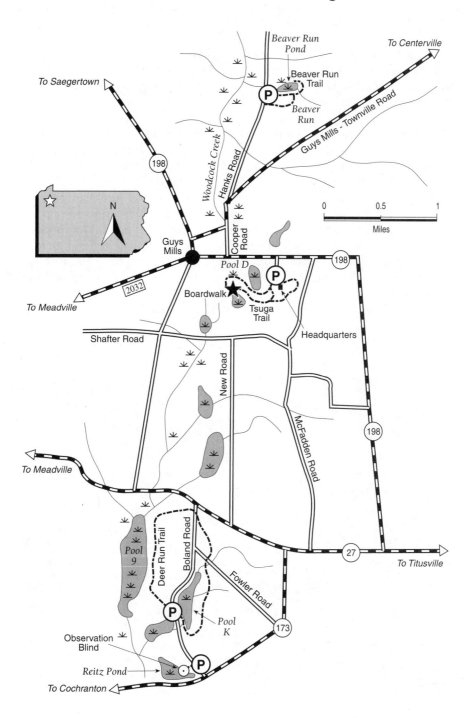

Year-round, except during the firearms deer season. Grounds: from a half hour before sunrise to sunset. Office: 8 a.m. to 4:30 p.m. Monday through Friday.
For information: Erie National Wildlife Refuge.

Finding the trailhead: Pennsylvania highways 27, 198, and 173, all pass through the Sugar Lake Division. From Meadville, go east on PA 27 and State Route 2032 to Guys Mills. From there, continue east 0.8 mile on PA 198, and turn south for the headquarters.

The hikes: Start the **Deer Run Trail** off Boland Road: From the junction of PA 27 and dirt Boland Road (2 miles west of Mount Hope, 9 miles east of Meadville), go south on Boland Road for 1.1 miles. Find parking on the right, the trail on the left.

Hike south along the levee of "Pool K," locating the trail sign past the fishing access for persons with disabilities. Geese, ducks, and herons occupy shore, shallows, and the pool's small humped islands. Woods claim the east rim of the pond, while silvered snags, mats of pond lily, and a cattail expanse contribute to viewing. To the west stretches an herb-and-forb flat secluding a smaller pond and wetland. Songbirds deliver a cheery address, while swallows dart for bugs.

By 0.2 mile enter a thick mixed woodland, with oak, maple, birch, beech,

Tsuga Nature Trail boardwalk, Erie National Wildlife Refuge.

ash, and black cherry. Hemlocks create a hiccough in the otherwise deciduous tour. Small footbridges cross flowing, seasonal drainages. The trail rolls, topping a low wooded plateau. Admire fern, Mayapple, and Mayflower. Markers guide hikers and cross-country skiers.

During a slow descent, pass from planted pines to an open field of thigh-high grasses, peppered with daisy and clover. A mowed track advances the trail. Atop the next low hill, scan the refuge mosaic and then descend to Fowler Road. Hike left along the road for 250 feet to pick up the trail on the right, passing through a shrub corridor.

Amid the edge communities, find field vegetation intermingled with young aspen and maple. At 1.6 miles cross Boland Road, skirting a field of waist-deep grasses to return to woods. Keep to the mowed track, passing between field and woods, traveling the outskirts of Pool 9. Beyond a small wildlife pond at 2.75 miles, reach a 2-track and follow it left to return to trail parking (3 miles).

While in this area, hike the **Observation Blind Spur**. Drive south 0.5 mile on Boland Road, finding parking on the right. Here a 0.3-mile round-trip spur leads to the wildlife-viewing blind. Travel through woods, bypassing a large multi-trunked black cherry, before a peninsular shrub corridor enfolds the closing passage. The 3-sided, roofed structure has diagonal-slit windows for overlooking vegetated Reitz Pond. Spy waterfowl and note their habits.

For the **Tsuga Nature Trail**, start to the right of the headquarters building (pick up the interpretive brochure at headquarters or kiosk). Nine stations mark the tour; encounter all of them prior to the loop cutoff.

From the kiosk, hike a wide, wood-shavings lane entering a mixed hemlock-deciduous woods, edging a grassland. Mayapple and sensitive fern dress the floor. Next pass from dense shoulder-high shrubs to a meadow's edge. Habitat changes occur in rapid succession. Soon follow a 2-track overlooking an artificial pond (Pool D), coated by aquatic vegetation.

At 0.4 mile turn left, touring transition habitat with dogwood and other flowering shrubs, coming to a boardwalk. Bullfrog, turtle, and red-winged blackbird enliven a stage of cattail and rush. Amid the wetland-bridging habitats, find aspen, hawthorn, apple, honeysuckle, and goldenrod.

At 0.6 mile, reach the more extensive boardwalk spanning a snag-riddled beaver pond, noisy with frogs and plied by geese. Duckweed and grass vegetate the bases of the snags. Dark glassy waters braid the vegetation.

Resume amid a moist woodland with skunk cabbage, touring the unblazed but well-defined trail. Enormous old trees add to travel, including a trio of hemlocks (0.8 mile). "Tsuga," the name for the trail, comes from the scientific name for eastern hemlock, *Tsuga canadensis*—the state tree.

Amid a choked, dark hemlock grove come to the cutoff junction, 1 mile. To shorten the loop go straight, returning to the headquarters in 1,000 feet. For the full loop, bear right crossing a footbridge over a small muddy drainage. Hemlocks continue to enfold the trail, with birch and beech amid their ranks. At 1.5 miles, emerge from a young deciduous woods at a pair of benches to view pond and ridge. A left on the mowed grade returns you to the headquarters (1.6 miles).

Reach the **Beaver Run Trail** by turning north off PA 198 onto Cooper Road, 0.4 mile west of the headquarters turnoff. Go 0.5 mile and bear left on dirt Hanks Road to find trailhead parking on the right in a little less than a mile.

Leave the southeast corner of trail parking, traveling a mowed path between aspen. Within 200 feet is an overlook to Beaver Run Pond, with its open water and mats of lily. Sumac, maple, black cherry, hornbeam, and shrubs enclose the trail as it rounds the pond basin. Beyond a skunk cabbage-and-sensitive fern wetland come to the 0.25-mile junction: To the right lies the loop; straight holds a spur.

Proceed forward, still in woods, edging the floodplain; then push through a crush of growth in the bottomland. Aspen and dogwood rise amid the tangle. Cross Beaver Run, touring a low ridge separating Beaver Run Pond and an auxiliary wetland. Here hornbeam and witch-hazel provide the signature look; at the nose of the ridge, choked hemlocks reign. The trail halts at pond level (0.5 mile), with an overlook of the vegetated water.

Backtrack to the 0.25-mile junction (0.75 mile), and complete the clockwise loop (now a left) or retrace the first 0.25 mile of travel. The loop return visits young deciduous woods, ancient maples, and a few big black cherry trees before arriving at an open, but managed field of waist-deep grasses. Rim the right side, aiming for a hiker symbol. A second hiker symbol then points left to a gate at the foot of the slope. Reach Hanks Road and go right 100 feet to end the hike at the trailhead (1.1 miles).

4 Oil Creek State Park

OVERVIEW

This 7,100-acre northwest Pennsylvania state park celebrates the oil boom and the birth of the petroleum industry, but its natural features equally stir visitors. Trails travel the steep-walled wooded canyon enfolding 13.5 miles of quiet-bending Oil Creek, along whose banks oil wells, boom towns, refineries, transportation centers, and cemeteries sprouted in the 1860s. To the north, the park adjoins Drake Well Museum, situated at the site of the first oil well, brought in by Colonel Edwin Drake in 1859.

General description:	The linear routes that parallel Oil Creek (West Side Trail, East Side Trail, Bike Trail, and even the seasonally operating Oil Creek and Titusville Railroad) lend themselves to circuitous tours. The woods along the West Side Trail cradle artifacts from the petroleum era; the Bike Trail travels back in time via interpretive panels. With some 70 miles of hiking, theme, and interpretive trails in the park, the West Side Trail-Bike Trail Loop marks just the beginning.
General location:	The park spans from the southern outskirts of Titusville to a point 4 miles north of Oil City.
Special attractions:	Oil Creek; Petroleum Centre, with visitor information, depot, picnic area, and bike rental; dispersed petroleum era artifacts; interpretive features; broadleaf forests, steep hollows, charming waterfalls, wildflowers, wildlife, and fall foliage.
Length:	West Side Trail–Bike Trail Loop, 22-mile loop: West Side Trail, 12.5 miles one-way; Bike Trail, 9.5 miles one-way.
Elevation:	West Side Trail, 500-foot elevation change; Bike Trail, 100-foot elevation change.
Difficulty:	West Side Trail, moderate to strenuous; Bike Trail, easy to moderate.
Maps:	State park brochure; Oil Creek hiking and bike trail fliers.
Special concerns:	2 hike-in camp areas (1 on each side of the creek) offer overnight Adirondack-style shelters. Each area holds 6 shelters available for single-night stays. Hikers must make advance reservations and pay a fee; contact the park office. The Drake Well Museum, the Oil Creek and Titusville Railroad, and bicycle rental concession are separate fee facilities; contact each for its season, hours, and rates. Find toilets at Petroleum Centre, hike-in camps, and Miller Farm Picnic Shelter.
Season and hours:	Year-round, daylight hours.
For information:	Oil Creek State Park.

Finding the trailhead: Find Petroleum Centre (the main park entrance and southern terminus to the loop) off Pennsylvania 8, 1 mile north of the borough of Rouseville; signs mark the turn. Reach the northern loop terminus out of Titusville: From the PA 89–PA 8 junction in Titusville, go south on PA 8 for 0.3 mile and turn left on East Bloss Street at the sign for Drake Well Museum. Go 1 mile reaching Jersey Bridge Parking.

The hikes: For this **West Side Trail–Bike Trail Loop** start at Jersey Bridge Parking, passing through the gateway at the south end of the lot for the **West Side Trail**. A crush of riparian greenery enfolds the hiker path as it passes above Oil Creek. Yellow blazes mark the trail; white blazes signal side routes.

Ascend a boardwalk ramp from the floodplain, cross over the Bike Trail, and continue up the slope, settling into a southbound contour at 0.3 mile. Maple, tulip, hemlock, big oaks, and hickory contribute to the canopy; diverse ferns and wildflower, the understory. Bird songs raucous and sweet drift over the trail. Deer, squirrel, wild turkey, skunk, and even a black bear may be encountered. Oil Creek remains but a glare beyond the trees. Soggy spots commonly mark the tour.

At 1.1 miles, passage through a shrubby corridor allows downhill looks to Oil Creek. The trail rolls mainly along the upper slope, periodically topping wooded plateau or dipping through hollow. At 2 miles be alert for the double blaze signaling a switchback. Ahead lies a signed junction; proceed right toward Miller Farm, crossing the Spring Run bridge. An old discarded barrel records the area's petroleum heritage.

At 3.25 miles, come to the white-blazed **Lower Miller Falls Bypass**, which later rejoins the West Side Trail. This route travels a more overgrown path, thrice crossing Miller Run. Discover rusting oil relics enmeshed with greenery: barrels, cables, rigging, compressors, and associated engines. Keep alert for the easy-to-miss 300-foot spur to Lower Miller Falls, a 15-foot broad, lacy falls skipping through a dark hemlock hollow. A cable strung between trees warns travelers back from the precariously steep slope. At 3.8 miles rejoin the West Side Trail southbound. (During high waters, delay taking the

Trail shelter, Oil Creek State Park.

Oil Creek State Park

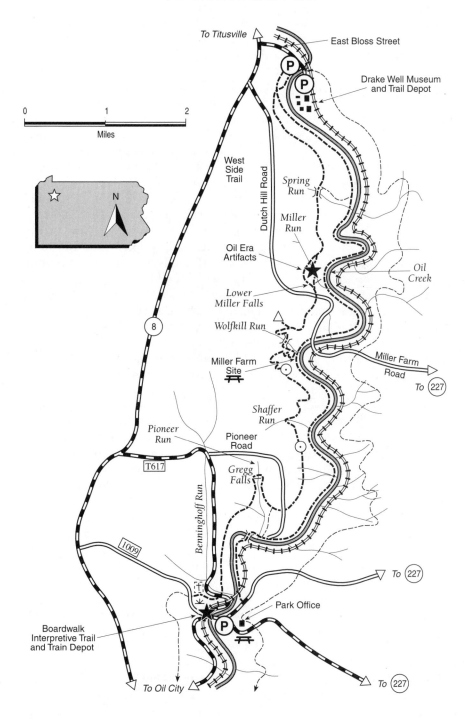

To Titusville

East Bloss Street

Drake Well Museum
and Trail Depot

West
Side
Trail

Dutch Hill Road

Spring
Run

Miller
Run

Oil Era
Artifacts

Oil
Creek

Lower
Miller Falls

Wolfkill Run

Miller Farm
Road

Miller Farm
Site

To 227

Shaffer
Run

8

Pioneer
Run

Pioneer
Road

Gregg
Falls

T617

Benninghoff Run

1009

To 227

Park Office

Boardwalk
Interpretive Trail
and Train Depot

To Oil City

To 227

To 227

0   1   2
Miles

N

bypass until 3.8 miles, opting for a round-trip spur to the falls and oil-era relics without having to wade.)

At 4.6 miles, find the 400-yard white-blazed detour to Wolfkill Run Shelter Site. Ahead, the West Side Trail follows Wolfkill Run downstream to a footbridge crossing. It then remains in the shade of the run coming out near Miller Farm Picnic Shelter and the Bike Trail (5.3 miles). Here, the West Side Trail curves south back into the woods. Hikers who wish to shorten the loop to 10 miles, may return north via the bikeway to Jersey Bridge Parking.

Switchbacks lead southbound hikers back to the plateau; hemlocks shade the ascent. Soon after, find an artificially maintained opening for an upstream view at a long straightaway of Oil Creek with Miller Farm Bridge. On the tour ahead, stay alert as the blazed route passes back and forth from old road grades to trail. Shaffer Run and an area of gigantic rocks mark off distance. At 7.9 miles reach a signed overlook.

At 9 miles, cross Pioneer Road for a pleasant woods stretch. The ground splashes of yellow paint warn hikers of protruding cables and pipes. At 9.4 miles come to the next marked junction; stay the West Side Trail southbound, following Pioneer Run upstream, crossing it just above charming Gregg Falls. From a pair of ledge overhangs, this falls spills in 20-foot streamers. Big beech trees and a ribbed and plated cliff add to the setting.

After 10 miles, encounter some corrugated tin buildings, a small tower, and slat-barrel tanks. In another mile, tour a shrubby regenerating woods—an area salvage-logged following the tornado of May 1985. Cross Benninghoff Run and State Route 1009, for a grassy wade and sunny travel. At 11.8 miles find a stone-block foundation encircling gravestones dating to 1818. A 100-foot detour right on a 2-track finds more headstones semi-buried in the tall grass.

Continue following blazes and wading the deep grasses, coming to a boardwalk over a small wetland. Bypass more rusting artifacts upon exiting at gravel Township Road 617. Here turn left for Petroleum Center and the loop; the West Side Trail still proceeds south. Bypass the **Wetland Trail**, the flag-stop train depot, and **Boardwalk Interpretive Trail** (its pictorial and verbal panels relate the lay of the former town, Petroleum Center).

At 12.5 miles, find the **Bike Trail** on the east side of the Oil Creek bridge. The park office, picnic area, restrooms, and drinking water, all lie farther east (uphill) along the road. Bear left for the Bike Trail, which begins as a multi-use road.

The official 8.5-foot-wide asphalt bikepath begins at 13 miles, with a modest grade, as it pursues Oil Creek upstream. Mileposts mark off distance; interpretive panels present the past. Aspen, sycamore, elm, birch, oak, silver maple, black and pin cherries, hemlock, and a tangle of vines shape the bordering woods. The route skirts wildlife ponds active with turtle, frogs, and dragonflies. Where the bikeway passes under the railroad bridge, find picnic tables.

Enjoy partial to full shade with looks at pretty Oil Creek, a slow, gently bending canoe-water supporting rainbow and brown trout. Among the oil-history panels, there is information on the tornado of 1985. The rich riparian aisle, smooth trail surface, history panels, and occasional tables and benches welcome walkers. Despite the trail's popularity, hikers still enjoy solitude; naturalists, plant and wildlife discovery.

At 14 miles, cross the bicycle bridge over Oil Creek, taking time to admire the water. The trail now remains on the west shore; a soggy floodplain often distances the trail from the creek. At times hikers may spy or hear the excursion train on the east shore. The bikepath follows an old 1860 steam-engine grade. At 15.5 miles, overlook a bend of Oil Creek. A canoe, fly fisherman, or heron may add to the scene.

At 17.25 miles, reach the Miller Farm Picnic Shelter, and then cross Miller Farm Road (unpaved). More wetlands contribute to the tour, as do occasional creek views. This serene and richly wooded creek canyon little hints at its industrial past. Only a century ago, the hillsides were denuded, webbed by roads, dotted by wells, shrouded in smoke, and choked with oil fumes.

Near the end of the tour, view the lawns, artifacts, and oil structures of Drake Well Museum. The trail then descends, entering Jersey Bridge Parking, 22 miles.

By starting the tour at Jersey Bridge, hikers may return either by foot, bike, or train. Before starting your outing, investigate train schedules and times for the flag stop at Petroleum Centre Station. Or inquire about bike rentals and their return deadline. The **East Side Trail** offers yet another return option for foot travelers.

5 Shenango Trail System

OVERVIEW

For the most part, the Shenango Trail and its associated side trails travel the public lands of Shenango Reservoir, a U.S. Army Corps of Engineers project. Explore the eastern shore and floodplain of Shenango River and a remnant of the Erie Extension Canal (1841 to 1871), which brought commerce to the region. Walk sections of the remarkably well-preserved towpath-levee, previously trodden by mules pulling canal boats. Keen-eyed travelers may detect locks or loading bays. Kidds Mill Covered Bridge, at the northern terminus, dates to 1868. Restored, the wooden-truss bridge spans 120 feet.

General description:	The white-blazed Shenango hiking trail explores riverine wetlands and woods along Shenango River and the historic canal. Kidds Mill Trail now replaces the forsaken northern mile of the 8-mile Shenango Trail for a more relaxed, woodland stroll.
General location:	In Mercer County, upstream from Shenango River Lake, 8 miles northeast of Sharpsville; 4 miles south of Greenville.
Special attractions:	Historic covered bridge, canal, and towpath; the sleepy canoe water of Shenango River; a rich riparian habitat of wetlands and woods; wildflowers; wildlife.
Length:	Lower Shenango Trail, 7.6 miles round trip; Kidds Mill Trail, 2.5 miles round trip.
Elevation:	20-foot elevation change between the lower and upper trailheads of the Shenango and Kidds Mill trails.
Difficulty:	Lower Shenango Trail and Kidds Mill Trail, both easy.
Maps:	U.S. Army Corps of Engineers, Shenango River Lake brochure. Or purchase trail map and guide from Shenango Conservancy; it leads hikers to historical sites.
Special concerns:	While annually maintained by the Shenango Outing Club, the northern half of the Shenango Trail is often unwalkable as the fertile, wet bottomland gives rise to unruly vegetation. Thru-trail hikers must have a gung-ho attitude and good sleuthing skills to complete the tour. Expect skin-tearing bramble and rose, beaver-raised wetlands, and bushwhacking through shoulder-high shrubs. Biting insects further raise the ante, but wildlife sightings are likely.
	While blazes have mostly disappeared from the northern stretch, the bridge improvements and fence step-stiles remain intact. Raised towpath sections offer brief reprieves from the floodplain struggle. About a mile of this stretch below River Road traverses private land. Pass respectfully, keeping to the line of the trail.
	Be alert for poison ivy on all sections of trail. When Shenango Reservoir exceeds 900 feet in elevation, the Lower Shenango Trail may suffer some flooding; phone the U.S. Army Corps of Engineers about lake levels. Watch out for turkey hunters during peak wildflower months.
Season and hours:	Spring through fall, daylight hours. Hikers should avoid the trail in summer, due to mosquito population.
For information:	Shenango Outing Club or Shenango Lake Resource Manager.

Shenango Trail System

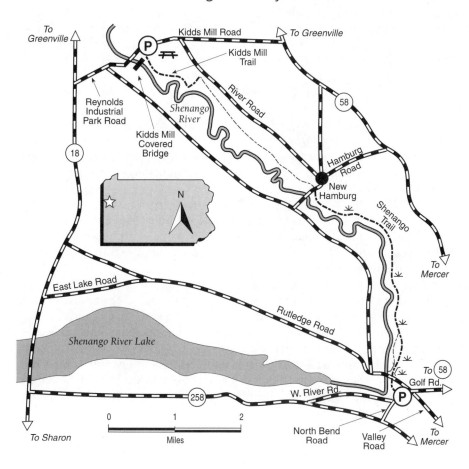

Finding the trailhead: Reach Kidds Mill Covered Bridge and Park (the northern terminus), going south from Greenville on Pennsylvania 58 for 4 miles and turning west on Kidds Mill Road/State Route 4012 for 2.3 miles. The park is on the left. From Hermitage, go north on PA 18 from its junction with U.S. Highway 62 for 8.3 miles. Turn right (east) on Reynolds Industrial Park Road/SR 4012, which becomes Kidds Mill Road as you reach the park in 0.8 mile.

To reach the southern terminus for the Shenango Trail, from the junction of PA 18 and U.S. 62 in Hermitage, go north on PA 18 for 6.4 miles. There turn right (east) on Rutledge Road, which later becomes Valley Road near Big Bend in 5 miles. Go 0.4 mile more and turn right off Valley Road onto gravel North Bend Road. Trailhead parking lies on the left.

The hikes: For **Lower Shenango Trail**, hike north through the trail gateway opposite the parking area on North Bend Road. An elevated sign indicates "New Hamburg, 4 miles"—normally the midpoint, but for this hike the turnaround destination. Blazes are absent at first, but a mowed path leads the way. Travel a valley floor-riparian transition habitat, bringing together elm, aspen, walnut, honeysuckle, dogwood, poison sumac, and wild grape. Milkweed and other field flowers adorn the way.

At 0.2 mile, pass under the Valley Road bridge, viewing the slow, murky waters of Shenango River. Big Bend Fishing Access occupies the opposite shore. There fisherman frequently put in; canoeists take out. Soon after cross a small, but lively suspension bridge spanning an unnamed stream; use the guide wires to keep your balance. Silver maple, elm, and locust trees line the banks. Along this stretch of the Erie Extension, the river served as part of the canal.

In 100 feet, the thin, overgrown **Towpath Trail** branches left, hugging the river, before rejoining the Shenango Trail at 1 mile. Keep to the Shenango Trail, now sporadically blazed. Maple, cherry, spruce, and pine contribute to the woods, while the occasional bramble nods into the trail. Find a comfortable, modest upstream ascent.

At side creeks, the trail forks, with the wider horse path veering off to a fording site; stay the hiker path for a log or footbridge crossing. Be careful on the spans when wet. Deer, raccoon, mink, beaver, turtle, heron, cedar waxwing, and kingfisher may grace a tour. Now and again, the trail edges closer to the sleepy river for viewing.

As the trail passes back and forth from floodplain to towpath, unmarked routes and 2-tracks may introduce confusion; keep toward the river. Skunk cabbage bogs, reeds, and sensitive ferns variously add to the tour; some big sycamores are also present.

Past a canal footbridge at 1.9 miles, hikers encounter a jungle growth of shrubs, topping the shoulder. Wriggle through the mesh, coming to a stately ancient maple. There look for the next white blaze and complete the push through vegetation, emerging at 2.1 miles. Ahead lies a wide grassy lane. Hike left a couple strides to pick up the northbound trail on the right; remain on the track to view the river.

Wetland and woods frame travel as the towpath presents a picturesque, relaxing tour. At 3.1 miles pause for a farewell look at the river and notice the rockwork in and near the side drainage. A hawthorn woodland follows. At 3.8 miles reach an abandoned paved lane, turn right, and in 15 strides round a gate. This marks the turnaround; nearby find a small midway parking area off Stamm Road.

If the trail has received recent maintenance, hikers may wish to proceed north. To do so, cross an old bridge, round a red-and-white barrier, and turn right on Hamburg Road. In a few feet, follow a 2-track left. At 4 miles, look for a trail gateway on the right, indicating "Kidds Mill Bridge, 4 miles."

The tour holds similar wetland-woods beauty, distanced from the river until 6.4 miles. From 5.4 to 6.4 miles, tour at the edge of private property. At

6.75 miles, follow Kidds Mill Trail, passing closer to the river; the northern mile of the Shenango Trail is no longer maintained. The hike ends at Kidds Mill Park at the east end of the covered bridge (8 miles).

Start **Kidds Mill Trail** at Kidds Mill Park, hiking south (downstream) from the levee of the covered bridge. Light blue or blue-and-white blazes point the way. Pass between river and wetland to explore the forest flat of the floodplain. Black cherry, hornbeam, sycamore, oaks, and maple contribute to a varied umbrella; jewelweed often dresses the floor. The 2-foot-wide trail offers clean, easy travel.

At 0.5 mile, the trail briefly nears the river, only to drift away; continue on the blazed route. Walnut trees find favorable habitat. At 0.8 mile cross a side-channel bridge to travel the river bank, rich and green. The trail ends at a signed junction with the Shenango Trail (1.25 miles). Wildlife can offer surprises along the way.

Allegheny National Forest Region

This region holds the state's lone national forest and some of the state's few remaining roadless wild areas, clearing the way to some exceptional hiking. A stirring roster of discovery awaits: lush second-growth forests, intriguing rocky domains, steep hollows, cascading streams, bountiful swamps, Allegheny Reservoir, the largest intact old-growth forest remaining in the eastern United States south of Maine, and the belly and rim of the Grand Canyon of Pennsylvania—Pine Creek Gorge. Rhododendron and mountain laurel embroider the landscape. Small communities are interspersed throughout the area.

6 Tracy Ridge–Johnnycake Loop

General description:	This all-day or overnight hike strings together Tracy Ridge Trail, part of the North Country National Scenic Trail, and Johnnycake Trail. Tour a broad ridge plateau and visit Allegheny Reservoir before pursuing sparkling Johnnycake Run upstream.
General location:	18 miles west of Bradford.
Special attractions:	Rich and varied second-growth forest, a roadless wilderness, sterling runs, reservoir access, rock features, wildlife, fall foliage.
Length:	10 miles round trip.
Elevation:	Find a 900-foot elevation change, traveling between the ridge plateau at 2,245 feet and the reservoir, 1,328 feet.
Difficulty:	Moderate.
Maps:	Johnnycake/Tracy Ridge Trail brochure (sometimes stocked at trailhead kiosk).
Special concerns:	Dispersed no-trace camping allowed; pitch no camps within 1,500 feet of the reservoir's treeline. Late fall and spring, the trails serve hunters as well.
Season and hours:	Year-round, depending on winter snows.
For information:	Bradford Ranger District, Allegheny National Forest.

Finding the trailhead: From the junction of U.S. Highway 219 and Pennsylvania 346 in Bradford, go west on PA 346, following the signs for Allegheny Reservoir through town. Go 13.7 miles and turn left (south) on PA 321. In 2.6 miles find Tracy Ridge Trailhead and its parking on the right. When

Tracy Ridge–Johnnycake Loop

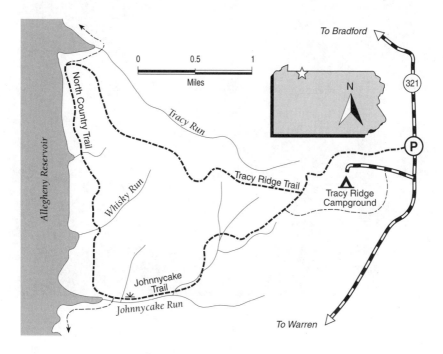

open, Tracy Ridge Campground (0.4 mile south) offers an alternative start. Find its developed trailhead off the campground entrance road.

The hike: From the PA 321-Tracy Ridge Trailhead, hike west on a worn foot track parting a grassy lane. Birch, hickory, oak, and maple shape the aisle. In 1,000 feet bear left at an arrow, entering a tight forest of silvered snags, young black cherry, and striped maple. The forest quickly transitions to tall oak and maple. Blue "i" blazes and white plastic markers show the way.

At 0.5 mile bear right, continuing to tour the broad plateau of Tracy Ridge. Striped maple and young American chestnut are interspersed throughout the woods. Ahead, traverse an area of large outcrop slabs and boxy boulders—a network of vaults and short tunnels, decorated in moss and fern. Historically, Indian hunters used such rocks for shelter. Tracy Ridge Campground lies but 300 feet away. At 1 mile, cross over a wooded lane descending from the campground and spy the green"i" blazes of the 2.5-mile **Interpretive Trail**.

Come to a Y-shaped loop junction at 1.4 miles. To the left travels **Johnnycake Trail**; to the right, **Tracy Ridge Trail**. Go right for a counterclockwise tour, initially keeping to the ridge plateau. The oak-maple forest remains spatially open, lacking a midstory. Enjoy penetrating looks into the forest; deer often steal away in the distance. The plateau welcomes carefree strolling. Rainy and humid days bestow an aura of mystery on the area.

Allegheny Reservoir, Allegheny National Forest,

After 3 miles, the trail veers left for a measured angling descent off Tracy Ridge, passing through an oak-huckleberry woodland. At 4.1 miles, within sound of Tracy Run, meet the **North Country Trail** (NCT), marked by white "i" blazes and blue plastic diamonds. A brief detour to the right offers an open look at vast, tree-rimmed Allegheny Reservoir and access to a deep drop-off for swimming. Bear left on the NCT to continue the loop.

Round the hillside, passing 100 feet above the reservoir, which is isolated by a steep forested slope. Springs give rise to skunk cabbage and muddy the trail. The trail progresses in the rolls and spurts of a moderate climb. Unnamed side runs race across the path; stones provide dry crossings. By 5.5 miles, the slope gentles, and grasses dress the woods. Picturesque rocks add to the forest views. Cross the cascading ribbons of Whisky Run just ahead.

Descend from Whisky Run, approaching the reservoir near the mouth of Johnnycake Run (6.3 miles). Here view the green-hued bay, spying fish weaving through the water. Hike 0.1 mile upstream from the mouth of Johnnycake Run, where a sign on the opposite shore indicates the fording that continues the NCT southbound. To conclude the loop, forgo crossing and instead proceed upstream on the **Johnnycake Trail**, once again following white "i" blazes and blue diamond markers.

An old woods road degraded by runoffs forms the trail along the valley bottom for a comfortable, shady tour. Maple, ash, and hemlock favor the coolness beside fast-racing Johnnycake Run. To the left spans a meadowy young woods with apple, hornbeam, and hawthorn. Pockets of wet meadow and thick marsh grass will also be seen.

By 7 miles, you will begin crossing the forked waters and runoff tributaries of Johnnycake Run, sometimes wading, still ascending. At 8 miles a cross-canyon view through the woods presents a waterfall on a Johnnycake side tributary. Where diamond markers and paint blazes direct you to alternate routes, follow the diamond markers—these are the improved re-routes. At 8.4 miles the Interpretive Trail joins the Johnnycake Trail on the right. At 8.6 miles, you will come to the conclusion of the loop; bear right, retracing the initial 1.4 miles to the trailhead.

7   Morrison Trail

General description:	This circuitous tour travels through varied forest, effusive mountain laurel passages, and bouldered areas, with a side-trail visit to a shoreline camp on the Kinzua Creek Arm of Allegheny Reservoir.
General location:	16 miles east of Warren.
Special attractions:	Hike-in campground, Allegheny Reservoir, mixed second-growth forest, crystalline runs, unique rock features, wildlife sightings, mountain laurel blooms (mid- to late June), fall foliage.
Length:	12.4 miles round trip, with spur to Morrison Hike-in/ Boat-in Campground.
Elevation:	Travel between a rim elevation of 2,000 feet and a reservoir elevation of 1,328 feet.
Difficulty:	Moderate.
Maps:	Morrison Trail brochure, sometimes stocked at trailhead.
Special concerns:	Dispersed no-trace camping is allowed; pitch no camps within 1,500 feet of the reservoir's treeline and no camping at the trailhead parking lot. Late fall and spring, this trail serves hunters as well.
Season and hours:	Year-round, depending on winter snows.
For information:	Bradford Ranger District, Allegheny National Forest.

Finding the trailhead: Find the marked trailhead parking area on the south side of Pennsylvania 59, 16 miles east of Warren; 26 miles west of Smethport.

The hike: Follow the wide forest trail south for a slow descent through a tall maple-oak complex adorned with hay-scented fern. These ferns grow with abandon—deer find them distasteful. Black cherry and small hemlock fill out the forest. At 0.5 mile reach the Y-shaped loop junction near a large boulder; go right for a counterclockwise loop. Blue "i" blazes and white diamond markers point the way.

Morrison Trail

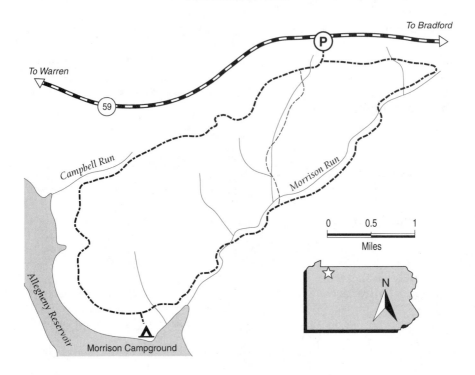

To Bradford

To Warren

P

59

Campbell Run

Morrison Run

Allegheny Reservoir

Morrison Campground

0   0.5   1

Miles

N

At 0.75 mile stone-step across an upper fork of Morrison Run and bear right up the slope, avoiding an abandoned section of trail ahead. Where diamond markers and blazes disagree, follow the diamond-marked trail.

Encounter the first mountain laurel passage at 1 mile. A porcupine may waddle by, deer may flee, or a woodpecker may telegraph its location. The song of upper Morrison Run drifts through the forest. Laurel alternately disperses and crowds the trail. Seasonally, dogwoods add an umbrella of bloom.

Enjoy a rolling meander; dark boulders contribute to the laurel-woodland enchantment. At the T-junction at 1.6 miles, follow the marked trail left along an abandoned woods road. At the Y-junction at 2.4 miles, bear left for 0.1 mile and then veer right, once again slowly descending.

The descent accelerates after the trail crosses the head of Campbell Run. It again travels fragments of woods roads as it pursues the run downstream. Iceberg-like rocks rise amid the forest, while birch, ash, and beech vary the ranks.

Near the bottom of the slope, look for the trail to turn left. Travel amid a dark, mature second-growth hemlock-beech forest on a more difficult trailbed. The trail then rolls, topping the divide between Campbell and

Morrison runs. As the trail rounds toward Morrison Run, spy the glint of Allegheny Reservoir.

Pass through an area showing half-a-dozen elephant-sized boulders to descend via a large grassy woods road. At 5.1 miles, the trail turns left off the descending grade to follow the slope, weaving through yet another rock field.

Where the slope flattens out, travel a habitat of hawthorn and highbush blueberry, with a meadow-grass floor. Oozing mud, low branches, and thorny bushes can impede travel. At 6.3 miles, reach the signed junction for Morrison Campground. Proceed forward to hike the loop; detour right to visit the campground and Morrison Bay in 0.2 mile. Interspersed amid the shoreline trees find 40 boat-to/hike-in campsites with vault toilets and a pump for drinking water. From camp, view the serial ridges framing the reservoir and descending to its shores.

To resume the loop at 6.7 miles, bear right, quickly cross the run near the campground, and pass through serene forest. Next, hike along either woods lane or bank, pursuing the attractive Morrison Run upstream. During high waters, the run becomes braided, and following the blazes may require several fordings. Keep to the north shore of the main run.

At 8.6 miles, prior to the West Fork's confluence with the main stem, you will see the cut-off trail to shorten the loop, heading uphill to the left. Proceed forward, crossing the West Fork, for the full 12.4-mile tour.

Enjoy a relaxing jaunt closely paired with scenic Morrison Run. Ferns contribute to the bank's beauty. At 9 miles comes the first of four main-stem crossings; wading may be necessary during high water. The trail still ascends. Boulders now contribute to the stream and woods.

White-tailed deer, Allegheny National Forest.

At 10.5 miles return to the north shore, touring a high-canopy forest with a fragrant fern floor. After a brief, steep ascent, you reach the rim plateau (10.8 miles), crossing a side drainage. Maple and oak again rule, but are interlaced with laurel. Tulip and cucumber trees may shower their lofty blossoms onto the trail. Top the next rim tier, closing the loop at 11.9 miles. Bear right to return to the trailhead.

8 C. Lynn Keller Trail

General description: Some 9 miles of interlocking foot trail explore 13,200-acre State Game Lands Number 37, which adjoins the Tioga-Hammond reservoir tract—a U.S. Army Corps of Engineers project. This relaxing circuit explores the Ives Run drainage, traveling the sometimes-steep wooded slopes and traversing the summit plateau of Bald Hill.

General location: 13 miles northeast of Wellsboro.

Special attractions: Mixed forest, meadow-shrub habitat, mountain laurel, berry bushes, a seasonal vista, wildlife sightings, and bird watching along the nearby 2.6-mile Rail Trail (open September through March; take the gravel road on the right as you approach the administration building).

Length: C. Lynn Keller Trail, 8 miles round trip.

Elevation: Travel from 1,100 feet near Hammond Lake to a summit elevation of 2,142 feet atop Bald Hill.

Difficulty: Moderate.

Maps: Trail flier (generally stocked at trailhead) or consult trailhead mapboard.

Special concerns: Following heavy rains expect to encounter soggy stretches on the final leg of the loop. While seldom seen, timber rattlesnakes are found in the area. Spring and fall, hunters share the State Game Land.

Season and hours: Spring through fall, daylight hours. Ives Run Recreation Area: 8 a.m. to dusk for day use.

For information: U.S. Army Corps of Engineers, Tioga-Hammond Lakes.

Finding the trailhead: Follow Pennsylvania 287 North/U.S. Highway 6 West out of Wellsboro, remaining on PA 287 North. Go 11.8 miles and turn right for Ives Run Recreation Area. Proceed straight on Ives Run Access Road for 0.8 mile, meeting Stephenhouse Road. Locate the main trailhead and its parking area off Stephenhouse Road near the intersection. Find alternative accesses at Ives Run Campground and farther south off Stephenhouse Road.

The hike: Starting from the main trailhead, hike east following the orange-circle blazes; elsewhere remnant yellow blazes also signal the trail. With a steep 0.1-mile climb, enter an easier stretch beneath a varied umbrella of oak, maple, birch, beech, hemlock, and witch hazel. Green shoots pierce the leaf mat. Mountain laurel and fern pockets vary the views.

Bypass a wooden lattice cylinder, and traverse a grassy wildflower clearing. An old jeep trail then continues the tour as it returns to woods and begins to climb. At 0.5 mile come to a signed junction. To the left lies the campground; bear right for the scenic vista and loop. Songbirds, red efts, turkey, deer, grouse, and even a black bear may offer fleeting companionship.

C. Lynn Keller Trail

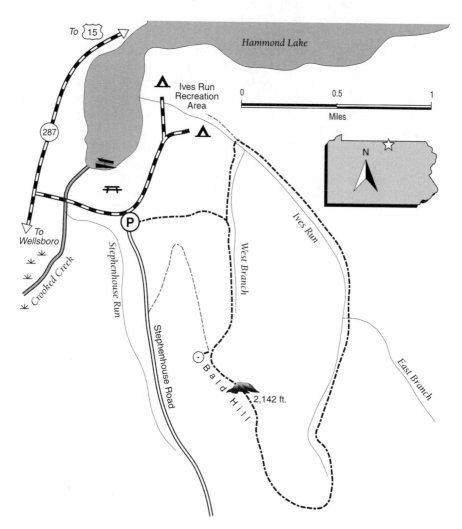

As you climb, you lose the background drone of PA 287. Tall mountain laurel congests the midstory, while planted pines pierce the forest canopy. By 1 mile ascend beside the rocky, barely trickling West Branch Ives Run; here the climb intensifies and becomes rocky. Be careful when the ground is wet or leafy. The climb eases above the drainage head.

At 2 miles top Bald Hill, finding a ridgetop junction. Straight now leads to the vista; a left continues the counterclockwise loop; right leads to southern Stephenhouse Road access. Go straight, descending amid pine-oak woods and berry bushes, reaching the natural vista ledge in 250 feet. The ledge extends comfortable seating and seasonal views. Admire the immediate forest and backdrop ridge, the rimming bracken fern, and columbine color.

Resume the counterclockwise loop, with a relaxing ridgetop stroll, passing amid oak-maple woods. Berry bushes, laurel, witch hazel, and striped maple weave a rich midstory. Early morning hikes often have an ethereal quality as sunbeams deflect through the morning mist. Travel a broad grassy track with attractive fern shoulders before turning left at 3.5 miles for a mild descent.

Cross the fern-clad head of Ives Run drainage, once again enjoying the classic beauty of gray birch and beech. A gnarly old multi-trunked maple nudges the trail as hikers arrive at the first of a series of springs, which support jewelweed. After rains, expect to do some tricky stepping or outright slogging between 4.2 and 5.25 miles. The woods lend serenity, while Ives Run adds its steady, gentle voice.

At 5.25 miles cross the East Branch Ives Run. Hemlocks precede this running water. More sopping travel may follow, as a grassy lane or old jeep trail advances the tour amid woods of small-diameter shad, hophornbeam, and hornbeam. In places, apple and other fruit trees hint at an old orchard. Hickory and ash represent the big trees. Be alert for wildlife.

With a slight rise find dry footing (6.7 miles), just as the tour turns left off the jeep trail. Now follow a blazed path through transition meadow and hawthorn-elm woodland. Over-the-shoulder looks present the ridge of Bald Hill. Reach the next junction in 7 miles. To the right lies the campground; turn left to return to the main trailhead.

Explore an alder-shrub transition habitat, coming out at Ives Run. Next trace the cobble-bottomed run upstream to the crossing at 7.1 miles (sometimes a wading). Forest then houses the trail as it ascends to close the loop, 7.5 miles. Turn right at the loop junction to return to parking, 8 miles.

9 Hickory Creek Wilderness

OVERVIEW

This 8,663-acre roadless area in Allegheny National Forest represents the sole landlocked federal·wilderness in all of Pennsylvania, New York, Ohio, Maryland, and New Jersey. Pennsylvania's only other designated wilderness consists of the seven Allegheny River Islands. A loop trail bounded by East and Middle Hickory creeks explores the gently rolling wilderness terrain of ridge plateaus and creek valleys. Traverse a quiet realm of hardwood and hemlock forests and broad meadows, shared by deer, porcupine, raccoon, fox, pileated woodpecker, turkey, black bear, and more. Faint skid roads, woods roads, and an abandoned rail grade hint at former logging camps that pre-date the wilderness. The area was logged in 1837 and again after 1910.

General description: An all-day or backpack hike celebrates the calm and beauty of Pennsylvania's prized wilderness.

General location: 15 miles southwest of Warren.

Special attractions: Mature second-growth forest, thick meadows, fish-supporting runs, wildlife sightings, fall foliage.

Length: Hickory Creek Trail, 12.1 miles round trip.

Elevation: Travel from a trailhead elevation of 1,900 feet to an elevation of 1,500 feet at both Jacks and Coon runs.

Difficulty: Moderate.

Maps: Hickory Creek and Allegheny River Islands Wilderness brochure (seasonally available at trail register).

Special concerns: In keeping with the wilderness spirit and to provide a challenge for hikers, intentionally faint yellow blazes (sometimes spread far apart) mark the way. Portions of trail may be difficult to follow after the trees drop their leaves or when the trail first opens in spring. Once regular foot traffic begins, find fairly easy travel. Note the blazes both ahead and behind you for clues. Off-trail exploration requires a map and compass.

As in any federal wilderness, no bikes and no motorized vehicles are allowed. Hikers may pitch dispersed no-trace campsites; keep them 200 feet away from streams and trails. Limit stays to 2 days per site, and keep party size small. Hunting occurs October through December and April and May.

Season and hours: Spring through fall for hiking, with winter cross-country skiing.

For information: Bradford Ranger District, Allegheny National Forest.

Hickory Creek Wilderness

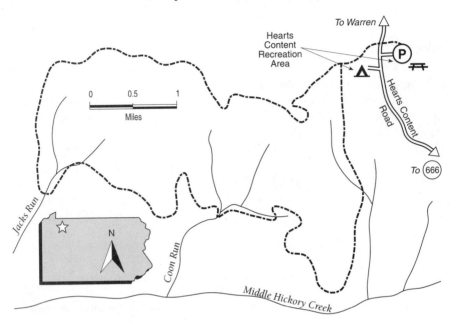

Finding the trailhead: At the intersection of U.S. Highway 6 and Mohawk Avenue in Warren, go south on Pleasant Drive, following the signs for Hearts Content. In 10.7 miles, keep left on oiled State Route 2002, as the main road curves right. Go another 3.5 miles and turn left for Hearts Content Scenic Area. On the left find a large gravel parking lot and access to Hickory Creek Wilderness; no camping at trailhead.

The hikes: From the northeast corner of trail parking, enter a regimented red pine plantation, following the yellow "i" blazes on a diagonal course northwest to SR 2002. At 0.2 mile cross the road and pass under a powerline to travel through a mature second-growth forest of black cherry, beech, maple, ash, and oak. The wide path now allows easy strolling.

At 0.5 mile come upon a trail register and mapbox, with the loop junction for **Hickory Creek Trail** 100 feet beyond it. To the right begins the north-side tour; straight is the south-side one. Go right for a counterclockwise trip, descending and rolling amid a deep woods of young hemlock and mixed deciduous trees. From the trail, spy mountain laurel growing at the grove's lighted outskirts. Where the trail returns to mature hardwoods, many of the trees show multiple trunks.

The wilderness extends a stress-erasing calm. At 1.3 and 1.7 miles, cross over faint logging roads. Rotting stumps recall a forest of old. The rolling trail shows a general downhill orientation. Leaf mat dominates, with a few

Jacks Run, Hickory Creek Wilderness, Allegheny National Forest.

A Mushroom in the Hickory Creek Wilderness, Allegheny National Forest.

fern pockets; large mushrooms commonly pierce the duff.

At 2.7 miles step over a rock, avoiding a tracked path that passes in front of it. Where the trail next descends, pass amid some mossy, solitary, and jumbled rocks. By 3.5 miles snags create a more open cathedral. Ahead travel the rim, overlooking the forested drainage of East Hickory Creek, again finding fuller woods. The overhead leaf pattern engages.

Descend touring the foot of the slope, with its meadowy forest floor. At 5.3 miles, cross hemlock-shaded 5- to 10-foot-wide Jacks Run either by fortuitous log or by wading. A previously used campsite lies near the crossing; avoid the paths branching from the camp.

Upon crossing, follow a time-healed railroad grade pursuing Jacks Run upstream; a few ties remain in place. Skirt open meadows, ducking under a multi-trunked hornbeam. Cross back over Jacks Run, traversing a deep-grass meadow where hidden fawns await their mother. With a third crossing, ascend away from Jacks Run, reaching a saddle (6.4 miles).

Next cross a broad, straight clearing recalling a one-time artillery range. Woods again bring shade. As the trail descends from the saddle, grape vines—both woody and fruit-bearing—entangle the trees; tulip poplars find habitat on the moist lower slope.

At 7.5 miles, follow Coon Creek downstream, cross, and parallel the waterway back upstream. Deep, narrow pools hold small fish. Pass amid meadow-edge woods, finding springs muddying the way. Cross a head fork of Coon Run at 8 miles to ascend along a scenic woods road for the next 0.4 mile. Stay alert for the blazes pointing the tour off the road and through a drainage dip. A fern understory complements the dark tree trunks. A more meandering ascent follows.

By 9.25 miles travel the upper slope and rim above the Middle Hickory Creek drainage. More sunlight penetrates the forest here. The trail again rolls. At 10.6 miles cross an old road grade and follow a side drainage upstream through hemlock forest. Here, find the 1st rocky stretch of the tour.

Where the trail tops out, bear left again crossing a woods road. Hemlocks once more create a deep-woods aura. At 11.6 miles close the loop; bear right to return to the trailhead, 12.1 miles.

10 Hearts Content Interpretive Trail

General description:	2 interlocking interpretive loops pass amid towering old-growth trees, offering a neck-craning tour. Signs identify tree species, compare bark, explain succession, and discuss the forest's evolution. The initial 0.25-mile loop offers wheelchair and stroller access. An audio tape may be checked out at the ranger district or in summer, from the host at Hearts Content Campground.
General location:	15 miles southwest of Warren.
Special attractions:	121 acres of virgin forest, springs draining to the headwaters of West Branch Tionesta Creek, a logging display, ferns.
Length:	Fully Accessible Loop, 0.25 mile; Long Loop, 1.25 miles.
Elevation:	The trails show minimal grade, touring at an elevation of 1,800 feet. Find less than a 5 percent grade on the fully accessible loop.
Difficulty:	Easy.
Maps:	Hearts Content Scenic Area Interpretive Trail brochure.
Special concerns:	During wind storms, beware of falling branches. Find a toilet and drinking water at the trailhead/picnic area. No camping or fires in the Scenic Area.
Season and hours:	Spring through fall, with winter cross-country skiing.
For information:	Bradford Ranger District, Allegheny National Forest.

Finding the trailhead: At the intersection of U.S. Highway 6 and Mohawk Avenue in Warren, go south on Pleasant Drive, following the signs for Hearts Content. In 10.7 miles, keep left on oiled State Route 2002, as the main road curves right. Go another 3.5 miles and turn left for Hearts Content Scenic Area. On the left find a large gravel parking lot, with limited parking at the picnic area/trailhead at road's end.

Hearts Content Interpretive Trail

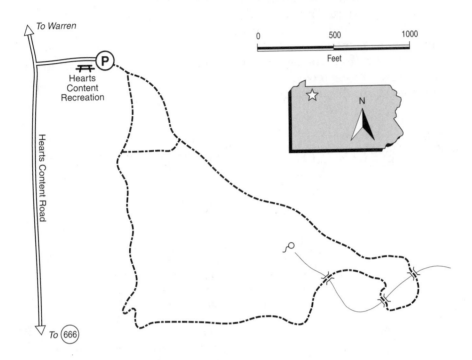

The hike: This trail salutes a tiny, but significant remnant grove of 300- to 400-year-old trees, including white pine, eastern hemlock, American beech, black cherry, and sugar maple. The scenic area won National Natural Landmark distinction in 1977. Trees tower 100 to 150 feet above the forest floor and boast diameters of 4 feet.

Intriguing snags pierce the skyline, hinting at natural catastrophes that opened the stand allowing the young white pines and other light-loving species to gain a foothold. A severe drought in 1644, followed by years of fire, gave the giant white pines of today their initial start. This grove is a looking glass to the past, pre-dating the pioneers and the saws that came with them.

The wide, crushed-limestone trail starts at the east end of the picnic area. An information kiosk and display on logging marks the start. Note the squaring of the exhibit pine; it shows how trees were readied for transportation and floated as river rafts to mills and markets.

Giant beech and oak frame the trail's start. Beech bark disease steals the normally smooth skin of some of the beech trees. Biologists estimate the large beech in this grove will most likely disappear in twenty years.

In 50 feet, you will reach a sensory panel on tree bark and the loop junction; bear left for a clockwise tour of the shallow basin and its gallery of big trees. More logs and stumps open the forest cathedral. Respect the integrity of this ancient grove.

Near a fenced site protecting regenerating forest from deer, the 0.25-mile **Fully Accessible Loop** turns right. Keep going straight to take the **Long Loop**, entering the heart of the big-tree area. Elsewhere, overbrowsing deer have stolen the young forest shoots, while ferns, distasteful to them, thrive.

A forked-top white pine joins the hemlock towers. Discover the former standing height of a tree now tumbed beside the trail by pacing it off. The trail is one for slow touring, reflection, and appreciation. More pines fill out the cathedral as the trail descends. A younger, lower-story forest pierced by the big trees now creates more shade.

At 0.5 mile find a bench seat and tablet honoring the lumber company founders who gave the government the first 20 acres of this celebrated grove. A spring bubbles forth here, feeding a small wetland. Cross a footbridge over the stream and begin the loop return.

The majesty of the big trees continues. Songbirds and squirrels visit the grove. The lofty tops sway in the wind; more severe winds have stolen the crowns of some trees. Black-and-orange beetles favor the large conches on the gnarled trunks. More footbridge crossings follow, as the trail doubles back on itself.

After the footbridge at 0.7 mile, look for a large beech snuggled into the trunk of an old-growth pine. The slow uphill return finds black cherry trees joining the mix. At 0.8 mile big trees ring a bench. Near the next pair of benches, study a woodpecker-drilled snag. At 1.2 miles, proceed either straight for the picnic area, or right and then left to close the loop and return to the trailhead.

11 Minister Creek Trail

General description:	This popular hiker circuit explores the woodland and rock features of Minister Creek drainage.
General location:	14.5 miles southwest of Sheffield.
Special attractions:	Attractive Minister Creek, boulder realms, vista, hike-in primitive camps, mountain laurel, fall foliage, access to North Country National Scenic Trail.
Length:	8.5 miles round trip, including round-trip spur to Deer Lick Camp.
Elevation:	Travel between 1,240 feet at the trailhead and 1,700 feet at the overlook.
Difficulty:	Moderate.
Maps:	Minister Creek Trail brochure.
Special concerns:	Spring and late fall, hunters share the trail. There is no overnight camping at the trailhead parking lot, and hike-in camps have no amenities. On summer weekends, the parking lot can fill; find more tranquil visits midweek and off-season.
Season and hours:	Year-round, depending on winter snow.
For information:	Bradford Ranger District, Allegheny National Forest.

Finding the trailhead: From the village of Sheffield, follow Pennsylvania 666 west for 14.5 miles. There find trail parking on the left, Minister Creek Campground on the right. The trail heads north off PA 666 just west of the campground entrance.

The hike: Hike a wide, ascending trail through beautiful, full forest, bearing right on a limited-access road at 0.1 mile. Maple, hemlock, black cherry, beech, and basswood continue to frame the way, but provide only scattered shade. White diamonds and faded blue "i" blazes mark the route.

Ascend to road's end (0.5 mile), where a foot trail resumes. Conglomerate boulders now add to the woods. Just ahead come upon the signed loop junction; go right for a counterclockwise tour descending to the creek bottom. A left offers the quickest route to Minister Valley Overlook.

A fairly steep descent delivers hikers to the valley floor. At 0.7 mile pass a mammoth boulder adorned in moss and ferns and wrapped by the snaking roots of a yellow birch. Previously used hike-in camps dot the flat. Cross a footbridge over Minister Creek, at 1 mile, admiring its beauty.

A steady, contouring ascent follows. Roots web and buckle the trail, while stones ease the crossings of routinely wet sites. Mayflower, oxalis, whorled aster, and partridge berry contribute to the forest mat. Enjoy stolen looks at Minister Creek until 1.3 miles. Amid a field of boulders, admire the pebbly conglomerate and dressy fern caps.

After tagging a high point, descend coming to the Deer Lick Camp spur, marked by yellow "i" blazes heading left. This 1-mile, round-trip detour

Minister Creek Trail

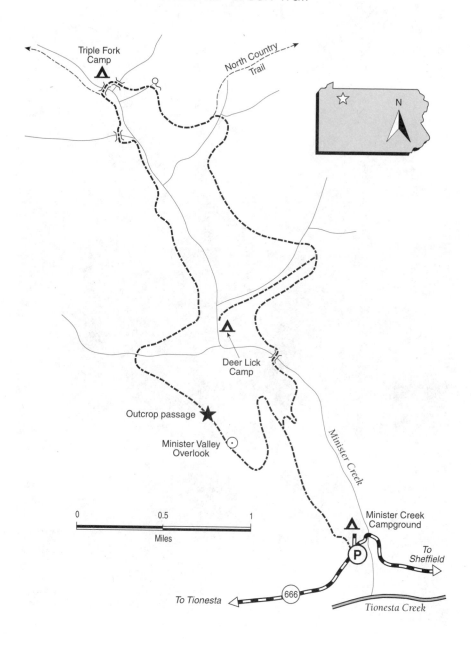

Triple Fork Camp

North Country Trail

N

Deer Lick Camp

Outcrop passage

Minister Valley Overlook

0   0.5   1

Miles

Minister Creek

Minister Creek Campground

To Sheffield

666

To Tionesta

Tionesta Creek

Ferns along the Minister Creek Trail, Allegheny National Forest.

descends amid forest and grass-fern meadow, reaching a flat dotted by black cherry and used by overnight campers. Minister Creek courses nearby, flowing 15-feet-wide and reflecting the hues of its rocky bed.

At 2.8 miles resume the counterclockwise tour, crossing a drainage to ascend the opposite slope. Here find boulder outcrops the size of barns. Ferns race to the boulders' feet and bigger black cherry and maple grow in their midst. Secondary paths wiggle away to a crest of the imposing rock. Discover tiers, weathered ribs and hollows, and perhaps a fossil.

Cross several small side drainages, leaving behind the rocks at 3.6 miles. Upon crossing a slightly larger tributary, find the first of two junctions with the blue-diamond marked **North Country National Scenic Trail** (4 miles). Hike left on a shared section of trail.

Descend, stepping across a beautiful, big spring feeding a clean-flowing stream. Next spy a few apple trees before the bridge crossing of Minister Creek (4.6 miles). Triple Fork Camp occupies the flat on both shores. Cross the next headfork via a bridge and part company with the North Country Trail, which ascends to the right.

Remain along the broad creek flat, touring meadowy plain and forest, following Minister Creek downstream. At 5 miles an arrow points right. Enter a hemlock grove to cross a tributary bridge. Pursue this last fork downstream to its confluence with the main stem and then follow the main stem downstream.

At 5.3 miles ascend away from the hemlock-shaded creek bottom, advancing via spurts of climbing. Return to the now-familiar broadleaf forest. At 6 miles traverse the upper reaches of the slope for a mountain laurel interlude. Dip and ascend through a drainage gouge to tour the next, impressive realm of boxy boulders, deep fissures, fern shelves, weeping mosses, and a 50-foot-high cliff.

Keep to the diamond-marked route, as side trails explore the area. At 6.8 miles pass through a broadened mossy fissure, 8 to 10 feet wide and 100 feet long—an impressive natural funhouse. Next, admire the dizzying vertical drop of the overlook rock, prior to ascending to its top (7 miles). The flat-topped rocky overlook affords a natural view of the wooded ridges of Minister Creek watershed. Mountain laurel dresses the edge of the rock. Songbirds serenade guests.

Hike past the overlook and descend stone steps, passing through an interesting collection of overhangs and dark grottos. Watch footing when rocks are wet; arrows help point the way. By 7.3 miles return to woods for a lazy, switchbacking descent. Close the loop at 8 miles, and retrace the initial 0.5 mile to trailhead parking.

12 Sizerville State Park

OVERVIEW

Five short trails explore 386-acre Sizerville State Park and a portion of Elk State Forest. Abutted by nearly 461,000 acres of state forest (Elk and Susquehannock), this small park contributes to a vital open-space and wildlife corridor. The east and west branches of Cowley Run thread the park. In 1917, the first pair of beaver were successfully reintroduced on the East Branch, after years of trapping had eradicated the large rodent from the state of Pennsylvania. Cowley Run supports both stocked and native trout. The state's lone elk herd roams the area wooded hills of Elk and Cameron counties.

General description:	The selected 3 hikes present the area, offering clear-flowing runs, the narrow valley, steep wooded slopes, and shady hollows.
General location:	7 miles north of Emporium.
Special attractions:	Vista, woodland and riparian wildflowers, fishing, natural and planted woods, fall foliage.
Length:	Sizerville Nature Trail, 3-mile loop; Bottomlands Trail, 1 mile round trip; Nady Hollow Trail, 2-mile loop.
Elevation:	Sizerville Nature Trail, 700-foot elevation change; Bottomlands Trail, minimal elevation change; Nady Hollow Trail, 400-foot elevation change.
Difficulty:	Sizerville Nature Trail and Nady Hollow Trail, both moderate; Bottomlands Trail, easy.
Maps:	State park brochure.
Special concerns:	Within the park, canted trailbeds put a strain on ankles. During hunting seasons, wear bright colors.
Season and hours:	Spring through fall.
For information:	Sizerville State Park.

Finding the trailhead: From the junction of U.S. Highway 6 and Pennsylvania 155 in Port Allegany, go south on PA 155 toward Emporium. In 15.7 miles, find the main entrance to Sizerville State Park on the left (east) side of PA 155. Locate parking for Sizerville Nature Trail on the west side of PA 155, 0.3 mile north of the main entrance; a wooden sign marks the site.

The hikes: For a counterclockwise tour of **Sizerville Nature Trail,** follow the slate blue blazes, rounding a gate to the right. Parallel PA 155 north, ascending a reclaimed logging road through a mixed woods of maple, oak, birch, beech, black cherry, and hemlock. In 0.1 mile ascend a foot trail heading left. It overlooks the often-waterless Arnold Hollow. Numbered posts remain from when a brochure accompanied this trail.

Sizerville State Park

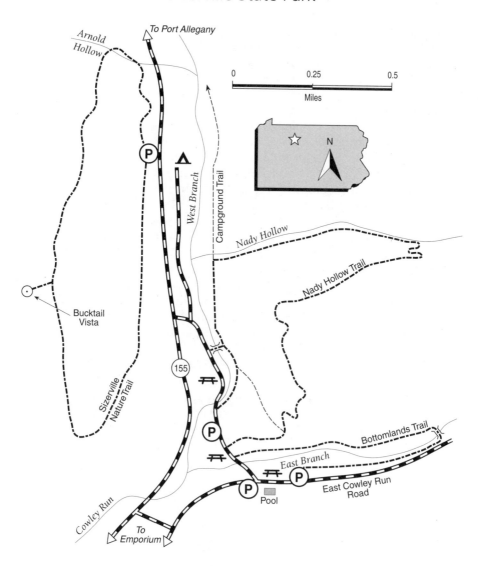

Find a steep ascent along the hollow, whose cool shade gives rise to violets, nettles, ferns, oxalis, and jack-in-the-pulpit. A covey of partridge may spook upon hearing your approach; deer abound in these woods. Large black cherry and ash may capture your attention here, causing your to walk with heads tilted back. At 0.4 mile pass a huge boulder capped in greenery. As the ascent eases, look for the trail to bear left.

At 0.6 mile, stroll the ridge. After touring a grove of 3-foot-diameter white pines, pass into a stand of large black cherry trees. At 1.1 miles reach an old logging road, softened by grasses and fern, for a steady, gradual descent. At 1.6 miles, come to a junction. The spur to the right leads to Bucktail Vista in 0.1 mile. Twin-trunked oaks frame the passage to this window-cut viewpoint. Overlook the Portage Branch of Sinnemahoning Creek, its layered ridges, and valley fields and farmhouses.

Resume the counterclockwise tour along the logging road at 1.8 miles. Despite the forest's young age, continue to enjoy full shade. Along the lower, southern-exposed slope, oaks dominate. After rounding a ridge nose (2 miles), mixed woods shadow the contouring descent. Problematic muddy spots can occur at 2.2, 2.4, and 2.8 miles. End at 3 miles.

The **Bottomlands Trail** starts off the day-use road in the picnic area 0.1 mile north of the pool. Look for a wooden sign and the pink-blazed trail.

Travel at the foot of the wooded east slope, edging the picnic area. Upon reaching East Branch Cowley Run, stroll the bank. Hemlock, maple, oak, black cherry, pine, and ash shape the forest. Nettles, hog peanut, Christmas fern, and jack-in-the-pulpit favor the run, as do hawthorn and hornbeam. The East Branch is a tiny, pleasant stream, skipping over bedrock.

Next travel a raised trail above a lush grassy flat. Dressy pockets of 4- to 5-foot-tall interrupted fern precede the East Branch footbridge. Trees bend over the waterway; erosion has exposed their roots. Traverse a fern- and goldenrod-filled field to cross a narrow footbridge over a deep side channel secluding fish and frog (0.5 mile). From there retrace your steps. Or, follow a mowed lane along East Branch Cowley Run downstream, skirt the pool area, and return to the trailhead (1 mile).

Locate the wooden sign and start for **Nady Hollow Trail** 1,000 feet north of the sign for Bottomlands Trail. Leave the east side of the park road, ascending stairs and passing through a mature pine plantation. Orange blazes mark the Nady Hollow Trail; green marks the **Nady Cutback Trail**.

At 0.1 mile, look for the cutback trail to head left. Proceed straight, ascending sharply amid mixed deciduous woods. At 0.2 mile follow the orange blazes, veering left; a blue-blazed trail streaks straight up the slope.

Ascend briefly to travel a higher hillside contour. Woody vines entangle the trees. Ferns and oxalis (blooming in early to mid-June) don the slope. Find the forest pretty and lively. At 0.8 mile pass beneath a big double-trunked black cherry. More of the dark, scaly barked trees enhance travel.

Reach Nady Hollow and turn left for the loop, descending steeply alongside the trickling stream. Tall maple, jack-in-the-pulpit, and violet grow along the hollow. The trail then pulls away to meet the boardwalk of the white-blazed **Campground Trail**.

Bear left on a joint section of trail, finding a better trailbed along the lower slope. At 1.5 miles come to a fork. Here, cross the bridge over the West Branch Cowley Run and bear left through the picnic area to return to the trailhead. Or, remain with the white blazes of the Campground Trail for a rolling tour along the lower wooded slope, pursuing the West Branch downstream. Where the Campground Trail enters the picnic area (1.75 miles), bear left to return to trailhead. Either way completes the tour at 2 miles.

13 Susquehannock Trail System

OVERVIEW

This rolling, long-distance hiker trail swings an impressive oval through Susquehannock State Forest, visiting Ole Bull and Patterson state parks, Hammersley Wild Area, and Cherry Springs Fire Tower. On this Allegheny Mountain tour, explore a terrain of moderate relief, with long, even-height ridges cut by sparkling runs that host native brook trout. Maple and beech dominate the second-growth hardwood forests, joined by impressive black cherry, stands of hemlock, and planted pine or Norway spruce. Oaks so familiar farther east are notably fewer here. The more open stretches showcase the state flower—the mountain laurel.

General description:	This long-distance loop and its associated spurs offer comfortable travel, incorporating existing foot trails, old and new logging roads, and abandoned logging railroad grades. Although road crossings (mainly forest roads) come at regular intervals, minimal road travel is needed to complete the circuit. Allot at least a week to tour the entire loop; travel is mostly on public land. With multiple access points, shorter hikes and loops are possible. Be aware that side trails can vary in quality and not all have markers.
General location:	South of U.S. Highway 6, 8.5 miles east of Coudersport, 13.5 miles west of Galeton. The loop twice crosses Pennsylvania 44 and dips southeast of PA 144.
Special attractions:	Full forests, a handful of views, Cherry Springs Fire Tower, access to the Donut Hole Trail and Black Forest Trail System, wildlife sightings, flagstone outcrops, mountain laurel, fall foliage.
Length:	84-mile loop.
Elevation:	Find the high point, elevation 2,545 feet, between miles 82 and 83; the low point, elevation 1,050 feet, when crossing Kettle Creek at Cross Fork.
Difficulty:	Easy to strenuous, depending on the length and section of the Susquehannock Trail System (STS) traveled.
Maps:	Susquehannock State Forest; Susquehannock Trail Club's Guide to The Susquehannock Trail System, with maps.
Special concerns:	Respect private property, pitching no camps. On public land, thru-trail hikers must secure a free permit for any overnight camping; contact Susquehannock State Forest. Thru-trail and overnight hikers who start from Ole Bull State Park (the

southern gateway), must first contact the park office, supplying details of the hike, name, address, and license plate number. No bikes, no horses, and pet owners should consider leaving dogs at home as porcupine incidents are common along the STS. Although rattlesnakes do occur in the area, encounters are rare.

Season and hours: Year-round, depending on snow. District Office: 8 a.m. to 4 p.m. daily.

For information: Susquehannock State Forest; The Susquehannock Trail Club; Potter County Recreation Inc.

Finding the trailhead: Find the northern gateway, south off U.S. 6, 13.5 miles west of Galeton, 8.5 miles east of Coudersport; take the turn for Susquehannock State Forest District Office. From the marked overnight parking area on the south side of the district office access road, hike east on the dirt road, locating the orange-blazed STS in 0.25 mile.

Find the southern gateway at Ole Bull State Park off PA 144, a couple miles south of Oleona, 17.5 miles south of Galeton. Locate other main accesses at Cherry Springs Fire Tower, Prouty Place Picnic Area, and Patterson State Park (consult the state forest map).

The hikes: For a clockwise tour of the STS (blazed with orange rectangles), start from the northern gateway off U.S. 6, following the orange blazes left (east) at the loop junction. The trail skirts the southern boundary of Denton Hill State Park, as it explores the hardwood forest of the ridge plateau for its first 4 miles. At 2.3 miles, a short vista spur on the left offers a northern perspective. Watch for the STS blazes where all-terrain vehicle trails cross the trail, to keep on course.

The Susquehannock Trail Club does an admirable job in maintaining and blazing the STS. After 4 miles, Jacob Hollow signals the first key descent, as the trail drops down to cross Lyman Run Road (6.6 miles) and soon after Lyman Run. A 1-mile detour east along the road leads to Lyman Run State Park and a lake. Striped maple, fern, and club moss commonly dress the forest, with bee-balm and jewelweed coloring the drainages. In fall, the forest's impressive array of hardwoods showers a mosaic of colored leaves on the trail.

From Lyman Run, make a steep 0.5-mile ascent, returning to ridge travel; another view sidetracks visitors on the uphill. Muddy and rocky sites periodically trouble hikers. Remain on the ridge until mile 10, then descend to cross Sunken Branch Road and the West Branch Pine Creek. The next uphill roll leads to PA 44 and Cherry Springs Fire Tower (13.7 miles). Ascend the rickety 8-story tower at your own risk; the nearby attractive rock cabin is off-limits to the public. Vertically oriented hay-scented ferns create a fuzzy sea at the foot of the tower; mountain laurel decorate the hilltop.

A slow descent follows, as the STS parallels Hogback Hollow and Bolich Run downstream; look for beaver sign. Deer, swallowtail butterfly, and grouse

Susquehannock Trail System

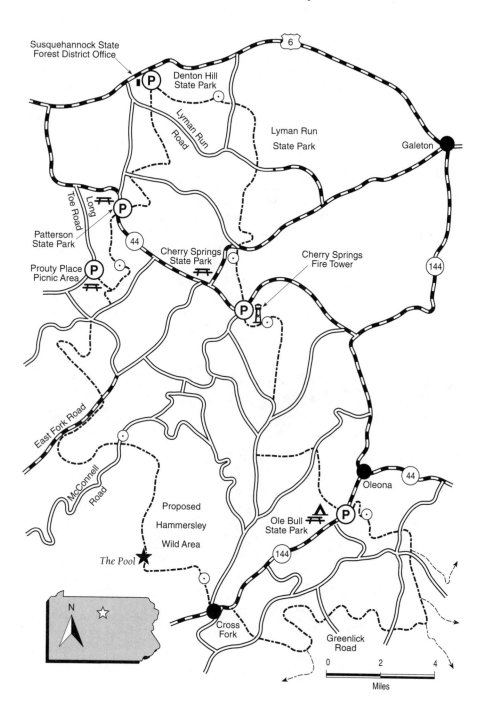

may divert attention. The forest engages throughout. At 19.3 miles cross Bolich Run and hike a stretch of road at Abbott, before turning east back into forest at 21 miles, to follow Cherry Run upstream.

Next, pass over the ridge and chase Ole Bull Run downstream to Ole Bull State Park (26.5 miles), where camping, a small lake, and amenities are available. Where the STS meets a dirt road upon entering the state park, a 0.2-mile side trail, **Castle Vista Loop**, leads to an interpretive sign and what remains of a "castle" foundation and its retaining wall. Here, in 1852, concert violinist Ole Bull had hoped to settle a colony of his fellow Norwegians, but years of hardship forced their disbandment. A bench seat offers a Kettle Creek overlook. Bluebirds sometimes visit the site.

Follow the STS through Ole Bull State Park, crossing an attractive footbridge over Kettle Creek. The STS then traverses the picnic area, crosses the park road north of Ole Bull Lodge, and ascends steps to PA 144.

On the opposite side of PA 144, the trail again rolls through mostly leafy forest, entering the gentle quiet of Spook Hollow (31 miles). Pine and spruce plantations vary views. At 32 miles and again at 34.2 miles, link trails branch away to the **Black Forest Trail System**; the latter (southern) link offers the shortest access.

Enjoy comfortable travel with a modest gradient. At 35.7 miles, reach the junction with the 56-mile **Donut Hole Trail** and bear right, hiking a 9-mile joint section of trail. Quickly enter a steep drop en route to the Left Branch Young Woman's Creek. Next, cross the creek and forest road, pursuing Lone

Susquehannock Trail sign, Susquehannock State Forest.

Hollow to a saddle passage (38 miles). As the trail rolls upward, laurel clad the ridge.

After Greenlick Run hosts the tour, look for the STS to cross Greenlick Road, travel a pipeline corridor, and descend along yet another run, before the Donut Hole Trail departs left (downstream) at Porter Branch (44.5 miles). Remain with the STS following Porter branch upstream. Climb up and over a hill to enter Cross Fork for the next stretch of road travel and the crossing of Kettle Creek.

In Cross Fork, thru-trail hikers find stores and motels. Watch for blazes on sign posts, guardrails, and rocks, pointing the way through the village and southwest along PA 144. Be alert for where the trail turns right off PA 144, swinging its way homeward.

Encounter more mountain laurel and chestnut oaks atop the ridges, as the trail enters the Proposed Hammersley Wild Area. Locate a vista at 51.2 miles; reach Hammersley Fork at 54 miles. A gradual ascent along the fork leads once more to the ridgetop, bypassing a popular deep basin dubbed "the Pool." Leave the proposed wild area at McConnell Road, 60 miles.

The trail then descends from the ridge, pursuing Gravel Lick Run downstream to the East Fork Sinnemahoning Creek and the start of private lands (62.5 miles to 64 miles); pass respectfully. The STS parallels the creek before crossing the waterway and East Fork Road. Soon after, it leaves private land.

As the trail again climbs, reach an area of flagstone quarries and outcrops. More rolling adventure follows. After traveling along Stony Run, return to the ridge plateau (68 miles). The trail now stays along the ridge or upper drainage reaches. At 72 miles, a blue-blazed side trail leads to Prouty Place Picnic Area off Long Toe Road. Keep to the STS, locating a forest view at 73.5 miles.

Once more pass from hollow to ridge, reaching charming Patterson State Park, which borders both sides of PA 44 at 77 miles. Here, find a small pavilion, as well as open picnic tables, primitive toilets, and seasonally a water pump. The STS leaves the north end of the picnic area at a sign for the **Plantation Trail**, 1 of the former trails contributing to the greater STS.

Resume the ridge-run tour, completing the west side of the loop. Tag the high point at 82.5 miles, remaining on the ridge plateau to close the loop at the northern gateway, 84 miles.

Thru-trail hikers should consider purchasing the *Guide to The Susquehannock Trail System*, with its accompanying maps. It provides point-to-point description, identifies re-routes, and may help hikers navigate through areas where nature may have stolen the trail.

14 West Rim Trail

General description: This spectacular 30-mile linear trail for the most part hugs the West Rim of Pine Creek Gorge—the Grand Canyon of Pennsylvania. Tour relaxing woods and secure striking views. While thru-trail hiking is popular, the 3 selected day hikes encapsulate the West Rim story.

General location: 8 miles southwest of Wellsboro.

Special attractions: Pine Creek Gorge vistas, varied woods with areas of impressive big trees, mountain laurel and fern, bird and wildlife sightings, colorful fall foliage.

Length: Barbour Rock Nature Way, 1.2 miles round trip; Bradley Wales-Burdic Run Section, 7-mile shuttle hike or 12.6 miles round trip; Gundigut-Steel Hollow Section, 3.2-mile shuttle hike or 5 miles round trip.

Elevation: The West Rim Trail travels between 850 feet and 2,020 feet in elevation, with Barbour Rock Nature Way showing a 75-foot elevation change, the Bradley Wales-Burdic Run Section showing a 100-foot elevation change, and the Gundigut-Steel Hollow Section showing a 200-foot elevation change.

Difficulty: Barbour Rock Nature Way, easy; Bradley Wales-Burdic Run Section, moderate; Gundigut-Steel Hollow Section, easy to moderate.

Maps: Tioga State Forest; West Rim Trail.

Special concerns: Salt-craving porcupines are a trailhead annoyance. Scattering moth balls around the vehicle helps deter them from coolant hoses. Thru-trail hikers may wish to use the shuttle services of Pine Creek Outfitters (See Appendix D). Phone a few days in advance to discuss pick-up/drop-off arrangements. Most hikers choose to tour south to north, being dropped off at the southern terminus, having their parked vehicle waiting for them at the Outfitters's parking lot in Ansonia (0.75 mile north of trail's end).

Presently, thru-trail hikers may camp a single night per site without obtaining a permit; for stays exceeding a single night, contact Tioga State Forest. Camping is prohibited at the Bradley Wales State Forest Picnic Area, at either trail terminus, or within 100 yards of buildings. Keep back from the rim; and stay off the rimrock.

Season and hours: Spring through fall for hiking.

For information: Tioga State Forest.

West Rim Trail

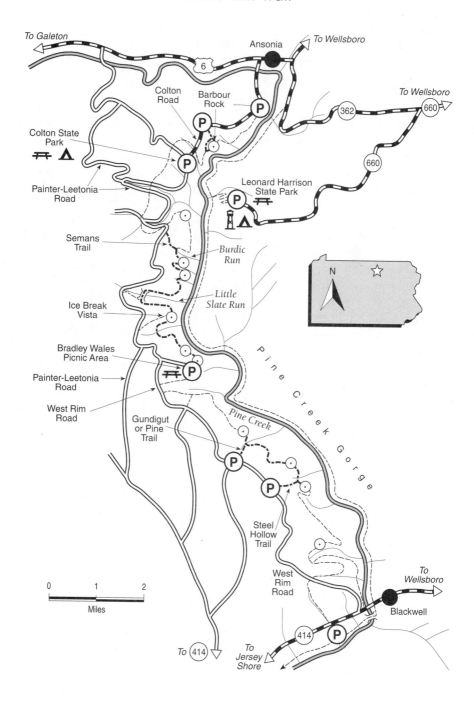

Finding the trailhead: In Ansonia, turn south off U.S. Highway 6 on Colton Road, finding the northern terminus in 0.5 mile; Barbour Rock Trailhead and day parking in 3 miles.

For the two other day hikes, continue south on Colton Road 3.1 miles, turning left on Painter-Leetonia Road, still heading south. Go 3.2 miles on Painter-Leetonia Road, finding the Semans Trail (Burdic Run access) opposite O'Conner Trail, a dirt road. An open slope offers parking for a handful of vehicles.

Again continue south, turning left on West Rim Road in another 4.4 miles. In 0.9 mile, turn left on Bradley Wales Road to reach the Bradley Wales trail access in about a mile, or stay on West Rim Road to reach the Gundigut or Pine Trail access (opposite Mine Hole Road) in 4.6 miles. The Steel Hollow access lies 1 mile farther south on West Rim Road.

Thru-trail hikers find the southern terminus and parking off PA 414, 2 miles south of Blackwell.

The hikes: Orange blazes mark the **West Rim Trail**; blue blazes mark the access trails, passing between rim and forest roads.

The blue-blazed foot trail of **Barbour Rock Nature Way** heads east, making a lasso tour of West Rim, snaring a classic canyon view prized by photographers. Travel an attractive leafy woods of beech, birch, oak, hophornbeam, witch hazel, and striped maple. In season, mountain laurel, Mayflower, trillium, and starflower dot the way with bloom. Stepping stones traverse soggy sites.

At 0.25 mile reach the loop junction; stay the well-tracked path straight ahead to reach the brink of the rim at 2 viewing sites edged by wooden rails (0.5 mile). A few pines dress the rim. Overlook the twisting Grand Canyon of Pennsylvania, sculpted by the current of pristine Pine Creek. Steep treed flanks elegantly frame the waterway, with areas of pinnacles and protruding red rock. The canyon contours are engaging. Far below, an abandoned stretch of Penn–Central Railroad hugs the east bank offering a first-rate rail trail (See hike 15).

Hike south past the blue blaze marking the loop return to gain yet another view in 0.1 mile. Here the steep, eroding sedimentary cliffs create a natural window. View the bulging and cupping canyon walls. In summer the canyon glories in green; in autumn a multi-hued palette calls hikers back.

Return north to the marked loop to complete the clockwise tour, enjoying patches of sunlit fern and tall forest. A few gray birch lend accent. Benches en route to and from the rim offer places to enjoy shade, bird songs, and the rustling of leaves. Close the loop and return to the trailhead, 1.2 miles.

The **Bradley Wales–Burdic Run Section** of the West Rim Trail offers a vista-packed rim tour, with a mild gradient and splendid forest. From Bradley Wales Picnic Area, hike 0.1 mile east on dirt road to reach the rim. There, turn north (left), finding the first vista in 30 yards. Rockwork and iron shape a scenic overlook, with grand up- and down-canyon views. Ad-

The view from Barbour Rock, Pine Creek Natural Area, Tioga State Forest.

mire a lazy-S bend on Pine Creek, treed islands and points, slow-water reflections, and the eastern cliffs.

Track the orange blazes north for a gently rolling tour near the rim. Hemlocks initially claim the cathedral, intermixed with birch and oak. At 0.3 mile tag the second formal vista, similarly set off by rock and railing. Overlook a shrub slope, with a gray birch rising center stage. Fog may reveal and conceal the canyon in a game of sleight-of-hand.

Gaps in the woods offer cross-canyon glimpses. At 0.5 mile, a lichen-stained flagstone outcrop rises next to the trail. Tall hardwoods with a striped maple midstory now shape the corridor. At 1.25 miles tour the foot of a fern-clad slope below Pine Creek Vista on West Rim Road.

Cross the rocky streambed of Ice Break Run (1.7 miles); jewelweed and nettles line drainages. Next, ascend to Ice Break Vista and another blue access trail heading west for Painter-Leetonia Road, at 2.25 miles. A wooden railing defines this vista atop a fast-plummeting point; the best views lie downstream.

Toad, red eft, towhee, turkey, deer, and porcupine may share the sylvan splendor, as the West Rim Trail follows a retired jeep trail north. Find a level tour, drawing away from the rim. The song of Pine Creek blends with lilting bird arias. At 3.3 miles, bypass another access trail to cross the footbridge over Little Slate Run; campsites dot its shore. The trail then curves right.

Hemlock, birch, and beech shade the trail, with swampy pockets marking travel. Fern abounds, while mountain laurel is notably absent. Where the trail returns to the rim, young beech close ranks. Cross intermittent Tumbling Run (4.7 miles), before reaching the fourth view atop a bald rim nose; a few oaks partition the view. Admire a downstream bend, a fire tower atop East Rim, the bold treed flanks, and shimmering Pine Creek.

Avoid rocky juts as the trail proceeds north and the woods again fill out with young beech. A scenic area of big hemlocks then spans to and beyond Horse Run. After 5.6 miles, towering hardwoods regain dominance. Ahead, reach a campsite with a rustic backpacker table; a few strides downslope from the camp locate a view, but not one to rival the earlier ones.

At 6.3 miles above Burdic Run, blue blazes signal **Semans Trail**—the selected ending access spur. Round-trip hikers retrace your steps (12.6 miles). Shuttle hikers follow the spur out to Painter-Leetonia Road (7 miles), traveling woods, fern slope, and homestead meadow. For a longer shuttle option, hike the West Rim Trail as it descends north, cross Burdic Run, and round to a sixth vista. The trail then swings back to meet Semans Trail at Painter-Leetonia Road.

For the southern rim sampler, hike the **Gundigut–Steel Hollow Section** of the West Rim Trail. It holds a single fine view on a splendid mountain laurel journey. Hikers, however, may opt to add bookend views via short detours north and south along the West Rim Trail. The mountain laurel is what sets this tour apart. With the vista detours, add another mile to the hike's round-trip or shuttle distance.

Southbound, begin at the **Gundigut or Pine Trail access spur**. This 0.5-mile trail descends east to meet the West Rim Trail; continue straight at the initial fork. A jungle of mountain laurel braided with witch hazel or chest-deep bracken ferns constricts the trail—an exquisite gauntlet when abloom.

Meet the West Rim Trail where it arcs away from the rim, and turn south (right). Or, to add the northern bookend view, detour left for an easy ascent, reaching a narrow, artificially maintained view in 0.3 mile. There find a cross-canyon look at the East Rim and rural hilltops, while the canyon bottom remains a mystery.

Southbound from the Gundigut junction, the trail rolls on, following the contour of the slope, and passing amid tall forest and full mountain laurel. In places, striped maple drape the trail. The trunks of gray birch contrast with the abundant green.

Pass a campsite in an open flat, at 1 mile (1.6 miles, if you took the northern vista detour). Then slowly descend, traversing an open woods and sea of waist-high bracken fern. Beyond another camp, ascend a faint jeep trail, turning left at 1.3/1.9 miles. More light penetrates near the rim.

At 1.6/2.2 miles, blue blazes mark a 100-foot spur to the main vista. Find an exciting tunnel view overlooking laurel and the wooded west flank to admire the reddish cliffs of the East Rim. A building afternoon thunderhead may bestow drama.

Resume the southbound journey, touring similar woods with brushing laurel and few big-toothed aspen. Upon crossing the headwater springs of Steel Hollow, reach the junction post and blue blazes for its access-trail (2.5/

3.1 miles). Here shuttle hikers exit, round-trip hikers turn around. To add the southern bookend view, hike south 0.2 mile to overlook another laurel slope, viewing the folding canyon ridges. The height of the laurel makes this a standing-only view.

The 0.7-mile **Steel Hollow Trail** ascends through an open forest, wet with springs, reaching an old road for a gentle, winding stroll to West Rim Road.

15 Pine Creek Rail Trail

General description:	This outstanding segment of rail trail, still in its infancy, follows the east bank of Pine Creek, exploring the belly of the Grand Canyon of Pennsylvania. This segment of rail trail represents the flagship of an even greater proposed rail trail that would span 62 miles between Wellsboro Junction (Pennsylvania 287) and Jersey Shore.
General location:	7 miles southwest of Wellsboro.
Special attractions:	Pristine Pine Creek and its canyon, a portion of which is recognized as a National Natural Landmark; fishing for trout and small-mouth bass; nesting bald eagles; wildlife sightings (perhaps even an elusive fisher, recently reintroduced to the area); ferns and wildflowers; seasonal cascades; colorful fall foliage.
Length:	20 miles one-way.
Elevation:	The trail shows a 300-foot elevation change between its two trailheads.
Difficulty:	Easy to moderate, depending on length and allotted time.
Maps:	Tioga State Forest; West Rim Trail.
Special concerns:	Dispersed primitive camping is allowed by permit only within an 8-mile stretch of the canyon between Burdic Run and Steel Hollow; secure permits in advance from the Tioga State Forest District Office. Thru-trail hikers may wish to use the shuttle services of Pine Creek Outfitters (See Appendix D); phone a few days in advance to discuss pick-up/drop-off arrangements.
	Exercise no-trace travel, respect posted closures for eagles, and respect private property. Use utmost care with regard to sanitation to protect the integrity of the canyon and the scenic waterway. Find toilet facilities at the Darling Run Trailhead (northern terminus), Tiadaghton Primitive Campground, the Blackwell boater-access, at Rattlesnake Rock Trailhead (southern terminus), and at Hoffman Farm primitive camp area south of Blackwell.

Season and hours: Year-round, with winter cross-country skiing.
For information: Tioga State Forest.

Finding the trailhead: Find the northern trailhead on Darling Run Road, southwest off PA 362, 7.3 miles west of Wellsboro (take PA 660 west to PA 362), 1 mile south of Ansonia. Find shared southern terminus parking for Pine Creek Rail Trail and the West Rim Trail, 2 miles south of Blackwell, off PA 414. A boater's access to Pine Creek lies on the east side of the PA 414 bridge in Blackwell; avoid parking there.

The hike: North-central Pennsylvania boasts some of the most remote wilds in the state and, for that matter, in the entire eastern United States, with the Grand Canyon of Pennsylvania being the sterling prize. A superb lineup of trails explores these wilds. Look for this newcomer to assume a place at the roster's forefront.

Pine Creek Rail Trail follows an abandoned stretch of Penn-Central Railroad, resurfaced in crushed limestone and open to foot and bike travel. Sections of parallel trail serve horseback riders. For its total length, the railroad levee remains about 30 to 40 feet higher than the creek.

For a downstream tour from the northern (Darling Run) terminus, turn left upon descending the access ramp. A line of tall pines and an herbaceous floodplain initially isolate the trail from Pine Creek. On the left, a fuller woods offers a buffer between the trail and PA 362. Gold finch, towhee, and a glorious chaos of bird songs accompany an early morning start.

By 0.2 mile view a broad, slow bend of Pine Creek as the floodplain narrows. Elsewhere, moderate whitewater and lengthy quiet spells characterize the waterway, as the trail and creek remain closely paired. From the start, it is clear why Pine Creek won Pennsylvania Scenic Rivers System distinction.

Ahead, a sign cautions no camping for the next 5 miles. Wildflowers dress the shoulders of the corridor, with poison ivy amid the mesh of Virginia creeper. With much of the tour open and sun-drenched, carry plenty of water and wear sun protection. Anglers on foot or bike are common passersby. Hawks and vultures soar the thermals, while a heron stealthily stalks its prey.

Closer to shore find elm, ash, birch, and sycamore, with hemlocks and a different assortment of hardwoods claiming the canyon slope. Side drainages count off distance. By 1.9 miles a few private residences dot both sides of Pine Creek; keep to the trail. At 2.2 miles, a sign along the creek warns canoeists and rafters of Owassee Rapids downstream. While out of view, the amplification of the rapids' sound brings excitement.

A few concrete pillars, wooden posts, and rusted pins recall the railroading days. Deeper in the canyon, admire the red-rock palisades piercing the leafy and spired cathedral. At 3.2 miles enter state park lands. At the rail bridge over the cascading Little Fourmile Run (4 miles), look for the steep **Turkey Path** to arrive from Leonard Harrison State Park, atop the East

68

Pine Creek Rail Trail

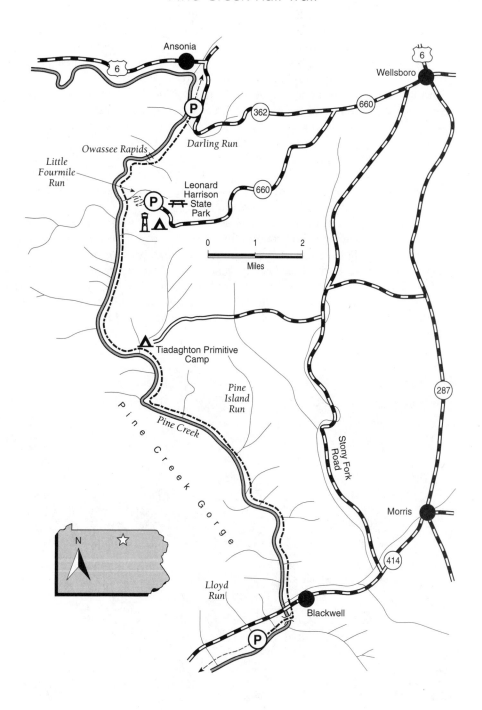

Rim. Here, too, find an easy access path to the rocky shore of Pine Creek—a satisfying turnaround for most day hikers. State park and private lands now claim the west shore. Exit the park, 4.7 miles.

Pine Creek flows broad over a rocky stream bed. Generally its waters reach only knee-deep, with a few 4-foot-deep pools enticing anglers to dance their fly-lines to them. Rich green grasses dress the shore. An upheaval of logs strewn across the floodplain hints at past floodwaters.

Throughout the tour, find tried access paths dipping to shore—some more sensible than others—and scenic shoreline changes, with wetlands enlivened by frogs and red-winged blackbirds. By 7.2 miles the floodplain again broadens, with a built-up ridge now secluding the creek.

Rock-ledge features, 25- to 40-feet-high, frame the gently bending tour; tulip poplars add their signature leaves. At 8.3 miles cross a larger side drainage, reaching Tiadaghton Primitive Camp (permit required), with restroom, water pump, and a scenic camp flat.

Downstream encounter more locust and box elder, and pass a few more residences at Tiadaghton. The rail corridor then narrows, losing the associated service road/horse trail. Over-the-shoulder looks present new perspectives on Pine Creek and better capture a sense of the canyon.

After 10 miles, taller ledges line the trail, with more woods spreading to shore. Here too, view a West Rim cliff. Deer, porcupine, pileated woodpecker, bluebird, kingfisher, merganser, scarlet tanager, and bald eagle may

Pine Creek, Pine Creek Natural Area, Tioga State Forest.

make the list of sightings. The eagles are the pride of the canyon.

At 13 miles cross the rail bridge over Pine Island Run. Maple, oak, and hickory remain familiar shade sources. Next, view a glassy straightaway on Pine Creek, where rainbow and brown trout, and rock and small-mouth bass slip through the water. After passing a sign showing no camping downstream, a tree border again alternately conceals and reveals the creek.

A side trail at 15.6 miles descends to a flat rock for admiring Pine Creek. Farther downstream a grassy island adds to views. Dripping mosses cloak the cliffs. Private residences signal that Blackwell lies just ahead; keep to the trail.

At 18 miles, reach the boater-access in Blackwell. To reach the southern terminus, continue downstream 0.2 mile, cross the reclaimed railroad bridge over Pine Creek, and travel the west shore the remaining way. Find an open corridor of sumac, birch, locust, and box elder, with grassy meadow flowing to Pine Creek; trees later bring shade.

Amid areas of sunken grade, admire the long straightaway of the rail trail. The floodplain grasses virtually consume deer wading in their midst. A planed overlook rock at 19.8 miles presents a scenic rocky point, attractive cove, and dark pools on Pine Creek, for a 1st-rate sign-off to the tour. Take the spur angling uphill to the right at 20 miles (prior to the Lloyd Run bridge), to end at the PA 414 parking.

16 Beaver Meadows Recreation Area

OVERVIEW

Centerpiece to this Allegheny National Forest recreation area is 34-acre Beaver Meadows Lake, created in 1936 as part of the Works Progress Administration (WPA). A network of five interlocking trails totaling 7.1 miles explores the natural woods, pine plantation, and grassy-fern savanna of the lake periphery. An innovative floating boardwalk crosses the inlet for an up-close wetland/lake perspective—a sight generally reserved for canoeists.

General description:	2 short loop hikes encapsulate the recreation area, exploring quiet Beaver Meadows Lake and touring the gentle terrain above Salmon Creek, the lake's scenic meandering outlet.
General location:	25 miles north of Brookville.
Special attractions:	Diverse habitat, lake and creek fishing, bird and wildlife watching, boardwalk, flowering shrubs, protected blueberry patches.
Length:	Beaver Meadows Loop, 3.5-mile loop, with Lakeside Loop spur; Salmon Creek Loop, 1.3 miles round trip.

Elevation:	Trails show less than 100 feet of elevation change.
Difficulty:	Both, easy.
Maps:	Beaver Meadows Hiking Trail System brochure.
Special concerns:	Following heavy dew or recent rains, rain pants or chaps help keep legs dry while hiking amid the deep grasses of the savanna or lake shore. During the spring and late-fall hunting seasons, wear bright colors.
Season and hours:	Year-round, depending on snow.
For information:	Marienville Ranger District, Allegheny National Forest.

Finding the trailhead: From central Marienville turn north off Pennsylvania 66 onto North Forest Street/Forest Road 128. Go 3.8 miles and turn right on FR 282 for Beaver Meadows Recreation Area. Find all trails starting near the dam in 0.8 mile; find a day-use parking area on the right, east past the picnic area. A 37-site campground serves overnighters.

The hikes: Beaver Meadows Lake represents the heart of the recreation area; its companion trail, **Beaver Meadows Loop**, the heart of the hiking network. While accessible from the day-use parking lot, start at the dam for early lake views and a counterclockwise tour. As the trail system is laid out in a four-leaf clover pattern, this tour may be extended by adding any one or

Beaver Meadows Lake boardwalk, Allegheny National Forest.

Beaver Meadows Recreation Area

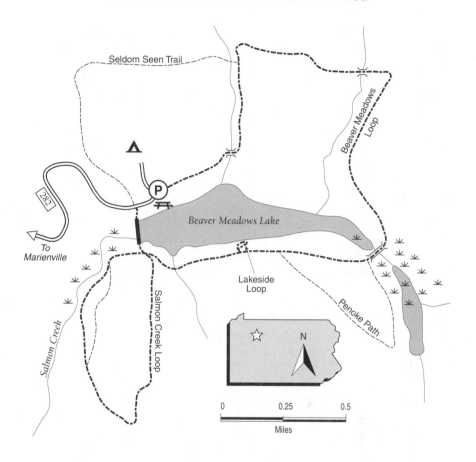

Seldom Seen Trail

Beaver Meadows Loop

282

P

Beaver Meadows Lake

To Marienville

Lakeside Loop

Salmon Creek Loop

Salmon Creek

Penoke Path

N

0   0.25   0.5

Miles

all of the site's four other loop tours: **Salmon Creek Loop**, **Lakeside Loop**, **Penoke Path**, and **Seldom Seen Trail**. For this tour, the lone addition will be the Lakeside Loop.

Round the boulder barricade to traverse the grassy-topped dam. Flowering shrubs dress the right side of the tour, Beaver Meadows Lake the left side. Below the dam, the dark release waters of Salmon Creek meander through a textured wetland.

Amid its low, rolling terrain, the long east-west lake presents a scenic shrub-and-grass shore. Attractive mats of aquatic vegetation complement the dark water plied by ducks and geese. A heron may study the shallows. The lake fish consist of bluegill, pumpkinseed, yellow perch, bullhead, and a few bass.

Upon crossing the spillway bridge reach a 4-way junction: Hiking left along the lakeshore advances the loop; the paths right and straight ahead form the Salmon Creek Loop. Proceed left, traveling amid pines with an understory of young maple, beech, hawthorn, serviceberry, fern, and bramble. White diamonds mark the way.

Next alternately pass between view-obstructing spruce and bracken fern clearings. At 0.5 mile, detour left for the **Lakeside Loop**, making a clockwise tour, closer to shore. Blue arrows and disks help point the way. On a narrow footpath, wade through the thick grasses, ferns, and flowering shrubs to win an open look at the lake. At times the vegetation overwhelms the trail, so be alert for arrows. Close the Lakeside Loop, bear left to return to Beaver Meadows Loop, and once on it, resume the counterclockwise tour.

At 0.8 mile and again at 1.25 miles meet the 1.1-mile Penoke Path, which swings southeast exploring more savanna. Forgo this side trip, remaining amid the fern meadows and stands of spruce and black cherry. At the 2nd Penoke Path junction, encounter fenced blueberry plots—an effort to deter browsing deer (A larger plot lies along the Seldom Seen Trail). Ahead reach the boardwalk at the east end of the lake.

The 0.1-mile-long boardwalk wins over visitors with the sights it affords and its innovative construction. Tall poles and vinyl palettes with water-release holes fashion the walk. When lake/marsh waters rise, the boardwalk simply climbs the poles. The release holes handle the displaced water. Enjoy open lake views and a close look at the textured inlet marsh, including knee- to waist-high aquatic grasses and a mosaic of wildlife channels.

From the boardwalk, enter a more sheltered woods habitat, rolling farther from shore. Here, hikers may notice the harvest mound of a squirrel, the knocking of woodpeckers, or the serenade of songbirds. Be careful of wet roots. By 2.1 miles return to a tree-dotted bracken fern expanse; ferns may attain shoulder height. Cross a footbridge over a hemlock shaded inlet. Then slowly ascend; here hay-scented ferns seasonally perfume the air.

After touring a pine plantation, bear left at 2.8 miles on a former logging railroad grade. A large meadow spans right. In another 0.1 mile meet the 1.2-mile Seldom Seen Trail; it heads right, offering an alternative return to the trailhead. For Beaver Meadows Loop proceed straight on the railroad grade. Where the loop descends from the grade, cross footbridge and log corduroys weaving back toward the lake to complete the tour at the day-use parking lot (3.5 miles).

For the **Salmon Creek Loop**, retrace the 1st 0.1 mile of Beaver Meadows Loop, but bear right upon crossing the dam for a counterclockwise tour along the lake outlet. Travel a piney woods interspersed with black cherry, overlooking the outlet-drained meadow. Blue diamonds mark the tour.

At the trail split (0.2 mile), the right fork (the primary trail) tours closer to Salmon Creek, offering an overlook of the 8-foot-wide waterway and the grassy plain it parts, before swinging left up the hill. The path straight ahead explores the heart of the red pine plantation with its rhythmic array of trunks and tall bracken fern. Both paths merge at 0.4 mile, with a closing glance toward Salmon Creek—a waterway favored by beavers.

Continue the counterclockwise tour. Red pine needles beneath the green ferns vary the forest look. At 0.6 mile, swing left, still ascending amid plantation. Hay-scented ferns replace the bracken ferns. Deer may bound away in flight. Before long, the loop again swings left, descending and meandering amid pine and a small alcove of spruce. Close the loop 1.2 miles, return to the trailhead 1.3 miles.

17 Buzzard Swamp Trail System

OVERVIEW

At this Allegheny National Forest hiking and wildlife viewing area, closed roads, reseeded tracks, and foot trails explore a gentle, mostly open terrain dotted by 15 pond impoundments and numerous pothole wetlands. The site proves a critical stopover for migrating waterfowl on the Atlantic flyway. Porcupine, rabbit, deer, bear, coyote, beaver, snapping turtle, osprey, and bald eagle likewise find habitat.

General description: Some 9.6 miles of trail explore Buzzard Swamp; the 2 selected hikes aptly present the wildlife area. The South Loop skirts the wooded thicket of the propagation area, journeys along and between ponds and wetlands, and tours levee and meadow, offering opportunities for wildlife viewing and fishing. The Songbird Sojourn Interpretive Trail concentrates travel within an attractive hardwood grove, with sightings of woodland creatures.

General location: 20 miles north of Brookville.

Special attractions: Wildlife viewing; fishing for bass, perch, crappie, catfish, and bluegill; meadows, ponds, thickets, and forest; wildflowers; 40-acre propagation area, providing vital nesting and rearing habitat for wildlife.

Length: South Loop, 3.7-mile loop; Songbird Sojourn Interpretive Trail, 1.6-mile loop.

Elevation: Both trails show minimal elevation change.

Difficulty: Both easy.

Maps: Buzzard Swamp Wildlife Viewing and Hiking Area brochure; Songbird Sojourn pamphlet (seasonally stocked at trailhead; best to secure a copy from the Marienville Ranger Station, 2 miles north of Marienville on Pennsylvania 66).

Special concerns: Entering the 40-acre propagation area is forbidden; visitors will find this area well marked in the field and on maps. As much of the travel is in open meadow, carry an area map with you. Junction stakes correspond to the map's letter codes. Hikers may port motorless boats to the ponds; find the nearest pond 1 mile from the trailhead. Allow wildlife a respectful safety margin. Spring and late-fall, hunting occurs. Come prepared for insects. No amenities.

Season and hours: Year-round, depending on snow.

For information: Marienville Ranger District, Allegheny National Forest.

Finding the trailhead: From PA 66 in Marienville, turn south on South Forest Street/State Route 2005. Go 1.2 miles, turning left on Forest Road 157 (an improved dirt road), opposite a National Forest Service/Pennsylvania Game Commission sign. Reach the graveled parking lot in 2.3 miles. Trails leave from the northwest and southwest corners and from the east end of the lot. For alternative touring, a northern trailhead is located 2.5 miles east of Marienville off Lamonaville Road.

The hikes: For a counterclockwise tour of the **South Loop**, begin at the southwest corner of the parking area (Junction A), hiking gated FR 378 south. Black cherry, birch, maple, spruce, pine, apple, beech, honeysuckle, fern, and wild rose weave a thick, diverse protective habitat for wildlife; keep to the trail. A thin waterway weaves back and forth beneath the road, flowing through culverts. Red efts sometimes venture forth from the wetland shoulder it feeds.

Vegetation gaps amid the propagation area allow swamp glimpses, with

Pond 6, Buzzard Swamp Trail, Allegheny National Forest.

Buzzard Swamp Trail System

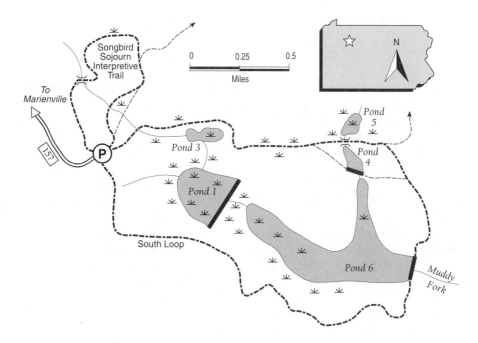

mist sometimes lifting from the water. Despite the forest fullness at the sides of the trail, the overhead cathedral remains open. At 0.7 mile, reach the open grassy meadow sprawling north to Pond 1, its open water often busy with geese. Low rounded ridges shape the backdrop, snags claim one end of the pond. Encounter the first of a handful of interpretive signs; this one on waterfowl migration. Scopes and binoculars enrich touring.

The single-track affords flat, comfortable hiking. Young aspen, maple, and beech now edge the route. At 1.1 miles secure the next open viewing of the ponds and the Buzzard Swamp interior. Nearby, cattails dress a tiny circular pond; beyond lies the more extensive open water of Pond 6. A dozen or more artificial potholes dot the perimeter meadow. The trail now alternates between meadow and wooded aisle.

By 1.75 miles, a grassy track leads to the levee, dam, and spillway crossing at Pond 6. View a small grassy island and reflections of snags. The concrete spillway feeds a pretty tree-lined waterway, with aquatic plants mottling the surface. Amid the expansive meadow straining north, find an open scatter of black cherry trees. Such open travel is unusual in the land of Penn's Woods. Hawkweed, daisy, and a myriad of other wildflowers decorate the grasses.

At Junction B (2.1 miles), proceed forward past the levee cutoff on the left, to travel the east perimeter of Pond 4. Look for beaver lodges, scent mounds, nesting boxes, and popular roosts. Swallows dart about, and the heavy scent of moist grass hangs in the air. Reach Junction C (2.4 miles), and bear left to close South Loop. To visit the northern chain of ponds, proceed straight, keeping your map handy.

For the loop alone, hike left along the gravel jeep trail of closed FR 157, passing between ponds 4 and 5. Amid the channel, look for sunfish in the dark, murky water; bullfrogs direct your attention elsewhere. Butterflies and moths flit about the wildflowers and travelers's ankles. Pass a large grove of young aspen, and soon after gain modest shade.

At 2.75 miles the cutoff trail from Junction B arrives on the left; keep to the gravel road. The route skirts the small auxiliary ponds north of Pond 1. Deer may be spied browsing along shore, protected by the propagation area. After 3 miles, leave the pond/meadow core of Buzzard Swamp, passing amid forest-transition habitat. The Songbird Sojourn Interpretive Trail branches to the right just as the hike ends at the east end of the parking lot (near the kiosk, 3.7 miles).

For the **Songbird Sojourn Interpretive Trail**, hike east past the kiosk, turning left at the attractive Songbird Sojourn trail sign to follow the 17 numbered stations in order. Silver diamonds identify the route, as do some blue cross-country ski markers. Follow the grassy track for 0.1 mile, then turn left on foot trail. At the stepping-stone crossing of a small drainage, admire the tall interrupted ferns of shore. Travel amid hardwood forest, planted spruce and pine, and a transition habitat near a tiny wildlife pond, steamy with transpiration-evaporation.

At Post 5 (0.4 mile) bear left, following markers. At 0.5 mile, again bear left; the trail to the right accesses the northern swamp and its chain of ponds. Follow a small drainage uphill to edge a wildflower opening, still remaining in woods. Black cherry, maple, beech, birch, ash, shad, and hornbeam enfold the tour. With a slow descent, begin a mildly rolling, woodland meander. Pass a spring and salamander pond, and revel in the forest tranquility. Leaves float lazily to the ground.

Cross a small footbridge (1.2 miles), passing through open woods with single and multi-trunked trees. Deer may frequent the apple trees in a clearing off to the right. Emerge from the shady woods at the northwest corner of trail parking, 1.6 miles.

18 Cook Forest State Park

OVERVIEW

Threaded by the Clarion River, this hallmark 6,668-acre Pennsylvania state park protects one of the largest old-growth white pine and eastern hemlock forests in the eastern United States. The ancient trees clad fully a third of its total acreage, with three large groves: Cathedral, Swamp, and Seneca. Some 30 miles of interlocking trail explore ancient and second-growth forest, the Clarion River, Toms Run, and plateaus of rhododendron and mountain laurel. Top a rocky vantage (Seneca Point) and historic Cook Fire Tower to survey the park's majesty.

General description:	The trail system presents a variety of round trip, loop, and shuttle-hike options; the selected five hikes provide a strong appreciation for the park.
General location:	13 miles northeast of Clarion.
Special attractions:	Primeval forest; Clarion River; 1929 fire tower; freshwater and mineral springs; rhododendron, laurel, and dogwood blooms; swinging bridge; wildlife; fall foliage; 1976-tornado legacy.
Length:	Nature Trail, 0.25-mile loop; Forest Cathedral Hike (tours Longfellow and Birch trails), 3 miles round trip; Joyce Kilmer Trail, 3.5 or 4 miles round trip; Fire Tower Loop (linking the Hemlock, Deer Park, Seneca, and Birch trails), 4.2-mile loop; Rhododendron Trail, 3 miles round trip.
Elevation:	Nature Trail, flat; Forest Cathedral Hike, 200-foot elevation change; Joyce Kilmer Trail, 300-foot elevation change; Fire Tower Loop, 400-foot elevation change; Rhododendron Trail, 300-foot elevation change.
Difficulty:	Nature Trail, Forest Cathedral Hike, Rhododendron Trail, all easy; Joyce Kilmer Trail and Fire Tower Loop, moderate.
Maps:	State park brochure.
Special concerns:	Control pets on leash at all times. Trails in the park are unblazed, but remain easy to follow for the most part. Find trail junctions signed and the occasional arrow indicating a direction change. No camping along trails. Within the park, overnight camping is restricted to Ridge Camp Family Campground or the organized group tent camping areas.
Season and hours:	State Park: year-round. Day-use: 8 a.m. to sunset. Hiking: spring through fall, with winter hiking or cross-country skiing popular.
For information:	Cook Forest State Park.

Finding the trailhead: On Pennsylvania 36 reach the park, 7 miles south of Leeper or 16 miles north of Brookville. Vowinckel Road/State Route 1015 represents the main north-south artery through the park; it leaves PA 36 north of the Clarion River Bridge and park office at Cooksburg.

The hikes: For the **Nature Trail**, turn east off Vowinckel Road at the sign for Sawmill Area and Pool. Prior to reaching the Sawmill Area, turn left on a dirt road, signed for the Nature Trail. In 0.25 mile reach the paved wheel-chair-accessible parking lot, with nearby open-area parking for general public.

This 0.25-mile paved circuit offers a first-rate window to what makes Cook Forest so special. Leisurely pass amid old-growth and second-growth trees, touring a dark eastern hemlock forest with huge beech, oak, and black cherry. Listen to the whisper of a breeze in the lofty treetops and succumb to relaxation. Amid the impressive big trees, downfalls and stumps harken to bygone days; logging ended in Cook Forest in 1915.

For the **Forest Cathedral Hike** and **Joyce Kilmer Trail** start at the historic Log Cabin Inn Visitor Center, near the intersection of Vowinckel Road (SR 1015) and Toms Run Road. Both hikes begin on the **Longfellow Trail**, starting uphill to the right of the visitor center.

Forest Cathedral Hike travels Forest Cathedral Natural Area. Here discover old-growth white pine and hemlock trees exceeding 300 years in age, 200 feet in height, and 3 feet in diameter. These trees date to the time of William Penn, Pennsylvania's first governor. On the **Longfellow Trail**, skirt a picnic area and "Tree of Peace" planted by the Mohawk Nation Council of Chiefs. Beautiful big hemlock, birch, and white pine engage from the start. The wide, well-traveled Longfellow Trail is the most popular gateway to the park's old growth.

At 0.1 mile visit Memorial Fountain; mosses and lichen adorn its attractive stonework. Only the occasional road noise intrudes on the forest solemnity. Rustic log benches invite a slow-paced appreciation. Towering snags as well as live trees tickle the sky; tilt your head back to gain a full measure of the forest. Alphabet-labeled trails (A through G), as well as other named trails, branch from or cross over the tour; keep to the Longfellow Trail.

Next visit the "windthrow" area of 1956, where a storm of cyclonic intensity leveled many of the evergreen giants within a 4-acre site. Downfalls have since been removed, but the openness of the forest now stands testament to the event. Watch quietly; a pileated woodpecker may emerge from a snag.

At 0.5 mile, the **Indian Trail** heads left; along it find the plaque denoting the National Natural Landmark standing of these woods, given in 1967. The Longfellow Trail continues forward, rolling along the forested slope. Amid hollows find massive beech trees, in addition to the evergreens. Mossy rock slabs and the rare appearance of a rhododendron vary viewing.

Angle downhill, meeting a footbridge spanning Toms Run (1.2 miles), but forgo crossing. Instead follow the east shore of Toms Run downstream to add a visit to the park's swinging bridge (1.5 miles). Cross here and turn right on the **Birch Trail** for the loop's upstream return.

Cook Forest State Park

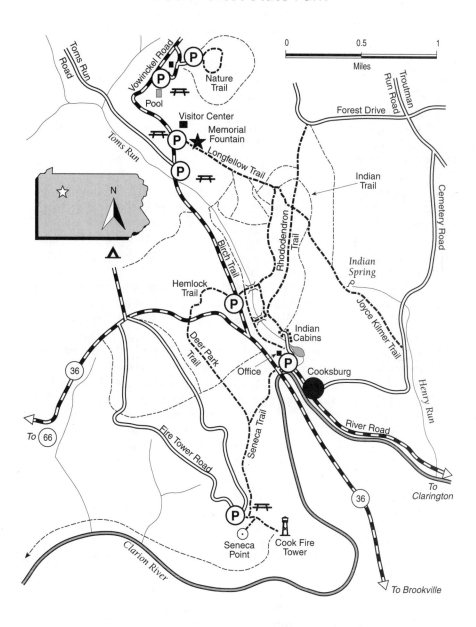

This trail overlooks Toms Run, passing below Vowinckel Road. Hike amid big hemlock and ancient birch, enjoying accents of hay-scented fern and rhododendron. The birch trees attain sizes seldom witnessed.

Where the trail approaches the road, pass through the small parking area, serving the **Hemlock Trail**, and descend a set of earthen steps. Tag the west bank of Toms Run and cross the bridge (1.8 miles). The 15-foot-wide tannin-colored water captivates onlookers. Retrace the Longfellow Trail to the trailhead, 3 miles. Or, explore the alphabet-spurs.

To hike the **Joyce Kilmer Trail**, retrace the first 0.5 mile of the **Longfellow Trail**, turning left on the **Indian Trail** for 50 feet. Then, turn right to begin the actual Joyce Kilmer Trail which travels a higher contour through Forest Cathedral Natural Area. Study junction signs to keep to the path. More of the spectacular big trees, snags, and snaking roots keep eyes darting. The leaves of beech and black cherry complement the evergreen boughs. Look for mosses and conches on stumps; some ghost trees show a twisted, silvered wood grain.

Find an easy to moderate ascent or rolling tour, with the trail bed gradually narrowing. As the trail explores the forest of upper Henry Run, briefly stroll a dense pine plantation (0.9 miles).

At 1.1 miles, bear right for a slow descent to Indian Spring—a 6-inch gurgling spout housed in a boulder cleft (1.25 miles). With a slight descent meet the **Bridle Trail** at 1.75 miles. Given that the Joyce Kilmer Trail now leaves the old growth, many hikers choose to turn around here.

Hikers who remain on the trail pass into second-growth hemlock forest, with many trees showing multiple trunks. A grassy floor and oaks complete the character change. Cross under a small powerline to end at Cemetery Road (2 miles). Return as you came or explore an intersecting trail.

For the **Fire Tower Loop**, start at the small trailhead turnout on the east side of Vowinckel Road/S.R. 1015, 0.3 mile north of the PA 36 - S.R. 1015 junction. On the **Hemlock Trail**, ascend the west side of the road, passing through a dark, full forest of big hemlock, birch, and pine—the Seneca old growth. Hay-scented ferns color the slope toward a small drainage. Pursue it upstream, soon being diverted away from a washout.

At 0.5 mile cross PA 36, to continue the tour on **Deer Park Trail**. The tornado of July 11, 1976, swept this area, culling trees, stealing evergreen crowns, and bringing light to the forest floor. The chaos and crash must have been thunderous. A tumbled tree near the trail allows hikers to physically pace off its former height.

Generally the trail is well-tracked, but a few places may cause you to stop and study. Clearings of hay-scented fern alternate with younger forest. Find mossy boulder-jumbles and guiding orange arrows. At 1.3 miles cross the **Mohawk Trail**, again passing amid stately trees. The trail is more meandering than the park map would indicate.

Rhododendron interweaves the forest, as oaks and maples join the ranks. Here meet the **Seneca Trail** (1.5 miles). To the right adds a visit to Seneca Point and Cook Fire Tower; a left completes the loop.

Go right to add the vistas and explore the best floral realm in the park. As the Seneca Trail gently rolls along a plateau, view grand displays of rhododendron, later adding mountain laurel and dogwood, for three floral seasons. At 1.75 miles come to a junction: The left path travels a scenic arbor of rhododendron and rock. Where the path straight ahead meets a wide lane, follow it left. Both lead to the picnic area atop Fire Tower Road, 2 miles (Fire Tower Road (a one-way loop), may be reached off PA 36, for an easier 0.5-mile, round-trip hike to Seneca Point and Cook Fire Tower.)

From the upper end of the picnic area parking lot, ascend 200 feet to the plateau, reaching a fork. Hike 0.1 mile to the right to reach the natural sandstone outcrop of Seneca Point for a vegetation-framed view of the Clarion River. Footbridges span the widened rock fissures. Hike left 0.1 mile to reach the 70-foot fire tower. Views overlook the Clarion River and Toms Run and pan the Allegheny forest beyond. Mount the tower at your own risk, heeding the posted 10-person limit. As the stairs spiral skyward, piece together a 360-degree view.

After pocketing both vistas, return to the picnic area (2.5 miles), and retrace your steps to the loop junction, 3 miles. Remain on the Seneca Trail, descending steeply away. Revisit the big hemlocks joined by rhododendron, snags, and stumps. At 3.4 miles overlook the Clarion River, flowing at the foot of the slope. The roadway bustle below breaks the woodland spell. Watch your footing where the mineral springs have been captured in small pipes.

At 3.6 miles, the Seneca Trail bears left (upstream); a spur leads downstream 200 feet to a rocky shore and closer look at the popular canoe water. At the foot of the slope, cross the road to Cook Forest Park Office, where restrooms are available. Round in front of the park office, go past the children's fishing pond, and ascend the loop road back toward PA 36, turning right on the gated trail prior to the stop sign (3.8 miles). This is the **Birch Trail** which parallels Toms Run upstream to trailhead parking on Vowinckel Road, 4.2 miles. Bluish-green lichen tint the bark of the ancient birch trees.

The **Rhododendron Trail** begins off the end of the Indian Cabins Loop. Park near Cook Forest Park Office and hike past the children's fishing pond to reach this area of historic cabins. These cabins, built from salvaged American chestnut by the Civilian Conservation Corps, are on the National Register of Historic Places.

Hike the east shore of Toms Run upstream amid a hemlock-birch forest, passing the swinging bridge at 0.1 mile. Mossy boulders dot the forest floor. At 0.25 mile, ascend into Forest Cathedral Natural Area and the enchantment of the big trees. Showings of any kind of understory greenery, including rhododendron, are rare. Enjoy a straightforward tour, noting junction signs.

With the climb, younger hemlock and beech generate a midstory. Rocks and logs invite contemplation. At 0.9 mile, spy an impressive pair of twin beech trees, sadly marred by carved initials. The trail halts at dirt Forest Drive (1.5 miles); return as you came.

19 Fred Woods Trail

General description:	This comfortable family trail swings a lasso across the summit plateau of Mason Hill. Pass through woods, fern meadow, and laurel-and-berry fields; explore rocky realms; and visit natural overlooks.
General location:	30 miles west of Renovo.
Special attractions:	Vistas; rocky slots, hollows, and overhangs; mountain laurel; wildlife sightings (look for elk in the old clearcut at the center of the loop); fall foliage.
Length:	5 miles round trip.
Elevation:	Find minimal elevation change traveling the summit plateau, elevation 1,900 feet.
Difficulty:	Easy, with a 0.5 mile of moderately difficult rocky footing.
Maps:	Fred Woods Trail map.
Special concerns:	Spring and late fall, hunting occurs. When climbing through the rocks, be alert for rattlesnakes.
Season and hours:	Spring through fall.
For information:	Elk State Forest.

Finding the trailhead: From the junction of Pennsylvania 120 and Pennsylvania 555 in Driftwood (28 miles west of Renovo; 18 miles south of Emporium), go west on PA 555 for 0.9 mile and turn right on dirt Mason Hill Road. Although passable for most conventional vehicles, expect some rough patches with rocks wearing through the road surface. Follow Mason Hill Road for 3.7 miles to find the marked trailhead on the left; parking for a handful of vehicles on the right. When wet, investigate the parking before pulling off the road.

The hike: This wide trail, which honors a forest foreman, starts amid a stand of hemlock. Orange blazes mark the way, few at first, then becoming more regularly spaced. Maple, oak, and striped maple later contribute to the bordering woods. Cross a grassy swath of a logging road, and at 0.4 mile, traverse a fern field dotted by birch, maple, and hemlock. As the trail curves out of the meadow, spy a stone wall off to the left.

A scenic open forest of hardwoods with a grass and fern floor now hosts travel; low berry bushes flank the trail. The openness of the woods and gentle terrain allow hikers to scan a broad area for deer and other wildlife. A spring can muddy the trail. At 0.8 mile reach the loop junction. Keep right, remaining on the wide hiker lane for a counterclockwise tour. Soon after, the trail angles across a even wider grassy logging road. A congested younger woods follows.

At 1 mile, pass the first hemlock-shaded array of rocks as a footpath advances the tour. Rock slabs and boxy outcrops become common forest additions. Ahead bear left, passing through a broadened rock fissure. Some

Fred Woods Trail outcrop, Elk State Forest.

Fred Woods Trail

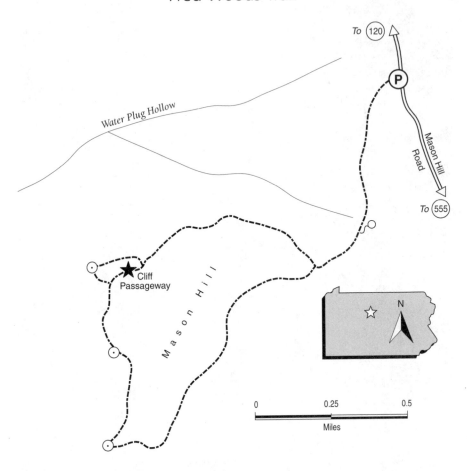

of the sandstone shows weathered, raised veins and peculiar ruffles, resembling features within a cave.

At 1.4 miles, enter an area of mountain laurel, finding dogwood and cucumber (a magnolia), which also blooms. Beyond lies a realm of rocks 12 to 20 feet high, with intriguing hollows, nooks, squeezes, and overhangs—a natural funhouse for children and the childlike. At 1.7 miles, hikers have the option of journeying amid the rocks or skirting the perimeter for a more straightforward tour; the blazed paths again meet near the first vista, 2 miles.

Opting for the rocky spur, explore a split-level narrow passage. View an intersecting fissure, venture beneath an overhang, and round a fallen rock, shaping a tight hiker-stile. Hemlocks grow from the sheer wall, while a few carved initials mar the sandstone. Follow blazes.

After emerging from the next slot, bear left and descend cautiously into the next assembly of rocks. A small hollow, 15 feet deep with a 3-foot ceiling may invite the smallest party members to snoop inside. At the fork at

1.9 miles, go right to find the vista and perimeter spur; left continues the loop.

Turn right, soon reaching a flat outcrop for a natural overlook of the forested watershed of Bennett Branch Sinnemahoning Creek, the rural valley floor, and Miller Run across the way. From here, the rocky-spur travelers backtrack; perimeter-spur hikers proceed straight, rounding away from the vista. At 2.1 miles, all hikers bear right to complete the counterclockwise loop.

An open maple-oak woods next hosts travel. Enjoy berry bushes and dogwood, before passing through a slot between 8-foot-tall outcrops and rounding right. At 2.4 miles come upon an easy to miss fork. Snuggled amid the rocks 100 feet to the right, find a scenic framed view overlooking a curvature of the Bennett Branch Sinnemahoning Creek. Early to mid-June, mountain laurel blooms enhance the image.

Resume the loop on a neatly narrow path amid a berry-laurel field, graduating to woods. At 2.9 miles, a 30-foot spur to the right leads to the final vista amid a small clearing with low berry bushes. Views pan the ridges shaping the Bennett Branch Sinnemahoning Creek. A silvered snag and weather pines may add to the presentation. Round the nose of the ridge keeping toward the edge of the plateau, and then at 3.5 miles, drift away to close the loop.

For the next 0.5 mile, find fewer of the large rocks and more rocks underfoot; be careful when rocks are wet or leaf-covered. Red efts may wiggle past the boot. The multi-trunked maples above a sea of ferns provides a soothing backdrop as the loop draws to a close at 4.2 miles. Retrace the first 0.8 mile to the trailhead.

20 S.B. Elliott State Park

OVERVIEW

Similar to much of Pennsylvania, climax pine and hemlock once clad this quiet 318-acre state park cradled in Moshannon State Forest. Today, find upland hardwoods and mature planted pine. At the end of the logging era in the 1920s, this site held a tree nursery, promoted by conservationist legislator, Simon B. Elliott. Still to this day, locals refer to the site as "the nursery." A system of lightly traveled hiking trails wanders the park's shady woods, picturesque meadows, and riparian environments.

General description:	A relaxing, most-of-the-day circuitous tour strings together several of the park's named trails, exploring the best the park has to offer.
General location:	9 miles north of Clearfield.
Special attractions:	Artificial pond, sparkling runs hosting native brook trout, mixed forest, mountain laurel, diverse ferns, blueberry fields, wildlife sightings, solitude.
Length:	Old Horse-Doctor's Fork-Rattlesnake Trail Circuit, 7.5 miles round trip, with opportunities to lengthen or vary.
Elevation:	Find a 420-foot elevation change.
Difficulty:	Moderate.
Maps:	Park map and S.B. Elliott State Park Hiking Trails brochure.
Special concerns:	Encounter soggy sites to negotiate and areas of brushing vegetation. Expect brief trail segments to go unmarked. During hunting seasons, wear bright colors. Although seldom seen, timber rattlesnakes do find habitat here.
Season and hours:	Spring through fall for hiking.
For information:	S.B. Elliott State Park.

Finding the trailhead: From Interstate 80, take exit 18 and go north on Pennsylvania 153 for 1.1 miles. At the sign for the park and Moshannon State Forest District Office, turn east (right) on Fourmile Road, and quickly bear right on Old Route 153. Reach the park in 0.8 mile.

The hike: Start the **Old Horse–Doctor's Fork–Rattlesnake Trail Circuit** next to site 22 in the state park campground; a sign and blue diamond signal the way. On the **Old Horse Trail** slowly descend amid tall maple-oak woods richly interwoven with mountain laurel—an enchanting tour during the mid- to late-June bloom. Bird songs ride the breeze, dismissing the intruding hum from Interstate 80. After crossing a faint road grade, impressive stumps recall the bygone forest.

At 0.3 mile, bear left for the marked tour; a well-tracked path journeys right. In another 100 feet again bear left to skirt a pine plantation on a wide grassy lane. Now watch for trail markers guiding the way through the laurel-blueberry meadow. Gain open views of the park's small levee-rimmed pond and its still-water reflections.

Cross a footbridge over the gurgling inlet brook and bear left near a meadow-isolated boulder. The trail now draws away from the pond, pursuing the inlet upstream, meandering through open woodland, mixed fern meadows, and a stump-dotted berry patch. Deer, fox, or turkey may divert attention.

Continue crisscrossing the inlet, following trail posts through the meadow. Dew-soaked vegetation can dampen pants; the midday sun can make things steamy. Stones help elevate feet in soggy sites. A pallet boardwalk then delivers hikers from the meadow.

S.B. Elliott State Park

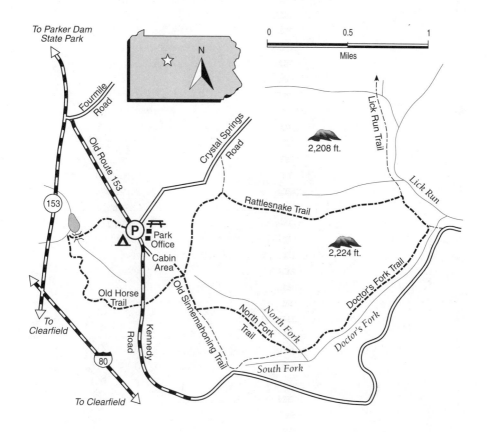

Here light penetrates the forest, feeding waist-high fern and adding dog-woods to the mix. After the inlet crossing at 0.9 mile, bear right upstream, and at 1.1 mile, bear left on a grassy lane reaching a dead-end dirt road and a trail post. Hike left on the road to resume the tour crossing over paved, lightly-used Kennedy Road (1.2 miles).

A wide grassy lane continues the tour; keep forward at 1.25 miles, where a secondary lane curves uphill to the right. The trail goes unmarked until the 4-way intersection at 1.6 miles; just keep to the lane.

At 1.6 miles find the loop junction: Go right on the **Old Sinnemahoning Trail** for a counterclockwise tour. Orange-circle paint blazes mark this trail. Ascend a soft grassy lane overlaced by maple and oaks, coming to a junction and hiker's choice at 2 miles. To the right the Old Sinnemahoning Trail leads to the **South Fork Trail** for a longer loop, passing through a regenerating burn. For this tour, go left on the **North Fork Trail** noted for its mountain laurel displays. The tour remains similarly blazed with orange circles.

Doctor's Fork, S. B. Elliott State Park.

The footpath descends and rolls, touring more of the beautiful woods. By 2.3 miles the laurel wins over travelers. Nearby, the North Fork, a disorganized stream, largely goes unrecognized. At 2.8 miles reach the next junction, marked by a 6-foot-tall wooden post. Here, the South Fork Trail arrives on the right; follow the **Doctor's Fork Trail** straight ahead. Crows may chastise an owl from its roost; woodpeckers tap out telegrams. Still the mountain laurel, blueberries, and varied ferns contribute to travel.

At 3 miles bear right, briefly traversing a disturbed area of old logging grades. The scenic water of Doctor's Fork soon restores the wilderness spell, shaded by birch, beech, and witch hazel. Tulip poplar and black cherry grow farther back from the stream. The trail seldom strays more than 100 feet from the fork; logs and rocks create scenic cascades.

After passing through a meadow opening, cross a small side water, reaching a junction on the shore of Lick Run (4.3 miles), just upstream from its confluence with Doctor's Fork. The loop now pursues the **Lick Run Trail** upstream. Hike along attractive Lick Run. At 4.6 miles the trail pulls up and away.

At 4.75 miles, reach the **Rattlesnake Trail** and follow it left to complete the loop. For the adventuresome, Lick Run Trail continues upstream, traveling a rockier trailbed and passing tempting berry patches, before reaching the headwater springs in another 1.25 miles.

For the loop alone, turn left following the Rattlesnake Trail for a steady, moderate climb angling uphill. Initially some large boulders punctuate the drainage-influenced forest. By 5 miles find only oak, maple, tulip poplar, dogwood, and chestnut oaks, with a mountain laurel midstory.

At the top of the slope, emerge at a small clearing and bear right on a grassy gaswell road. The aisle, at first open, later affords partial to full shade. Sassafras and cucumber magnolia join the ranks, but the laurel departs. Meet the **Old Horse Trail** at 6.3 miles, and turn left. To the right, the **Central Pennsylvania Lumber Company Trail** heads north 7 miles to Parker Dam State Park.

The Old Horse Trail extends a narrower grassy lane through similar woods, but goes unmarked. Avoid a second forest lane to the right; it returns to the day-use at an open field. Stay straight, hiking past the park cabins, to close the loop back at the 1.6-mile junction (7 miles).

From here, hikers may retrace the first 1.6 miles of the Old Horse Trail to end the tour. Or, turn right on the Old Sinnemahoning Trail, cross over Cabin Loop Road, and bear right upon meeting this road a second time at 7.2 miles. Hike the road out to the gate at 7.3 miles, ignoring a cabin spur to the right. Now bear left for the park road or cross through the day-use to complete the hike at (7.5 miles).

Pocono Mountains Region

This northeast region spans between the Alleghenies and the Delaware River and features a broad, flat, mountainous plateau sliced by deep-cut stream and river valleys. The Pocono landscape is one of flat horizons, its scenery one of beauty. Enjoy some of the state's finest waterfalls, large lakes and reservoirs, wetlands, and more of the state's signature woods. Despite the Poconos being a long-time favorite playground for residents of the mid-Atlantic states, hikers can still stroll to quiet corners and bask in the area's treasures.

21 Worlds End State Park

OVERVIEW

Amid the plateau country known as Sullivan Highlands in Wyoming State Forest, this 780-acre state park enfolds an S-bend on Loyalsock Creek. The park's name can be traced to the area's earliest road, which ran parallel to the creek, hugging the steep canyon slope. At the point where the creek hooks sharply back on itself, roadway travelers thought surely it spelled the "end of the world" for them.

Today, hikers find splendid discovery with ledge vistas, mazes of boxy boulders, sparkling runs and picturesque Loyalsock Creek, waterfalls, and tranquil woods. The long-distance Loyalsock Trail passes through the park, calling the more adventurous to don their backpacks.

General description:	The 2 selected day hikes travel to falls and vistas, incorporating some of the park's fine short trails and offering a peek at the 59-mile Loyalsock Trail.
General location:	7 miles northwest of Laporte, 2 miles south of the village of Forksville.
Special attractions:	Vistas, scenic waterways, waterfalls and cascades, rock features, wildlife sightings, fall foliage.
Length:	Double Run Nature Trail–Link Trail Hike, 4.1 miles round trip; Loyalsock Trail to Alpine Falls, 9.1 miles round trip.
Elevation:	Double Run Nature Trail–Link Trail Hike shows a 600-foot elevation change; the Loyalsock Trail to Alpine Falls has an 800-foot elevation change.
Difficulty:	Both, moderate.

Maps:	State park brochure.
Special concerns:	Expect some rocky, uneven footing along Double Run. Camping permits are required for the Loyalsock Trail; contact Wyoming State Forest. Overnight backpackers wishing to leave their vehicles at the state park, must first register with the park office and then park near the office.
Season and hours:	Spring through fall for hiking.
For information:	Worlds End State Park.

Finding the trailhead: From the intersection of U.S. Highway 220 and Pennsylvania 154 (just north of Laporte, 8.5 miles south of Dushore), travel north on PA 154, reaching the turnoff for the campground in 6.2 miles, Double Run Nature Trail in 6.7 miles, and the turnoff for the park office and High Rock/Loyalsock Trailhead in 7.1 miles.

Worlds End State Park

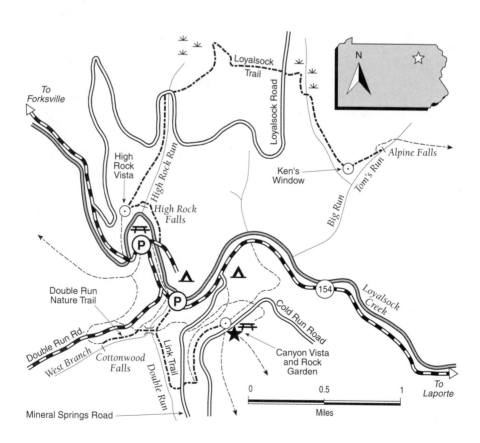

The hikes: The **Double Run Nature Trail** offers a fun streamside tour and serves as a springboard to 3 park destinations: Cottonwood Falls, Canyon Vista, and the Rock Garden. Visit any one or go for all three.

From the trailhead parking area off PA 154, hike south (upstream) on the green-on-white blazed trail, touring a wooded flat removed from Double Run. Where the trail pinches to the east bank of Double Run, find a charming cascade spilling through a broken bedrock ledge. Remain along the stairstepped stream.

At the bridge at 0.25 mile, reach the **Link Trail** (red cross on yellow disk) and a decision point. For Canyon Vista and the Rock Garden, follow the Link Trail left. To add a visit to Cottonwood Falls, proceed across the bridge.

For the falls tour, cross the bridge and quickly after cross a bridge over the West Branch Double Run. Now proceed upstream, tracking the green blazes of the nature trail, as the Link Trail turns downstream. Soon admire a pretty chute, with Water Beech Pool next addressing hikers. A 6-foot cascade empties into this tannin-steeped natural pool ringed by low ledges.

The trail continues to hug the creek. Where it forks, find both a poolside and overlook view of Cottonwood Falls (0.7 mile). This lacy, tiered veil spills amid a half-moon broken ledge; to its left view a tearful falls amid a mossy hollow. Return as you came for a 1.4-mile round trip, or backtrack (0.45 mile) to the bridge to continue the upstream tour to the vista and rocks.

For the full 4.1-mile hike, turn right, following the Link Trail upstream from the bridge (1.15 miles). Soon after pass the **Loyalsock Trail** (red dash on yellow). Travel is initially on what appears to have been an old cart path.

A blazed cross-country trek then takes the baton. Where the trail travels at water level, be careful on the wet rock. The stream's rippled sandstone and broken ledges shape a pretty flow. Jack-in-the-pulpit and fern-capped rocks accent the tour. With one last look at a cascade (1.8 miles), hikers switchback uphill to cross gravel Mineral Spring Road.

Rocky footing follows, as the trail weaves above the road. A natural cliff overhang foreshadows a rock garden yet to come. Maple, black cherry, and ash replace the hemlock and birch of Double Run drainage.

At 2 miles, the blue-blazed **Canyon Vista Trail** arrives on the left to share the remaining climb. Hemlock and beech dress the upper slope, as the trail angles to the ridgetop vista 2.4 miles. From this railed viewing site, peer across a steep shrub slope to the folding even-height ridges of the Loyalsock drainage.

Turn right, ascending away from Canyon Vista and its small picnic area to enter the Rock Garden in 0.1 mile. Here find a gallery of boxy 10-foot-tall outcrops. Broadened frost-formed fissures shape natural passages. When ready, retrace the Link Trail and the eastern-shore portion of the Double Run Nature Trail, returning to the trailhead, 4.1 miles.

For a tour of the acclaimed **Loyalsock Trail**, start at the High Rock Trailhead (on the left, after crossing the bridge over Loyalsock Creek, 0.2 mile east of the park office). With limited day-use parking at the trailhead, hikers may need to park near the park office and hike to the trailhead,

Alpine Falls, Wyoming State Forest.

following the signature Loyalsock Trail blaze (red dash on yellow). All overnight parking is next to the park office.

Ascend from Loyalsock Creek, passing beneath a leafy umbrella pierced by hemlock boughs. Beech, black cherry, maple, ash, and hornbeam contribute to the deciduous array. Besides the Loyalsock Trail blazes, the yellow disks of the park's **High Rock Trail** help point the way.

Where the trail dips to cross High Rock Run, rough secondary paths descend 100 feet along either shore for a view of a downstream falls; the west shore holds the better vantage. The 30-foot falls spills from an overhang and washes over a canted outcrop slope—a genuine falls during times of high water. At low water, its watery glaze brings out the color of the rock.

Upon crossing the run, the blazed trail enters a more intense climb, "stairstepping" and switchbacking up the rugged natural rock slope. A few flowering cucumber magnolia add to the forest. Atop a ledge shoulder, the blazed route switchbacks right, before rolling to High Rock Vista, 0.7 mile. A wooden rail signals the viewpoint.

Here overlook a chestnut-oak clad slope to the bending Loyalsock Creek drainage and park below. Autumn colors particularly recommend the destination. A few mountain laurel decorate the vantage in mid-June. Vultures sometimes soar the thermals; deer may pause themselves for a curious look.

From the vista continue on the Loyalsock Trail, which heads right, following a scenic, faint road grade; the High Rock Trail proceeds straight, eventually coming out on PA 154. Along the lower ledge of a boulder jumble, spy fern and rock-tripe lichen. Oaks dominate the upper canopy; where hemlocks cluster find richer shade. Nettles, violet, jewelweed, and berry bushes favor the marshy side drainages, as do maple, beech, and striped maple. After 1.3 miles overlook High Rock Run.

At 1.6 miles, angle across Loyalsock Road to tour east along the ridge; a large wooden sign indicates a partnership of landholders. Stay the well-blazed route, bypassing High Rock Spur, a gated jeep trail heading left. Enjoy a relaxing stretch through mixed, sometimes open woods. Gray squirrel, woodpecker, and porcupine may add to travel. At 2.1 miles, reach a T-junction at a woods road; turn right, following the blazes to cross back over Loyalsock Road, 3 miles.

Descend via foot trail through open, fern-dressed woods, soon skirting a snag-riddled, shrub-reclaimed beaver pond. Meander from hemlock stand to deciduous woods. At 3.3 miles cross Big Run via stones. An abandoned timber railroad grade next advances the trail; a thin traveled footpath parts the lush knee-high greenery. At 4.1 miles reach the "50-mile" marker for the Loyalsock Trail and Ken's Window, a clean aisle look out Big Run drainage.

The blazed route then descends through choked forest to follow another railroad grade upstream along Tom's Run. At 4.5 miles meet the falls spur marked by a red cross on yellow disk. Here forsake the Loyalsock Trail to follow the spur, crossing Tom's Run and hiking upstream 250 feet to view Alpine Falls. The generally whispering falls courses over platy sandstone ledges, spilling in tiers. A fractured cliff shapes its west wall, a steep forested slope the east wall. A clearwater pool catches its splash. Return as you came or resume the saga of the Loyalsock Trail.

22 Shuman Point Natural Area Hiking Trail

General description:	Exploring a Pennsylvania Power and Light (PP&L) natural area, this circuit travels a wooded peninsula on Lake Wallenpaupack, periodically reaching shore for lake views and relaxation.
General location:	3 miles southwest of Hawley.
Special attractions:	Lake access, fishing, mixed forest, colorful mushrooms, wildlife sightings, fall foliage.
Length:	3.5-mile loop.
Elevation:	Find perhaps a 100-foot elevation change.
Difficulty:	Easy.
Maps:	Shuman Point Natural Area and Beech House Creek Wildlife Refuge trail map (available at PP&L Visitor Center and at trailhead).
Special concerns:	No camping, campfires, or picnicking. Hunting occurs in spring and late fall.
Season and hours:	Spring through fall for hiking, dawn to dusk. No parking after 9 p.m.
For information:	Lake Wallenpaupack, Pennsylvania Power and Light Company.

Finding the trailhead: From Interstate 84, take exit 7 and go north on Pennsylvania 390 and 507, following signs for Lake Wallenpaupack. In 6.7 miles continue north, now following U.S. Highway 6 West. In another 1.1 mile, find the visitor center on the left. Go 0.3 mile more and turn left (west) on PA 590 to reach the marked trailhead and parking area in 2.1 miles.

The hike: This trail explores an undeveloped 250-acre wooded natural area along the northern shore of Lake Wallenpaupack. Stone walls on Shuman Point hint at the land's one-time use as farmland. The lake site holds historical interest being once owned by William Penn and later the property of James Wilson, a signer of the Declaration of Independence.

Built in 1926, the 5,700-acre manmade lake has 52 miles of shoreline. It captures the waters of Wallenpaupack Creek; *Wallenpaupack* is the Lenni-Lenape (Delaware) Indian word for "stream of swift and slow water."

From the kiosk at the west end of the parking area, round the boulder barricade and quickly veer left uphill on a blue-blazed foot trail for a counterclockwise peninsula tour. Find a steady, moderate gradient and rock-studded, but good trail. Maple, black cherry, and oak clad the lower slope, with huckleberry, sarsaparilla, young chestnut, oak shoots, and witch hazel filling out the woods.

At 0.25 mile top the rise amid a stand of white pine. Mats of moss and reindeer lichen add interest to the forest. The trail then descends through low-canopy oak woods. Deer, turkey, bear, and eft may number among the wildlife sightings. Colorful mushrooms or the colorless Indian-pipe may dot the forest floor. Winds enliven the canopy.

At 0.8 mile, avoid a spur heading right. As the trail flattens, glimpse the lake glare beyond the young woods. At 1.1 miles find the first 70-foot spur to shore, as the loop arcs left. The spur leads to a gravelly beach overlooking a large cove on Lake Wallenpaupack. Willow and birch frame the shore, while a large treed island and ring of even-height Pocono Mountain ridges contribute to the lake view.

Resume the counterclockwise loop, staying with the blazes. At 1.25 miles, access a half-circle beach with washed reddish gravels and flat-topped outcrops. The smooth seating invites sunning or lake admiration. From this lake vantage, wooded points pinch together, shaping a gateway to the dis-

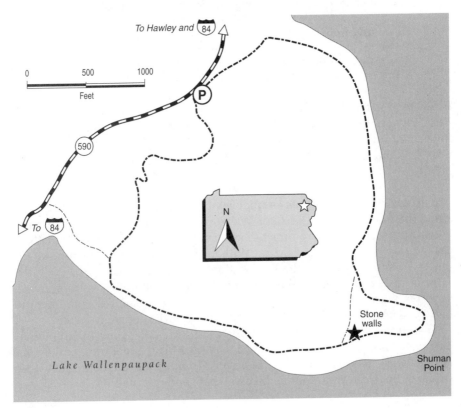

Shuman Point Natural Area Hiking Trail

tant lake waters. Kingfisher and heron are common sightings. A few dogwoods decorate shore. The loop then continues just removed from the lake edge, rolling up and away at 1.7 miles. Young maples alter the forest character.

Encounter fragments of stone wall, some more defined than others, coming to a blazed fork (2 miles): Bear right for the full loop; the path straight ahead is a cut-across for shortening the tour. At an intersection of the stone walls, take a moment to study the careful balance of the flat plates and round boulders. White pines again join the forest ranks.

The trail next approaches rim ledges but swings away, descending back to the lake, 2.4 miles. Here a 40-foot spur accesses a lake view that spans the blue waters to the dam. Continue the loop, passing trees larger in diameter, with the cut-across returning on the left. Rocky patches briefly mark travel. Where the loop arcs left at 2.75 miles, avoid a 100-foot spur to a tiny private dock.

At the junctions at 3.1 and 3.3 miles continue to bear left for the loop, strolling a scenic lane. Pass two especially noteworthy white pines, one with a triple trunk, before emerging on the east side of the parking area (3.5 miles).

23 Ricketts Glen State Park

OVERVIEW

This 13,050-acre state park is a shining prize of national merit, drawing visitors with its natural beauty and premier outdoor recreation. Although approved for national park status in the 1930s, the advent of World War II shelved its opening. The park joined the Pennsylvania state park system in 1942.

The Glens Natural Area—the park's sterling heart—won National Natural Landmark distinction in 1969. Amid the shady glens of Kitchen Creek drainage, discover 22 named waterfalls, old-growth trees exceeding 500 years in age and sporting diameters of 5 feet, shale cliffs, a boulder tunnel, chance wildlife encounters, and a superb network of trails by which to admire it all.

General description:	A lollipop-shaped tour explores The Glens Natural Area, joining several named trails along Kitchen Creek drainage. The tour offers close-up views of the named and unnamed waterfall features. A short hike at the southern extreme of the natural area rounds up the final named falls.
General location:	25 miles west of Wilkes-Barre.
Special attractions:	A bombardment of exciting waterfall images, captivating forest, wildflowers, fall foliage.
Length:	The Glens Natural Area Hike, 7.4 miles round trip; Adams Falls Hike, 0.2 mile round trip.
Elevation:	For The Glens Natural Area Hike, find a 1,250-foot elevation change. For Adams Falls Hike, the elevation change is minimal.
Difficulty:	The Glens Natural Area Hike, moderate; Adams Falls Hike, easy.
Maps:	State park brochure.
Special concerns:	Expect muddy and rock-studded stretches, rock stairs, and some awkward stepping along the shale canyonsides overlooking the falls; boots strongly recommended. Due to the popularity of the trail, midweek and off-season visits allow for more leisurely hikes and a full appreciation of the falls and their setting. Hikers planning to walk the upper falls loop alone, should know the upper trailhead parking lot fills rapidly in summer, requiring hikers to park near the park office and walk the dirt roadway to the trail's start.
Season and hours:	Spring through fall, daylight hours.
For information:	Ricketts Glen State Park.

Finding the trailhead: From the junction of Pennsylvania 309 and Pennsylvania 415 in Dallas, go north on PA 415 for 2.2 miles and turn west on PA 118. Remain on PA 118 for 16.5 miles reaching "The Glen Entrance" (lower trailhead), with trail parking on both sides of the highway.

For the upper trailhead, from the junction of PA 118 and PA 487 in Red Rock (1.5 miles west of the PA 118 trailhead), go north on PA 487 for 3.5 miles and turn right for the Lake Jean Area. Go 0.3 mile, turn right on the dirt access road just past the Lake Rose Park Office, and follow the dirt road for 0.6 mile to the marked falls trailhead.

The hikes: The Glens Natural Area Hike strings together the Kitchen Creek, Glen Leigh, Highland, and Ganoga Glen trails. From the PA 118 trailhead, follow the **Kitchen Creek Trail** north (upstream) along west bank of Kitchen Creek: A crosswalk accesses the trail from the southern parking lot; a bridge accesses the trail from the northern lot.

The wide, well-traveled trail travels the broad canyon bottom, overlooking the tea-colored clearwater and its rocky bed. Overhead tower big hemlock, birch, and ancient snags, with an interweaving of maple and ash. Nettle-

Ricketts Glen State Park

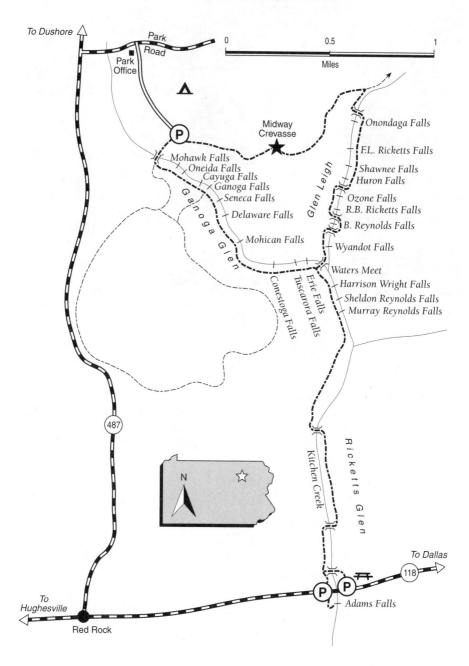

Mohawk Falls, Ricketts Glen State Park.

lookalikes, ferns, and sarsaparilla brush green to the floodplain. Footbridges cross Kitchen Creek at 0.2 and 0.9 mile, with a third bridge crossing a side water at 0.6 mile.

Upon return to the west shore at 0.9 mile, look for the trail to drift apart from the creek as the canyon gains definition. At 1.4 miles arrive near the top of 16-foot Murray Reynolds Falls, spilling through a rocky cleft. The rounded rock at the head of the falls forces the water to spout up. The whorled bedrock likewise adds visual interest.

Just upstream beckons 2-tiered Sheldon Reynolds Falls; enjoy views from base, side, and top. Next comes the graceful shower of 27-foot Harrison Wright Falls spanning the breadth of the creek ledge, but Kitchen Creek deserves acclaim even in its gentler moments. Stairs now ascend the slope leading to the loop junction at Waters Meet (1.8 miles).

Cross the West Branch bridge for a counterclockwise tour of the upper canyon, now on the **Glen Leigh Trail**. Natural rock steps advance the tour past engaging Wyandot Falls, secluded amid a dark hollow. The trail then crosses the East Branch Kitchen Creek between Wyandot Falls and 40-foot B. Reynolds Falls, which shows a rubble base and west shore overhang. Big birch rise amid the hemlocks, with jewelweed and witch-hazel gracing the creek-hugging trail.

At 2 miles cross the footbridge below R. B. Ricketts Falls. Complemented by a cascading and weeping side drainage, this falls serves up a lovely union of water, rock, and greenery. More deciduous trees shade the tour as hikers pursue the artful, twisting East Branch upstream. Next find Ozone Falls tucked away in a corner.

Again cross a footbridge. Here, admire the folding together of the platy cliffs, as switchbacks and stone steps lead the way. Ahead the spiral-and-tiered waters of 41-foot Huron Falls mark off distance. Upstream view a cliff grotto, as the trail ascends stairs toward Shawnee, F. L. Ricketts, and Onondaga falls. The platy shale serves both as a canvas for and sculptress of the showering waters.

At 2.6 miles cross a bridge, continuing the ascent along the East Branch; old-growth trees and impressive snags command attention. At 2.8 miles comes the next junction; go left on the **Highland Trail** to continue the falls loop. The trail upstream leads to the cabins area.

The Highland Trail journeys west to meet the West Branch Kitchen Creek. Stroll a relaxing woodland of beech, birch, black cherry, and striped maple, finding a mild uphill grade. In places, flat stones ease the crossing of muddy spots; elsewhere hikers must slog through. Despite the busy hiker thoroughfare, bear have been sighted prowling through ferns.

Pass a split-rock ledge, coming to a narrow passage (Midway Crevasse), amid the jumbled sandstone blocks. The Highland Trail then remains flat and shady. Where it meets **Ganoga Glen Trail** at 4.1 miles, bear left. To the right lies the upper trailhead (0.1 mile).

With the descent, the sound of the West Branch urges hikers to pick up their stride for the next parade of falls. Short, steep grades punctuate travel. At 4.2 miles, bear right per a sign and soon after cross a footbridge. At the next junction, a left continues the Ganoga Glen Trail and Natural Area tour; to the right travels the **Old Beaver Dam Road Trail**.

Downstream from this junction find the first cascade-waterfall series on the West Branch—37-foot Mohawk Falls. A steep set of rock steps descend alongside its lacy veil, ledge cascade, and skirt of skipping water. A classic beauty, Oneida Falls continues the watery story.

The side-by-side streamers of Cayuga Falls precede the glen's tallest falls, the 94-foot Ganoga Falls, which reveals a different persona, depending on angle. Look for a spur to the left leading to the base of the falls for a full-length view. This stately waterfalls generates its own breeze and nurtures a wall of greenery with its spray.

The countdown continues with Seneca, Delaware, and Mohican falls. With the beautiful zigzagging waters, it is difficult to tell where one falls ends and the next begins. Side streams likewise arrive in cascades. The 17-foot Conestoga Falls, the billowing lace of 47-foot Tuscarora Falls, and elegant Erie Falls end the exciting tale as the loop draws to a close at Waters Meet, 5.6 miles.

From here, backtrack downstream along the Kitchen Creek Trail, renewing acquaintance with the first three waterfalls and the beauty of Kitchen Creek. End the tour at 7.4 miles.

For the **Adams Falls Hike**, descend the path at the north end of the southern trailhead parking area off PA 118, hiking toward Kitchen Creek. In

0.1 mile, overlook 36-foot Adams Falls, spilling snowy white through a recessed drop where the cliffs fold together; the keyhole look engages. By traveling atop the rocky vantage, view the swirling chute that escapes the upper plunge pool and the potholes it fills. The chasm sets this falls apart from the ones upstream.

24 Bruce Lake Loop

General description:	This hike follows a maintenance road and a foot trail, touring 2,845-acre Bruce Lake Natural Area, crossing the isthmus of Egypt Meadow Lake and encircling Bruce Lake.
General location:	25 miles east of Scranton.
Special attractions:	Bruce and Egypt Meadow lakes; swamps; flowering rhododendron, mountain laurel, and sheep laurel; blueberries; wildlife sightings; fall foliage.
Length:	6.8 miles round trip.
Elevation:	The trail has less than a 100-foot elevation change, traveling between 1,700 and 1,800 feet in elevation.
Difficulty:	Easy.
Maps:	Delaware State Forest; Promised Land State Park.
Special concerns:	There is no camping, but visitors may hunt or fish in season, with valid licenses. Hikers, take precautions during hunting seasons. Carry insect repellent and expect areas of brushing vegetation. Pass softly and practice no-trace wilderness ethics.
Season and hours:	Spring through fall for hiking; daylight hours.
For information:	Delaware State Forest.

Finding the trailhead: From Interstate 84, take exit 7 for Promised Land State Park and go south on Pennsylvania 390. In 1.5 miles find marked trailhead parking on the left.

The hike: Round the stone pillar and entry gate, traveling closed, mildly rolling **Bruce Lake Road** (a woods-road trail), east into Bruce Lake Natural Area. The occasional blue blaze marks the way.

Logged of its towering pine and hemlock in the late-19th century, then ravaged by fire, the natural area now sports a low-canopy hardwood cloak. Pass amid maple, oak, and hickory, with a complement of hemlock, laurel, a handful of rhododendron, fern, sassafras, and sarsaparilla. A few spruce appear where the trail approaches the southern edge of snag-riddled, shrubby Panther Swamp. Despite the wooded fullness at the trail's shoulder, the overhead cathedral remains open.

At 0.4 mile, stay on Bruce Lake Road; to the right travels the footpath of **Brown Trail** for a longer loop option. Before long, cross the bridge over the

Bruce Lake Loop

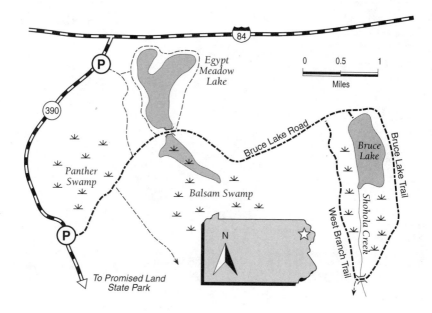

outlet of Panther Swamp to find the next trail junction. Here **Panther Swamp Trail** heads north to **Egypt Meadow Road** (another hiker avenue accessing the natural area). Again stay with Bruce Lake Road. By 0.75 mile the woods to your right take on a wetland character.

At 0.9 mile reach the picturesque mirror-dark waters of Egypt Meadow Lake; a secondary path travels north along its west shore. Built by the Civilian Conservation Corps in 1935, Egypt Meadow Lake measures 48 acres, with open waters spanning north of the isthmus, vegetated waters grading south to 100-acre Balsam Swamp. A narrow neck and bridge shape the lake isthmus. Water lilies and reflection rocks add to northern lake views; ducks, frogs, and herons animate the southern lake.

As Bruce Lake Road gradually ascends away from Egypt Meadow Lake, find the trees more draping and occasionally spy rock outcrops and glacial rock deposits. At 2.1 miles keep to Bruce Lake Road, hiking past the **West Branch Trail** (the loop's close) on the right.

Unmarked spurs now lead to the Bruce Lake shore. Spring-fed 56-acre Bruce Lake occupies a glacier-melt depression or kettle. More of the white-blooming lilies adorn this broad natural lake, with highbush blueberry and mountain laurel adding flourish to its rim. The flat Pocono Plateau sculpts a level skyline of trees. Additional spurs break away to the lakeshore, arriving at attractive grassy flats.

At 2.5 miles, the roadway narrows and bends right, signaling the start of **Bruce Lake Trail**, although no sign indicates it as such. Turn right for a clockwise perimeter tour of Bruce Lake, passing amid an oak-and-blueberry

Bruce Lake, Bruce Lake Natural Area, Delaware State Forest.

complex. More secondary trails branch away to the lake glare, with the last one occurring at 2.7 miles, near a disabled pump.

Mountain and sheep laurel now intermingle with the low and highbush blueberry, squeezing the trail to boot-width. Despite the woods stealing lake views, the berry walk engages, especially when the bushes hang heavy with fruit. Glimpse the marsh and open water at the southern extent of Bruce Lake; here snags rise amid the oaks. Now cross the outlet bridge and in a couple of strides turn right on the West Branch Trail to close the loop.

This trail offers a similar narrow footpath stroll through brushing vegetation, with the laurel more numerous and the forest fuller. Initially enjoy looks toward the marsh and red maples. A slight elevation gain allows for such looks before the wooded lake buffer again builds. No spurs access the west shore. At 4.7 miles, return to Bruce Lake Road and turn left to end at the trailhead, 6.8 miles.

25 Pinchot Trail, Northern Loop

General description:	A northern loop tour of the 23-mile Pinchot Trail System explores the Pocono Plateau, visiting an observation tower and an intriguing spring. Pass amid pink-and-white splendor, as the mountain laurel attains peak bloom mid- to late June, indulge in the tasty bounty of the area's highbush blueberries mid-July to August, or enjoy the fire-blaze of autumn-colored leaves in October.
General location:	12 miles east of Wilkes-Barre.
Special attractions:	Observation tower for a Pocono panorama; flowering laurels and grasses; blueberries; mixed hardwood forest for vibrant autumn color; swamp, meadow, and springs; solitude; wildlife.
Length:	11.2 miles round trip.
Elevation:	Find a 450-foot elevation change, with the high point atop Big Pine Hill (2,250 feet), the low point at Painter Creek crossing (1,800 feet).
Difficulty:	Moderate.
Maps:	Pinchot Trail System; Lackawanna State Forest.
Special concerns:	Find the trail system blazed at 100-foot intervals. Blue marks the Pinchot Trail, red the connecting trails. Overnight travelers must secure a camping permit from Lackawanna State Forest District Headquarters or Thornhurst Forest Foreman's Office (1.5 miles east of the trailhead). The maximum stay per any single site is 2 nights; limit hiking party to 4 people. No swimming or wading; check posted rules for campfires. As rattlesnakes find habitat here, watch hand and foot placements and look before you sit. Seasonally, springs overflow parts of the trail.
Season and hours:	Spring through fall.
For information:	Lackawanna State Forest.

Finding the trailhead: From Interstate 80, take exit 43 and go north on Pennsylvania 115 for 5.7 miles, passing through Blakeslee. Then, turn right on State Route 2040/River Road for Thornhurst, 4.5 miles. Go 0.3 miles past Thornhurst, turn left on S.R. 2016/Bear Lake Road to reach the trailhead on the right in 4 miles.

The trail may also be accessed via I-380: Take exit 6, go north on PA 435, and west on River Road (here SR 2013) to Bear Lake Road, and turn right.

The hike: Named for Gifford Pinchot, the first chief of the United States Forest Service, the **Pinchot Trail**, together with its associated trails, offers tranquil touring amid the varied habitats of the Pocono Plateau, with numerous hike options.

For this northern loop tour, ascend north via the **Powder Magazine Trail**, part of the Pinchot Trail (blue blazes). Pass amid a semi-open forest of maple, oak, birch, and sassafras, with both mountain and sheep laurel, bracken fern, highbush blueberry, and low berry shrubs. Stepping stones ease travel across a soggy site. Soon after, reach a trail register, where maps are often available.

At 0.5 mile come upon the loop junction. Here, turn left on the red-blazed **Pine Hill Trail** for a clockwise tour of the state forest, returning via the Powder Magazine Trail straight ahead. Find the foot trails well-cut and maintained with some protruding roots and rocks, but generally they allow for carefree strolling. Deer, woodpecker, cedar waxwing, and songbirds offer brief interludes. As June wanes, both kinds of laurel and a beautiful flowering grass add to travel.

Past a planted stand of spruce, reach the next signed junction. Here the **Frank Gantz Trail** (also blazed red) heads left, offering alternative loop travel. Proceed forward on Pine Hill Trail. Tackle the brief challenge of a rock field, tour amid hip-high fern and shrubs, and skirt a rocky ledge and knoll, before meeting a forest road at 1.5 miles. Detour left on the road to visit Pine Hill Observation Tower atop Big Pine Hill; the loop continues directly across the road.

At 1.6 miles reach the 2-story tower for a 360-degree panorama of the flattened, tree-clad Pocono Plateau, with just a few higher hilltops punctuating the terrain. Overlook the Delaware and Susquehanna river drainages, with the shining sliver and dark basin of Bear Lake to the south. In the fall, the mosaic of changing leaves brings a sense of texture to the leafy stage. Day hikers find the tower a satisfying, 3.2-mile, round-trip destination.

For the full loop, return to the point where the Pine Hill Trail crosses the forest road and resume the tour north (a left at 1.7 miles). The trail gradually ascends near some whitish-gray rocks, touring similar forest. In many areas, the low canopy, snag-riddled woods owes its stature and character to the plateau's depleted minerals—the aftermath of a series of fires in the post-logging era. The trail then tops out and descends, meeting a closed road grade. Turn left, rounding the gate at 2.1 miles.

The branches of black cherry, maple, and oak lace over the grassy lane, with tall laurel and some American chestnut adding to the trail's border. At 2.75 miles, proceed forward to meet the blue blazes of the **Scrub Oak Trail** (2.8 miles), which now continues the loop to the right. Ignore the orange-diamond markers on the left at 2.75 miles.

While easily passable, this foot trail at times cries out for a manicure. Pass from low-stature forest to tall oaks and maples. A couple of rocky sites mark travel. With a mild rolling ascent, cross Pittston Road (another forest road at 4 miles); keep to the blue blazes. Here the **Painter Creek Trail** takes the relay pass.

Glimpse a marshy area beyond the woods to the left, and encounter a few spruce amid the woodland. At 4.25 miles, hikers have an option: Either keep to the blue-blazed Pinchot Trail, traversing the top of a wooded pla-

Pinchot Trail, Northern Loop

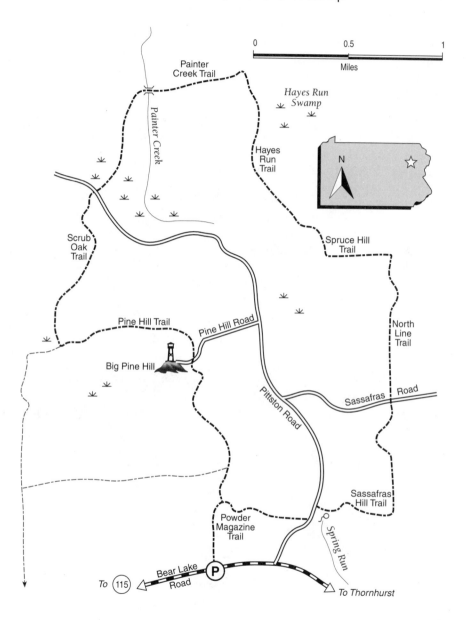

teau, before making a plummeting descent to Painter Creek, or take the red trail for a direct descent along the creek. To prevent further erosion of the steep drainage slope, opt for the red creekside spur.

At 4.75 miles rejoin the blue-blazed route near the forest boundary, and bear right to cross the log footbridge over Painter Creek. Here the waterway flows through a picturesque dark hemlock cove. Look for blue blazes, pointing out an ascent. With a rolling tour find a rocky spring, introducing the signature bloom and leaf of the tulip poplar. The trail remains near the forest boundary.

At 5.4 miles swing right, still tracking blue blazes. A downed post likely signals another trail-name change, but all hikers really need to remember now is to stay the blue blazes. Sheep laurel abounds, lending its own seasonal flourish when the mountain laurel parades out pink-hued blooms. Alternately travel open woods and shady pockets. Hayes Run Swamp below to the left remains a mystery. Birch, shad, and pitch pine dot the woodland.

At a junction post amid a grassy opening (6.4 miles), turn left on a grassy lane, staying with the blue blazes. A foot trail then advances the loop, as the trail arcs right at 6.5 miles. Expect some rocky footing, climbing to a low rocky hilltop; a sheep laurel and berry flat lie below to the right.

Pass a second rocky cap, touring amid fern-filled woods. At 7.2 miles, turn right for a straight-line tour, still vacillating between sun and shade. At 7.5 miles, looks left find a small wetland. The trail then descends a canted

Pine Hill observation tower, Lackawanna State Forest.

outcrop and divides a clover-grass meadow, meeting Sassafras Road.

Cross this forest road for a dazzling mountain laurel tour. Scenic stands of sassafras and white birch likewise recommend travel. The easy trail allows eyes to roam. As the trail dips and the woods fill out, the laurel disperses. A couple more rocky fields call hikers to attend their footing.

At 9.75 miles reach a spring, gurgling beneath and up through the rocks. From it, Spring Run, a full-fledged creek emerges. A towering white pine and its braided root contribute to the mystical scene. Day hikers who travel the loop in reverse will find the spring a satisfying destination.

Next meet Pittston Road a second time and follow it left for 0.1 mile to pick up the blue-blazed Powder Magazine Trail on the right, for the closing leg of the loop. Initially find a rocky trailbed, with framing laurel, birch, and meadow habitat. Pockets of shade offer reprieve from the open-woods travel. Cross a small rocky spring and close the loop at the red-blazed Pine Hill Trail (10.7 miles). Keep to the blue blazes, retracing the first 0.5-mile of the Powder Magazine Trail to return to the trailhead, 11.2 miles.

26 Painter Swamp–Stillwater Natural Area Hike

General description:	This barbell-shaped tour swings a circuit around Painter and Big Bear swamps, with the latter located in Stillwater Natural Area. This 1,931-acre native area has been set aside to prosper relatively undisturbed. During the Civil War, deserters and draft dodgers hid out in the swamps. Keen-eyed hikers may detect shack remnants amid the dense growth.
General location:	12 miles southwest of Milford.
Special attractions:	Swamps; hardwood and conifer forest; flowering azalea, rhododendron, mountain laurel, and sheep laurel; a beaver dam; wildlife sightings; fall foliage.
Length:	8.6 miles round trip.
Elevation:	Find a mildly rolling trail, traveling between 1,300 and 1,400 feet in elevation.
Difficulty:	Moderate, due to rocky footing.
Maps:	Thunder Swamp Trail System (generally stocked at the trailhead mapbox during hiking season); Delaware State Forest.
Special concerns:	This hike is part of the 45-mile Thunder Swamp Trail System. Identify the main trails by blue blazes; connector trails by red blazes. Hikers may backpack camp; secure a free permit from Delaware State Forest. When applying by mail, submit the request 10 days prior to a visit. Carry a backpacker stove,

drinking water, and insect repellent.

Season and hours: Spring through fall for hiking.

For information: Delaware State Forest.

Finding the trailhead: From the junction of U.S. Highways 6 and 209 in Milford, go south on U.S. 209 for 7.9 miles and turn right on Pennsylvania 739 North. Go 1.1 miles and turn left on Silver Lake Road, heading toward Porters Lake. Go 7.4 miles, turning left on dirt Flat Ridge Road (0.7 mile past the Edgemere Ranger Station). Find the marked trailhead on the left, in another 1.9 miles.

Alternatively, take exit 8 off Interstate 84, going south on PA 402 for 8.8 miles. There, turn left (east) on Silver Lake Road, go 3.9 miles, and turn right on Flat Ridge Road to reach the trailhead in another 1.9 miles.

The hike: Follow the red-blazed path heading east, touring a multistory forest of red maple and white, black, and chestnut oak. Sarsaparilla invades the grasses, while low, angled rocks penetrate the trailbed, straining ankles. At 0.1 mile, reach the Painter Swamp loop junction and turn right for the west shore tour. During high water, hikers should forgo the loop, keeping to the east shore to avoid the beaver-dam crossing at the outlet. Both shores hold similar merit.

To the right, the trail hugs the west shore of this large swamp, passing within 50 feet of the snag-pierced, shimmering open water. Vegetated is-

Painter Swamp, Stillwater Natural Area, Delaware State Forest.

Painter Swamp–Stillwater Natural Area Hike

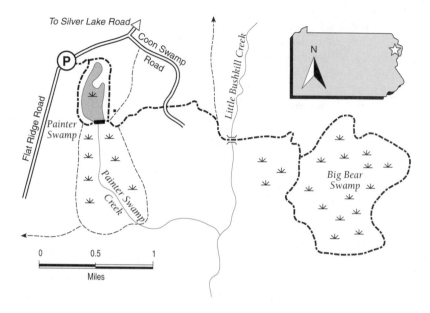

lands; pockets of aquatic grass, rush, and cattail; and mats of lily pad embroider the stage. Heron, frog, turtle, splashing fish, and swallows call for the raising of binoculars. With a flush of autumn color, the fully wooded perimeter ups the ante. Highbush blueberry and sheep laurel favor the shoreline.

At 0.4 mile, a rock slab offers swampside seating and an invitation to relax (when insects cooperate). At the 0.6-mile junction, turn left for Stillwater Natural Area; the path ahead leads to Lake Minisink. Now, the shoreline opens up, adding azalea to the mix of shrubs.

Next cross Painter Swamp Creek (the swamp outlet), via a makeshift bridge and the sticks and mud of a beaver dam. A few sloshing steps seem unavoidable. Just beyond lies a junction. Here, turn right, hiking along a jeep trail for 20 strides, to pick up the semi-masked foot trail on the right. While it is blazed, stay alert.

At 1 mile, bear left for the natural area as a second path to Lake Minisink branches right. Blue blazes now guide the way. Encounter a couple of quick turns: go right at the T-junction and left at the fork. At 1.6 miles pass a register box, coming out at Coon Swamp Road. Keep to the blue blazes, angling across this restricted access road.

Enjoy a pleasant woods meander on the foot trail, encountering a few spring-soaked bottom areas. Bird songs, a breeze, and lighting changes add to the relaxation. On higher plateaus, bracken fern reigns; in moist depressions, blueberry and huckleberry. Past Coon Swamp Road lose much of the rockiness.

At 1.8 miles, turn right for the Big Bear Swamp tour of Stillwater Natural Area; to the left, a red-blazed loop explores the area's northern block. Stay with the blue blazes, descending to a footbridge crossing of Little Bushkill Creek (2 miles). With islands of greenery, the shallow waterway flows smooth and dark. Geranium and violet adorn its banks, mountain laurels dress the woods as the trail draws away. Spy low rock ledges as a carriageway advances travel.

At 2.4 miles turn left, following blazes upstream along a creek to the point of crossing. At 2.7 miles reach the loop junction for Big Bear Swamp. Go left for a clockwise tour, once again traveling a grassy woods lane, but stay alert for the foot trail on the right that continues the tour, at 3 miles.

Travel amid a woods void of swamp glimpses, coming to a 10-foot-high rock ledge. Where it ends, mount the low plateau. Snags now open the skyline. Pass between woodsy flats and low rock tiers. By 3.8 miles, spruce, birch, rhododendron, and highbush blueberry signal the swamp is near. In places spy the wetland floor, green with sphagnum moss, fern, and bog grass.

The circuit continues, mildly rolling. Where oaks reclaim the tour, again spy pockets of mountain laurel. At 5.5 miles meet a woods lane and follow it right, passing through posted private property to close the loop (6 miles). Turn left, backtracking to Painter Swamp (7.8 miles). There, turn right to complete the Painter Swamp circuit along the east shore, enjoying new perspectives. End at the trailhead, 8.6 miles.

27 Delaware Water Gap National Recreation Area, Dingmans Creek Area

OVERVIEW

This 70,000-acre national recreation area (NRA) spans the Pennsylvania and New Jersey shores of a 40-mile stretch of the Delaware Wild and Scenic River. At the southern end of the park, view Delaware Water Gap, where the Delaware cuts an S-shaped chasm through 1,400-foot Kittatinny Ridge. Throughout the corridor, find exceptional river recreation. Within the river's vital watershed, hikers explore wooded slopes, Pocono plateaus, and picturesque ravines. Sparkling waterfalls, mature eastern hemlocks, and rhododendron dress the side-creek canyons. Trails of varying length and difficulty are present in the NRA.

General description:	2 popular short loop trails visit the waterfall galleries along Dingmans Creek: at Dingmans Falls Visitor Center and at George W. Childs Picnic Area (Fulmer Falls).
General location:	8 miles south of Milford off U.S. Highway 209.
Special attractions:	5 dramatic waterfalls, scenic Dingmans Creek, dark hemlock forests, early July rhododendron blooms, chance wildlife sightings.
Length:	Dingmans Falls Nature Trail, 0.75-mile round trip (fully accessible); Fulmer Falls Loop, 1.2-mile loop.
Elevation:	Dingmans Falls Nature Trail shows 150 feet of elevation change; Fulmer Falls Loop, some 200 feet of elevation change.
Difficulty:	Dingmans Falls Nature Trail, easy; Fulmer Falls Loop, easy to moderate.
Maps:	Dingmans Falls Nature Trail; the Delaware Water Gap: Selected Hiking Trails brochure.
Special concerns:	Keep to the trail, do not disturb natural objects, and no swimming. During peak travel season, the visitor center parking lot frequently fills. Note: A new bridge for Dingmans Falls Road will keep Dingmans Falls Visitor Center and Nature Trail closed to the public through 1998.
Season and hours:	Spring through fall, daylight hours. Dingmans Falls Visitor Center: daily 9 a.m. to 5 p.m. April through October; weekends November and December; and closed January through March.
For information:	Delaware Water Gap NRA.

Finding the trailhead: From the junction of U.S. Highways 6 and 209 in Milford, go south on U.S. 209 for 7.9 miles, reaching the intersection with Pennsylvania 739 North.

For Dingmans Falls Visitor Center and trailhead, remain on U.S. 209, continuing south another 0.2 mile. There turn right (west), following Dingmans Falls Road for 0.8 mile to visitor center/trail parking.

For George W. Childs Picnic Area, turn right on PA 739 North. Go 1.1 miles and turn left on Silver Lake Road, heading toward Porters Lake. Find the first Childs Park access in 1.7 miles, the second 0.1 mile farther west, and the third by turning left on Park Road in still another 0.1 mile.

The hikes: The popular **Dingmans Falls Nature Trail** heads upstream from the visitor center building. Footbridges twice cross Dingmans Creek, allowing for loop travel between the 80-foot Silver Thread Falls on a side tributary and the 130-foot Dingmans Falls on Dingmans Creek.

Travel the cool, dark mystery of the hemlock-clad ravine, crossing the 1st bridge to begin the tour with a visit to Silver Thread Falls. This elegant shimmery ribbon spills through an eroded shale crevasse. Hemlock, birch, and beech contribute to its tranquil, shady bower.

Next proceed upstream to the second bridge, admiring the waters and bedrock of Dingmans Creek. Upon crossing, arrive at a junction. Here the loop swings left (downstream); upstream, the trail forks to a pair of Dingmans Falls vistas.

Rhododendron, Delaware Water Gap National Recreation Area.

Delaware Water Gap National Recreation Area, Dingmans Creek Area

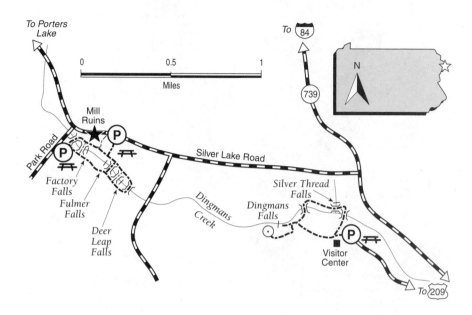

Bear right to reach the lower boardwalk platform for a full-face view of this exciting multi-directional, multi-tier, forceful white surge. When the falls attains full glory, billows of mist shroud the canyon. Dry-season visits present a much altered face. Crowning hemlocks, fanning deciduous, and rhododendron complement the union of water and shale. Dingmans Creek quickly gentles the churned water.

Enjoy the views of Dingmans Falls as you ascend the stairway to the upper viewing site. Also, admire the mossy bedded outcrop shaping the trail. A bi-level viewing deck presents the top of the falls and a grotto along the opposite wall. Return to the loop junction and proceed downstream; rustic benches invite pause. End at 0.75 mile.

For **Fulmer Falls Loop**, find 5 footbridges spanning Dingmans Creek, facilitating loop travel and presenting new perspectives on the area's 3 falls: Fulmer, Factory, and Deer Leap.

Starting from the first (easternmost) parking lot for George W. Childs Picnic Area, descend the slope to the creek's north shore and bear right (upstream), reaching a fenced viewing area. Here obtain a side perspective overlooking two-thirds of the 70- to 80-foot drop of Fulmer Falls. Following rains, admire a thundering plummet and the pounding of rock.

Continue upstream passing through the picnic area of the north shore, for a counterclockwise loop. Next, admire the 30- to 40-foot shimmery pyra-

Dingmans Falls, Delaware Water Gap National Recreation Area.

mid of Factory Falls. Below the second Childs parking area, discover ruins from an old mill. The plunging waters of Dingmans Creek powered early-day industry in the Delaware River Valley. View stone walls 10 feet high.

Continue upstream to the uppermost bridge for the full 1.2-mile loop, overlooking more of the creek. Spruce, hemlock, pine, hickory, maple, and oak weave shade. On the south shore, the trail drifts from the creek. Find more groundcover and some mountain laurel. Log-braced earthen steps then return hikers to Dingmans Creek, for a glimpse at the head of Fulmer Falls. Due to canyon angles, the appreciation is primarily aural.

Avoid bridge crossings, proceeding downstream to Deer Leap Falls. A detour onto the footbridge at the head of this falls provides a stirring perspective on the steep canyon drop and the gash carved into the stream shelf. Cross the lower-canyon bridge for the close of the loop and a view of 15- to 18-foot Deer Leap Falls. Ascend, traveling wooden stairs and rounding slope. Cascades add to the upstream tour. Close the loop at Fulmer Falls and return to parking, 1.2 miles.

28 Delaware Water Gap National Recreation Area, Pocono Environmental Education Center

OVERVIEW

Straddling the Pennsylvania–New Jersey shore of the Delaware Wild and Scenic River, this popular 70,000-acre national recreation area (NRA) extends exceptional scenery, 1st-rate river recreation, hiking trails, and an acclaimed residential environmental-education center. Occupying a former honeymoon resort amid the quiet beauty of the Pocono Plateau, Pocono Environmental Education Center (PEEC) holds classes and offers walks and talks designed to increase environmental awareness; for these, visitors must register and pay a fee. But the PEEC also boasts a fine series of short, interlocking trails open free to the public.

General description:	3 hikes travel several of the site's 6 color-coded named trails visiting ponds, waterfalls, a vista, fossil bed, mixed woods, streams, and rocky ledges.
General location:	Off U.S. Highway 209, 12 miles south of Milford, 15 miles north of East Stroudsburg.
Special attractions:	Delaware River Valley–Kittatinny Ridge view, waterfalls, wildlife ponds, wetlands, flowering shrubs, wildflowers, marine fossils, rock ledges, fall foliage.
Length:	Two Ponds–Tumbling Waters Trail, 3 miles round-trip; Fossil Trail, 1.3-mile loop; Sunrise–Scenic Gorge Trail, 4 miles round-trip.
Elevation:	Two Ponds–Tumbling Waters Trail, 200-foot elevation change; Fossil Trail, 300-foot elevation change; Sunrise–Scenic Gorge Trail, 150-foot elevation change.
Difficulty:	All, moderate.
Maps:	PEEC trail map and interpretive brochures (modest charge for some printed materials).
Special concerns:	Come prepared for ticks and poison ivy. Find trails well-blazed with generally good beds. Use care on 1 precarious ledge descent/ascent along the Sunrise–Scenic Gorge Trail; a guide rope aids travelers over the challenge. Keep to the trails, and no collecting within the park. Hikers may seek out fossils, but they may not remove any of them.
Season and hours:	Spring through fall for hiking, daylight hours.
For information:	Pocono Environmental Education Center.

Finding the trailhead: From the junction of U.S. Highways 6 and 209 in Milford, go south on U.S. 209 for 12.6 miles and turn right (west) on Briscoe Mountain Road at a PEEC sign. In 0.8 mile bear right on Emery Road to reach the main building and parking lot in 0.1 mile. Trails radiate out from here.

The hikes: Start the **Two Ponds–Tumbling Waters Trail** on the boardwalk across Emery Road from the main building. An interpretive brochure pairs up with the white-blazed Two Ponds Trail; orange blazes mark the Tumbling Waters Trail.

Travel a shrub-enclosed boardwalk for 50 feet to a wildlife blind. There wooden panels open to the shrubby environment and inhabiting birdlife of Front Pond. Pass an artificial bat roost and, next, edge a field, spying a decomposition graveyard, conveying the evils of litter and waste. At 0.25 mile, angle right across Briscoe Mountain Road.

Travel from locust woods to pine-spruce plantations, descending to Pickerel Pond. Stone walls crisscross the trail system. Elongated, even-width Pickerel Pond shows an edge of submerged grasses and a rim of planted conifer with hardwoods. Follow the blazes rounding the pond's right shore. A few beaver gnawings or the noisy pass of a kingfisher may draw atten-

Delaware Water Gap National Recreation Area, Pocono Environmental Education Center

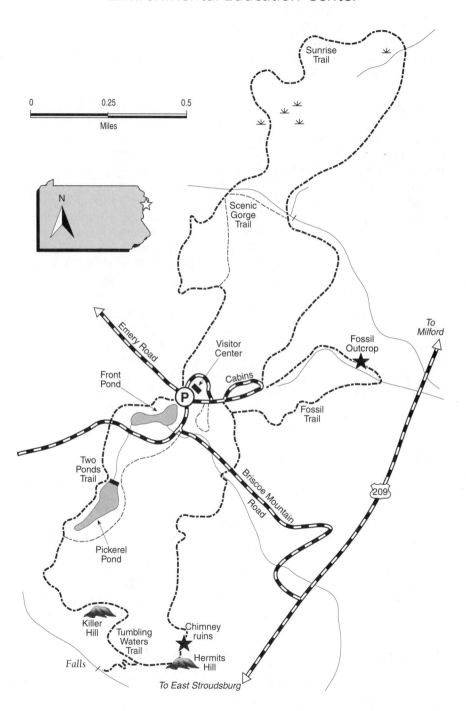

tion.

Veer away from the pond, coming to a junction (0.6 mile). Here the white Two Ponds Trail swings left, returning to the center for a 1.5-mile round trip. Proceed forward, tracking the orange blazes to complete the Tumbling Waters tour. Travel oak-maple woods and encounter the occasional large hemlock or forgotten white pine. As the trail rolls and contours, hear the whisper of a stream in the below ravine. Hemlocks become more prevalent as the trail tops "Killer Hill," 1.2 miles. Descend and round to the falls spur, 1.5 miles.

The loop bears left; while the falls spur switchbacks downhill to the right. Two falls actually grace the ravine. Glimpse the upper portion of the 1st falls, before reaching the bottom of the ravine for a full-face view of the 2nd falls. This parted 50-foot tiered veil enchants, with fanned ferns and rhododendron. Do not go cross-country for a better view of the 1st falls.

Resume the loop (1.7 miles). With a fairly steep ascent through low-stature oaks, come out atop the open sandstone outcrop of Hermits Hill. Overlook Delaware Gap, the long, wooded rise of New Jersey's Kittatinny Ridge, and a series of distant blue shadows. Occasionally, a hawk circles overhead. During fall migration, kettles of hawks spiral skyward.

Continue across the top of Hermits Hill, turning left at an old stone foundation and fireplace. Descend and later bear right, touring a woods road through a choked pine-deciduous woods; again bear right at the fork. Scenic old maples entwined by Virginia creeper now frame travel. Tiger lilies grow where the trail again crosses Briscoe Mountain Road.

Next travel the narrow footpath amid a open shrub-wildflower habitat. Ascend, encountering red cedars. At 2.8 miles, bear right, descending to the next pine plantation; be alert for this easily missed turn. The blue-blazed **Fossil Trail** then arrives on the right, sharing the closing distance. Emerge on the cabin campus road opposite Cabin 10. Hike left along the road to return to the main building (3 miles).

For the **Fossil Trail** start opposite Cabin 10 (0.1 mile east of the main building). A sign and blue blazes point the way; an interpretive brochure identifies features keyed to the numbered blocks along the trail. Travel the shared distance with the orange Tumbling Waters Trail through mixed forest, before bearing left and ascending and rounding a rocky knoll. Deer may pause for a curious look. Next, skirt a small wetland, where frog or muskrat may be spied. Ahead, keep to the blue blazes, as the trail passes through a maze of tracked paths.

With a fairly steep descent, travel amid taller forest and cross a small drainage and then a ravine to reach the base of the fossil-bearing outcrop cliff. An interpretive board identifies, each of the marine fossils found here. Crinoids, fingertip-sized circular depressions, seem particularly numerous. Also discover brachiopods and trilobites. Generally a previous traveler will have left some fossils near the sign, cluing what to look for; remember no collecting.

Now ascend steeply, paralleling the ravine upstream. The trail emerges

Red eft, Delaware Water Gap National Recreation Area.

at the campfire talk/amphitheater site, near the end of the cabin campus loop; bear left following the road past the dining hall. Keep left to close the loop at 1.3 miles, return to the main building and parking, 1.4 miles.

For the **Sunrise–Scenic Gorge Trail**, start at the bridge north of the main building, near Cabin 1, ascending through a red pine plantation. Dogwood and young maple grow amid the pines. Yellow blazes indicate the Sunrise Trail; red, the Scenic Gorge Trail.

Where the trail tops out, bear right, skirting a small outbuilding. An oak-huckleberry woodland claims the plateaus on this rolling tour; taller forest of white pine and mixed hardwoods the dips. Birds pair melodic notes to the shuffle of the boot. As the trail bottoms out at 0.4 mile, stay the yellow-blazed trail, bearing left for the longer loop. In another 0.1 mile, watch for the trail to turn right.

The trail twice passes through a flattened stone wall, before the red trail returns at 0.9 mile. At the upcoming ravine, stay with the yellow trail, making a stone-hop crossing; here the red trail turns right following the ravine. Cross a slow drainage and stroll along the foot of a low slope with a scalloped-ledge crest. The trail again climbs and dips.

At 1.5 miles come to a steep descent at a pair of ledge overhangs. A guide rope assists hikers down the upper half; a sure boot helps you negotiate the skidding gravels of the lower slope. Upon reaching the base, turn around to admire the jutting ledges. A hemlock woods next hosts travel. Mayapple and jack-in-the-pulpit lend spring accents.

Again the trail rolls before entering a straight-arrow course, passing a 15-foot-tall rock chimney and dipping to skirt a meadow and skunk cabbage bog. At 2.5 miles, edge a small wetland and round a hemlock slope to follow a small brook downstream. Cross it, and ascend along a second drainage. Cross this drainage above a picturesque corner falls to again meet the red trail.

Now pursue dual blazes, following the joined creek waters downstream. Small tiered cascades and low rock banks shape a mini-gorge. At 3.25 miles, a larger cascade and 10-foot-high mossy rock walls forge a final gorge impression. The trail then ascends away, reaching oak-pine habitat for a comfortable stroll back to the PEEC.

Reach the campus loop below Cabin 49 and bear right. Upon meeting the next paved road, again bear right. Hike past Cabin 10, the Fossil Trail's start, and the stone-ring pledge site to return to the main building, 4 miles.

29 Susquehanna Riverlands

OVERVIEW

At this Susquehanna River education and recreation site, jointly operated by Pennsylvania Power and Light (PP&L) and the Allegheny Electric Cooperative, three of the four land parcels extend hiking: Council Cup (above the east shore) and on the west shore, the Wetlands Nature Area and Riverlands Recreation Area. Each has its signature offering.

General description:	Hikes at Council Cup offer Susquehanna River overlooks and an upland woods stroll. The superb Wetlands Nature Trail System travels along river, marsh, swamp, and the North Branch Canal. The Riverlands Area completes the offering with a pair of hikes: One explores an artificial pond and the historic canal; the other the river.
General location:	5 miles northeast of Berwick.
Special attractions:	Susquehanna River; the historic North Branch Canal (1831-1900); wetlands, swamps, and marsh; riparian and upland woods; wildflowers; wildlife; fall color.
Length:	Council Cup Hikes: South Loop, 0.25 mile; North Loop, 0.8 mile; Wetlands Nature Trail System, 1-mile loop; Towpath Trail, 1.7-mile loop; Riverside Trail, 1-mile loop.
Elevation:	Find a modest roll to the Council Cup Hikes, touring at 700 feet in elevation. Find the river floodplain trails all flat, at 400 feet in elevation.
Difficulty:	All easy.
Maps:	Susquehanna Riverlands and Wetlands Nature Area brochures.

Susquehanna Riverlands

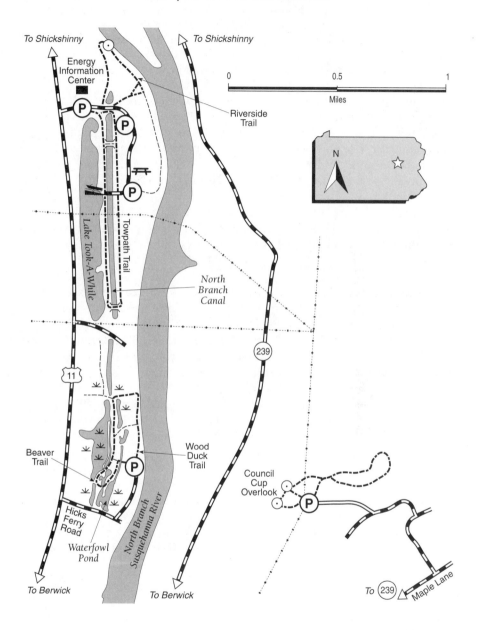

To Shickshinny

To Shickshinny

Energy
Information
Center

Riverside
Trail

0   0.5   1
Miles

N

Lake Took-A-While

Towpath Trail

North
Branch
Canal

239

11

Beaver
Trail

Wood
Duck
Trail

Council
Cup
Overlook

Hicks
Ferry
Road

Waterfowl
Pond

North Branch
Susquehanna River

To Berwick

To Berwick

To 239   Maple Lane

Special concerns:	Seasonally, carry insect repellent and netting. Beware of poison ivy. No pets or fishing in the Wetlands Nature Area, and no swimming or wading at any area. Register upon entering the wetlands.
Season and hours:	Generally spring through fall for hiking, 8 a.m. to dusk.
For information:	Susquehanna Riverlands.

Finding the trailhead: At the junction of U.S. Highway 11 and Pennsylvania 239 South in Shickshinny, go south on PA 239 for Council Cup. In 5.9 miles, turn left on Hobbie Road at Wapwallopen. Following signs, go 1.9 miles and turn left on Maple Lane. Go 0.6 mile on Maple Lane and again turn left. Drive 0.5 mile more, and turn left. Then, go 0.3 mile and turn right on the gravel road indicated for Council Cup Scenic Area to reach parking in 0.4 mile.

For the west shore offering, proceed south on U.S. 11 from Shickshinny. In about 4 miles, turn left for the Energy Information Center/Riverlands Recreation Area. Find Susquehanna Wetlands on the left, 1.4 miles farther south.

The hikes: For the **Council Cup Hikes**, hike west into the mixed upland woods from the northwest corner of trail parking. A wide grass and then gravel path ascends modestly. Reach a chain-link fence and bench overlooking the bluff escarpment of Council Cup (0.1 mile). To the right lies the **North Loop**; to the left the **South Loop**. From the bench, view the Susquehanna River Valley, its rural floodplain, small communities, and a tower of steam above the nuclear power plant.

The South Loop holds additional views. Come to a 2nd bench in another 0.1 mile. It lends new perspective on the river valley and extends looks north at the cliff profile. The view opens up when the trees lose their leaves. From here, the trail swings back into woods. Ascend amid oak, maple, tulip, hickory, sassafras, hophornbeam, and pitch pine. Close the loop, emerging near a utility tower at the south end of the parking area, 0.25 mile.

The North Loop initially remains along the bluff rim, but the forest blocks any views. In another 0.1 mile, traverse a utility corridor where lines extend an open-aisle look toward the river. Afterward, faded blue blazes mark the woods-shaded trail. Proceed forward, where a trail branches right at 0.25 mile. Soon after, reach a blazed junction: Go left; the main woods road ahead marks the return of the loop.

Make a slow descent passing through areas of white pine and birch, coming to a 4-way intersection (0.5 mile). The path ahead and the one to the left both dead-end; go right, still following faint blazes. At 0.6 mile complete the loop. Proceed forward a couple hundred feet and turn left to end at the northeast corner of trail parking.

Reach the **Wetlands Nature Trail System**, 0.6 mile east off U.S. 11, via Hicks Ferry Road. Three trails tour the natural area: **Wood Duck Trail**, **Spice Bush Short-cut**, and **Beaver Trail**. Interpretive panels introduce natural and cultural history. Leave from the northeast corner of the parking area, returning near the kiosk.

The Wood Duck Trail tours the field-and-forest habitat of the west bank Susquehanna River, passing ruins from an old coal dredge. When water levels are low, look for eel walls along the riverbed. In the early 1900s, these V-shaped 2-foot-high stone weirs funneled eels together for easy harvest. Beautiful old-growth ash, maple, and oak shade the way. Long ago, the Iroquois Indians walked this path en route to council meetings.

At 0.2 mile, the Spice Bush Shortcut heads left. Continue forward for the full 1-mile loop. Follow the broad, smooth-coursing Susquehanna River north upstream. In another 0.1 mile, turn away from the river, merging with a service road to edge a marsh. Cattails, snags, and a surface of duckweed contribute to the rich wetland, while frog, turtle, muskrat, and dragonflies lend animation.

Variously framing the trail's shoulder find honeysuckle, highbush blueberry, azalea, and sensitive fern. Next, reach the North Branch Canal and turn left following the towpath along its east bank. Duckweed, overhanging trees, sunning turtles, and snags likewise define this once vital transportation corridor. Mules plodded this path, pulling cargo boats of coal to fuel early Philadelphia industry.

Birch, hickory, tulip, and locust add to the treed edge, as the towpath passes between canal and marsh. Sedge, rush, arrowhead, and loosestrife vary the wetland tapestry. Haughty geese may voice prior claim to the trail. At 0.5 mile, the Spice Bush Shortcut arrives on the left. Continue forward on the towpath; culverts link the marsh waters.

Next view a sleepy bend on the retired canal. In 200 feet, the Wood Duck Trail turns left, returning to the parking lot for a 0.7-mile tour. Proceed forward on the towpath (now the Beaver Trail), for the full 1-mile loop. Enormous trees, tangled woods, and wetlands continue to dazzle. Ahead reach a bench near an intersection; views pan east toward the cliffs of Council Cup. Keep to the towpath.

At a 4-way junction (0.7 mile), turn left, leaving the towpath. Pass a skunk cabbage bog and again turn left for the closing leg of the loop. Here a 50-foot detour straight ahead adds a look at Waterfowl Pond—an open water with small shrub islands and cross-pond views toward Council Cup. Now pass a beaver-cut stump, interpretive sign, and birch swamp, before turning right to end at the trailhead kiosk.

Several parking areas within Riverlands Recreation Area access the **Towpath Trail**. Start this hike from the trail parking lot just east of the Energy Information Center. A trail kiosk marks the site. Hike south along the west bank of the historic canal. A fine cinder surface makes the flat 8-foot-wide towpath ideal for exercise walkers. Silver maple, black locust, oak, and dogwood edge the trail, screening looks at the murky canal water. Noise from U.S. 11 rivals the chorus of birds and croaking frogs.

Cross a breach between the canal and artificial Lake Took-A-While. Now look for the first of three bridges to cross the canal at 0.2 mile. Keep to the western towpath. Looks west find a billow of white steam from the power station. Alder, willow, and ash join the tangle of trees. View Canada geese, swallows, kingfisher, turtles, and fish. An angler may cast a line for bass. At 0.8 mile cross the southernmost bridge over the canal, and trace the east bank north to close the loop.

While looks at the canal remain similar, field, woods, and a developed recreation area now abut the trail. Birders find ample reason to raise their binoculars. At 1.25 miles, pass a boat launch area and interpretive sign on the North Branch Canal. Beyond, find restrooms and tables amid the developed park. Keep to the towpath, coming out at the park road. Turn left to close the loop at trail parking, 1.7 miles.

From the same parking area (east of the Energy Information Center), look on the north side of the road for the signed **Riverside Trail.** For a clockwise tour, hike north along the west bank of the nearly-dry canal. Travel a scenic grassy lane shaded by silver maple, dogwood, black cherry, elm, and ash; the floodplain boasts some big trees. Virginia creeper, sassafras, poison ivy, and waist- to chest-high jewelweed color the plain. Beware of roots.

The trail bends riverward (0.4 mile), reaching the blinding light of a pipeline corridor. There, turn right, following the grassy riverside aisle; shrub thickets rise at its border. From a riverside bench, admire the smooth, brownish-green Susquehanna River and enjoy the shade trees of shore. A fairly fast, even current transports bubbles downstream.

Strawberries, wildflowers, ducks, herons, and tiny toads may add to discovery. Keep to the mowed path to avoid poison ivy. At 0.75 mile and again at 0.8 mile, side trails branch right; follow either of these to close the loop. Where the paths merge in 200 feet, continue west edging a field to come out on the east shore of the North Branch Canal, 1 mile.

30 Lehigh Gorge Trail

General description:	Part of Lehigh Gorge State Park, this abandoned stretch of the Jersey Central Railroad welcomes multiple-use recreation along the Lehigh River.
General location:	West of Interstate 476, between White Haven and Jim Thorpe.
Special attractions:	Overlooks and access to a changeable, class III whitewater river; exciting gorge; sheer cliffs; a spectacular rhododendron showcase; fishing; side-creek waterfalls; wildflowers; wildlife; fall foliage.
Length:	15.5 miles one-way from White Haven to Penn Haven; 21.5 miles to Glen Onoko.
Elevation:	Find an easy, comfortable grade, descending from 1,200 feet to 600 feet in elevation.
Difficulty:	Easy to strenuous, depending on length.
Maps:	State park brochure.
Special concerns:	No overnight camping or swimming. Mileage markers and benches ease travel, with toilets at White Haven, Rockport, and Glen Onoko. Park officials regularly patrol the trail; locate the park office at Rockport. Midweek visits are quieter. Timber rattlesnakes may be spied.
Season and hours:	Year-round, 8 a.m. to sunset. Snow may linger in the gorge until early May.
For information:	Lehigh Gorge State Park.

Finding the trailhead: From Pennsylvania 940 in White Haven, turn south onto Main Street prior to reaching the White Haven Shopping Center. At the end of Main Street, turn left, and then bear right on an improved-surface road heading south. Reach trailhead parking, 0.5 mile.

For the Rockport Access, follow PA 940 south from White Haven, turning left on Lehigh Gorge Drive/State Route 4010. Follow S.R. 4010 to S.R. 4014 and turn left passing through the village of Rockport to the park office and trail access.

For Glen Onoko Access Area, from the junction of U.S. Highway 209 and PA 903 in Jim Thorpe, go 0.4 mile north on PA 903, turning left on Front Street, which becomes Coalport Road. In 0.3 mile, turn left on the gravel access road; reach parking in another 1.7 miles.

The hike: For a north-to-south downstream tour begin at White Haven: Round the gate and hike south, traveling the west bank of the Lehigh River. Swallows dart from nests in the trestle crosswork. Crushed stone surfaces the wide railbed. Despite a varied woods of aspen, maple, sumac, oak, cherry, and birch, find an open cathedral, with canyon shadows for shade.

From here to Sandy Run, the park service encourages fishing; farther downstream rafting numbers may cause conflict. Hear the rush of the Lehigh River, but gather only token looks. To the right sandstone and siltstone cliffs rise above the corridor. Enjoy showers of rhododendron bloom in early July; other times, admire the large radial leaves.

The trail travels some 50 feet above the river, often with a steep bank slope. A handful of secondary trails branch to the waterway—some border on the insane. Bikes are not allowed off the main trail. Pine and hemlock join the leafy gallery.

At 1.1 miles, cross Tannery Road, pass through a small parking area, and proceed downstream. At 1.5 miles, a foot trail crosses the rail trail, descending 200 feet to a shoreline outcrop or sandy beach. The song and face of the river may change from calm to agitated. Side creeks cascade to the river, marking off distance. Cross-canyon views present the opposite treed rim, an active railroad, and features of shore.

Despite the trail's popularity with cyclists, hikers find ample solitude. Their slower mode of travel allows for wildlife viewing and a better appreciation of the gorge and river. Deer, porcupine, snake, scarlet tanager, frog, and hawk, each may break the hypnotic spell of this gently bending river tour. A few mountain laurel appear, but cannot rival the rhododendron display—one of the best in the state.

Now and then, uncover clues to the abandoned railroad or another transportation milestone—the Lehigh Canal, which had 29 locks between White Haven and Jim Thorpe. Prior to Sandy Run (3 miles), travel a sunken grade and pass a small landslide. Mid-March through June, river-runners may negotiate the rapids at the run's mouth.

Past Leslie Run (5.1 miles), a 40-foot-wide meadow isolates the trail from the canyon cliff. The river flows calm and brown between sets of riffling water. At the Mud Run distance marker, a wide side trail descends to the shrubby floodplain and thin dirt shore. From shore, view the lively confluence and framing arch of Mud Run Bridge across the way.

On rare occasions, an impressive cicada hatch enlivens the tour, with clicking-excitement. Honeysuckle, highbush blueberry, and brier may win notice. Look for the trail to grade closer to the river approaching Rockport (9 miles), where three boat launches descend to shore. Admire a zigzagging falls and cascading Indian Run on arrival; an open river overlook on departure.

View another falls sheeting over a cliff at 9.2 miles, with a round stone tower set back in the hemlock darkness. Vegetated islands and the occasional boulder alter the river's image or flow. At 11.4 miles reach the Drakes Creek distance marker, a bench, and another hiker's path to the river. Drakes Creek arrives on the east shore.

In another mile it is Stony Creek, parting the east shore, and downstream looks better present the gorge. Once again find a 50-foot slope to the river, as the aisle becomes more open. Tour beneath exposed cliff, with sumac, young trees, and wildflowers. As a trade-off for the increased sun and heat, find unobstructed river views.

Lehigh Gorge Trail

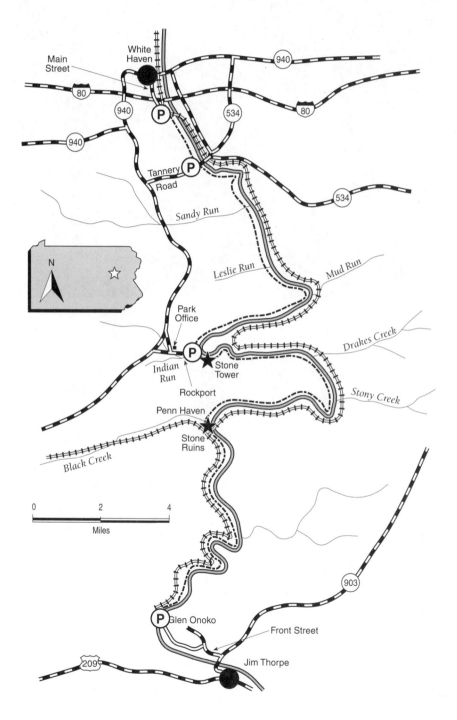

Lehigh River, Lehigh Gorge State Park.

Beyond a pretty side creek, pouring through a cove of laid stone (15.2 miles), find a natural outcrop that overlooks the river. Approach cautiously and be sure of the ground beneath your boot, as erosion is trying to make this pinnacle an island. Admire an upstream bend, the rocky east shore, and a dizzying look down to the water. No diving.

At 15.5 mile, reach Penn Haven, where the active Conrail line crosses the river to travel the west shore. To the right above Black Creek, stone ruins hint at an old incline plane. Officially-speaking, Penn Haven marks the southern terminus for the tour, as crossing gates have yet to offer a safe means over the railroad tracks. For now, turn back here.

When the crossing gates are in place, hikers will find a thru-trail to Jim Thorpe. Meanwhile, hikers and cyclists who choose to cross the active railroad tracks do so at their own risk.

The tour downstream from Penn Haven is sandwiched between river and railroad. The river helps you forget the downward-beating sun. But eventually trees of the floodplain steal all river looks. Downstream, the rocky bank of the railroad track grades higher, rising some 10-feet above the trail. Past Bear Creek (18 miles), hikers again find paths to shore.

In about a mile, pass beneath an old river suspension bridge. The railroad then grades lower approaching Glen Onoko. Round the gate to enter this popular access, 21.5 miles. The tour continues through the parking area, along gravel road, and on paved surface streets reaching the Jim Thorpe terminus, but this addition has little merit for foot travelers.

Valleys of the Susquehanna Region

This vital puzzle piece features the north-central Black Forest Region of Pennsylvania and the Susquehanna River drainage. Trails tour the perimeter of the Allegheny Mountains and explore the bold ridge arcs of the central state. Travel rich forests and old-growth groves, tag natural vista outcrops and manicured vista sites, and explore flagstone outcrops and mountain laurel realms. Here too, discover the lowland domain at Montour Preserve with Lake Chillisquaque.

31 Naval Run–Black Forest Trail Loop

General description:	Accessing a central portion of the extensive 42-mile Black Forest Trail (BFT), this rolling tour passes back and forth between scenic drainages and wooded ridges, visiting numerous manicured vistas. Start at Naval Run Trail for a clockwise tour, concluding above Slate Run. The final 2 miles occur on road but overlook Pine Creek.
General location:	25 miles northwest of Jersey Shore.
Special attractions:	Rich and varied forest, vistas, cascading runs and hollows, mountain laurel, wildlife sightings, fall foliage, a genuine sense of Pennsylvania "wilderness."
Length:	17-mile loop.
Elevation:	Travel between 800 feet near Pine Creek to more than 2,100 feet atop the ridges.
Difficulty:	Moderate backpack; strenuous day hike.
Maps:	Black Forest Trail map and guide (by the Tiadaghton Forest Fire Fighters Association; the forest district office will explain how to order); Tiadaghton State Forest.
Special concerns:	Presently an overnight permit is unnecessary for primitive camping, but hikers should sign the area trail registers. Avoid building fires; carry a backpacker stove. Fires are prohibited at mountain vistas. Slate Run is open for fly-fishing only. The BFT is blazed at regular intervals with orange circles; its associated trails with blue circles.
Season and hours:	Spring through fall for hiking.
For information:	Tiadaghton State Forest.

Naval Run–Black Forest Trail Loop

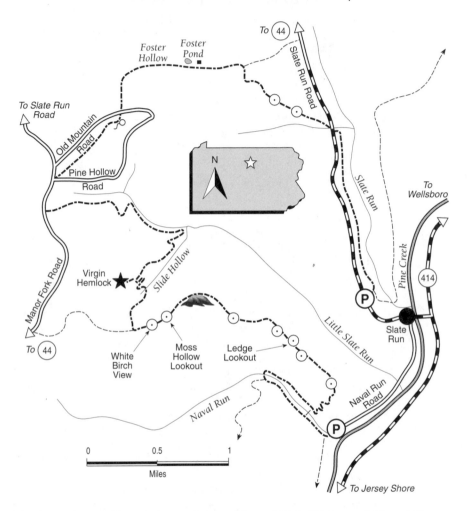

Finding the trailhead: From the junction of U.S. Highway 220 and Pennsylvania 44, west of Jersey Shore, go north on PA 44 for 11.9 miles, turning east on PA 414 for another 13.8 miles. At the village of Slate Run, turn west to cross a Pine Creek bridge, coming to a marked T-junction. Turn left to reach the Naval Run Trail at a barricade in 1.2 miles. Find parking for a handful of vehicles. Additional parking may be reached by going right at the T-junction on Slate Run Road.

The hike: For the **Naval Run Trail**, step over the barricade and follow a closed dirt road to cross skipping Naval Run via stones or a plank (0.1 mile). Meet a second woods road on the opposite shore and follow it upstream. A steep fern-and-hardwood slope sweeps uphill to the left. The drainage cool supports conifers.

134

At 0.3 mile glimpse a tiered 12- to 15-foot cascade slipping over bedrock amid a ledge amphitheater. Avoid the precarious trail descending to it. Downstream, the run engages with broad pools linked by pinched waters. More hemlocks now weave a dark hollow character.

At 1 mile find the **Black Forest Trail**, and follow the orange blazes right for Gas Line Road; the left leads to Hemlock Mountain. Descend the slope and cross Naval Run via stones or wading to ascend and pursue the opposite slope downstream. Gain a new perspective on Naval Run, touring a similar woods. Rains bring forth red efts and toads. After tendering a 2nd-look at the 0.3-mile falls, the BFT turns uphill for a well-designed switchbacking ascent.

At 2.2 miles a trailside ledge may suggest a breather. Dogwoods interweave the woods of oak, maple, and beech. Ahead top and follow a side ridge before resuming the ascent. At 2.75 miles, a berry-clad slope presents the 1st view of the tour. Overlook Pine Creek, with Half Dome rising above it, for a 1,360-foot vertical relief.

Top the main ridge and trace its spine left. At 3 miles, a 50-foot spur on the left reaches flat rocks and an opening to Hemlock Mountain. The pines of the vantage slope complement the view on clear days, compose the view on misty ones. Days of low humidity find this vista-packed tour at its finest.

Resume the tour along the ridge. Here small-diameter oaks, berry bushes, and a few scorched mountain laurel fashion a low cover. Reach the Ledge Lookout spur for a view on the opposite side of the ridge. The site's rocky point and clearing present a landscape of rounded leafy crowns. Return to the BFT, ascending to the next ridge level, now on shady woods lane. On the left at 3.3 miles, add a Naval Run vista. At 3.5 miles, the BFT turns left on foot trail.

Find a trail register, where the BFT serves up a Pine Creek Gorge view (3.9 miles). As the BFT continues, several secondary trails wiggle away; follow the blazes. At 4.25 miles, hike left on a sun-exposed 2-track lined by chestnut oaks and tall laurel. Here the blaze interval lengthens, so stay alert. At 4.7 and 4.8 miles find back-to-back vistas on opposite sides of the ridge: Moss Hollow Lookout and White Birch View.

At 5 miles reach Slide Hollow and turn right; the blue **Gas Line Trail** continues forward. Descend steadily amid fuller forest, finding a campsite at the head of Slide Hollow. The BFT now follows the hollow downstream, weaving back and forth across the rocky drainage; watch your footing. At 5.6 miles, a sign points hikers left out of the drainage.

Switchback to a ridge, coming to the junction with the **Bicentennial Trail** (5.9 miles). Here the BFT hooks right, touring atop the ridge. But first, detour 800 feet on the Bicentennial Trail for an audience with an impressive virgin hemlock, measuring 4 feet in diameter. A few other big trees grow in its shadow.

Resume the BFT, soon descending along a ridge with attractive white birch amid the forest. Glimpse neighboring ridges as the descent steepens. By 7.2 miles, briefly tour alongside the cool richness of lower Slide Hollow.

Above its confluence with refreshing Little Slate Run, the BFT swings left briefly sharing a portion of the **Little Slate Run Trail**. Pursue a former road grade upstream. At 7.75 miles ascend a side hollow, admiring its mossy bed, high-canopy forest, and few rhododendron.

At 8 miles, cross over the hollow to hike downstream and out of the drainage. Old corduroys and roots help hikers keep their feet dry. Again birch complement the forest. At 8.75 miles, meet lightly used Manor Fork Road (a forest road), and follow it right, resuming on footpath where Manor Fork Road intersects Pine Hollow Road (9 miles). Travel through pine plantation, emerging in a laurel-laden open forest. With a mild descent, cross a secondary forest road in another mile.

Keep to the BFT, heading toward Foster Hollow on a meandering forest trail. At 10.4 miles descend along another small, rocky hollow until an arrow points right. This leads to the upper reaches of Foster Hollow. Hike upstream, enjoying pine-hemlock shade and a few tiny pools. Then skirt stark Foster Pond and the private hunting camp (11.5 miles).

Stay the orange blazes, traveling an aesthetically pleasing woods with multi-trunked trees and a sea of bracken fern. At 12 miles, the BFT heads right as the **Fill Trestle Trail** heads straight. At 12.1 miles a re-route advances the BFT through similar open woods. Reach a northern rim, for the 1st of a series of views, as the trail descends the nose of the ridge. Flagstone outcrops bring added interest; views now sweep the Slate Run drainage. Poison ivy dots rocky nooks.

At 13.4 miles, follow a hollow out to Slate Run Road and turn right to pick up the BFT where it descends to follow Slate Run downstream. Enjoy varied woods of hemlock, birch, beech, maple, oak, and tulip poplar, touring a wide woods lane midway between Slate Run and Slate Run Road. While sounds of the run contribute to the relaxation, it remains a mystery.

At 15.1 miles, orange blazes ascend the slope to road shoulder parking; turn left on Slate Run Road, following it and Naval Run Road back to the starting trailhead (17 miles). Pine Creek hosts the road tour. When temperatures rise, look for trout to collect at the mouth of Little Slate Run.

32 Golden Eagle Trail

General description:	This rolling-woods circuit tours the drainages of Bonnell and Wolf runs, topping the dividing ridge for a couple of superb natural vistas, looking out over the Pine Creek drainage and Wolf Run.
General location:	20 miles northwest of Jersey Shore.
Special attractions:	Vistas, scenic drainages, flagstone outcrops, hints at an old quarry and logging camp, mountain laurel, wildlife, fall foliage.
Length:	9 miles round trip.
Elevation:	Travel between 800 feet at the trailhead and nearly 2,200 feet on the ridge between Bonnell and Wolf runs.
Difficulty:	Strenuous.
Maps:	Golden Eagle Trail; Tiadaghton State Forest.
Special concerns:	Overnight camping is prohibited. Expect some rugged sections of travel. Due to multiple crossing of the two runs, avoid hiking during times of high water.
Season and hours:	Spring through fall, daylight hours.
For information:	Tiadaghton State Forest.

Finding the trailhead: From the U.S. Highway 220–Pennsylvania 44 Junction, west of Jersey Shore, go north on PA 44 for 11.9 miles, turning east on PA 414 for another 11.3 miles. Locate the trail heading east at Bonnell Run, with trail parking on the west side of PA 414 at Clark Recreation Access (midway between the villages of Cammal and Slate Run).

The hike: On the south shore of Bonnell Run, step over the turnout barrier and hike the unmarked foot trail heading upstream. As the trail angles up slope, find a posted notice "No Horses." An old road grade now advances the tour. Large-diameter trees contribute to the varied hemlock-deciduous complex, while mosses paint the forest floor green. Enjoy Bonnell Run overlooks and its refreshing song.

Keep alert for a junction at 0.3 mile. The path to the left descends to a chute and cascades amid a small gorge on Bonnell Run. The paths straight ahead and to the right form the loop of **Golden Eagle Trail**. Turn right, ascending first toward the vista ridge, now following orange circle blazes.

Berry bushes replace the showy drainage moss, as the trail tours an oak-hickory-maple woodland. At 0.6 mile edge a grassy meadow frequented by white-tailed deer. The trail then switchbacks left on a grassy jeep trail, for a snaking ascent. A fuller forest weaves more complete shade.

By 0.8 mile, a footpath continues the tour, angling and contouring up slope. Where the trail tops out, 1.3 miles, arrows point the way right for a steep descent along the dividing ridge between Bonnell and Wolf runs. Outcrops shape a ragged crest.

At 1.5 miles a spur to the right leads to an outcrop jut and the first vista. Be careful when descending the rock, as there is little room for false steps. Enjoy a grand view of the Wolf Run drainage with Watson Fork and the beautifully folded treed ridges, green in summer; a kaleidoscope in fall.

Resume the descent, tagging Ravens Horn (1.6 miles), a vantage named for the jet-black birds that commonly roost here. A scenic flagstone block affords seating, with looks up Wolf Run, down Pine Creek, and across at an attractive long saddle to a conical peak. Watch footing on this flaking rock.

More of the eroded flagstone pedestals mark the ridge as the trail approaches the third vista (1.75 miles). Neighboring growth censures this view, but the first two excel. Follow orange blazes along the left side of the outcrop, admiring the crossbeds, hollows, and fissures. Striped maple grow amid the rock.

At 2 miles, the trail plunges steeply from the ridge, entering switchbacks. As it settles into a steady contouring descent, hear Wolf Run at the foot of the slope. At 2.2 miles, a second PA 414-access spur arrives on the right. Proceed forward. Amid the drainage, encounter fern, hog peanut, nettles, sarsaparilla, and Mayapple. Serial cascades, chutes, and deep pools accent the sandstone bedding of Wolf Run.

At 2.5 miles, the trail begins crisscrossing the run. Beware the sidewalk-like sandstone can prove slippery when wet. The bedrock records ripples from an ancient sea, while hemlock and birch hug the run. At 2.6 miles, look left to view a domino scatter of rectangular flagstone tablets, recalling

Ravens Horn, Golden Eagle Trail, Wolf Run Wild Area, Tiadaghton State Forest.

Golden Eagle Trail

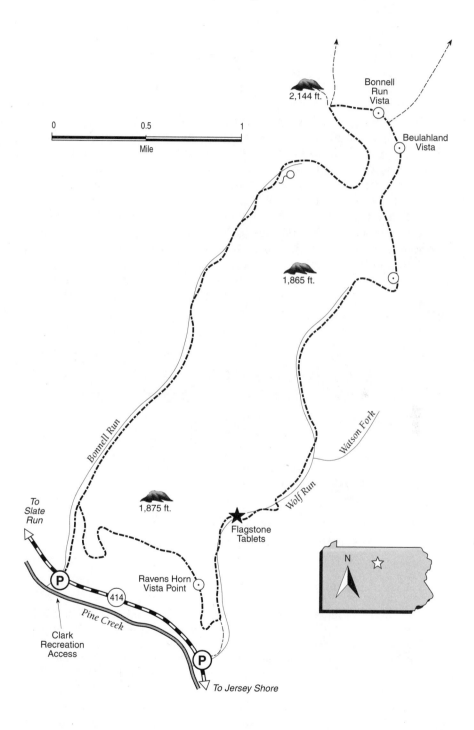

0   0.5   1
Mile

Bonnell
Run
Vista

Beulahland
Vista

2,144 ft.

1,865 ft.

Watson Fork

Bonnell Run

Wolf Run

1,875 ft.

To
Slate
Run

Flagstone
Tablets

P

414

Ravens Horn
Vista Point

N

Pine Creek

Clark
Recreation
Access

P

To Jersey Shore

an old quarry. On this zigzagging upstream tour, water level dictates the number of crossings. Amid big pine and hemlock (3.8 miles), discover an old stove left from a logging camp.

Where the path grows undefined, stay alert for blazes. By 4.1 miles ascend away from the drainage. As the trail steepens, a spur to the left leads to a mountain laurel-and-berry clad vista slope. Soon after top a broad ridge. Turn right at 4.9 miles to follow a wide grassy swath maintained by the Game Commission. Reach Beulahland Vista, elevation 2,180 feet. A vulture may grace the northeast panorama.

At 5.25 miles, turn left on an intersecting grassy lane to reach the next view—Bonnell Run Vista. Here, peer out Bonnell Run to Pine Creek and its west ridge. At 5.5 miles again turn left, following a saddle to Bonnell Run and returning to footpath. To the right the secondary-looking **Hilborn Trail** leads to Pine Creek. With a steep, loose rock descent, travel an oak-mixed woods, with laurel and berry bushes.

By 6 miles descend the dry headwater hollow of Bonnell Run, weaving back and forth across the drainage. Springs dampen the sides. Slowly gain a trickling flow and later a reliable stream. Downfalls complicate travel. While blazed, the trail now has a cross-country character. At 8.2 miles reach the woods road on the left (south) side of the creek for a straightforward journey out the canyon. Close the loop at 8.7 miles, end the hike at PA 414, 9 miles.

33 Cherry Ridge Trail

General description:	This split-character woods loop tours aptly named Cherry Ridge. Maintaining an untamed charm throughout, it begins easy but degrades to a rigorous log scramble before drawing to a close.
General location:	20 miles north of Williamsport.
Special attractions:	Attractive woods of black cherry and beech; solitude; wildlife sightings of deer, bear, turkey, and porcupine; wildflowers.
Length:	5.7-mile loop.
Elevation:	The rolling trail passes between 2,100 and 2,200 feet in elevation.
Difficulty:	1st half and closing distance, easy, with a strenuous middle distance.
Maps:	Tiadaghton State Forest; Tiadaghton State Forest Old Loggers Path and Hawkeye Cross Country Ski Trails.
Special concerns:	Secure a permit from the district office for primitive backpack camping. On the latter half of the tour, a broader blaze interval and taxing downfalls

Cherry Ridge Trail

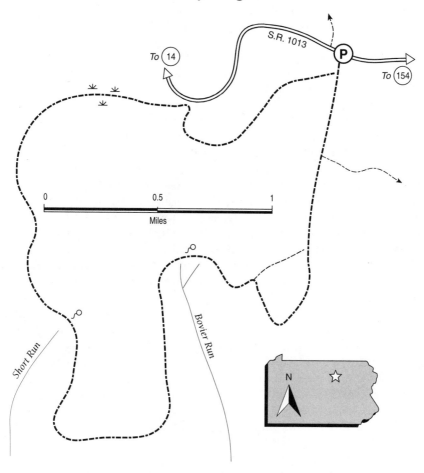

complicate travel; newcomers to hiking should avoid this leg, as it will only frustrate. Seasonally, expect some soggy trail segments.

Season and hours: Spring through fall for hiking.
For information: Tiadaghton State Forest.

Finding the trailhead: From the village of Shunk (12 miles south of Canton), go west on State Route 4002 where Pennsylvania 154 enters a curve. At Tompkins Corners in 2.5 miles, the road name changes to SR 4003/1015. Continue another mile and turn left for Masten on improved-dirt SR 1013. At the Y-junction in 1.1 miles, bear right to find gated Krimm Road (the trailhead) on the left in 0.6 mile. Park to the sides of the gated road; do not block gate.

The hike: Hike south on Krimm Road, rounding the gate. On the right, find blue-blazed **Cherry Ridge Trail.** The orange blazes straight ahead mark the **Old Loggers Path** (a 27-mile circuit through the eastern block of Tiadaghton State Forest), and the closing leg for the loop. Go right, touring counterclockwise.

Travel a vegetation-narrowed woods road with a gentle gradient, for a relaxing tour. Large black cherry trees exceeding 2 feet in diameter dominate the woodland. Beech, striped maple, and sugar maple weave amid the dark, scaly trunked giants. Tall wispy ferns grow at their feet.

The occasional low-swinging branch or small log to step over contributes to the trail's raw charm. The forest sameness brings about a hypnotic quality. Subtle changes and discoveries are hallmarks of this tour.

At 1.3 miles, pass through a small meadow clearing, as hemlock and birch join the forest ranks. The black cherry loses its dominance. Sphagnum moss betrays seasonal wet spots. The corridor broadens, and the blazes become farther spread but remain sufficient to reassure and guide hikers.

Travel a brief area of cobbles before the trail curves left at 1.6 miles. At 1.8 miles pass below a scenic multi-trunked black cherry, sporting both living and dead trunks. Starflower, Mayflower, and other delicate spring blooms dress the trail's shoulders. A few unmarked side trails branch away; watch for the guiding blue blaze at or near each junction.

At 2.75 miles, the terrain reveals rock slabs and ledges above the trail, with a gentle wooded slope below. Striped maples favor the area of rocks. Blazes point hikers across a couple of springs, before returning to the woods road travel. At the fork at 3.75 miles, blazes mark the upper fork, but the prongs merge in another 0.2 mile.

Larger fallen trees obstruct and confuse the line of travel. Stay alert, noting the last spied marker, in case you need to backtrack in search of the trail. The hike still extends woodland serenity and solitude, only now with added challenge and exercise. At 4.1 miles cross a couple of seasonal rocky drainages, returning to a better stretch of woods road with a defined 2-track. Enjoy a re-emergence of ferns along the path's shoulders and beneath the trees.

In 0.5 mile, as the 2-track curves left uphill, go right touring a longer-retired woods road. Then at 4.75 miles, turn left on another 2-track, briefly hiking alongside an electric fence. Continue straight on the 2-track.

At 5.4 miles, the orange-blazed Old Loggers Path arrives on the right from the ghost town of Masten (a former logging town, now marked only by a sign); find a register near the trail junction. Resume forward now on the joint Old Loggers Path/Cherry Ridge Trail to conclude the loop at the gate, 5.7 miles.

34 Little Pine State Park

OVERVIEW

At this 2,158-acre park along Little Pine Creek, trails explore the shore of the free-flowing creek and the reservoir floodplain, mount the steep forested flanks of the enfolding Appalachians, and meander along the broad summit plateau. Discover routes that both challenge and entertain, and others that invite Sunday strolling for nature study. In the logging era, springtime floods on Little Pine Creek transported rafts of logs to downstream mills. During Hurricane Agnes in 1972, the waters overflowed the dam, modifying the landscape.

General description:	The selected 4 hikes explore much of the park: Buttonball Nature Trail, Carsontown Trail, Lakeshore Trail, and Love Run–Panther Run Loop.
General location:	12 miles north of Jersey Shore.
Special attractions:	Creek and reservoir access, flagstone outcrops, vista, mountain laurel and wildflowers, diverse wildlife sightings, colorful fall foliage.
Length:	Buttonball Nature Trail, 0.5 mile round trip; Carsontown Trail, 0.85-mile loop or 1 mile round trip (depending on trail condition); Lakeshore Trail, 3.6 miles round trip; Love Run–Panther Run Loop, 5.5-mile loop.
Elevation:	Buttonball and Carsontown trails, minimal elevation change; Lakeshore Trail, 100-foot elevation change; Love Run–Panther Run Loop, 1,150-foot elevation change (high point, 1,900 feet, low point, 750 feet).
Difficulty:	Buttonball, Carsontown, and Lakeshore trails, easy; Love Run–Panther Run Loop, strenuous.
Maps:	State park brochure.
Special concerns:	Trailside camping in the state park is prohibited; camp only at designated sites within the family campground. Floods can alter the floodplain trails. Expect rigorous, steep pitches and inclines along Love Run–Panther Run Loop. Color-coded blazes distinguish the trails.
Season and hours:	Year-round.
For information:	Little Pine State Park.

Finding the trailhead: From the junction of U.S. Highway 220 and Pennsylvania 44, west of Jersey Shore, go north on PA 44 for 10.4 miles, turning right on State Route 4001. Go 3.2 miles to reach the campground entrance (and Buttonball Nature Trail), 3.5 miles to reach the dam (and Lakeshore Trail), 4.3 miles to reach Love Run Trailhead, 5.6 miles to reach Panther Run Trailhead, and 6.4 miles to reach Carsontown Trailhead.

The hikes: Look for the **Buttonball Nature Trail** to head downstream, upon crossing the bridge to enter the campground. Passing between the campground and Little Pine Creek, this trail offers a fine riparian walk with ample opportunity to get close to the water. By 0.1 mile sycamores dominate the flat, joined by pine, hornbeam, and ash. The creek flows broad, flat, clear, and tea-colored, drawing trout fishermen.

The shore grows cobblier, approaching an attractive grassy point isolating the free-flowing stream from a stagnant back water. Reeds push up amid the cobble; beautiful grassy mounds adorn the point and far shore. Spy kingfisher, heron, and swallow. Return as you came, 0.5 mile.

The **Carsontown Trail** travels along a snaking section of Little Pine Creek upstream from the Little Pine Lake reservoir. Its floodplain relates the tale of the power of water and resilience of nature.

From the trail sign, hike a mowed swath across the grassy canyon bottom. Wallflower, sweet clover, and other wildflowers decorate the knee-high grasses. Lone-standing pine, willow, or hornbeam spot the meadow. Often, a marvelous chorus of bird songs rides the breeze. At the loop junction in 50 feet, bear left for a clockwise tour.

Travel the upper edge of the floodplain, touring meadow or meadow-dressed woods, crossing a footbridge over Schoolhouse Run. Markers count off 0.1-mile increments. Along the woods lane, discover deer tracks. At the 0.4-mile post, the trail swings toward Little Pine Creek. Tour the outskirts of a sycamore stand to reach this scenic braided waterway. Some sycamores reach 3 to 4 feet in diameter.

Beyond the 0.5-mile post, floods can steal the trail. Hikers may then backtrack or pick their own downstream return, often including a rock-hopping or wading of Schoolhouse Run. Note how the racing floodwaters straightened the upstream bend to overflow the plain, tumbling trees, distributing uprooted debris, and shifting cobbles and rock.

For the **Lakeshore Trail**, start at the parking area near the dam (avoid blocking the gate when parking). Traverse the dam for a length-of-the-lake view and then turn left, touring north along the east shore of artificial Little Pine Lake. Descend to a grassy flat, where a fisherman's path branches left. Views upstream feature the enfolding wooded ridges. In the field, swallows dart after insects.

By 0.4 mile travel amid woods, finding the 1st of the red blazes. The 5-foot-wide, mildly rolling trail has a carriageway character and ease. Enjoy a leafy cathedral of maple, oak, hickory, and beech, with punctuations of white pine. While the lake remains visible, a steep forested slope denies access. At 0.9 mile, a cross-bedded flagstone outcrop partially overhangs the trail. A few springs muddy the path.

Prior to reaching often-dry Naval Run, the blazed trail turns left and descends to floodplain level. Here overlook the marshy upper end of the lake. Frog, goose, mallard, and kingfisher animate the scene. The trail then crosses lower Naval Run and grades back uphill into transition forest. Here find an open spacing of pine and hickory above a grassy floor. Below, watery channels web the floodplain.

Little Pine State Park

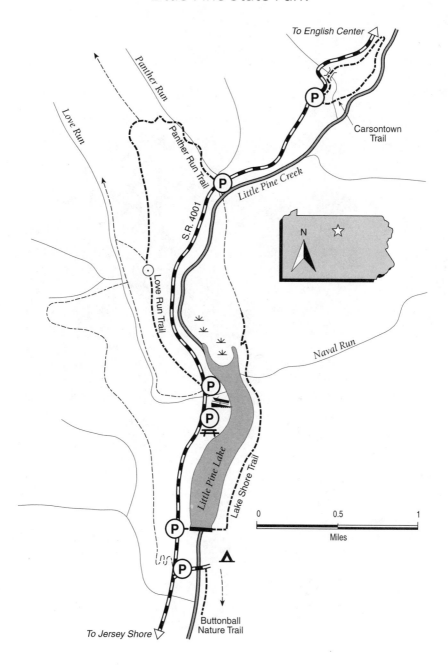

To English Center

Panther Run

Love Run

Panther Run Trail

S.R. 4001

Love Run Trail

Little Pine Creek

Carsontown Trail

N

Naval Run

Little Pine Lake

Lake Shore Trail

0   0.5   1
Miles

To Jersey Shore

Buttonball Nature Trail

Love Run Trail, Little Pine State Park.

With a switchback at 1.6 miles, return to the floodplain, touring a cropped-grass path between waist- to chest-deep grasses. Cross a culvert over a muddy side channel and edge a sycamore stand. Near the metal "trashboom," which keeps debris out of the reservoir (1.8 miles), nettles win a stronghold and the trail loses definition. Turn around, returning to the dam.

For a clockwise tour of the **Love Run–Panther Run Loop**, start at the Love Run Trailhead, hiking west on closed Love Run Road for 50 feet to find the marked trail on the right. A large hiking sign rests amid the hemlocks. Travel amid an oak, hickory, and maple forest, with a leaf mat floor. Woody vines string between the trees, and aspen dot the canopy. Initially find the foot trail blazed by a green T on white background, later by a straight green blaze.

Enter a steady climb, with a few sharp, angled bursts. By 0.2 mile, reach the mountain laurel belt of the slope, for a showy July display. Mosses pierce the decaying leaves, while small pines rise amid the laurel. Next stroll a ridge spine marked by ragged flagstones. With the climb, the oak and pines lose stature. Amid the outcrops, spy startling profiles, anvil overhangs, windows, and gravity-defying balancing acts.

Where the trail crosses a flat of broken rocks between the outcrops (an old quarry site at 1.2 miles), detour left to top a rocky point for a view overlooking the treed watershed of Little Pine Creek. An oriole may adorn a nearby branch. After snaring the vista, follow a fragment of woods road to the marked Y-junction, 1.25 miles.

A left leads to Love Run Road for an alternative loop, returning to the same trailhead. For this tour, turn right following the dual blaze of the orange **Mid State Trail** and yellow **Panther Run Trail**. Continue the ascent, now amid a tight aisle of pine, hickory, and oak, with mountain laurel and berry bushes.

At 1.6 miles, top the ridge and pursue the blazes north along it. At first, narrow, the ridge presents downward looks over both steeply dropping slopes. The ridge itself extends a relaxing stroll. Small toads, drumming grouse, and scratching birds may raise diversion. As the ridge broadens, travel a dense field of mountain laurel.

Depart the Mid State Trail at 2.5 miles, turning right, remaining on the yellow Panther Run Trail for a treacherous descent. Despite switchbacks, attend to footing. Ferns replace the laurel, and maples abound, shading Panther Run drainage. At 3 miles, the trail contours the steep run slope downstream. A cut trailbed provides surer footing.

A washout at 3.5 miles, then puts hikers on a bypass route that travels through stinging nettles. Its price may be higher than that of hiking downstream via the rocky streambed. The blazed trail continues crisscrossing the stream, before assuming a higher line of travel above the run. Come out at a steep eroded descent to S.R. 4001 (4.2 miles); be careful. Upon reaching the road, turn right to close the loop back at Love Run Trailhead, 5.5 miles. From the roadway, overlook Little Pine Creek and Little Pine Creek Lake.

35 Loyalsock Trail to Smiths Knob

General description:	This short, but fairly challenging sampling of the 59.3-mile Loyalsock Trail travels steep flank and summit plateau, snaring both cleared and natural vistas. Wander amid laurel and Mayapple, and visit the impressive sandstone outcrop and cliff of Smiths Knob.
General location:	10 miles northeast of Montoursville.
Special attractions:	Smiths Knob, Loyalsock Creek panorama, mountain laurel and forest wildflowers, wildlife sightings, fall foliage.
Length:	3.6 miles round trip or 4.7 miles, adding an end loop.
Elevation:	Find a 1,150-foot elevation change between the trailhead (770 feet) and Smiths Knob (1,920 feet).
Difficulty:	Moderate to strenuous.
Maps:	Tiadaghton State Forest; The Alpine Club of Williamsport map and trail guide to the Loyalsock Trail.
Special concerns:	Obtain camp permit at district headquarters. Loyalsock Trail has a signature red dash on yellow blaze or LT-disk markings; its alternate routes or bypasses show a red X on yellow disk. Also encounter blue access trails and white unmaintained trails. Expect steep inclines and pitches, and be especially attentive, when rounding Smiths Knob.
Season and hours:	Spring through fall for hiking.
For information:	Tiadaghton State Forest.

Finding the trailhead: From Interstate 180/U.S. Highway 220 at Montoursville, go north on Pennsylvania 87 about 10 miles, and turn east on improved-dirt Little Bear Creek Road. Go 0.8 mile to find road-shoulder parking for the trail, near the bridge to Little Bear forest headquarters.

The hike: From the headquarters entrance, hike 200 feet west along Little Bear Creek Road to follow the Loyalsock Trail (LT) north up the hill. A sign for Smiths Knob marks the start. White pine, mixed oaks, aspen, hemlock, and maple rise above the hiker-only trail. Cross the road to the ranger's residence and find a trail register.

The assault on the wooded slope steepens, quickly drawing out of the conifers and into the mountain laurel belt. Hear Little Bear Creek below and the wind rustling through the canopy. Find the foot trail in good condition and well-used. Woodpecker, songbirds, and soaring vultures enliven the air. A flattening of the trail allows hikers to catch their breath before the next charge. In places, striped maples win root.

Where the trail flattens out and follows the rim of the slope (0.7 mile),

Loyalsock Trail to Smiths Knob

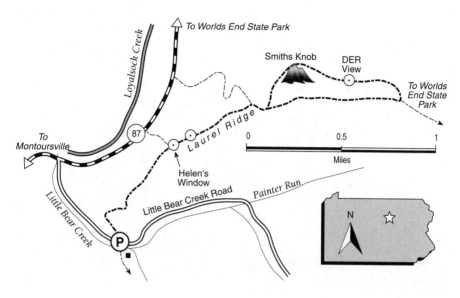

find Helen's Window and a white trail descending to PA 87. Overlook a clearing to a long straightaway of Loyalsock Creek and the framing even-height ridges. A jagged wildlife snag pierces the clearing. Flat rocks provide gallery seating, while hemlocks offer shade. A second clearing at 0.8 mile overlooks the wooded flanks of the neighboring ridges, for a fine autumn mosaic.

Atop this shoulder of Laurel Ridge, find the trail rocky and ample laurel to give credence to the name. Where the trail drifts away from the rim, the rocks disappear and large chestnut oaks and low berry bushes frame a gentle walk. At 1.3 miles, meet a blue-blazed horse trail (a woods road arriving from PA 87), and follow it right for 0.1 mile to pick up the foot trail of the LT on the left. Note the red X disks on the woods road ahead; these mark the optional loop return.

The LT presents a sharp climb to the summit spine of Laurel Ridge. Birches briefly add to the forest. Hornbeam and Mayapple favor the lofty flat. A clearing at 1.6 miles offers a view south-southeast toward Allegheny, Red, and Tar Kiln ridges parted by the drainages of Little Bear Creek and Painter Run.

Tag the ridge high point and descend, coming upon the blue circular sign for Smiths Knob (1.8 miles). The cliff creates a natural gap for admiring the wooded countryside, rural Loyalsock Valley, and the lichen whitewashed cliff itself, plunging 30 to 50 feet. Keep back from the edge, and no horseplay. Vultures soar at hikers' feet.

From Smiths Knob, hikers have the option of returning as they came for

Smiths Knob view, Tiadaghton State Forest.

a 3.6-mile round trip, or proceeding on the LT to meet the red X trail, adding a loop to the tour. For the loop, continue the ridge descent, hugging the cliff and easing over and between rocks. Use care on this brief treacherous stretch.

An easy foot trail then travels along the north rim of the slope. Enjoy an attractive forest cathedral with old-growth maples and oak, tulip, and hemlock. At 2.1 miles pass the marker for "DER View"; this peek through the tree trunks may easily go unnoticed but for the sign.

Drift from the rim, finding the red X trail at 2.4 miles. Follow it right, departing the LT, which curves left. Laurels again dress the tour, and a deer's curiosity may cause it to linger. Round a vernal pond and turn right on the woods road of the blue horse-trail. At 2.8 miles, red X disks point hikers off the horse trail onto a lower parallel route, only to return to the woods road at 3 miles. Close the loop at 3.3 miles and retrace the LT to the trailhead 4.7 miles.

36 Chuck Keiper Trail, East Loop

General description:	This hike explores the offering of the eastern component of the 50-mile, double-looped Chuck Keiper Trail System (CKT). Travel mixed woodlands, picturesque hollows, meadow, and burn habitat. The CKT follows old logging grades and named foot trails, bridged by some road travel.
General location:	35 miles west of Williamsport, 30 miles north of State College.
Special attractions:	Solitude; rhododendron, laurel, and dogwood blooms; vistas; wildlife sightings; fall foliage.
Length:	25.6-mile loop, with Big Rocks Vista detour.
Elevation:	This rolling trail shows a 1,200-foot elevation change, with a low point of 1,100 feet at Hall Run and a high point of 2,300 feet atop Barneys Ridge.
Difficulty:	Strenuous.
Maps:	Chuck Keiper Trail; Sproul State Forest.
Special concerns:	At present, backpack camping is allowed without a permit, but regulations in the works may call for that to change. Check with the forest district headquarters for an update; such permits are free. During high water, hikers may need to wade larger runs. Forest roads regularly intersect or advance the CKT, allowing hikers to partition the loop; consult the Sproul State Forest public-use map.
Season and hours:	Spring through fall for hiking.
For information:	Sproul State Forest.

Finding the trailhead: From the junction of Pennsylvania 120 and Pennsylvania 144 South in Renovo, go south on PA 144 for 9.8 miles and turn right (west) on a dirt road opposite Swamp Branch Road for the trail. At the fork, go left 0.1 mile to find parking atop a vista plateau; access the Chuck Keiper Trail off the right fork for a clockwise tour.

The hike: From the parking area, survey the Fish Dam Run Wild Area, and then follow the 2-track bearing right up the slope away from the trail kiosk. Where the jeep trail curves, take a quick left past a stand of pines to follow the orange blazes of the CKT along an open meadow swath. Wildflowers sprinkle the grasses of Barneys Ridge. Young maples grow to the side. While hikers lose views of Fish Dam Run Wild Area, looks east present Coffin Rock Fire Tower.

The CKT then gently descends from Barneys Ridge, passing amid an area of bigger trees for shade. Reach Barneys Ridge Road (0.8 mile), and follow this dirt forest road left for a sunny walk, despite framing trees. At 1.2 miles reach a sign for Big Rocks Vista.

This 0.4-mile, round-trip detour to the right travels woods road and foot trail beyond a rock barricade to an area of large outcrops. A slot allows fairly easy access to the top, although views are limited. Laurel adorns the site, but graffiti and broken glass prove strong detractors. Resume the main hike at 1.6 miles, bearing right.

At 2 miles, bear right on Dry Run Road, passing amid hardwoods and berry bushes. Then at 2.2 miles, turn right following a grassy lane uphill for an easy stretch on both eyes and feet. Sassafras, laurel, and witch-hazel shape the gateway. As the jeep trail arcs right, proceed forward on footpath; watch for blazes on trailbed rocks and trees.

The CKT now dips into the cool, full-canopy forest of Drake Hollow for a steady, sometimes steep descent on **Drake Hollow Trail**. Ferns abound. Where the trail crosses to the right bank, an old road bench offers easier footing, with the occasional obstacle of nettles or springs. At 3.7 miles, a side drainage reveals a seasonal waterfall or weeping wall. Downstream the hollow shows more reliable water, with cascades dressing the bedrock. Hemlock, birch, tulip poplar, and rhododendron accent shore. At 4.8 miles, cross back to the left bank to exit onto PA 144 (5.1 miles).

Cross Drake Hollow bridge, ascending along PA 144 south for 0.9 mile. Generally the sun's angle affords some shade, and the bending route keeps traffic both low and slow. At 6 miles, turn left following the CKT blazes, now on **Diamond Rock Hollow Trail**. Descend and cross the gravelly stream of Hall Run to follow the north shore of Diamond Rock Run upstream. Cross this run at 6.2 miles; the lower drainage shows varied woods. The stepped run proves a pleasing host.

At 6.5 miles encounter sections of improved trail, as the CKT pursues the headwater fork to the right. Crisscross the fork and eventually walk the rocky drainage itself. Be alert, or the rocks and masking leaves could lead to a twisted ankle. With a steep burst of climb, reach a jeep road (7.5 miles) and ascend it left. Turkeys may startle hikers. Striped maple, sassafras and berry frame the way. Meet Petes Run Road, another dirt forest road, at 7.75 miles.

Turn left on Petes Run Road to resume the CKT on the right in 200 feet, quickly crossing a utility line corridor. Return to fern-floored forest for a moderate descent, crossing the upper drainage of Boggs Hollow at 8.2 miles. A worn cartpath advances the trail. Next enter a bowl where several headwater streams meet. Twice cross the run to continue downstream along the left bank. The trail draws above the run as the slope steepens. Rhododendron accent the tour.

Cross springs and side tributaries, dropping down to cross Boggs Hollow and follow its right bank downstream (10.5 miles). Jewelweed, violets, nettle, and Mayapple grow along the drainage. The trail next rolls, traveling a contour well above the run. At 11.8 mile enter the recess of a large side drainage and follow this tributary upstream.

At 12.5 miles, cross the right headwater fork to follow the left fork upstream. The trail then charges out of the drainage, passing amid drier forest

Chuck Keiper Trail, East Loop

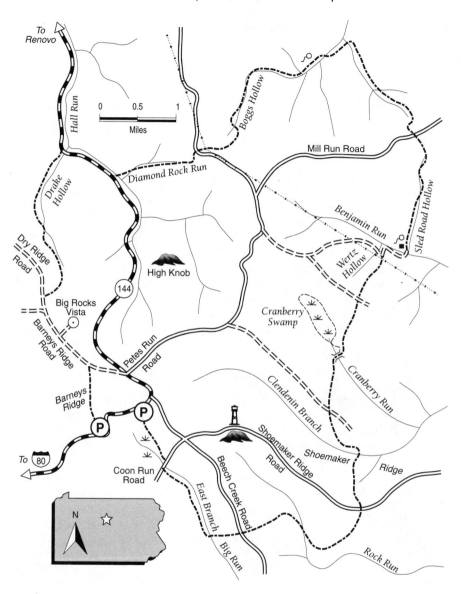

intermixed with laurel. Cross Mill Run Road (13.3 miles), finding the blazed path (a grassy secondary jeep trail) just to the right of a gated jeep road. The grassy path descends fairly sharply for Sled Road Hollow. The blazes are farther spread with laurel and berry bushes sometimes hiding them until the last minute.

At 13.8 miles the jeep trail fades, entering a meadow; look for a blaze at the far end. A foot trail then descends to the rocky head of Sled Road Hollow, where a soothing hemlock darkness cloaks travel.

The CKT hopscotches between banks of the bending hollow, before settling on the west bank for an easy stroll. Laurel and mushroom seasonally enhance travel, as the trail nudges the pine-oak forest. Pieces of old lane and foot trail advance the hike downstream. Tour meadowy shore and pine stand, crossing the foot of a descending logging road (14.8 miles).

Keep amid the meadow and mixed woods of shore, cross a muddy side spring, and pass a piped spring. At 15.1 miles follow the orange blazes along a 2-track, hiking past a small white building; keep out, no camping. Cross the road bridge over Benjamin Run to meet a dirt forest road, Sled Road Trail; turn right.

Briefly follow Benjamin Run upstream, staying on the road as it curves left past a mesh fence at a gas pipeline. Again, blazes occur farther apart. Ascend past some buildings (state forest camps), proceeding straight on a wide grassy swath where the road hooks right.

Another ascent follows, gradually growing steeper. Cross a powerline

Fire zone, Chuck Keiper Trail, Sproul State Forest.

corridor (15.7 miles), returning to woods. Laurel join and later replace the trail's edge of small pines. Top the ridge at 16.4 miles and cross a dirt forest road. Soon after the trail again dips, passing amid a wealth of laurel and berries. At 17.3 miles cross a footbridge over Cranberry Run, and head left downstream. Upstream to the right lies Cranberry Swamp Natural Area, but currently no marked trail accesses it. Seasonally, insects bother both hikers and deer.

Be sure to carry plenty of drinking water for the hot stretch ahead. With the next ascent, enjoy another profusion of laurel. This is now **Four Ridge Trail**; it tops out (17.8 miles), touring a burn habitat. Find hundreds of silver snags, thick berry bushes, laurel, and young sassafras, maple, and pine. Stakes help guide hikers. Songbirds favor the site, and views pan the neighborhood of flat-topped ridges.

At 18.3 miles cross a jeep trail/firebreak, entering semi-open forest for a slow descent to the Clendenin Branch (19 miles). Cross via stones, passing a campsite. With a brief burst of climb, the grade eases. Cross a small drainage near another state forest camp, and then ascend foot trail and jeep road to cross Shoemaker Ridge Road (19.8 miles).

In a select cut, knee-high fern, laurel, and berry bushes brush passersby. Descend to cross Rock Run, coming out near a building. Follow the closed jeep road through an opening to the right. Amid this clearcut maintained for wildlife, the vegetation grows waist-deep. At 21.1 miles bear left. The trail re-enters forest at 21.6 miles. Where it nears another state forest camp structure, meet a jeep track and follow it out to Beech Creek Road (21.75 miles).

Now hike a grassy lane into open forest, descending to a gentle drainage. At 22.1 miles reach a marked junction with **CKT, West Loop**. Turn right, hiking upstream along a typically dry drainage to cross attractive East Branch Big Run on a decaying log bridge. Walk up the East Branch, crossing it twice more on rotting log bridges. Mossy rocks dot the stream.

The gentle terrain shapes an easy walk away from the run. Discover a few larch and white pine, as low quartzite boulders litter the forest floor. Leave the boulder field, arriving at Coon Run Road (23.7 miles).

Turn right to pick up the CKT on the left in 0.1 mile, now traveling **East Branch Trail**. Return to woods, skirting the headwater marsh of East Branch Big Run, a large shrubby flat with a few cattails. Old yellow blazes linger. Travel a disturbed zone where a tornado thrashed about trees, and cross a deep, thin headwater. More tornado-disturbed forest follows and then open grasses.

Navigate blaze to blaze, crossing a wide grassy swath at 24.9 mile to reach PA 144 at an old foundation—"State Camp" on maps (25 miles). Turn left of PA 144, hike 0.6 mile, and turn right on a dirt road, returning to the trailhead. The West Loop proceeds south along PA 144.

37 Montour Preserve

OVERVIEW

Cradled in the broad Appalachian valley between Montour Ridge and Muncy Hills, this 966-acre Pennsylvania Power and Light (PP&L) preserve invites outdoor recreation and nature study. At the heart of the preserve lies 165-acre Chillisquaque Lake, an important waterfowl stopover on the Atlantic Flyway. Historically, the Muncy–Mahoning Indian Path passed through what is now the preserve. Today, a fine series of interlocking hiking trails welcome contemporary boots.

General description: Five hikes incorporate many of the trails and spotlight the preserve's cultural and natural history. Interpretive panels and brochures help unfold the story.

General location: 10 miles north of Danville.

Special attractions: Visitor center with habitat dioramas; lake and wildlife ponds; meadow and riparian-valley woods; Devonian fossil pit; maple sugar shack; flowering shrubs, wildflowers, and pond lilies; wildlife sightings, with peak waterfowl migration in late March; colorful fall leaves.

Length: Chilisuagi Trail, 4.25-mile loop or 6.2-mile loop with side trips to Ridgefield Point and the restricted-access blinds (secure permits prior to start); Goose Woods/ Braille Trail, 1 mile round-trip (0.4 mile for Braille Trail alone); Wildlife Management Trail, 0.75 mile round-trip; Laura Smith Trail of History, 0.25-mile loop; Fossil Pit Trail, 0.2 mile round trip.

Elevation: Find a minimal elevation change along the trails; preserve lands range between 550 and 650 feet in elevation.

Difficulty: Chilisuagi Trail, moderate; all others, easy.

Maps: Montour Preserve brochure; individual trail booklets (generally available at each trailhead).

Special concerns: Entry permits are required to cross the designated wildlife refuge to access the preserve's 2 wildlife blinds; inquire at the office for a permit and key. No pets, no bikes, no swimming, no collecting (except at the fossil pit), and no overnight camping. Keep to designated trails and heed area and State boating and fishing rules.

Season and hours: Year-round, sunrise to sunset. Office and Visitor Center: 9 a.m. to 4 p.m. weekdays, with weekend hours: 9 a.m. to 4 p.m., May through September only.

For information: Montour Preserve.

Montour Preserve

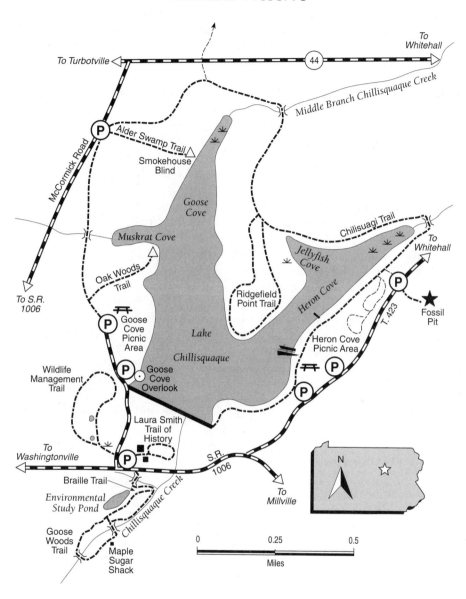

Finding the trailhead: From Interstate 80 west of Bloomsburg, take exit 33 and travel north on Pennsylvania 54 West toward Washingtonville. Following signs for the preserve, in 4.6 miles turn right on PA 254, go 0.5 mile, and turn left on State Route 1003. Go another 3.6 miles and turn right on SR 1006. In 0.5 mile, turn left to find the Visitor Center and its associated trailheads in 0.1 mile, Goose Cove Overlook Parking in 0.5 mile, and Goose Cove Picnic Area in 0.7 mile.

For the Fossil Pit, stay on SR 1006, driving past the visitor center turnoff. In 0.5 mile bear left on Township Road 423 toward Heron Cove Boat Launch and Picnic Area. Park on the right opposite the Bluebird Trail in another mile.

The hikes: Hikers may access the **Chilisuagi Trail** at the Goose Cove and Heron Cove recreation sites or from Goose Cove Overlook Parking. Starting from the latter, round the gate to cross the dam for a counterclockwise tour. Enjoy cross-lake views at the surrounding low wooded rises, the tongue dividing the Chillisquaque Lake coves, and the preserve mosaic. Loons, swallows, and geese are common sightings. "Chillisquaque" means "song of the wild goose."

In 0.5 mile, bear left on a gravel lane, continuing to round the lake. A myriad of thistle, pea, daisy, clover, chicory, and milkweed colors the grass-land. At 1 mile, pass through groomed Heron Cove recreation site, finding restrooms, water, tables, a fishing dock, and boat launch. Hikers may spy a turtle's head piercing the lake surface.

The tour resumes amid maple, elm, and hawthorn, with hedgerows of flowering shrubs and poison ivy separating the trail from the open field. Later a marsh habitat with cattails and the lively notes of red-winged black-birds and frogs extends right. Still enjoy filtered looks left at the lake.

At 1.3 miles, reach an interpretive panel and the 0.75-mile **Bluebird Trail**, heading right. Continue the lake tour, counting down the numbered interpretive panels. The aisle grows more shaded with scenic old maples. Lake views are now of the cattail extent of Heron Cove. Cross an inlet bridge, and continue passing interpretive stations and bench seats. Keen-eyed hik-ers may note the toothy evidence of beaver.

View Jellyfish Cove and tour a tall hickory-oak woodland to meet the **Ridgefield Point Trail** (1.8 miles). Turn left to add this stroll, exploring the dividing lake tongue, touring field and forest. Follow the mowed/raked track, for a clockwise tour. Side mowings facilitate wildlife, creating a braided habitat. Discoveries may include a beaver lodge of mud and sticks, the noisy passage of a turkey, or deer tracks in the soft sand of shore. Conclude this side trip at 2.6 miles, turning left on the Chilisuagi Trail.

The lake trail now shows a mild roll, passing amid mixed woods and skirting wild and groomed fields, removed from Chillisquaque Lake. At 3.25 miles, cross the bridge over Middle Fork Chillisquaque Creek.

Where the mowed track of the 1.5-mile **West Branch Trail** heads right (3.5 miles), stay the gravel lane ahead. Young transition woods and open meadow prescribe a sunny stroll. Hawks and cardinals grow the bird watcher's roster.

Near McCormick Road (4.1 miles), find a gated entry to the restricted wildlife refuge and **Alder Swamp Trail** (Trail 10 on the preserve map) to Smokehouse Blind. Hikers must possess a permit to add this 0.7-mile, round-trip tour. Travel a transition-woods aisle to the enclosed blind, with camouflaged windows and viewing cut-outs for scopes and camera lenses. Overlook the head of Goose Cove.

Resume the lake tour at 4.8 miles, crossing the inlet creek to Muskrat Cove. At 5.25 miles, the mowed swath of the **Oak Woods Trail** (Trail 9; entry permit required) passes through field and oak-hickory woods, meeting a service road near Muskrat Blind (5.5 miles). This larger blind looks out to Muskrat Cove and a shrubby island and has viewing on 3 sides.

Back at the Chilisuagi Trail (5.75 miles), turn left to come out at the developed Goose Cove recreation area. Proceed south through the area or along its entrance road to conclude the loop at Goose Cove Overlook Parking, 6.2 miles.

Three hikes start next to the visitor center: the **Goose Woods/Braille Trail**, the **Wildlife Management Trail**, and **Laura Smith Trail of History**.

Start the **Goose Woods/Braille Trail** at the Braille Trail sign in the parking lot. Quickly cross S.R. 1006, traveling a wood shavings path framed by young forest of elm, ash, and dogwood, with honeysuckle, Virginia creeper, jewelweed, and rhododendron. Cross a footbridge and begin a clockwise tour, passing alongside the Middle Branch Chillisquaque Creek. A guide rope leads travelers; wooden beads along the rope signal interpretive signs in both Braille and large print.

The framing woods and trailside vegetation show great variety. Jet-black and neon-colored damselflies hover above the stream. At 0.2 mile the Braille Trail swings right to complete its loop along a lily pond. Proceed forward for an upland woods tour of Goose Woods Trail (no guide rope). This trail too concludes along the pond.

Cross the creek bridge to reach the Sugar Shack, where visitors learn about the making of maple syrup in late February-early March. Other times, just enjoy the big maples. Continue along the creek bank, learning about the natural and cultural history of the area. Then cross back over the creek, viewing billows of vapor from the site's steam electric plant.

At 0.6 mile reach the lily pond to complete the tour, following the Braille Trail along the east shore. Pink and white pond lilies, cattail, bulrushes, and soothing reflections of clouds add to the pond's charm. A muskrat may part the still water. Re-enter woods, close the loop, and return to the visitor center, 1 mile.

Start the marked **Wildlife Management Trail** on the west side of the preserve road, opposite the entry to the visitor center. Croaking frogs announce their presence in a small cattail pond to the right. In less than 0.1 mile, reach another wildlife pond and the loop junction; go left for a clockwise tour. Travel the mowed track, passing amid field, meadow, transitioning shrubs, pine plantation, and elm-oak and maple woodlands. Find the trail mostly sunny. Deer, dragonfly, red-winged blackbird, and songbirds may provide companionship. Pass a butterfly garden, and turn left upon closing the loop to return to the center.

For the 0.25-mile **Laura Smith Trail of History** follow the point-to-point description in the trail brochure, hiking past the Victorian farmhouse, now the PP&L Preserve Office. The circuit visits an herb garden and rusting farm equipment and overlooks Chillisquaque Creek, before returning to the center. The pamphlet ties images from the present to the past. Even on this short hike, hikers may spy deer, woodchuck, and songbird.

For the **Fossil Pit Trail**, hike east off Township Road 423 for 0.1 mile, reaching the quarry slope. The shale holds evidence of an ancient sea, dating to the Devonian Period 395 million years ago. An interpretive board and brochure identify the fossils by shape and name. Collect corals, lamp shells, cephalopods, and crinoids (plant-like animals). Search amid the freshly exposed shales; the more serious seeker should come with a clay knife or hammer and a paint brush to clean the fossils. At this shadeless site, bring plenty of drinking water and wear a hat. Be careful of the sharp-edged shale.

38 Mid State Trail

General description:	This long-distance, north-south trending hiking trail lays a loose sash across the middle of Pennsylvania. The Mid State Trail (MST) travels up Pine Creek Valley and rolls against the grain, passing up and over the serial arced ridges of the central state. While the MST is incomplete, this hike features some 168 adjoining miles.
General location:	The trail runs north-south between Blackwell on Pennsylvania 414 and the village of Water Street on U.S. Highway 22.
Special attractions:	Fire towers and natural vistas, a section of the Great Island Indian Path, an abandoned railroad tunnel, mixed forest, mountain laurel, solitude, fall foliage.
Length:	168 miles one-way.
Elevation:	The rolling trail has a total elevation change of 25,000 feet, passing from ridgetops in excess of 2,400 feet to valley bottoms less than 550 feet in elevation.
Difficulty:	Easy to strenuous depending on length and selected section of trail.
Maps:	Mid State Trail Association maps and *Guide to the Mid State Trail in Pennsylvania*.
Special concerns:	Find overnight camping within the developed campgrounds of the state parks (at usual fees) or on state forest lands outside the natural areas and away from Penns Creek where it passes between Cherry Run and Poe Paddy. Secure a free overnight permit from the appropriate state forest district headquarters. As water is not dependable along the full-length of the tour, carry adequate amounts

Mid State Trail

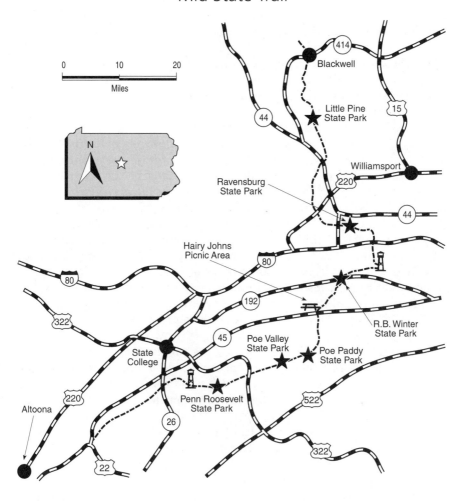

between known water sources; purify all trail sources. Thru-trail hikers will need to plan for resupplying, what to do in case of an emergency, and arrange for pick-up at the end of the trail; the *Guide to the Mid State Trail in Pennsylvania* offers hints. Find the MST orange-blazed with official distances expressed in metric units; side trails have blue blazings. Pass respectfully on private lands.

Season and hours: Spring through fall for hiking.

For information: Tioga, Tiadaghton, Bald Eagle, Rothrock, and Buchanan state forests; Mid State Trail Association.

Finding the trailhead: Access the northern end of the MST at Blackwell off PA 414; the current southern terminus at the corner of U.S. 22 and State

Route 4014 east of Water Street. Find midway accesses at state parks and highway crossings.

The hike: Mostly utilizing footpath and old roads, the Mid State Trail travels mainly on public lands, with a few private properties bridging trail fragments. Pass through five state forests, half a dozen state parks, state forest picnic areas, a state game land, and a handful of natural areas, enjoying a mostly forested tour with occasional views and stretches along waterways. Volunteers do a fine job maintaining the trail.

The MST crosses creeks, forest roads, highways, and an interstate highway, as it cuts across Pennsylvania. Roadways allow hikers to partition the tour into manageable segments. The lightly used MST has won the nickname "Wildest Trail in Pennsylvania."

On this rigorous journey, namedropping Pennsylvania ridges becomes routine. The MST passes through hemlock and mixed hardwood forests and sites of plantation pine, while touring the ridge flanks and drainages. Atop the flat-topped ridges, find low stature oaks, laurel, and berry bushes.

On a north-to-south trek, the Grand Canyon of Pennsylvania launches the tour. Start south from the community of Blackwell (Or add 2 days to hiking by starting at Ansonia and following the **West Rim Trail** to Bohen Run.) Perhaps one of the bald eagles nesting in the canyon will salute your journey. At 2 miles, the MST tops Gillespie Point for an early view. It then rolls from hollow to run, with a stretch along Brown Fork.

State Game Lands 75, Wolf Run Wild Area, and Bark Cabin Natural Area (old-growth hemlock) advance the tour from mile 5 to mile 18, still in the Pine Creek countryside. Enjoy a view from Oregon Hill (11 miles). If you pitch a camp along this stretch, be sure it lies outside the state game land.

By 21 miles, the MST passes through Little Pine State Park, meeting and sharing a leg of the yellow-blazed Panther Run Trail for a ridgetop journey. Laurel enriches the tour. Detour left where the Panther Run Trail ends to find an old flagstone quarry flat and an outcrop overlooking Little Pine Creek Valley. The MST now heads left on closed, dirt Love Run Road, crosses Love Run, and shares the trailbed with two additional park trails, before crossing Little Pine Creek at the park campground off State Route 4001 (25.3 miles).

Southbound, the MST parallels Little Pine Creek away from the park, before making a rolling ascent. Rugged Houselander Mountain with its vista opportunities then takes the baton at 36 miles. Upon descent, cross PA 44 and ford Pine Creek at Camp Kline (38 miles); this crossing requires low water. In the future, an old Conrail bridge will allow for an easier crossing. MST blazes already lead to this bridge, but keep to the fording until the bridge is made trail-safe.

The trail again rolls pursuing runs up and downstream, snaring views along Nepley Ridge, and crossing Big Springs Road (45 miles). The MST then descends, passing through the 1st stretches of private land at about 48 miles. On this stretch the MST passes through Woolrich near the factory outlet store and traverses lands owned by Woolrich Woolen Mills and others.

Mid State Trail railroad tunnel, Bald Eagle State Forest.

Cross PA 150 at 50.8 miles and travel roads to the West Branch Susquehanna River bridge. Cross, hike east along River Road East, and then continue weaving via roads through West Branch Valley. Sights along this stretch include a roadside marker for a Delaware Indian Village, a side-road marker for Fort Horn (1777), and remnants of old canal. As the MST ascends, leaving private land (56 miles), find foot trail. Traverse the scree slopes of Round Top (57 miles) to win rewarding views of the West Branch, Allegheny Front, and Gates of Pine Creek.

Continue tracking the weaving route of the MST, hiking along Ramm Road for a spell. Where the MST next descends, walk the Great Island Indian Path. Today, an old road replaces the original footpath, but it is one of the few areas where history has not been paved over. Reach PA 880 and follow the blazes to enter Ravensburg State Park (64.3 miles). From the park, the MST ascends Big Mountain, entering the ridge-hopping phase of travel. Where it levels out, tally more views.

The trail then dips to cross White Deer Creek (about 71 miles), followed by a more modestly rolling stretch. At 76 miles, a span over Interstate 80 advances the MST. At 81 miles visit Sand Mountain Fire Tower. Hikers may ascend the 12-story tower. Beware: the landings lack protective cages; use railings, heed posted numbers, and no horseplay. A 360-degree view awaits, combining farmland, rural towns, the folded ridges traveled by the MST, and the beauty of Penn's Woods. The MST then eases downhill and trends southwest, traversing Bake Oven Mountain.

Where the trail meets PA 192 (84.2 miles), travel pine plantation and deciduous woods, overlook dammed Halfway Lake, and admire the scenic outlet of Rapid Run in R.B. Winter State Park. Next ring up travel on Brush, Shriner, Sharpback, Buffalo, and Winkelblech mountains, interrupted by a dip to cross Pine Creek (Centre county's, not Lycoming's). Views are denied until Winkelblech Mountain (94 miles).

Where the MST passes through Hairy Johns Picnic Area and crosses PA 45 (95.5 miles), find the trail well-blazed, but sometimes absent a tracked path. Snare views atop Thick Mountain before descending via Cherry Run to the attractive Penn Central Railroad Grade along Penns Creek. At 108 miles, pass through Paddy Mountain via the abandoned tunnel. Only an arc of light at the far end breaks the darkness. At the culvert-like opening, hikers may need to stoop.

From the tunnel, travel a private drive and forest road, pursuing MST blazes to Poe Paddy State Park. Find amenities at the park, before making a rocky climb to travel Long Mountain. Here vistas present Penns Creek. At mile 112, a trail leads to Poe Valley State Park.

Between the Millheim–Siglerville Pike and Stillhouse Hollow, the MST thrice crosses Greens Valley, a pretty, tree-overlaced, gurgling stream. A rocky ascent follows. Once again atop Long Mountain, gather southern views from Chickadee Rocks and Big Valley Vista. Then dip to pass under U.S. 322 in a culvert (123 miles).

Now the MST follows the grain of the long, flat ridges, smoothing out the tour. At 130 miles, reach Penn Roosevelt State Park, with its small pond. Next follow Detweiler Run downstream before climbing to the top of Thickhead Mountain. Along this mountain find Indian Wells Overlook, lauded as one of the best vistas in the state (136 miles). Here and beyond, gather views of Bear Meadow Natural Area, before reaching Little Flat Lookout Tower.

Extensive flat-topped Tussey Mountain, with only a brief cut down to Shaver Creek for water, next advances the southbound MST from mile 141 to mile 163. At the Shaver Creek-cut, hikers have the option of keeping to the mountaintop.

While possessing rugged, often rocky footing, Tussey Mountain serves up a feast for the eyes with frequent vantages overlooking the natural scree and talus slopes. Chestnut oak and striped maple dress the ridge, interwoven with berry bushes and laurel. At 148 miles find Jo Hays Vista parking north of the MST's crossing of PA 26. Here, overlook State College, the valley flat, and multi-hued green and gold fields.

The next 15 miles host perhaps the finest vista stretch of the tour, but the descent from Tussey Mountain to Little Juniata River holds little to recommend it. The descent traverses areas disturbed by quarry and cutting. Present plans call for some rerouting and for growing the trail south, perhaps utilizing **The Lower Trail**. Meanwhile end at the corner of U.S. 22 and SR 4014. An isolated southern leg of trail, north of the Maryland border, tours Buchanan State Forest.

Thru-trail hikers should purchase guide and maps from the Mid State Trail Association, for point-to-point directions. For alerts to the latest re-routes and extensions, consult the Keystone Trails Association Newsletter or visit the web site at http://www.reston.com/kta/kta.html.

39 Tall Timbers Trail

General description:	This trail tours the Swift Run drainage, passing through the old growth of Snyders-Middleswarth Natural Area, reaching the mature second growth of Tall Timbers Natural Area. Despite its length, the trail has a wild aspect.
General location:	30 miles east of State College.
Special attractions:	Remnant forest of old-growth hemlock, white pine, and hardwoods, recognized as a National Natural Landmark; rhododendron and laurel; solitude; clear-flowing Swift Run.
Length:	3.8 miles round trip, with options to extend or shorten the hike.
Elevation:	Find a 400-foot elevation change between the picnic area (elevation 1,342 feet) and the upstream turnaround.
Difficulty:	Moderate.
Maps:	Bald Eagle State Forest.
Special concerns:	No overnight camping. These adjoining natural areas along Swift Run hold a superb set of ridge-run loop options, but they have fallen to neglect. The underlying trailbeds remain in place along Swift Run and atop the ridges of Thick and Buck Mountains. With scouting and bushwhacking, experienced hikers can still chart and walk a loop.
Season and hours:	Spring through fall.
For information:	Bald Eagle State Forest.

Finding the trailhead: From central Mifflinburg, go west on Pennsylvania 45 for 8.5 miles, turning south on PA 235. Remain on PA 235 for 8.7 miles, turning right (northwest) on Timber Road/Swift Road in Troxelville. It begins paved changing to dirt. In 3.6 miles bear left for Tall Timbers. In another mile veer right, entering rustic Snyders-Middleswarth Picnic Area to find the trailhead. A stone monument for the National Natural Landmark signals the start of the upstream tour.

The hike: On the north shore of Swift Run, hike upstream past the monument on well-defined, but unmarked **Tall Timbers Trail**. Immediately enter the old-growth realm. Downed trees and limbs strew the banks and slope of Swift Run. Enjoy birch of admirable size, with neck-craning looks

Tall Timbers Trail

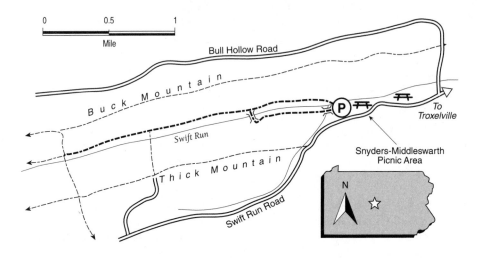

at the hemlocks marching up slope. Mayflower, fern, and hobblebush contribute to the drainage bottom.

At 0.2 mile pass beside a hemlock and later a snag, both of impressive girth and height. A cut passage in a fallen giant better demonstrates the tree's diameter. The gossiping run puts a musical score to the tour. Where the trail forks at 0.4 mile, the left prong leads to a footbridge and south-shore return for a 1-mile loop. Remain on the Tall Timbers Trail to view the upstream forest, with its laurel and rhododendron.

Light trickles through the old-growth forest, owing to clearings left by the tumbled and snapped trees. The uphill gradient remains easy. Discover a few enormous white pines amid the hemlocks and hardwoods; a scattering of pine cones may signal a search for the source. A few rhododendrons now dot the drainage. Encounter logs to step over or duck under and curtains of living boughs to step through, all part of the natural area's signature.

At 1 mile the trail grades higher, touring some 30 feet above the run. At 1.2 miles stay alert. Here an unmarked path descends left to cross Swift Run, where a side trail then ascends to **Thick Mountain Trail** for a southern ridge return. Carry a map for this 3-mile loop option, which includes some road travel. For the chosen hike, continue upstream along the north shore.

At 1.4 miles mountain laurel pinches the trail, while a bounty of rhododendrons decorate Swift Run. The uncut woods show greater variety, and hiking virtually becomes cross-country. Still, enough feet pass this way that hikers can usually view the line of travel and find tracked bypasses around the worst of the downfalls. Seasonally, the floral blooms adequately reward the added expenditure. Other times, hikers will have to weigh the merits of continuing.

At 1.8 miles, again be on the alert. Here a tracked path heads uphill to the right to **Buck Mountain Trail**, with a less recognizable trail descending left to cross Swift Run. On the south shore of Swift Run, a couple of white blazes point out the ascent to Thick Mountain Trail (angle left). Both ridge trails offer opportunities to vary or extend the tour. As the struggle of drainage-bottom travel only increases, turn back or ascend here.

For this hike, retrace the Tall Timbers Trail, returning to the footbridge crossing at 0.4 mile (3.2 miles). Cross and follow the trail downstream along the south slope, gaining a new perspective on the old-growth canyon. The trail rolls along the flank of Thick Mountain, staying between 50 and 100 feet above Swift Run, but the separating slope denies stream views. Again find logs to negotiate and rock studding, but the forest continues to enchant. At 3.7 miles, descend and cross a footbridge over a nearly equal-sized side tributary. Mossy boulders add to its beauty. Next bear left to cross the road bridge over Swift Run, returning to the trailhead (3.8 miles).

40 Tunnel and Iron Horse Trails

General description:	These adjoining trails explore second-growth forest and meadow habitats, tracing a remnant of railroad history (late 1800s to early 1900s).
General location:	40 miles west of Harrisburg.
Special attractions:	Diverse second-growth forest, clues to the railroading past, wildflowers, wildlife sightings, fall foliage.
Length:	10.4-mile loop; 1-mile loop for Tunnel Trail only.
Elevation:	Travel between 850 and 1,700 feet in elevation.
Difficulty:	Moderate.
Maps:	Iron Horse Trail brochure; Tuscarora State Forest.
Special concerns:	Red blazings indicate the Iron Horse Trail; blue the Tunnel Trail. Hikers may camp overnight along the Iron Horse Trail, but not within Big Spring State Park or on private lands along or near the trail. Contact the district headquarters about permits. As the Iron Horse Trail often abuts and for 1 mile traverses private land, keep to the trail, pass respectfully, and obey posted restrictions. Flooding necessitated a re-route on the southern Iron Horse Trail; watch for blazes.
Season and hours:	Spring through fall for hiking.
For information:	Tuscarora State Forest.

Finding the trailhead: From Penna Turnpike Interstate 76, take exit 14 and follow Pennsylvania 75 north for 11 miles, turning east on PA 274. In

4.7 miles, turn right on dirt Hemlock Road to reach the marked trailhead and upper parking area for Big Spring State Park. For the park's main entrance and picnic area, go 0.1 mile farther east on PA 274. Find a 2nd trailhead on PA 274, 3.8 miles east of Big Spring State Park; 2 miles west of New Germantown.

The hike: On the south side of PA 274, the Iron Horse Trail incorporates grades from the Perry Lumber Company Railroad (1901 to 1905). On the north side of PA 274, travel fragments of the Path Valley Railroad—a failed venture, halted by the geology of Conococheague Mountain. The Tunnel Trail visits the site that spelled the end for Path Valley Railroad. Intended to extend 0.5-mile through the mountain, the tunnel penetrates but 100 feet. The site's metamorphosed rock (flint) resisted blasting, and with pay not forthcoming, the workers walked.

From the Hemlock Road trailhead, hike south across the road, following the **Tunnel Trail** for a counterclockwise tour. Pass amid oak, birch, hemlock, and laurel, paralleling Hemlock Road east. Fragments of the historic railroad grade advance the rolling tour. Where the trail curves left to descend (0.3 mile), proceed forward to view the abandoned tunnel amid the hemlock darkness. A fence denies a close inspection of the skyward-angled void.

Resume the Tunnel Trail, crossing Hemlock Road. Meander amid a tight young forest of birch and gum to reach the **Iron Horse Trail**/Perry Lumber

Iron Horse Trail, Tuscarora State Forest.

Tunnel and Iron Horse Trails

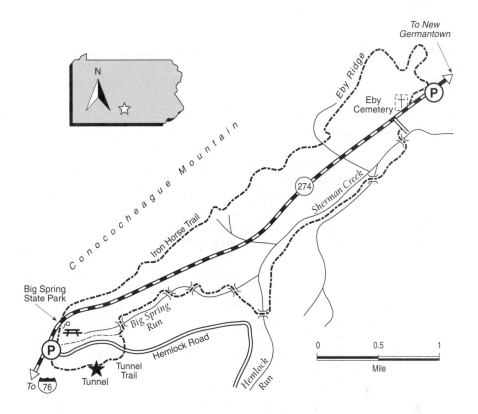

Company Railroad (0.75 mile). Turn left to complete the Tunnel Trail at Big Spring State Park (1 mile). Turn right for the 10.4-mile loop.

Red is now the guiding color for the long tour. The grade begins with areas of loose rock alternating with wet-meadow stretches. Ripples beneath the boot hint at the former railroad ties. Ferns favor the moist sites.

Before long, follow gurgling Big Spring Run downstream, crossing the stream four times via simple footbridges, some in disrepair. Encounter bigger oak, tulip, and maple trees, with islands of hemlock interrupting the hardwoods. Deer and small trout may be seen.

With the 4th crossing, ascend to skirt a private parcel. Where the trail tops out (2.3 miles), turn left per markers, touring a selectively cut forest. After a level passage, descend to cross a bridge over Hemlock Run at 2.6 miles. Along the trail ahead, patches of bramble and brier snatch at hikers. Keep to the trail, still edging private land.

At 3.1 miles bear right at Sherman Creek, following the waterway downstream. Born at the confluence of Hemlock and Big Spring runs, Sherman Creek hosts a more mature forest of maple, oak, hickory, tulip, ash, hemlock, and beech. At 3.6 miles, follow a jeep trail past a private cabin, cross a dirt forest road, and resume travel on a footpath marred from illegal motorcycle use.

Stay alert upon crossing a footbridge over an unnamed run. The actual trail proceeds forward, while a more worn path swings right. Cross a pair of pipeline corridors, keeping an eye out for blazes and ribbons, and then cross the Sherman Creek footbridge (4.7 miles). Admire the wide, clear, rocky waterway. Cross a secondary flow and bear right where the trail forks.

At 4.9 miles hike left on a narrow forest road. Where the blazed trail turns right to parallel PA 274 northeast, hikers may opt instead to hike along the highway to avoid the shrubs and poison ivy that overwhelm the trail. Look for the Iron Horse Trail to resume on the north side of PA 274 at the eastern edge of Eby Cemetery. This tiny rustic cemetery houses tasteful markers dating to the mid 1800s.

Continue northeast just removed from PA 274, coming to a marked junction opposite the lower trailhead (5.4 miles); bear left on the Path Valley Grade. With a gentle ascent, the trail meanders amid planted pine and spruce with hardwoods. Rains give rise to a gummy mud. Soon a raised grade hosts travel.

At 6.3 miles bear right to travel Eby Ridge. Atop the ridge, stroll a classic oak-and-wild berry forest. Western glimpses present impressive Conococheague Mountain. At 7.1 miles descend to follow a pipeline corridor left, wading through the deep grasses.

Turn right at 7.3 miles, hiking on an elevated railroad grade. Then descend sharply, cross a side drainage, and pass through another pipeline corridor, before returning to the grade. At 7.8 miles, proceed forward through a cut log. The grade, breached in places, still advances the trail.

Along the lower reaches of Conococheague Mountain, traverse posted private land (8.4 to 9.4 miles); no hunting, driving game, camping, or fires. Despite the young trees, enjoy a mostly shaded tour. Re-entering public land find mature forest.

The trail again rolls to skirt a private parcel, before it contours southwest along the wooded slope above lightly traveled PA 274. The trail then descends to cross PA 274 southwest of the main entrance to Big Spring State Park. Follow the blazed trail back to Hemlock Road (10.4 miles).

41 Hemlocks Natural Area

OVERVIEW

This 120-acre site, recognized as a National Natural Landmark, preserves an uncut drainage of original white pine–eastern hemlock forest—a habitat that once dominated much of the state of Pennsylvania. In this old-growth domain, hemlocks boast the greatest count. Here the state tree reaches heights in excess of 100 feet and diameters greater than 2 feet. The average age for the trees is between 300 and 500 years old. As the Patterson Run canyon spans only 0.25 to 0.5 mile across, it allows for an intimate acquaintance with the regal gallery.

General description:	A basic loop explores the drainage bottom and eastern hillside above Patterson Run, traveling the Hemlock and Rim trails. A detour downstream along the Laurel Trail takes visitors to a congestion of mountain laurel, before the path deteriorates.
General location:	40 miles west of Harrisburg.
Special attractions:	Old-growth hemlock and hardwoods; clear, cascading Patterson Run; mountain laurel; fall foliage.
Length:	Hemlock–Rim trails Loop, 1.5-mile loop; Laurel Trail spur, 0.6 mile round trip.
Elevation:	Find a 400-foot elevation change between the trailhead and the lowest Patterson Run crossing.
Difficulty:	Easy to moderate.
Maps:	Hemlocks Natural Area brochure; Tuscarora State Forest.
Special concerns:	No camping or fires in the Natural Area, along the bordering roadway, or at trailheads. Entry is by foot only. As the area is allowed to prosper undisturbed, hikers may expect downfalls, brushing passages, and minimal trail markings. Flooding necessitated a re-route, so watch for it.
Season and hours:	Spring through fall, daylight hours.
For information:	Tuscarora State Forest.

Finding the trailhead: From Penna Turnpike Interstate 76, take exit 14 and follow Pennsylvania 75 north for 11 miles, turning east on PA 274. In 4.7 miles, turn right on dirt Hemlock Road to reach the Hemlock Natural Area in 3.8 miles, the trailhead in 5.4 miles.

The hikes: Descend a deciduous-clad slope interspersed with hemlock; in autumn the evergreens provide splendid contrast to the flame-colored foliage of gum, birch, tulip, oak, and maple. A moderate grade leads to Patterson Run and the engaging big trees. Cross the bridge at 0.1 mile, com-

Hemlocks Natural Area

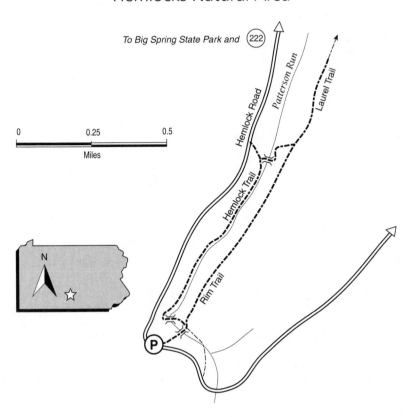

To Big Spring State Park and (222)

Hemlock Road

Patterson Run

Laurel Trail

Hemlock Trail

Rim Trail

0   0.25   0.5
Miles

N

☆

P

ing to a trail junction. To the left lies the **Hemlock Trail**; the paths right and straight ahead belong to the **Rim Trail**.

Go left on the lightly traveled Hemlock Trail, crossing back over Patterson Run on a second footbridge. A rustic bench welcomes hikers to pause and admire a grand union of images: the statuesque forest, a crystalline Patterson Run cascade, the mossy rocks and logs of the streambed, and the picturesque footbridge. Follow Patterson Run downstream. Ferns and mossy rocks fashion the drainage bottom; be careful not to turn an ankle amid the rocks. Sphagnum moss mats the wet spots.

Pass within feet of the run, admiring the series of 1-foot-tall cascades, but the towering hemlock, large birch, and snags draw eyes skyward. In this narrow canyon, witness the ongoing process of nature, with tumbled and snapped-top trees, snags and rotting logs, and renewing young forest.

At 0.8 mile find another trail junction. The path ahead ascends past a beautiful stand of big trees to Hemlock Road. The footbridge over Patterson Run launches the **Laurel Trail**, which then links to the Rim Trail.

Cross the footbridge, take a few strides downstream, and then contour up the eastern canyon slope, meeting the Rim Trail in 250 feet. For the loop alone, follow the Rim Trail right. To add a side tour to a dense grove of mountain laurel, remain on the Laurel Trail, heading left; the blooms arrive in late May to early June.

Opting for the spur, hike left touring 30 to 40 feet above the run. The trail extends new perspectives on the canyon, its forest, and the size of its trees. A few faint, but largely unnecessary blue blazes mark the route. Oak leaves shower the forest floor.

Pass from old growth to mixed hardwoods, with little fanfare (1 mile). Here laurel gains a footing. Where the trail starts to roll downhill, a dense growth of the flowering shrub encloses on the trail and travel becomes cross-country. The faint blazes are now necessary. Stop to overlook the laurel-rich slope. Then return as you came to the Rim Trail junction (1.4 miles).

The Rim Trail contours the eastern canyon slope upstream, overlooking Patterson Run and extending cross-canyon views. Hemlock needles and cones soften the narrow footpath. Where the trail ascends, small downfalls add to the effort. The trail passes from smaller hemlocks back into an area of big trees (1.6 miles); a sentinel pair of hemlocks announce the change. Patterson Run whispers 60 to 80 feet below.

The trail rolls and descends to close the loop back at the bridge, 2 miles. An upstream hike along the Rim Trail will extend the discovery. For this hike, cross the bridge and return to the trailhead, 2.1 miles.

Pittsburgh Region

In the rolling countryside near Pittsburgh, hikers can explore an exciting boulder-riddled creek gorge, a remnant prairie ecosystem, a wildflower reserve, wetlands, mixed woods, waterfalls, lakes, and reservoirs. Echoes to the past mark travel: a grist mill, a mineral springs spa dating to the early 1800s, a covered bridge, a farm, and a limekiln. Along the roadways, furnaces harken to the era of iron. Long-distance trails traverse the region, but with much of their distance crossing private land and subject to change, we have chosen not to include them.

42 McConnell's Mill State Park

OVERVIEW

A National Natural Landmark, this 2,529-acre park serves up the beauty and excitement of Slippery Rock Creek Gorge and the shady, charm of Hell Run. Worn 400 feet deep into the landscape, the gorge features enormous boulders both on shore and altering the creek flow. Trails parallel the distinctive waterways. Overlook the alternating whitewater and eddy-swirled calms of Slippery Rock Creek and the crystalline flow of Hell Run. A pair of the bridges that span Slippery Rock Creek allow hikers to partition the hike or walk a loop. The trails also visit a restored rolling mill—1 of the 1st in the nation; a covered bridge built in 1874; and a limekiln.

General description:	The creek-run trail system at this park welcomes round-trip, loop, or shuttle hikes.
General location:	40 miles north of Pittsburgh.
Special attractions:	Exciting, picturesque waterways, house- and elephant-sized boulders, waterfalls, fishing, historic sites, spring wildflowers, fall foliage.
Length:	Alpha Pass Trail, 0.5 mile one-way; Kildoo Trail, 2-mile loop; Slippery Rock Gorge Trail, 6 miles one-way; Hell's Hollow Trail, 0.8-mile round trip; Alpha Pass to Upper Hell's Hollow, 7.6 miles one-way.
Elevation:	Find a 400-foot elevation change between Alpha Pass and the confluence of Hell Run and Slippery Rock Creek.
Difficulty:	Moderate to strenuous, depending on length.
Maps:	State park brochure.
Special concerns:	Within the park there is no overnight camping and no swimming. Pets must be leashed and controlled. In this steep-sided gorge, expect areas of rugged, difficult footing, slippery wet rock, and side-drainage crossings. During hunting seasons, wear fluorescent colors. Blue blazes mark park trails.
Season and hours:	Spring through fall for hiking, daylight hours. Mill hours: 10:30 a.m. to 5:30 p.m. Memorial Day through Labor Day, with variable spring and fall hours.
For information:	McConnell's Mill State Park.

Finding the trailhead: From Interstate 79, take exit 29 for Moraine and McConnell's Mill state parks, and go west on U.S. Highway 422. In 1.7 miles, turn left (south) on McConnell's Mill Road, reaching the park office in less than 0.1 mile, Alpha Pass trailhead parking in 0.6 mile, and the Kildoo Picnic Area/Old Mill Access in 1.1 miles. For Hell Run, follow McConnell's Mill Road through the covered bridge, negotiating Lawrence County roads to the trailhead; consult the state park map/brochure (available at park office).

The hikes: For the **Alpha Pass to Upper Hell's Hollow Hike**, start at the Alpha Pass parking area. Hike the steep **Alpha Pass Trail** downhill; rustic pole railings help hikers keep their balance. Black cherry, maple, birch, hemlock, tulip, and beech shade the gorge.

At the fork at 0.1 mile, the main gorge trail swings left, heading downstream to the mill. A 0.3-mile, round-trip detour along the 2nd blazed route leads to Alpha Pass Falls. It descends to an impressive bouldery shore and noisy rapid along Slippery Rock Creek. From there, look for the path to cross and ascend along a side drainage, traveling root and rock steps to Alpha Pass Falls. This 30- to 40-foot falls consists of sparkling droplet chains spilling over cliff.

Opting to forgo the falls detour, keep to the gorge tour passing amid hemlock, birch, and mossy rocks. The boulders of the slope intrigue as they fold together shaping dark hollows, passages, and dens. Despite the rugged trailbed, many boots pass this way.

A stiff current remains, even where the 25-foot-wide Slippery Rock Creek quiets. Rafters and kayakers share the corridor; life-saving rings placed along the trail allow hikers to assist creek-runners in trouble. The trail rolls, near-

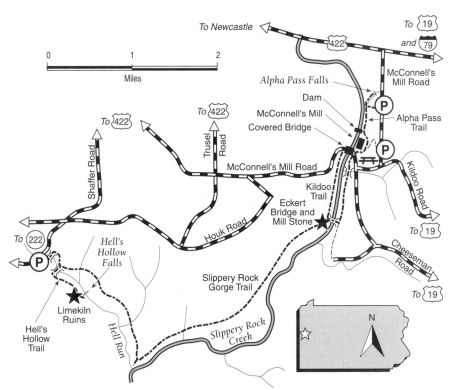

McConnell's Mill State Park

ing and then drifting away from the waterway. Benches welcome lengthier creek views.

At 0.5 mile (0.8 mile with Alpha Pass Falls spur), reach the mill area with its viewing decks. Overlook the dam, raceway, and spillway falls, with the historic covered bridge downstream. Find amenities and a natural spring. Here too, hikers may spy river travelers portaging around the dam.

The 2-mile loop of the **Kildoo Trail** next advances the gorge tour. Hikers may opt to keep to the east shore or pass through the covered bridge for a west shore downstream tour. For this description, keep to the east shore of the interpretive trail (brochure available at park office). While initially paved, wet mosses can still make for slippery footing. Enjoy the rich forest of the gorge and frequent creek views. Pocket sandy beaches mark shore; their location can vary depending on seasonal flooding.

A footbridge at 0.75 mile offers views at a bouldery side drainage with cascading chutes. Where the trail forks, keep toward the creek. Another turbulent, squeezed rapid brings amplified excitement to the tour. Before long, steps descend to a boaters take-out below Eckert Bridge.

Cross Eckert Bridge, closed to traffic. On the opposite shore (1.5 miles), turn left near a mill stone to continue the tour to Hell Run Parking, now on **Slippery Rock Gorge Trail**—part of the **North Country National Scenic Trail**. Or turn right to complete the Kildoo Trail, winning new perspectives.

The rugged Slippery Rock Gorge Trail promises a workout, touring the western gorge slope. A mix of elm, locust, tulip poplar, and oak enfolds the tour, with sycamore along the creek. Baneberry, fern, jewelweed, and witch-hazel weave the understory. Find poison ivy where more light penetrates.

The trail rolls to and from the creek, crossing side drainages and springs. An even flow of Slippery Rock Run parts the flats. By 2.1 miles the trail climbs to contour some 100 feet above the creek. Although the steep wooded slope censors views, the creek's song goes unrestrained. Be alert for switchbacks as the trail marches up a side ridge, passing amid tilted layered sandstones and small ledges. By the time the trail tops out, hikers have easily doubled the distance between trail and creek.

Along the upper slope, find a fairly easy woods stroll. Where the trail dips through an upper drainage, admire big-diameter trees. Clearings give rise to brushy passages and gorge overlooks. Wildflowers sprinkle the forest floor. Work the toe of your boot, as the trail switchbacks downhill to again contour some 100 feet above the creek. "Beech-lovers" find ample numbers of the prized tree; do not deface trunks. With steep pitches reach Walnut Flats (3.7 miles) and a trail distance sign.

Basswood, tulip poplar, and cucumber magnolia now interweave the forest. Proceed downstream, again contouring the slope, now above a quieter creek persona. Darker hemlocks contain the trail. At 4.8 and 5.6 miles find filtered looks at whitewater rapids. A few muddy trail sites require devised crossings. At 5.7 miles come upon another distance sign. Here a downhill detour (0.2-mile round trip) on unmarked trail delivers a confluence view of Slippery Rock Creek and Hell Run. Proceed forward for Hell Run Parking.

Slippery Rock Creek, McConnell's Mill State Park.

The hike now follows Hell Run upstream, contouring its north slope some 80 feet above the waterway. Cross an unmarked trail, staying the blazes, to descend to the rocky shore for a better view of pretty, babbling Hell Run. Blazes then return hikers to the rim.

View an attractive, dark, corner hollow with mossy rocks and a spring, before drifting away to travel a black cherry flat and later an oak-hickory woods interspersed with flowering shrubs. On the rolling descent, footbridges and boardwalks span side drainages. Reach the junction with **Hell's Hollow Trail** (7.5 miles). Go left across the footbridge to visit Hell's Hollow Falls (described below); proceed forward to end at Hell Run Parking (7.6 miles).

For **Hell's Hollow Trail**, hike 0.1 mile downstream from Hell Run Parking or reach it from the west end of Slippery Rock Gorge Trail. Cross the footbridge over Hell Run to follow the south shore downstream. Jewelweed, cardinal flowers, and nettles dress the stream; maple and elm overhang the banks.

Cross a bridge over a side tributary. The trail remains wide, with green shoulders, shaded by high-canopy forest. Enjoy fine old maples, hickory, black cherry, and basswood. Midway a bench seat overlooks a miniature gorge along Hell Run. Downstream view a bedrock slide, feeding a deep pool.

Where the trail forks, stay along the run, descending to the head of Hell's Hollow Falls and an arched opening to an old limekiln built amid the natural rock. A peek inside the kiln reveals a circle cut to the sky and 10-foot-tall walls. Stairs now descend to the base of the waterfall. The main watery drop spans 15 feet and measures 10 feet high, its white streamers dancing over rounded ledge. By negotiating streambed rocks, secure looks at the upper 3-foot cascade.

On the upstream return, a detour along the untraveled fork leads to the fenced top of the kiln. Hepatica and trillium seasonally adorn the site. Return to Hell Run Parking (0.8 mile).

43 Jennings Environmental Education Center

OVERVIEW

At this 320-acre environmental education center, visitors can tour and study a relict (prehistoric) prairie, similar to the classic prairies of the Midwest. About 2000 B.C., the prairie ecosystem spanned between the Rockies and the Appalachians, but climatic changes opened the door for forest succession. In the East all but handful of these prairies were claimed by deciduous woods.

The specialness of this site prompted the establishment of the first reserve in Pennsylvania for the protection of an individual plant species—the blazing star. This prairie dweller captured the attention of botanist Otto Emery Jennings and lends its name to the site's prairie ecosystem. In early August, be dazzled by the rose-purple radial blooms of the 4- to 6-foot-tall blazing star.

General description:	Interlocking nature trails explore the center's lowland and plateau woods, wetlands, and prairie ecosystem. The selected 4 hikes encapsulate the offering.
General location:	40 miles north of Pittsburgh.
Special attractions:	Relic prairie; one of the state's best wildflower shows; manmade wetland; bird watching; a swamp habitat suitable for a reclusive, endangered rattlesnake—the Massasauga; fall foliage.
Length:	Woodwhisper Trail, 0.25-mile loop; Black Cherry-Ridge Trails Loop, 1.4 miles round trip; Blazing Star-Prairie Loop Hike, 0.5 mile round trip; Massasauga-Deer-Oakwoods Trails Loop, 2.1 miles round trip.
Elevation:	Woodwhisper Trail and the Blazing Star-Prairie Loop Hike, both flat; Black Cherry–Ridge trails Loop and Massasauga–Deer–Oakwoods trails Loop, both less than 100 feet of elevation change.

Difficulty: Black Cherry–Ridge trails Loop, moderate. All
others, easy.
Maps: Environmental education center brochure.
Special concerns: Keep to the trails, and leave pets at home or control
them on a tight leash. Watch where you step or place
hands as the Massasauga rattlesnake dwells here. If a
snake is spied, keep a 6-foot safety margin. The snake
is reclusive by nature and is just as eager to avoid an
encounter as the hiker. While trails go unblazed,
junctions are signed.
Season and hours: Spring through fall for hiking, 8 a.m. to sunset;
Office: 8 a.m. to 4 p.m., weekdays.
For information: Jennings Environmental Education Center.

Finding the trailhead: From Interstate 79, take exit 29 and go east on U.S. Highway 422 for 5.6 miles. Turn north on Pennsylvania 528 and go 7.5 miles more to find the entrance to the prairie trails on the left. Less than 0.1 mile to the north, reach the center and woodland trails on the right.

The hikes: **Woodwhisper Trail** and **Black Cherry–Ridge trails Loop** start out the back door of the Environmental Education Center.

For the wheelchair-accessible **Woodwhisper Trail** begin on the boardwalk of the **Old Mill Trail**. A beautiful old oak presides over the oak, maple, birch, and black cherry woods. Rhododendron splash seasonal color through the midstory. Proceed from the end of the boardwalk on paved trail for 200 feet. There a gravel spur leads to a hexagonal gazebo. The gazebo overlooks a small wetland, consisting of an open pond, cattail marsh, and wetland meadow. While providing habitat for wildlife, this manmade wetland is also helping to cleanse Big Run of contaminating acids—the result of a burst seal on an upstream abandoned coal mine.

The tour then continues through similar woods, with Mayapple and clubmoss amid the ground flora. PA 8 overwhelms the whisper of the trees. The pavement ends at 0.2 mile, with a gravel spur returning to the center (0.25 mile). Wheelchair-users may wish to forgo this difficult gravel passage, returning instead as they came.

For the **Black Cherry–Ridge trails Loop**, bear right upon exiting the center, descend steps, and travel a gravel path through similar lowland woods, with witch hazel, a few elm, jewelweed, and ferns. Look for the **Old Elm Trail** to branch right as you approach the footbridge over Big Run (0.1 mile). Across the bridge, find the loop junction; go left for a clockwise tour.

Hike upstream, overlooking muddy-flowing Big Run. Green banks and areas of skunk cabbage and cardinal flower grace its course. At 0.2 mile, detour left 100 feet onto the bridge of the **Old Mill Trail** for a view of the old mill site. The remaining stone foundation blends into the woodland-run setting. From here, hikers may opt to return to the center via Old Mill Trail for a 0.4-mile loop.

Jennings Environmental Education Center

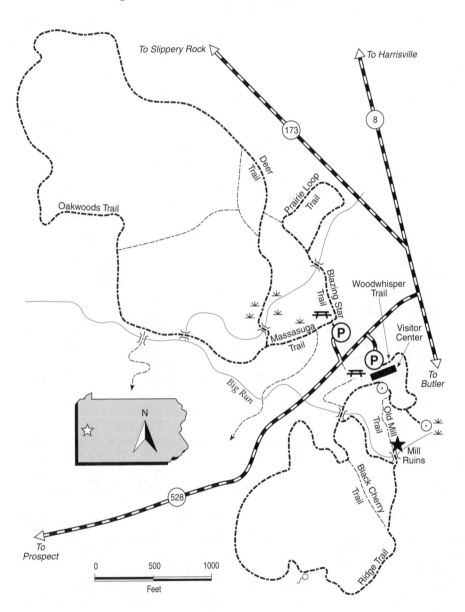

To Slippery Rock

To Harrisville

173

8

Deer Trail

Prairie Loop Trail

Oakwoods Trail

Blazing Star Trail

Woodwhisper Trail

Visitor Center

P

P

Massasuga Trail

To Butler

Big Run

Old Mill Trail

N

Mill Ruins

0   500   1000

Black Cherry Trail

528

Feet

To Prospect

Ridge Trail

To complete the Black Cherry–Ridge trails Loop, follow the steps up the rise at 0.2 mile to travel an earthen trail away from Big Run. Hickory and oak share ranks with the big black cherries. At the upcoming junction, turn right for a 0.75-mile loop on the Black Cherry Trail alone; bear left to extend the tour via the **Ridge Trail**.

On the Ridge Trail, tour the wildflower-shrub habitat of a utility corridor, quickly returning to a full multistory forest, vibrant with greenery. Songbirds, squirrels, and perhaps a skittish deer may provide a passing acquaintance. Keep right for the Ridge Trail. A few rocks embed the path; the ascent is mild. Cucumber magnolia and tulip poplar join the woodland, with grapevines snaking to the sunlight.

At 0.5 mile the trail tops out and rolls, passing a spring adorned by jewelweed and skunk cabbage. Half-a-dozen fern varieties contribute to the understory mantle. On the descent, pass back through the utility corridor, touring a less congested woods. A pileated woodpecker may startle hikers out of their woodland reverie.

Black cherry trees precede a footbridge leading to a T-junction with the Black Cherry Trail; turn left. Complete the loop (1.3 miles), and again turn left to cross Big Run and return to the center (1.4 miles).

Start the **Blazing Star–Prairie Loop Hike** and **Massasauga–Deer–Oakwoods Trails Loop** from the prairie trails parking lot on the west side of PA 528. Hike through the stone gateway.

In 100 feet the trails separate, with the Blazing Star Trail heading right, the Massasauga Trail heading left, and the picnic shelter straight ahead. Go right for the **Blazing Star Trail**. Prairie habitat sweeps away in both directions from the mowed path. View a dense growth of knee- to waist-high vegetation, with a parade of white, pink, purple, yellow, and red wildflowers announcing the passage of the seasons.

Young aspen and maple shoots rise amid the yellow primrose, yarrow, blazing star, and lily. Depleted glacial soils and a regimen of burning keep the forest in check. Beware of poison ivy. Interpretive signs introduce the area.

Cross a footbridge over a Big Run tributary. The flowing water gives rise to skunk cabbage, cattail, and cardinal flowers. Past the bridge, reach the 1st **Prairie Loop** junction and proceed straight for a clockwise tour, still hiking the Blazing Star Trail. At 0.2 mile turn right for the loop; the Blazing Star Trail ends at the **Deer Trail**, 150 feet ahead.

Enjoy a slow tour of the Prairie Loop. A hawkmoth, which hovers like a hummingbird, may draw study. Where the trail nears PA 173, a tree-and-shrub buffer holds back the visual distraction but not the noise. The intrusion only reinforces the foresight of the state in protecting this prairie island. Small burrows riddle the edge of the prairie. Close the loop (0.4 mile), and turn left retracing the 1st 0.1 mile to the parking area.

A left at the 100-foot junction puts hikers on the **Massasauga Trail** for the **Massasauga–Deer–Oakwoods Trails Loop**. Travel trimmed grass and gravel path, between herbaceous meadow and the framing shingle oaks and

Forest boardwalk, Jennings Environmental Education Center.

maples. Proceed forward at the four-way junction near an old oak. In a few strides, the **Glacier Ridge Trail** branches left. Travel mixed lowland woods with hawthorn and dogwood, spying a small wetland pond to the right. With a rolling descent, reach the signed loop junction (0.3 mile). Stay the Massasauga Trail, bearing right; the Oakwoods Trail holds the return.

Counterclockwise, the trail overlooks a skunk cabbage drainage and bog. A footbridge spans the thin flow. At 0.5 mile, the Massasauga Trail ends at the **Deer Trail** loop; choose either fork to continue the tour. Beyond the trees to the right lies Blazing Star Prairie. Keep to the Deer Trail to meet and follow the **Oakwoods Trail** (0.6 mile).

Amid the gentle woodland terrain housing this trail, ditches and depressions hint at old ore pits reclaimed by nature. The meandering trail strains to the property boundary. Surrender to the woodland's relaxing spell. Descend at 1.2 miles, and cross a drainage footbridge. At 1.5 miles the **Old Field Trail** arrives on the left; proceed forward.

Descend again to tour a low wooded flat, with hornbeam, hawthorn, and hazelnut. The collage of leaf shapes wins over travelers. Glimpse Big Run prior to reaching the 1.7-mile junction. Here the **Hepatica Trail** heads right, crossing Big Run on a footbridge. Continue forward for the loop, passing between Big Run and a skunk cabbage-lined side water. Soon cross a footbridge over the latter. Bog and run habitats continue to frame travel. Close the loop (1.8 miles) and turn right, backtracking the first 0.3 mile to trail parking.

44 Raccoon Creek State Park

OVERVIEW

At this 7,323-acre state park, hikers can tour the interlocking nature trails of an exceptional wildflower reserve, strolling both floodplain and bluff. Elsewhere, paths visit an historic mineral spring and explore a mature hardwood forest, overlooking Traverse Creek and manmade Raccoon Lake.

General description:	4 hikes present the area offering.
General location:	25 miles west of Pittsburgh.
Special attractions:	314-acre wildflower reserve, with more 500 species of blooming plants (April through October); Traverse and Raccoon creeks; Raccoon Lake; platy cliffs, mature trees, mineral springs, wildlife, fall foliage.
Length:	Max Henrici–Old Field Trails Loop, 1.5-mile loop; Jennings–Audubon trails Loop, 2.1-mile loop; Frankfort Mineral Springs Loop, 0.4-mile loop; Valley Trail, 2.5 miles round trip.
Elevation:	Trails all show less than 100 feet of elevation change.
Difficulty:	Max Henrici–Old Field trails Loop, Jennings–Audubon trails Loop, and Valley Trail, all moderate; Frankfort Mineral Springs Loop, easy.
Maps:	State park brochure; Wildflower Reserve map/flier.
Special concerns:	Within the wildflower reserve, there is no collecting, no smoking, no pets, no picnicking, and no bicycles. Beware of poison ivy. Mosquitos seasonally annoy. Watch footing on descents; at times, pathways can be muddy.
Season and hours:	Year-round, spring through fall for hiking. Wildflower Reserve: 8 a.m. to sunset.
For information:	Raccoon Creek State Park.

Finding the trailhead: From Pittsburgh go west on U.S. Highway 30 for 9.1 miles to reach Raccoon Creek State Park Wildflower Reserve on the right. Go 0.2 mile more and turn left, now following the park road west. Pass the beach turnoff in 1.7 miles, the picnic area in 2.8 miles, the campground in 5 miles, and meet Pennsylvania 18 in 5.7 miles. Locate the park office less than 0.1 mile north on PA 18. Locate parking for Frankfort Mineral Springs on the west side of PA 18, 0.3 miles south of the junction (0.4 mile south of the park office).

The hikes: Two loops introduce the Wildflower Reserve and access the site's other named trails for additional exploration: **Max Henrici–Old Field trails Loop** and **Jennings–Audubon trails Loop**. A month-by-month bloom schedule (available at the nature center) speeds rifling through the wild-

Raccoon Creek State Park

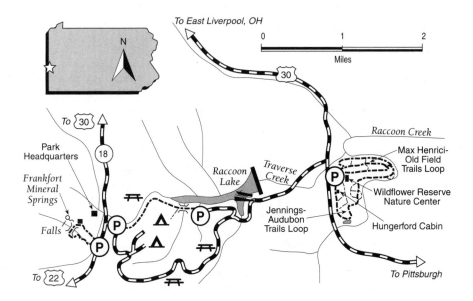

flower field guide. Wooden trail signs at the parking area and near the nature center identify starts for the hikes.

Look for the **Max Henrici Trail** as you approach the nature center. Bear left, as the **Audubon Trail** heads right. Travel a wide mowed lane between field and woods, hike past a park residence, and descend along a thin jewel-weed drainage to reach the Raccoon Creek floodplain. Hickory, elm, black cherry, maple, and walnut contribute to the woods. A rich, moist understory spills at their feet.

Skunk cabbage, Mayapple, trillium, and jack-in-the-pulpit seasonally grace a tour. Enjoy a myriad of leaf shapes, layers, and textures. Keep right, hiking past a trio of link trails to the **Old Field Trail**. At the foot of a bluff, come to a multiple junction at 0.6 mile: Uphill to the right lies the Audubon Trail; straight ahead is the **Jennings Trail**; and to the left, the **Old Field Trail** holds the selected loop return.

Go left, passing between an old field and Raccoon Creek. The creek flows broad and cloudy, with alternating muddy and green banks. Big sycamores overlook the proceedings. Morning sunlight floods the forest with beams and starbursts. Intricate spider webs attract attention. The tall meadow understory holds a host of blooms, appearing in sprays, multi-floral crowns, and single flowers—yellow, white, pink, purple, red, and orange.

Keep to the Old Field Trail, ignoring the link trails back to the Max Henrici Trail. Spurs to the right present creek overlooks. Muddy beaches may hold the tracks of deer or raccoon. Complaining crows and damsel flies add to travel.

At 1.2 miles, the Old Field Trail bears left; the **Travis Trail** heads right. As both merge prior to reaching the center, hikers have an option. Go right to enjoy more creek overlooks, including a deck view at the confluence of Traverse and Raccoon creeks. At 1.3 miles meet the Old Field Trail where it arcs, and turn right to close the loop in 250 feet. Retrace the hike's start to the center, 1.5 miles.

The **Jennings–Audubon trails Loop** pays tribute to two renowned naturalists: botanist Otto Emery Jennings and ornithologist John James Audubon. Find the start of the **Jennings Trail** behind the flagpole, and hike toward Hungerford Cabin. Ascend steadily amid planted pine and spruce. On the right in 200 feet, an impressive spreading oak rises in marked contrast to the tall, straight plantation trees. At 0.1 mile reach the Cy Hungerford Cabin, cross its porch, and continue the same line of travel to enter deciduous forest.

At the upcoming descent, shun the steep path that heads straight downhill; instead use the switchbacks. At 0.2 mile and 0.25 mile respectively, the Deer and Big Maple trails branch left. Noise from PA 30 and a flyway for the Pittsburgh airport makes conversation difficult.

As the Jennings Trail travels the edge of a bluff, come upon the **Ridge Trail**. Hikers may opt to descend via the Ridge Trail to tour along a wetland pond, passing below the platy cliff. Or, keep to the Jennings Trail for rim overlooks of the pond. Both paths merge prior to reaching Old Oak—now a snag, broken and bare of its bark (0.7 mile). Past the snag, travel floodplain woods via the Jennings Trail.

Beyond a skunk cabbage bog, the Big Maple Trail tags up on the left. Shortly after, stay left as the **Old Wagon Road** heads right. At 1 mile, a spur heads left to the parking area; again keep to the Jennings Trail. Even a slight elevation change can alter the vegetation mix. Muddy sites may now mark travel, but the cliff ledges, hollows, and protrusions engage.

In another 0.25 mile, the **Meadow Trail/Old Wagon Road** returns on the right. As the trail proceeds downstream, Raccoon Creek invites looks right. Big oaks grow at the foot of the cliffs, sycamores along the creek. Only a few roots drape the bare rock.

At 1.5 miles comes the next choice: Here, the **Beaver Trail** travels alongside Raccoon Creek (Note: wet weather can make this trail impassable.) The Jennings Trail keeps to the base of the cliff. At 1.6 miles, the trails again merge. With a farewell look at Raccoon Creek, the Jennings Trail halts at a multiple junction with **Max Henrici, Old Field, and Audubon trails**. Turn left, angling up the slope on the **Audubon Trail** to complete the selected loop.

Top the bluff plateau, traveling removed from the rim. Ahead the ridge narrows. Discover relaxing woods and upland flora. At 1.8 miles a spur descends right. At the cordoned junction at 2 miles, travelers of the Audubon Trail may take either fork. Meet the Max Henrici Trail at the side of the visitor center, completing the tour at 2.1 miles.

For the **Frankfort Mineral Springs Loop** start at the historical marker

Raccoon Creek State Park Wildflower Reserve.

and parking area west off PA 18. The mineral springs contain 15 different minerals, purported to have healing qualities. From the early 1800s through early 1900s, a resort and health spa served summer guests.

Cross the closed road bridge over a tributary of Traverse Creek and in a few feet turn left on a gravel trail. Wild grape flourishes along the tributary, songbirds harmonize in the treetops, and a moist woods flora grows at the foot of the trees. Hike upstream, crisscrossing the tributary waterway via culvert crossings. In places, flood has stolen the trailbed and accompanying rockwork.

At 0.2 mile, a footbridge crosses the creek for a frontal view of an 8- to 10-foot falls, veiling from a broken ledge and cupped in a rocky grotto. Hemlocks fan the sides of the grotto, while deciduous trees dress the rim. Ascend to view the weeping mineral springs, streaking the cliff orange. The natural rocks beneath the springs bear worn catch basins.

Next ascend to a view a restored stone building from the 19th-century health spa. Lilies grow to its side; a big oak wrapped in poison ivy stands sentinel. Buried in the tall uphill grasses lie other clues to the spa. Turn right on the old road for a loop return to the parking area (0.4 mile). Ancient oaks line the way.

For the **Valley Trail**, start at the west end of beach parking or from a marked trailhead on the north side of the park road, 0.2 mile east of PA 18, 0.5 mile west of the campground. For the latter, find parking 0.1 mile west of the trailhead.

For the more tranquil downstream tour, start at the western terminus off the park road and end at the beach. Pass through an egress in the guardrail, descending into woods on a narrow earthen path. Enjoy a full, mixed woods, as the rolling trail contours the slope above Traverse Creek. Sugar maple, birch, beech, ash, elm, cherry, and basswood contribute to the shady realm. Sharp pitches may steal footing.

Cross side waters and muddy sites via footbridges, devised means, or wading. Beautiful, big, mature trees are the hallmark of the tour. Woodland wildflowers, dogwood, and drainage cardinal flower, beebalm, and skunk cabbage lend accent. Collapsed shacks lie below the trail.

At 0.8 miles, a spur descends left to Traverse Creek and a "low road" to the beach. Keep to the Valley Trail, rounding between 60 and 150 feet above the creek, still enjoying the glorious gathering of big trees. Soon the glare of Raccoon Lake replaces Traverse Creek, and sounds of the lake bustle drift to the trail. At 1.2 miles, bear left, descending along the wide trail linking the campground and beach. Cross a footbridge and enter beach parking (1.25 miles).

45 Beechwood Farms Nature Reserve

OVERVIEW

Amid the low, rolling hills at the northern outskirts of Pittsburgh, the Audubon Society of Western Pennsylvania leases a portion of land from the Western Pennsylvania Conservancy. The leased site allows visitors to discover the region's traditional landscape, including abandoned fields, thickets, and forest. Within each microcosm discover the native plants and wildlife that make it special. Five miles of interlocking trail allow visitors to explore the reserve at their own pace. In spring and fall, the valley flyway hosts migrating birds.

General description:	2 loops help introduce the 134-acre reserve and provide access to the site's other trails for outward exploration.
General location:	In Fox Chapel, 8 miles northeast of downtown Pittsburgh.
Special attractions:	Wildlife pond, 40-acre Native Plant Sanctuary, wolf trees (candelabra-branched trees), a small waterfall, bird watching, spring and fall wildflowers and shrubs, educational programs, nature center/nature store.
Length:	Spring Hollow Walk, 0.6-mile loop, with spurs to pond and Treetop; Upper Fields-Meadowview-Pine Hollow Trails Loop, 1.6 miles round trip.
Elevation:	Spring Hollow Walk has a 100-foot elevation change. The rolling Upper Fields-Meadowview-Pine Hollow Trails Loop has a 150-foot elevation change and rings up 550 feet of cumulative elevation.
Difficulty:	Spring Hollow Walk, easy. Upper Fields-Meadowview-Pine Hollow Trails Loop, moderate.
Maps:	Reserve map.
Special concerns:	At this extremely popular site, the parking lot fills summer weekends. No bikes, no dogs, no picnicking. For each trail, the initial junction is well-signed, but the return may go unmarked. Keep to the path to avoid poison ivy. When wet the clay soils on Pine Hollow Trail prove slippery.
Season and hours:	Grounds: daily, dawn to dusk. Center: 9 a.m. to 5 p.m. Tuesday through Saturday; 1 p.m. to 5 p.m. Sunday; closed some holidays.
For information:	Beechwood Farms Nature Reserve.

Finding the trailhead: From Pennsylvania Turnpike Interstate 76, take the Butler Valley Exit (exit 4), and go south on Pennsylvania 8 for 3.1 miles.

There (north of Allison Park), turn left (east) on Harts Run Road (State Route 1010/State Route 1006), the Green Belt. Go another 3.5 miles, and turn right on Dorseyville Road to reach the reserve on the right in 0.2 mile.

Alternatively, from PA 28 take exit 5B, go north on PA 8 for 0.4 mile, and turn right on Kittanning Street in Etna. Proceed another 4.3 miles to find the reserve on the left. Leaving Etna, Kittanning Street becomes Dorseyville Road.

The hikes: For both hikes, round the front of the adjoining farmhouse and barn of Evans Nature Center, passing through a breezeway to reach the back. While in the breezeway, take a moment to admire the richly carved and hand-painted reserve signs. Carvings around the map depict the 4 seasons. Ahead, reach the trail-map kiosk and junction post.

For **Spring Hollow Walk** bear right, traveling a wide maintained path amid a clearing of Canada thistle, milkweed, Queen Anne's lace, and gold-

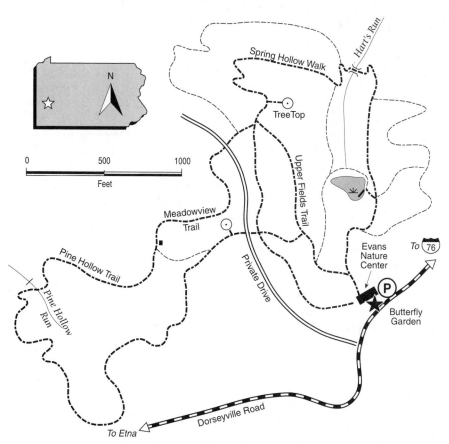

Beechwood Farms Nature Reserve

enrod. Monarch butterflies and hovering hawkmoths frequent the blooms. Ahead a few birch and silver maple edge the field of elbow- to shoulder-high vegetation. Keep to Spring Hollow Walk.

Soon view the cattail outskirts of the reserve's small pond, a nesting post, and backset area of full, rounded deciduous trees. Opposite **Toddler's Trail**, take a spur to the pond boardwalk and bench. Red and silver maple, along with spruce, edge the site; a few lilacs harken to the days of the farm. Hear croaking frogs and vibrating wings of dragonflies. Watch for turtles, fish, kingfisher, herons, and spotted sandpipers. Patches of duckweed, cattails, and a birch-and-willow vegetated island contribute to the acre pond's charm.

Back on Spring Hollow Walk, maples overlace the trail, later joined by oak, black cherry, and tulip poplar. Benches welcome visitors to sit and let the birdlife come to them. The reserve trails welcome slow, reflective travel. At 0.2 mile bear left, easing downhill to the Hart's Run crossing. Plaques identify tree and plant species.

Keep to Spring Hollow Walk, still passing named trails, including the lightly-traveled **Woodland Footpath**, with its stand of 250-year-old oaks and unusual wolf trees that show evidence of lightning strikes. On the walk, wild grape entangles the upper tree branches; grey-stemmed dogwood appears in the midstory. Past the midway point, an elevated boardwalk leads visitors to the octagonal observation platform dubbed "Treetop." From here admire the crowns of the surrounding oak, cherry, maple, and sassafras for a squirrel's eye view of the forest.

Resume counterclockwise travel of Spring Hollow Walk. Ascend back into meadow, proceeding forward at the 4-way junction with the **Meadowview and Upper Fields trails**. Fruit trees provide clues to a farming past. Wildflowers abound. On wide mowed lane, hike below the education center and past the Native Plant Sanctuary to close the loop at 0.6 mile.

For the **Upper Fields–Meadowview–Pine Hollow trails Loop**, head left on the **Upper Fields Trail** from the trailhead mapboard. Ascend through open field of Canada thistle, goldenrod, daisy, and grass. Cardinals may adorn the branches of nearby aspen. Later, shrubs rise amid the field vegetation. Keep left, hiking past the **Goldenrod Trail**. At 0.1 mile, come upon the unmarked loop junction. Proceed straight on the Upper Fields Trail for a counterclockwise tour. Soon after a spur heads right, leading to benches for group talks or wildlife viewing.

Cross **Spring Hollow Walk**, continuing the loop via the **Meadowview Trail**. Quickly pass the **Woodland Trail** and cross a paved, private drive to travel between meadow and meadow-transitioning woods. In some meadows, stringy orange dodder webs the vegetation. Elsewhere, showy orange butterflyweed attracts attention. Fruit trees grow amid the young woods of maple, sassafras, dogwood, ash, and hawthorn.

At 0.4 mile pass an abandoned pumphouse; approach quietly as wildlife may take sanctuary there. Beyond the pumphouse, bid farewell to the Meadowview Trail and hello to **Pine Hollow Trail**. Hikers may shorten the tour by staying on Meadowview Trail.

Wildlife pond boardwalk, Beechwood Farms Nature Reserve.

The Pine Hollow Trail takes a couple of marked bends, passing from woods to goldenrod-and-shrub meadows. Descend and cross Pine Hollow Run to find a seasonal 15-foot waterfall gracing a natural ledge on the right. With the following ascent, pass from leafy woods to red pine plantation (0.8 mile). A chaotic shrub midstory contrasts the order of the pines, while the whir from a windmill congers images of giant insects.

Continue the steady ascent, grading into a woods of mixed conifers and black cherry. The trail then rolls, leaving behind the plantation trees. Cross a bridle path and descend to return to the **Meadowview Trail**. Bear right for an ascent.

Prior to re-tagging the private drive, a vista spur heads left 100 feet. Overlook a meadow slope to spy flattened hilltops beyond the rimming trees, with the Allegheny and Ohio river valleys barely visible in the distance. Return to Meadowview Trail, cross the private drive, and descend to meet the Upper Fields Trail (1.5 miles). Bear right, retracing the initial 0.1 mile to the center.

Laurel Highlands Region

In the southwest corner of the state, hikers will find great diversity. They can trace the region's ridges, walking the superb Laurel Highlands Hiking Trail and the often-rugged Tuscarora Trail. Or stroll an exceptional rail trail paired with the whitewater excitement of the Youghiogheny (pronounced Yock-ah-gain-ee) River. A temperate-forest jungle of old growth and rhododendron at Alan Seeger Natural Area and the history of Friendship Hill also call hikers to explore. Find hideouts for solitude and lively, multiple-use recreation trails. Mountain laurel—the state flower—dresses nearly every site, giving credence to the region's moniker.

Toad, Stone Valley Recreation Area.

46 Stone Valley Recreation Area

OVERVIEW

At this 700-acre recreation area of The Pennsylvania State University, hikers find 25 miles of blazed trail open to the public. Paths explore forest, abandoned fields, thicket, lakeshore, and marsh. Amid the outdoor and rustic cabin setting, the facility also presents a full line-up of fee recreational and educational pursuits. At Shaver's Creek Environmental Center, the mission is "to interpret Penns Woods to all visitors"; live exhibits promote that end.

General description:	4 circuitous tours explore much of the recreation area, touring a variety of habitats.
General location:	10 miles south of State College.
Special attractions:	72-acre Lake Perez, marsh boardwalk, fishing, vista, environmental center, wildlife viewing, fall foliage.
Length:	Lake Trail, 2.5-mile loop (2.7 miles with the Grapevine boardwalk detour); Old Faithful-Mountain View Loop, 2-mile loop; Shaver's Creek-Wood's Route Loop, 3.9-mile loop; Woodcock Trail, 1-mile loop.
Elevation:	Lake Trail, 200-foot elevation change; Old Faithful-Mountain View Loop, 350-foot elevation change; Shaver's Creek-Wood's Route Loop, 250-foot elevation change; Woodcock Trail, less than a 100-foot elevation change.
Difficulty:	Lake and Woodcock trails, both easy; Old Faithful-Mountain View Loop and the Shaver's Creek-Wood's Route Loop, both moderate.
Maps:	Recreation area map; purchase at park office or equipment rental.
Special concerns:	The following are prohibited within the recreation area: pets, alcoholic beverages, swimming, fishing from docks, and overnight camping along trails or in parking areas. Find the trails color-coded, with numbered junctions corresponding to the map. Beware of poison ivy.
Season and hours:	Year-round, spring through fall for hiking. 8 a.m. to sunset.
For information:	Stone Valley Recreation Area.

Finding the trailhead: From U.S. Highway 322 in State College, take exit 1 and go south on Pennsylvania 26 for 11.2 miles. There turn right (west) on State Route 1029/Charter Oak Road, heading toward Mooresville. In another 1.6 miles turn left on the east entrance road for the recreation area, environmental center, and trailheads. Park at Mineral Industries (MI) Day

Stone Valley Recreation Area

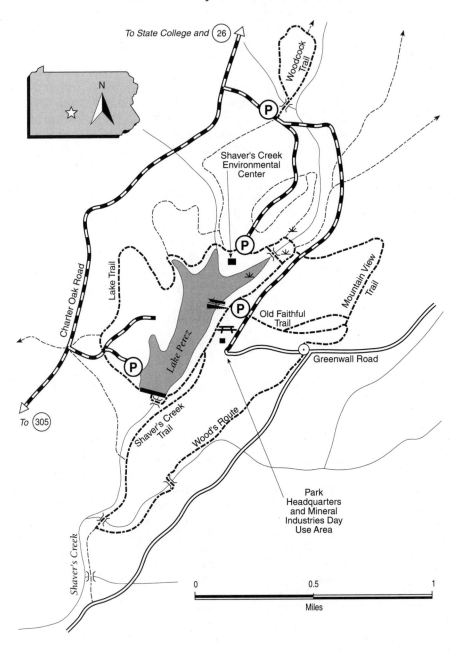

To State College and (26)

Woodcock Trail

N

Shaver's Creek Environmental Center

Charter Oak Road

Lake Trail

Mountain View Trail

Old Faithful Trail

Lake Perez

Greenwall Road

To (305)

Shaver's Creek Trail

Wood's Route

Park Headquarters and Mineral Industries Day Use Area

Shaver's Creek

| 0 | 0.5 | 1 |

Miles

Use Area for all but the Woodcock Trail, which has a separate trailhead near the turnoff to the environmental center.

The hikes: For a clockwise tour of the **Lake Trail** from MI parking, hike southwest along Lake Perez, traversing the lower end of the pine-shaded picnic area; orange blazes point the way. Enjoy glimpses at the attractive manmade lake with Tussey Mountain in the backdrop. Although shrubs build toward shore, anglers still find lake access.

Descend along the spillway, cross the outlet footbridge, and ascend a grassy slope to traverse the dam at 0.5 mile. Bear left upon leaving the dam to follow a grassy jeep track for a contouring hillside tour. Avoid the well-tracked secondary path closer to shore. Pass amid hawthorn, black walnut, hickory, tamarack, and pitch pine, with an entangling array of honeysuckle, wild grape, and poison ivy.

After tagging a high point (0.75 mile), descend to round a gate and cross the paved west entrance road. On the rolling tour, small meadow clearings interrupt the pine-deciduous woods, and shade can be precious. Pass through a utility corridor to share the way with the **Ironstone Trail** (dark-blue blaze). Beyond the next powerline corridor, pass a grouping of large sugar maples.

Return to the lake at 1.6 miles and bear left to round an inlet cove. Here hike past the red-blazed **Bluebird Trail**. Wildflowers sprinkle the forest's meadow floor. Farther along, the woods fullness again steals lake views. Keep to the orange/dark-blue blaze scheme until 2 miles, where the orange (lake) trail bears right only to be joined by a yellow-blazed trail before continuing solo.

Buildings precede arrival at Shaver's Creek Environmental Center (2.1 miles). Detour right to tour the center; a modest admission fee is charged. Find a museum, outdoor garden, live wildlife exhibits, and amenities.

Resume the Lake Trail, now wide, groomed, and accompanied by interpretive panels; ignore the other color-coded trails. Songbirds and woodpeckers divert attention while girdled trees and raised waters hint at beaver.

At 2.4 miles (at the second meeting with the red-blazed **Grapevine Trail**), detour right onto the 300-foot boardwalk to overlook the marshy end of the lake. Alder, dogwood, cattail, sensitive fern, gurgling water, frog, and fish, all contribute to the tale. Beyond the army of cattails lies the open lakewater. Resume the clockwise tour, and where the Lake Trail forks, take either path to end at MI parking (2.7 miles).

For **Old Faithful–Mountain View Loop**, look for junction post 18 opposite the entry to the MI Day Use Area and follow the indigo (lavender-appearing in the field) blaze of the **Old Faithful Trail** into a deep woods of hemlock, white pine, and oak. A spring on the left hosts Mayapple, skunk cabbage, and fern; some trees reach 2 feet in diameter. Ahead, take either blazed-fork to ascend to **Mountain View Trail** (0.5 mile).

Upon meeting the rose-blazed Mountain View Trail, turn left for the loop. To the right the rose blazes lead to Tussey Mountain View at Greenwall Road (about an 0.8-mile, round-trip detour). On the loop, pass an electric fence that keeps deer out of a regenerating select cut. The ridge ascent features younger woods, snags, and only partial shade. Later when oak, hickory, maple, and shad fill out the forest, glimpse the shadowy profile of the outlying ridges.

Eventually, a steep descent returns hikers to the hemlock-darkened lower slope. Cross the east entrance road at 1.5 miles, coming to the light blue blaze of the **Sawmill Trail**. Turn left, quickly meeting the orange-blazed **Lake Trail**, and again bear left to return to MI parking (2 miles). Conclude the tour amid floodplain woods.

For the **Shaver's Creek–Wood's Route Loop**, follow the orange blazes of the **Lake Trail** southwest through the picnic area to find the aqua-blazed **Shaver's Creek Trail**. Bluebird, duck, and goose animate shore while sailboats and rowboats weave across Lake Perez. At junction 24 veer left, angling past the picnic pavilion, to enter the woods. Travel a scenic woods road, where tulip poplar and cucumber magnolia shower their blooms in late spring and early summer.

From 30 feet above the lakeshore, gain just a hint of blue beyond the trees. Along Shaver's Creek outlet, the woods road grades lower; still track the aqua-blazes. Shaver's Creek flows sleepy and wide. The trail then traverses a wild meadow dotted with walnut trees to resume along the shady floodplain distanced from the creek.

At 1.5 miles cross a footbridge over a side tributary to meet junction 11. Go left on **Wood's Route** for the selected loop. By bearing right, a roadway return presents itself at junction 12. On the seldom-tracked footpath of Wood's Route, follow the tributary upstream. At 1.8 miles, a steep outcrop slope looms over the voiceless stream. Cross a footbridge and contour the hillside.

Where a younger deciduous woods claims travel, bear right crossing a tiny headwater. Hemlocks wane from the forest, and a couple more footbridges advance travel. Next parallel the roadway return of Shaver's Creek Trail, traveling an aisle through a red pine plantation.

At 3 miles, angle right across Greenwall Road to a vista bench on the rose-blazed **Mountain View Trail**. Across the valley, Tussey Mountain draws a striking wooded line across the sky. Differing hues of green hint at past forestry practices.

For the trailhead return follow rose blazes, contouring and descending to junction 15/17 (3.4 miles). From there, descend on the hemlock-shaded **Old Faithful Trail** (indigo blaze) to reach the park road and MI Day Use at 3.9 miles.

For the **Woodcock Trail**, hike east from the marked trailhead on the east entrance road. Blue and orange blazes initially mark the way; where they separate, keep to the orange blazes. Generally, find brochures at the start and/or interpretive plaques at each of the nine stations.

This site features abandoned farmland, critical for the woodcock to breed and nest. Elsewhere, development and encroaching woods have deprived the bird of such habitat. Along Shaver's Creek, explore meadow, wetland, shrub thickets, and young woods, with arrows guiding hikers through the shrub-meadow sites. Much of the tour is shadeless and the vegetation can create a sauna effect. Deer, turkey, squirrel, and even a bear may be spied.

47 Alan Seeger Natural Area to Greenwood Lookout Tower Hike

General description:	This hike combines the 0.6-mile Alan Seeger Trail, touring both spectacular old-growth forest and a rhododendron jungle, and the 2-mile Johnson Trail segment of the Greenwood Spur that ascends to Greenwood Lookout Tower atop Broad Mountain for a 360-degree central state panorama.
General location:	8 miles southeast of State College.
Special attractions:	Some of the oldest trees in Pennsylvania, natural arbors and tunnels of rhododendron (peak bloom early July), mountain laurel, accessible lookout tower, sweeping views, wildlife sightings, rustic picnic area.
Length:	5.2 miles round trip.
Elevation:	Pass from 1,000 feet in elevation at Alan Seeger Natural Area to 2,400 feet at Greenwood Lookout Tower.
Difficulty:	Moderate.
Maps:	Rothrock State Forest; the Mid State Trail Association's Mid State Trail System Map (map 203.1).
Special concerns:	No overnight camping. Blue blazes mark the Greenwood Spur and Johnson Trail.
Season and hours:	Spring through fall for hiking, sunrise to sunset.
For information:	Rothrock State Forest.

Finding the trailhead: From U.S. Highway 322 Eastbound at Laurel Creek Reservoir, turn west on Stone Creek Road and continue 7.3 miles for Alan Seeger Natural Area. Find the road paved. To access Stone Creek Road from U.S. 322 Westbound, travelers must make a U-turn at the next crossover point, some 2 miles west of Laurel Creek Reservoir.

Alternatively, from Pennsylvania 26 at McAlveys Fort, take Stone Creek Road/State Route 1023 east for 6.4 miles, traveling paved road.

The hike: Find the marked start for the **Alan Seeger Trail** south off Stone Creek Road near its intersection with dirt Seeger Road. To the left of the mapboard, a footpath enters the exciting, dark old-growth realm. Pass amid massive hemlock and white pine, with some hemlocks exceeding 500 years in age. The broad wooded flat invites carefree strolling, allowing eyes to roam and trace the trunks skyward. Plaques identify the interweaving tree species.

Alan Seeger Natural Area to
Greenwood Lookout Tower Hike

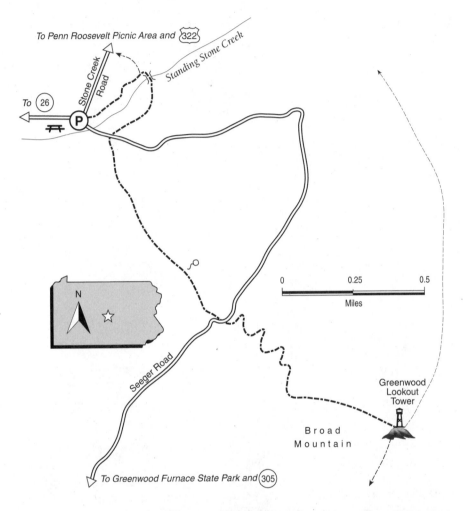

To Penn Roosevelt Picnic Area and (322)

Standing Stone Creek

To (26)

Stone Creek Road

P

Seeger Road

N

0   0.25   0.5
Miles

Greenwood
Lookout
Tower

Broad
Mountain

To Greenwood Furnace State Park and (305)

As the tour transitions into younger forest, arrive at the signed junction for the **Mid State Trail, Greenwood Spur**. To the left it offers northbound exploration. For the chosen tour, proceed forward on the Alan Seeger Trail and southbound leg of the Greenwood Spur. Virgin forest again enfolds travel, giving way to a chaos of rhododendron at a small drainage. Here admire the radial leaves, 10- to 20-foot heights, and seasonal pompom blooms of the rhododendron bushes.

Next cross a trio of footbridges over the braided water of Standing Stone Creek. Small trout dart through the clear water. Rhododendron still engage.

Cross Seeger Road at 0.6 mile and take the marked **Johnson Trail of the Greenwood Spur** to continue to the lookout. For the Alan Seeger Trail

Greenwood Lookout Tower, Rothrock State Forest.

alone, bear right on the road, returning to the trailhead (0.75 mile), or retrace your steps for an encore tour of the natural area.

En route to the lookout, proceed through tall forest of hemlock, pine, and oak, twice crossing a gurgling spring-fed stream. Squirrel and woodpecker enliven the treetops. Bigger trees in the forest impose a natural circle around themselves, perfect for paying homage. By 1 mile pursue a ravine upstream.

At the fork at 1.2 miles, the left spur leads to a spring in about 100 feet; the main trail bears right. Striped maples become a familiar sight as snags open the cathedral. Here the climb intensifies, with rocky sites. At 1.5 miles cross upper Seeger Road.

Switchbacks follow, passing amid rhododendron, laurel, mature birch, and leaning hemlock. Broad Mountain wildlife encounters may include deer, fox, and black rat snake. At the fourth switchback, spy a white birch with eight major trunks. Rocks displace beneath the boot.

As switchbacks end at 2.1 miles, laurel and blueberry bushes go on parade amid the semi-open, oak-hickory woods. On arrival at Greenwood Lookout Tower (2.6 miles), the blue-blazed trail heading south is the **Telephone Trail** to Greenwood Furnace State Park. The destination tower rises 9 flights; the crow's nest is closed to the public.

Scale the tower at your own risk, heeding posted numbers. From the upper landings, attain a full 360-degree view, overlooking the signature long, arc ridges of Pennsylvania; rural flats sprawl east. Fall brings a kaleidoscope of blazing color. Return as you came, retracing the Alan Seeger Trail for a grand old-growth finale (5.2 miles). Or turn left at 4.6 miles, hiking out Seeger Road to end at 4.75 miles.

For an altogether different and longer return, seek out the **Ross Trail**. It descends from the northeast corner of Greenwood Lookout Tower. Where it emerges at Stone Creek Road, turn left and hike the road back to the trailhead.

48 The Lower Trail

General description:	This relaxing, multiple-use, rail-to-trail hugs a river and passes through wooded canyon and rural countryside. Along it discover remnants of the Pennsylvania Canal (1830s to 1850s) and Petersburg Branch of the Pennsylvania Railroad (1879 to 1979).
General location:	Along the Frankstown Branch Juniata River between Alexandria and Williamsburg.
Special attractions:	Rail, canal, and quarry ruins; varied woods; periodic river access; fishing; wildflowers; bird and wildlife watching; fall foliage.
Length:	11 miles one-way.
Elevation:	Pass from 700 feet in elevation at Alexandria to 900 feet at Williamsburg.
Difficulty:	Easy to moderate, depending on length of hike.
Maps:	Rails to Trails, The Lower Trail brochure (generally available at trailhead).
Special concerns:	On spring and fall weekends, parking lots commonly fill. No overnight camping, and beware of poison ivy when venturing off trail. Between 4.75 miles and 5.1 miles, travel private property; pass respectfully, keeping to the trail. Mileposts count off distance. Find chemical toilets at the northern and southern terminus; bring water for the hike.
Season and hours:	Year-round, spring through fall for hiking. Daylight hours only.
For information:	Rails-to-Trails of Blair County, Inc.

Finding the trailhead: To reach the northern terminus (Alfarata Trailhead), from U.S. Highway 22 east of the village of Water Street at the west end of the Frankstown Branch Juniata River bridge, turn north on State Route 4014, and go 0.3 mile to find a large gravel parking area on the right. Find the southern terminus off Pennsylvania 866 at the corner of Liberty and First in Williamsburg.

The hike: For a north-south, upstream tour of this family-oriented trail, begin at the Alfarata Trailhead. Hike the 8-foot-wide crushed limestone path, gaining early overlooks of the sleepy Frankstown Branch Juniata River. The overlacing trees show great variety with silver maple, elm, black walnut, ash, box elder, and sycamore. Virginia creeper and poison ivy scale the trunks.

Pass under the U.S. 22 river bridge, where a mural decorates the concrete support and pigeons roost overhead. A large talus slope now marks the opposite wooded rim. While this early pairing with U.S. 22 intrudes, the river wins out.

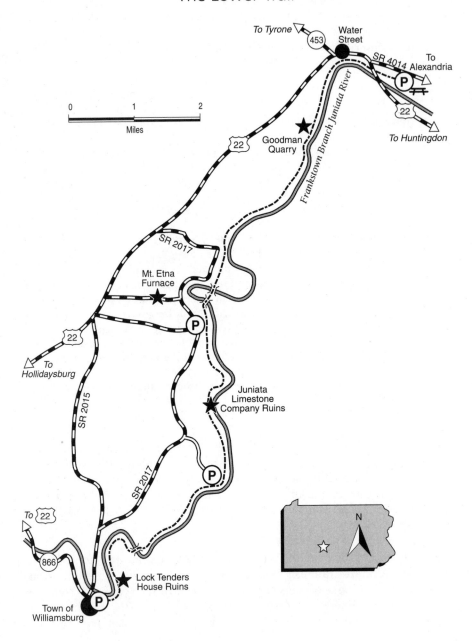

The Lower Trail

To Tyrone

453

Water Street

SR 4014

To Alexandria

22

To Huntingdon

Frankstown Branch Juniata River

0   1   2

Miles

22

Goodman Quarry

SR 2017

Mt. Etna Furnace

P

22

To Hollidaysburg

SR 2015

Juniata Limestone Company Ruins

P

SR 2017

To 22

866

Lock Tenders House Ruins

P

Town of Williamsburg

N

Bike riding, The Lower Trail.

Heron, swallow, goose, cardinal, bluebird, and woodpecker grow the roster of bird sightings. A local Audubon chapter made an official count for the corridor, identifying some 250 bird species. Benches dot the route, while joe-pyeweed, lily, yarrow, daisy, black-eyed Susan, and honeysuckle lend splashes of color to the bordering grasses. Steep angler paths descend to shore, but at 0.7 mile an easier path presents itself. A treed slope then builds to the right, vanishing U.S. 22.

Along the corridor, modest signs identify the historic sites. View channels, foundations, walls, white obelisks, and whistle-stop posts. At 1 mile the river narrows, showing greater energy. Small vegetated islands interrupt its flow. Tulip poplar, basswood, and cucumber magnolia add their signature leaves. With bicyclists but fleeting companions, hikers find ample blocks of solitude for reflection and wildlife watching.

At 2.5 miles, spy the parallel 20-foot-high concrete walls recalling the Goodman Quarry. At 3.5 miles, a cornfield isolates the trail from the river as a rolling field and barn contribute to looks right. Later, a shrubby floodplain steals the river view. Approaching a bench at 4 miles, admire a long straightaway of the scenic rail trail. At Fox Run, the lichen-etched stones of the arched bridge invite a look over the railing.

At 4.75 miles and 4.9 miles, cross back-to-back trestle bridges over a tight bend in the river. The first allows both up and downstream viewing; the second only a downstream view. Travel posted private land, coming to a small covered bridge, which overlooks a small waterway where turtles commonly sun. Beyond the covered bridge lies a midway access off gravel SR 2017, with tables, benches, and parking.

The harmony of wind, river, bird, and insect dominate. At a pair of benches past the 7-mile post, look for a footpath heading left into the floodplain. It leads to the nearly hidden 2-story concrete shell of the Juniata Limestone

Company. Be alert as you approach; sometimes fortunate hikers spy an agile black rat snake probing the concrete nooks for prey. At 7.7 miles, pass the trailhead parking at Cove Dale. Large sycamores captivate travelers.

Gain rock ledges to the right of the trail. Reeds grow riverside. A scenic old stonehouse and outbuildings lie beyond the fence (9.3 miles). Again cross the river, passing between crops or fields and river floodplain. The trail itself becomes more exposed. Discover the foundation of an old lock house and pause at a couple more river overlooks, before ending the hike at Williamsburg (11 miles).

49 Terrace Mountain Trail

General description:	This linear trail traverses the flank of Terrace Mountain, exploring the eastern slope and shore of Raystown Lake. Pass through Rothrock State Forest, Trough Creek State Park, and lands owned by the U.S. Army Corps of Engineers. The southern third of the trail lends itself to easy strolling, touring a closed management road for much of the way; on the northern two-thirds, find a prescribed, well-blazed route, but one often of cross-country rigor.
General location:	About 20 miles southeast of Altoona.
Special attractions:	Challenge and solitude, mixed forest, occasional lakeshore access and vistas, wildlife sightings, an ice mine, flowering shrubs, fall foliage, swimming at Tatman Run Recreation Area, fishing.
Length:	18.6 miles one-way, with logical break points at Trough Creek State Park and Tatman Run Recreation Area.
Elevation:	Travel between 800 and 1,700 feet in elevation.
Difficulty:	Strenuous.
Maps:	Rothrock State Forest; U.S. Army Corps of Engineers Raystown Lake map/brochure; Trough Creek State Park brochure.
Special concerns:	Backpackers may camp at the designated campground in Trough Creek State Park or at Paradise Point/Peninsula Camp, a boat-in/hike-in campground on the southern leg of the tour. For the latter, first prepay at Lake Raystown Resort (on the east shore, off Pennsylvania 994). Putts Camp (along the southern leg) is a Boy Scouts-only camp. Find the trail blue-blazed, with mileage markers and Terrace Mountain Trail (TMT) signings. Expect patches of poison ivy.
Season and hours:	Spring through fall for hiking.
For information:	Raystown Lake, U.S. Army Corps of Engineers.

Finding the trailhead: From the junction of U.S. Highway 22 and PA 26 in Huntingdon, go south on PA 26 for 14.1 miles, and turn left (east) on PA 994, crossing Raystown Lake. Go 4.5 miles to reach Tatman Run Recreation Area. Go 0.5 mile more and turn left on State Route 3031 for Trough Creek State Park and the northern terminus. Reach the park in 1.7 miles. Continue northeast through the park via gravel Paradise Road, reaching the northern trailhead at the junction of Paradise, Fink, and John Bum roads, 4.7 miles past Trough Creek Lodge. Locate parking north of gated Fink Road (the trail).

For the southern trailhead, stay PA 26 south all the way to PA 913; there turn east for Saxton. From the center of Saxton, continue east on PA 913 for 0.7 mile. There turn left on SR 3003 for Weaver Falls and Raystown Lake and stay on it. Locate the trail, a gated service road on the right in 1.5 miles, just before the bridge. A few cars can park without blocking the gate. Find additional parking and amenities at Weaver Falls Access Area across the bridge in another mile.

The hike: For a north-south tour of the TMT (counting down the mileposts), round the gate on dirt Fink Road to descend west for Raystown Lake. Initially no blazes mark the route. Maple, oak, birch, and locust frame the road while laurel, jewelweed, and fern crowd the shoulders. At a 2nd gate (0.3 mile), the blazes begin; keep to the road for a moderate descent. At a double-blaze and mile marker 17 (1.25 miles), turn left (south) off old Fink Road. Be alert as older blazes can blend with the shadows.

Basswood, tulip poplar, and ash join the maple along the lower slope. Spy squirrel, deer, turkey, songbirds, and perhaps even a wood turtle. A secondary jeep trail continues the contouring descent to 1.75 miles, where a TMT emblem and arrow point hikers left. The old jeep trail itself curves right reaching shore and a small bay in 0.4 mile, suggesting an early lake detour. Ignoring the temptation, proceed south.

At 1.9 miles bear right and then left following TMT markers to cross a rocky run via footbridges. Next angle left up the slope, negotiating a log-strewn oak rise, before finding the next faint jeep trail advancing the rolling TMT. The woods alternately show dominant oak or varied hardwoods. Only the bright westward lighting hints at the lake.

Find a rustic log bench at 2.6 miles. In another 0.5 mile, the jeep trail bends lakeward, descending parallel to a drainage. At the bottom of the grade, cross the drainage. Although the trail fails to reach the lake, it puts hikers within striking distance.

At a T-junction (3.6 miles), turn left following an overgrown grade atop a low bluff for the 1st open view of long, sculpted Raystown Lake. Across the lake, a wooded peninsula grades to Allegrippis Ridge and a backdrop of folded ridges. In exchange for such views, endure hip-brushing grasses, sunny travel, and the occasional stumble on unseen broken shale. The bluff grades from 50 feet to a mere 5 feet above the lake, but poison ivy invades near lake level.

Terrace Mountain Trail

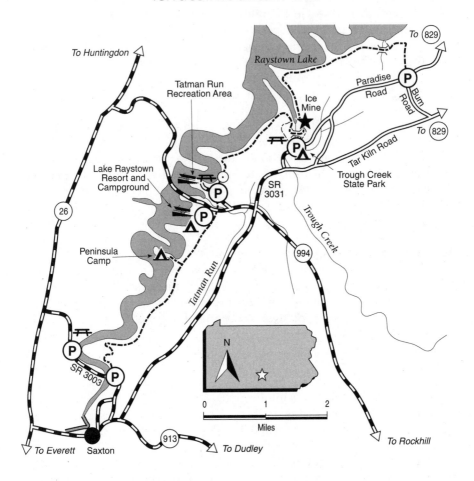

By 4.5 miles the trail turns away from the lake, passing amid some glorious big trees. Encounter thin drainages and rock piles from old, before passing through an egress in a stone wall. Ascend along the wall, bearing right per blazes and arrows. Black cherries rank among the bigger trees.

At the end of a more defined stone wall, resume contouring and descending south. The TMT now descends left off a side ridge, passes mile marker 13 (5.3 miles), and crosses into Trough Creek State Park. Round the rocky forest slope, coming to a steep bank descent (5.6 miles).

The TMT now travels an abandoned, tree-shaded, paved lane just above elongated Trough Creek Cove; a steep slope plummets to the water. Emerge at the developed park, rounding a gate and proceeding forward past the roof-covered ice mine (6.3 miles). From the railed sides, peer down at the folded rock of the mine, spying an adit from which cold air rushes. Stairs descend for a closer look.

Hike past the **Ice Mine Trail** and bear right on the closed gravel road, descending to cross Trough Creek on a footbridge above the dam.

From the bridge, ascend steeply to the gravel road of the TMT and bear right. Shrubs along the lower slope distance hikers from the shade-throwing trees. Overlook the spillway at 6.5 miles. Continue forward on the TMT as the orange-blazed **Brumbaugh Trail** heads left. Round a barricade and proceed on a contouring footpath. Here erosion suggests a potential reroute.

Resume traveling an overgrown lane above the lake. Then at 7.5 miles, ascend left to contour along the upper slope, only to descend along a steep drainage slope, returning within 100 feet of shore. Past an old shack (8.3 miles), find a steep climb, complicated sometimes by downfalls and slippery canted rocks covered by leaves.

Dip back toward the lake (9.6 miles), before again rolling uphill and descending along a steep, narrow side ridge (10.3 miles). A detour onto a point presents an overlook of the lake, its ridges, red shores, and Tatman Run Recreation Area. Descend, rounding south to the recreation area, again encountering a poison ivy stronghold.

At 11.1 miles, the TMT actually angles left into woods before coming out on the recreation area road, but sometimes unruly vegetation makes the trail difficult to find. Instead, follow the pipeline corridor, rounding to the swimming area and restrooms; find a water pump near the boat launch. When ready, hike up the road to the marked trailhead (11.5 miles) and resume the southbound tour to Weaver Bridge.

Wood Turtle, Terrace Mountain Trail.

Pass through full deep woods, crossing scenic tree-draped Tatman Run via footbridge. At 12 miles, cross PA 994, hike a few strides south on a grassy jeep trail, and cut left for the forest of oak, maple, beech, tulip poplar, and dogwood. Sound of the occasional boat reminds hikers they are still along the lake. Again snatches of old grade advance travel.

Continue the TMT count down, passing milepost 6. At 13.3 miles cross a trimmed grass road, and at 13.4 miles bear left on the single-lane dirt management road; to the right lies Lake Raystown Resort. The TMT now offers lake glimpses, but no access. Chestnut oak, locust, and hickory join the maple along the roadway. Poison ivy and Virginia creeper sometimes hide the blazes, but just stay on the road.

At 14.1 miles, a detour right leads to Paradise Point/ Peninsula Camp in 0.2 mile. There find a tree-shaded, grassy peninsula curving into the lake, bold lake views, and basic amenities. Resume the TMT south at 14.5 miles, for a rolling ascent. The woods show greater variety.

A dripping spring lies opposite milepost 4 (14.7 miles). Snags open the cathedral where the trail tops out and a slow descent follows. At 15.8 miles bypass Putts Scout Camp. By 16.5 miles, travel at lake level with waters lapping at the road bank.

The TMT again rolls, contouring some 100 feet from shore. With a moderate climb find more beech and rhododendron along the service road. Upon return to lake level, a heron or family of wood ducks may suggest a pause. Round the gate at 18.6 miles, exiting at the Weaver Bridge Trailhead on SR 3003.

50 Laurel Highlands Hiking Trail

General description:	Spanning 5 counties, this premier long-distance trail rolls across Laurel Ridge. It ranks as one of the best in the state and in the nation for its natural offering, its accessibility, and its amenities. The Laurel Highlands Hiking Trail (LHHT) has won national recreation trail distinction and is part of the Potomac Heritage Trail.
General location:	Along Laurel Mountain between the Youghiogheny River at Ohiopyle and Conemaugh Gorge near Johnstown.
Special attractions:	Mixed woodland, picturesque sandstone and limestone outcroppings, vistas, plant fossils, Adirondack-style overnight shelters, mountain laurel and rhododendron, meadow wildflowers, sparkling runs, wildlife, fall foliage.
Length:	70.1 miles one-way.
Elevation:	Travel between a low of 1,300 feet at both end points and a high of 2,950 feet at Seven Springs.
Difficulty:	Easy to strenuous depending on length and section of hike.
Maps:	Recreational Guide for Laurel Ridge State Park and the Laurel Highlands Hiking Trail brochure; the Sierra Club, Pennsylvania Chapter and Western Pennsylvania Conservancy's *A Hiker's Guide to the Laurel Highlands* (available for purchase from the Pennsylvania Chapter of the Sierra Club, P.O. Box 8241, Pittsburgh, PA 15217).
Special concerns:	Camping and fires are restricted to designated areas; an overnight camping reservation and fee are required. Contact Laurel Ridge State Park by phone or mail, 30 days in advance, with the date and location of entry; the leader's name, address, and phone number; and number in the party. Find a shelter/tent area every 8 to 10 miles along the trail. Yellow blazes mark the LHHT; blue, the side trails. Mileage monuments aid in charting progress and finding trail features. Poisonous snakes dwell here but are rarely seen. Park personnel recommend hikers avoid the LHHT during the 2.5 weeks of rifle deer hunting season. No bikes, no horses.
Season and hours:	Year-round, spring through fall for hiking.
For information:	Laurel Ridge State Park.

Finding the trailhead: 6 30-car parking areas (most with water) serve LHHT hikers, allowing for piecemeal travel. At major highway crossings, large wooden signs identify the LHHT.

Laurel Highlands Hiking Trail

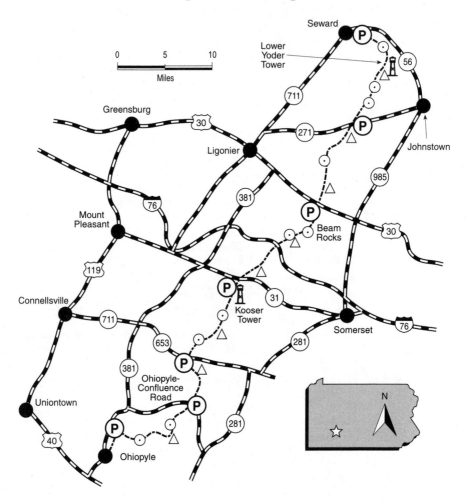

For the southern terminus, go 0.25 mile north from the Pennsylvania 381 bridge in Ohiopyle and turn east at a sign for Laurel Highlands Trail Parking. Go 0.7 mile on paved and gravel King Road to reach parking on the right.

Along the south shore of the Conemaugh River, find the northern terminus off PA 56, 7 miles north of Johnstown, 1.5 miles south of the borough of Seward. Signs indicate the turn.

The hike: For a south-to-north tour, from the designated parking lot north of Ohiopyle, follow the blue-blazed access spur to join the LHHT near milepost 1 and turn left. To the right the LHHT enters Ohiopyle at Garrett Street. Past the 1-mile mark, look for the trail to enter a rugged climb. Find the path regularly blazed and well-groomed.

Mixed hardwoods cloak the hillside, dotted by pockets of laurel. With a 750-foot elevation gain, acquire a Youghiogheny River overlook, with the bend at Victoria Flats and Sugarloaf Knob. The knob becomes a familiar face.

As the trail rolls northeast along the ridge, find more carefree strolling, with additional views when the trees drop their leaves. Rock Spring and Lick runs sound off distance. Besides woods, discover an old orchard and wildflower meadow. At 6.3 miles, locate the spur to the 1st shelter/tent area, south of the LHHT.

From the shelter junction, enter the most demanding climb of the tour, returning to the ridgetop (elevation 2,600 feet). At 8.5 miles a series of rocks extend vantages, broadening the view. Gentle rolls, outcrops, and rivulet-sized streams characterize travel. At 10.3 miles, Little Glade Run engages with its deep hemlock shade, mountain laurel, weeping overhangs, and small waterfall.

At 11.2 miles cross the Ohiopyle-Confluence Road at Maple Summit, with nearby parking for State Game Lands 111 (no water). Ahead enjoy a gentle, relaxing stroll amid a varied woods of oak, maple, hickory, cucumber magnolia, sassafras, and birch. The understory alternately shows meadow and woods flora. A series of clean-flowing streams recommend the leg.

A wind-disturbed area precedes the trail's arrival at a small lake (13.4 miles). Traverse the dam and follow the east shore, before crossing a dirt road. Larger trees now frame travel. Cross Harbaugh Run (15 miles), ascend past outcrops, and twice cross a closed logging road, before finding the next set of streams, each about a mile apart. While the rolling LHHT lacks great elevation changes, it can still present some brief steep pitches and rises.

Preceding the 18.5-mile spur to the next shelter community, travel full forest with patchy laurel, hobblebush, ferns, azalea, and sites of bramble. Weathered outcrop jumbles and ledges accent and prescribe travel. Distanced from the main traffic flow, the attractive trail shelters are the "Hiltons" of the outdoors and well worth the fee.

At PA 653 (18.8 miles), a short detour east on the road leads to the Laurel Ridge State Park office. Across the highway, find an old cemetery, pass more rock outcrops, and edge an open field with a microwave transmitter. At 21.3 miles overlook the Middle Fork Laurel Run watershed. Continue north along the ridge and then descend to cross log bridges over the four feeder streams to Fall Creek and later Grays Run.

Atop the ridge at 24.2 miles, a 0.3-mile spur leads to the Grindle Ridge Shelters. On the LHHT, a switchback descent reaches the cool drainage of Blue Hole Creek; the following ascent brings a valley overlook. Tag the highest point on the tour, traveling the bumpy ridge through private Seven Springs Resort; pass respectfully. West of the LHHT at 26.6 miles, an observation tower built by the resort presents a 360-degree panorama. The trail then crosses ski slopes before rolling to cross a paved road.

At a wildlife pond, skirt the east shore and at the saddle at 28.7 miles gain views both west and south. Ahead, travel a State Forest beltway through

Laurel Highlands Hiking Trail, Laurel Ridge State Park.

Roaring Run Natural Area. Encounter clearings with brushing vegetation and cross little-used gravel forest roads. Where the LHHT approaches Kooser Lookout, travel amid planted spruce and pine; lush ferns color the plantation floor. At 30.8 miles, reach the spur to PA 31 parking.

Pass from scrubby area to young woods, crossing PA 31 at the sign for Laurel Summit (elevation 2,728 feet). Soon after, cross quiet Old Route 31. Nearby stands the 1923 Somerset-Westmoreland County Line Monument. Continue north finding one of several nice areas of beech. At 32.5 miles reach the next shelter spur and begin climbing in spurts.

Roll through more stream valleys, before reaching the fenced bridge over Pennsylvania Turnpike Interstate 76. Upon crossing, look for the LHHT to take a switchback, dropping below a snowmobile trail. Bald Knob adds to views.

Before crossing dirt Hickory Flat Road (37.6 miles), pass amid a gorgeous stand of tall ferns and snag-riddled forest. Insects claimed these trees. At milepost 38 snare a rare view for this leg, and soon after pass the spur to the next set of shelters. A casual, fairly level woods stroll leads to Rector Edie Road.

From the base of Beam Rocks (41 miles), view the exciting collection of cliffs, crevices, ledges, and isolated boulders. Tracked side paths ascend the adjacent hillside to top the rocks, but rhododendron and laurel may obscure the way. Atop the jumble, gain dizzying looks over the edge, admire the woods below, and scan the terrain straining east. Beam Rocks often bustles with visitors as a short access trail leads to it from Laurel Summit Road.

Just shy of 43 miles find a trio of stream crossings at Spruce Run; be alert at the first of these as an unmarked side trail can mislead. Rocky passages characterize the next saddle. Cross US 30 (45.8 miles).

The trail rolls over small hills, meeting jeep trails and small streams. At 47.6 miles, cross the historic **Forbes Trail** (today a jeep trail). In 1758, during the French and Indian War, a colonial military procession of 6,000 men trod this path. The ensuing campaign helped decide control of the Ohio River forks.

South Branch Card Machine Run and Mystery Hill next mark off distance. When the trees lack leaves, find sporadic views. Enjoy another laurel-colored stretch and more rock passages before reaching the 0.7-mile spur to both PA 271 parking and the shelter/tent camping area.

At 56.8 miles cross PA 271 and hike north, rubbing elbows with cinnamon fern. Side trails break away west, entering State Game Lands 42 or Rachelwood Game Preserve (a research station). Scrubby areas continue to mile 60.

A rare roadway stretch advances the LHHT between miles 61 and 62. The trail then continues passing between woods and clearings. At 64.9 miles, a blue trail heads east to the Decker Avenue (northernmost) shelters. At just under 66 miles, spy radio towers to the east and visit Lower Yoder Fire Tower for a panoramic look at the Johnstown Area.

On the final 4-mile descent, overlooks of the Conemaugh River Gorge put a fine cap on the tour. Travel from Lower Yoder Lookout (elevation 2,600 feet) to the trailhead (1,300 feet). Powerlines can both open and intrude on views. At 68.4 miles, pass a quarry said to have provided stone for the rail bridge in Johnstown. In the 1889 flood, this bridge held. Tour amid full canopy forest to end at Seward Parking (70.1 miles).

51 John P. Saylor Trail, Middle Ridge Loop

General description:	This sampling of the John P. Saylor Trail System in Gallitzin State Forest explores the heart of Clear Shade Wild Area.
General location:	12 miles southeast of Johnstown.
Special attractions:	Hardwoods and hemlock, wetlands and meadow, picturesque springs, wildflowers, wildlife, solitude.
Length:	7 miles round trip.
Elevation:	Find about a 300-foot elevation change, with the low along Clear Shade Creek (2,300 feet) and the high point part way along the Middle Ridge Loop (2,570 feet).
Difficulty:	Easy to moderate.
Maps:	John P. Saylor and Lost Turkey Trails Map; Gallitzin State Forest.
Special concerns:	Secure an overnight camping permit, limit stays to 2 consecutive nights, and keep party size small. Locate camps at least 200 yards away from Clear Shade Creek; 100 yards from any other stream. In places, raised waters can make for sloshing travel. Seasonally, insects can be troublesome; take precautions for ticks. Orange blazes guide hikers on the John P. Saylor Trail. Mileposts on the 6-mile loop help hikers track progress.
Season and hours:	Spring through fall for hiking.
For information:	Gallitzin State Forest.

Finding the trailhead: From the junction of Pennsylvania 56 and Pennsylvania 160 in Windber, go east on PA 56 for 5.7 miles, turning south on gravel Shade Road (0.3 mile east of the State Forest Headquarters). Go another 1.6 miles, finding a trailhead turnout on the left for the Fisherman's Path, with parking for 5 vehicles and additional parking along the road shoulder.

The hike: Start on the yellow-blazed **Fisherman's Path**, descending a rock-studded foot trail to the orange-blazed **John P. Saylor Trail**. Pass amid a black cherry and beech woods, with an understory of ferns. An old mossy

214

Clear Shade Creek hiker bridge, Gallitzin State Forest.

John P. Saylor Trail, Middle Ridge Loop

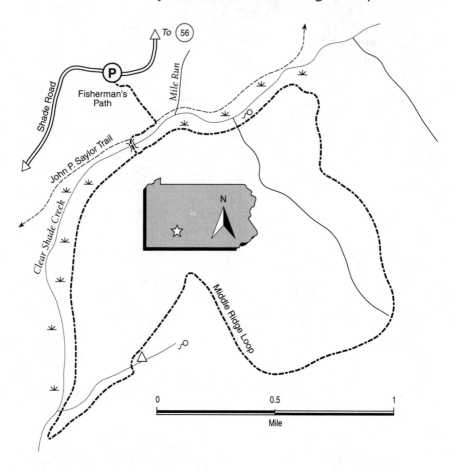

stump with a burl records the forest of old.

At 0.3 mile, turn right on the John P. Saylor Trail; here it also shows blue cross-country ski blazings. Just shy of 0.5 mile, arrive at the sign for **Middle Ridge Loop**, and turn left to cross Clear Shade Creek via a suspension bridge. Given the natural bounce of the bridge, have no more than two people on it at any one time. Hemlocks fan the clear-flowing stream. In 100 feet, reach the loop junction. Blazes head both straight ahead and along the grade to the right; proceed forward for a clockwise tour.

In a couple of strides, bear left on a second raised grade framed by black cherry, birch, maple, and witch hazel. Four varieties of club moss weave a forest miniature at boot level. Wetland depressions support sphagnum moss. The brushing grasses and ferns of the grade are in keeping with the wild area. Bird songs and the muffled voice of the creek blend for a soothing backdrop.

Cross a side tributary and near milepost 1 on the loop (1.5 miles into the hike), find a beautiful freshwater spring bubbling up. It immediately launches a 15-foot-wide stream coursing over a mossy bed with grassy banks and islands of aquatic plants. Beyond the spring, travel an eye-pleasing forest consisting of a wispy meadow floor, dark-trunked cherry, and thorny hawthorn.

Self-heal, buttercup, daisy, milkweed, and thistle dot color to the tour while butterflies and damsel-flies add winged signatures. The meadows variously show grasses, ferns, and a wetland flora with berry bushes. After a few soggy strides, look for the trail to swing right and ascend the slope of Middle Ridge. Black cherry dominates; a woodland flora at times replaces the ferns.

Top the ridge and enjoy a meandering stroll amid gentle terrain. Where leaf mat overtakes the trail, be alert for blazes. The trail cuts back on itself prior to reaching the 3-mile post (3.5 miles). Here, thin-trunked striped maples jail the few big trees and dark logs overlace the forest floor. The crashing passage of a black bear may emphasize the wilderness.

As the trail slowly descends, find the woods more mixed, with islands of hemlock amid the deciduous. Again soggy sites cause one to ponder strategies for keeping dry. Beyond milepost 4, travel a long fern-and-grass meadow, skirting an open-faced shelter with earthen floor and picnic table. Pockets of blueberry seasonally slow travel; some cattail and rhododendron lend interest and texture. Scan the meadow's length for a blaze on a distant tree and maintain the line of travel.

The trail then turns left for a log-crossing of a spring-fed side water flowing to Clear Shade Creek. Follow it downstream and bear right, to meet a grassy grade (5.2 miles). Turn right on the grade to cross back over the side stream.

Ahead stretches a straight-arrow, flat floodplain return, just removed from Clear Shade Creek. Pass mainly in the open, touring meadow and dispersed woods of aspen, hawthorn, and black cherry. The rippled trailbed betrays it was once a railroad. Breaches present wet footing.

Close the loop at 6.5 miles and backtrack, re-crossing the suspension bridge and turning right to pick up the Fisherman's Path. Return to the trailhead at 7 miles.

52 Grove Run–Fish Run Hike

General description:	This lopsided, barbell-shaped tour joins Grove Run Trail and Fish Run Trail, exploring the southern hills of Linn Run watershed. Travel lands of Linn Run State Park and Forbes State Forest.
General location:	20 miles southwest of Johnstown, 40 miles southeast of Pittsburgh.
Special attractions:	Mature forest, meadows, sparkling cascades, woodland wildflowers, wildlife, fall foliage.
Length:	8 miles round trip.
Elevation:	Travel between 1,800 feet at the picnic area trailhead and 2,620 feet at the ridge summit.
Difficulty:	Moderate.
Maps:	Grove Run and Fish Run trails map; Forbes State Forest.
Special concerns:	Within the state park there is no backpack camping and for all state forest lands, permits are slated to become regulation; contact the state forest headquarters to secure a free permit and ask where to park for overnight travel. Greenbrier grows in strongholds, and rattlesnakes dwell in this area but encounters are rare. Blue blazes and markers indicate the trail, but in places they are faint and few, requiring detective work. No bikes.
Season and hours:	Spring through fall for hiking. Linn Run State Park, 8 a.m. to sunset.
For information:	Forbes State Forest; Linn Run/Laurel Mountain Complex.

Finding the trailhead: From Ligonier, go 2 miles east on U.S. Highway 30 and turn south on Pennsylvania 381. Go 4 miles reaching the tiny town of Rector. There turn left on Linn Run Road for Linn Run State Park. Reach the entrance to Grove Run Picnic Area (the trailhead) on the right in 2.9 miles.

The hike: Start from the picnic area turnaround at the sign for **Grove Run Trail**. Ascend steadily pursuing intermittent Grove Run upstream, touring amid tulip poplar, maple, big beech, basswood, and birch. Witch hazel and striped maple fill out the midstory while large snags open the cathedral. The rich multistory forest erases all memory that these slopes were denuded of trees in 1909.

In places find trailside vegetation brushing and thorny. At 0.9 mile, cross a canted footbridge over Grove Run and admire a 2-foot cascade upstream. Avoid a secondary path that continues upstream. The primary trail hooks left past the bridge, before ascending and contouring away from Grove Run. Soon discover a seasonal cascade and 5-foot veiled falls along a feeder

Grove Run–Fish Run Hike

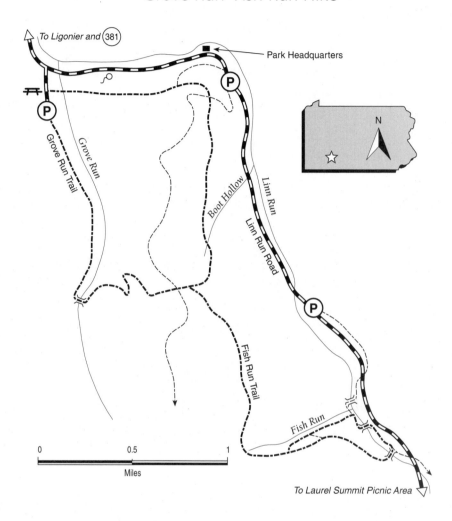

To Ligonier and 381

Park Headquarters

Grove Run Trail

Grove Run

Boot Hollow

Linn Run

Linn Run Road

Fish Run Trail

Fish Run

N

| 0 | 0.5 | 1 |

Miles

To Laurel Summit Picnic Area

hollow to Grove Run. Pursue the hollow upstream, before crossing it via stones. Attractive big trees complement travel. Much of the hiking season, some species of woods flora lends bloom.

The upper slope now holds older oaks, with young maple and birch and often unrestrained greenbrier. A hummocky moss adorns the path as it switchbacks. At 1.5 miles, sign in at the trail book.

Salvage logging (for removing insect-infested trees) intrudes on and muddles the trail. Still ascend, bearing right at 1.6 miles. The trail could use a few more blazes, but keep your line of travel to cross Quarry Trail (a dirt service road) at 1.7 miles.

Return to the natural woods of the summit, and at 1.8 miles, reach a signed trail fork. For a 4-mile loop tour of Grove Run Trail alone, bear left. To explore **Fish Run Trail**, turn right, later returning to this point to complete Grove Run Trail.

This stretch of the Fish Run Trail requires detective work; watch for trail markings both ahead and behind you and look for hints to the path. Clues may include fragments of wooden markers bare of color and even the tacks that held them in place. Travel a spatially open woods of mature oak, maple, and black cherry, wading through knee- to waist-high ferns. To the right lies an area of woods marked for a timber sale, so future tours could show changes in lighting and forest appearance.

By 2.5 miles travel a more open meadow, dotted by trees or snags, keeping right. In another 0.2 mile, descend to cross a headwater fork of Fish Run. Meet and descend an old grade (2.9 miles), likely associated with a logging/passenger rail line that once traversed the area.

At 3 miles, reach a blazed loop junction for the Fish Run Trail; keep to the grade for a counterclockwise tour. Once again, lower-elevation hardwoods shade travel. For the most part, better blazes guide hikers. Descend past a cut-across (3.2 miles) to cross a bridge over Linn Run at 3.6 miles.

The trail again forks: To the right, Fish Run Trail crosses Linn Run Road. For the chosen loop, go left (downstream), crossing a second bridge. A high-canopy forest overlaces rocky Linn Run. Keep an eye out at 3.8 miles for the blaze on the left signaling the loop's footpath return (Reach this turn about 150 feet before the third bridge.) The serial bridges recall the switchbacking route of the former railroad.

Travel a scenic, rock-studded footpath, passing amid unspoiled beech trees and overlooking a couple of Fish Run cascades, before coming to a T-junction with a lower cut-across grade. Turn right to close the Fish Run loop at the 3-mile junction, at 4.3 miles. A birch snag signs off the loop.

Retrace the obscure 1.2-mile upper ridge segment to return to the 1.8-mile junction with the Grove Run Trail (5.5 miles). There bear right to close the second loop on this barbell-shaped tour.

Descend following a headwater fork of Boot Hollow to begin a rugged, contouring return. The canted trailbed tests ankles, with descents coming in modest measure. Mature forest engages travelers. Woodpecker, turkey, and deer may offer distraction.

Snags disappear from the forest mosaic prior to the second crossing of Quarry Trail (6.8 miles). Continue contouring. At the marked junction at 7 miles, bear left for Grove Run Picnic Area. To the right lies Linn Run Road. Still the trail rolls and rounds the slope, before descending to cross Grove Run via rocks. With an ascent of the drainage slope, emerge at the picnic area between the restroom and turnaround. End at 8 miles.

53 Ryerson Station State Park

OVERVIEW

At this 1,164-acre park in southwest Pennsylvania near the West Virginia border, the centerpiece to recreation is manmade R.J. Duke Lake. In addition to fishing and boating, some 10 miles of trail explore the park's hillsides and floodplain. The park takes its name from a 1792 outpost—Fort Ryerson, which was constructed at the order of Virginia authorities to provide refuge during Indian raids.

General description:	3 loop tours present an overview of the park and its trail offering.
General location:	25 miles west of Waynesburg.
Special attractions:	Mixed southern hardwoods, a 300-year-old wolf tree, old cemetery, vistas, floodplain meadow, lake and creek access.
Length:	Pine Box Trail, 2-mile loop; Three Mitten Trail, 1.5-mile loop; Lazear Trail, 2.4-mile loop.
Elevation:	Pine Box and Three Mitten trails, each have a 300-foot elevation change. Lazear Trail has a 400-foot elevation change.
Difficulty:	All, easy to moderate.
Maps:	State park brochure.
Special concerns:	There is no trail camping; camp only in the park's designated campground. Poison ivy abounds. Find the trailheads and junctions marked, but no trail blazes.
Season and hours:	Spring through fall for hiking.
For information:	Ryerson Station State Park.

Finding the trailhead: From Graysville (about 15 miles northwest of Waynesburg on Pennsylvania 21), go west on PA 21 for 5.1 miles and turn left (southeast) on Bistoria Road/State Route 3022. Reach the park in another 0.8 mile: To the right lies the south shore day use and start for the Lazear Trail; straight on SR 3022 leads to the park office, campground, and starts for the Pine Box and Three Mitten trails.

The hikes: For **Pine Box Trail**, start from the parking area at Iron Bridge, opposite the intersection of SR 3022 and McNay Ridge Road (the campground road). Hike south across Iron Bridge, overlooking the North Fork of the Dunkard Fork of Wheeling Creek. Sycamore, locust, and willow shade the banks, with a thick meadow floodplain spanning to the southern hills. Upon crossing, turn left (upstream); to the right lies the **Iron Bridge Trail**.

Travel is shadeless along a broad mowed path. Amid the bordering tall-meadow vegetation, spy lily, fleabane, butter-and-eggs, goldenrod, nettles,

Ryerson Station State Park

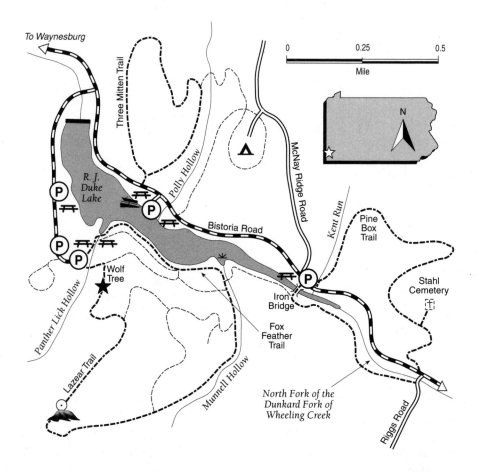

and Queen Anne's lace. Jewelweed grows closer to the water. Near the bridge, the creek flows as a broad cloudy band; upstream it becomes riffling, losing the reservoir's influence. Kingfisher, scarlet tanager, and crow divert eyes.

Where the mowed track forks (0.3 mile), stay right to angle up the wooded slope and overlook the narrowed floodplain to the creek. Via boardwalk, skirt a weeping rock; maple and box elder shade travel. Back on the meadow path, view rustic outbuildings of a neighboring farm and hike past a twin-trunked sycamore, before ascending to cross Riggs Road Bridge and then SR 3022.

Now hiking toward Stahl Cemetery, find a steady, moderate switchbacking ascent on an old wagon road shaded by big oaks. Amid a stand of spruce (1 mile), look for the Pine Box Trail to turn left. However, a 0.2-mile, round-trip detour straight ahead leads to Stahl Cemetery—an attractive multi-family hillside cemetery. Within the rustic rail fence, find stones that date to the mid 1800s amid the natural woods.

Resume the Pine Box loop as it contours downhill on a tree-shaded old road, crossing the head and later the foot of a steep ravine draining to Kent Run. Glimpse Kent Run and return to SR 3022. Cross the road and bear right to close the loop at trail parking, 2 miles.

Find the marked **Three Mitten Trail** across from Walnut Grove Picnic Area, 0.1 mile west of the park office. Park either in the day use area or at the office. Hike north up a barricaded woods road, drawing away from the reservoir.

In 100 yards, reach the loop junction and proceed forward for a clockwise tour. The vegetation reclaiming the old road is cropped low for easy walking. Elm, oak, and hickory contribute to the woods; honeysuckle and bramble to the shoulder mesh. With a moderate ascent, the trail wraps around the slope for early overlooks of the reservoir. Sizable oaks cause eyes to linger. Basswood, ash, maple, spruce, and walnut extend the roster.

The intrusive rumbling comes from nearby Holbrook Compressor Station. By 0.5 mile lose the drone from this station and descend. Tall straight trunks prove visually appealing. Bear right with the grade at 0.8 mile; to the left is **Polly Hollow Trail**, which travels past the campground. As the Three Mitten Trail maintains a fairly even contour along the lower slope, younger trees introduce a midstory. Close the loop at 1.4 miles, and bear left to end at 1.5 miles.

On the east side of the south shore's day-use parking area, above the boat rental and pavilion 3, a sign indicates the path for the **Lazear and Fox**

Stahl Cemetery, Ryerson Station State Park.

Feather trails. Head right from the mapboard, ascending amid the maple-tulip poplar woods of the lower slope. At 0.1 mile reach a 4-way junction. An unmarked service road heads left, the Fox Feather Trail takes the center fork, and the **Lazear Trail** heads right.

On the Lazear Trail, tour a spruce-mixed hardwoods forest, hiking past a large oak with spreading branches. Then at 0.3 mile, discover the acclaimed "wolf tree." This 300-year-old oak grew up in a clearing, which accounts for its low-level candelabra branching. The celebrated oak shows a 5- to 6-foot diameter and totally dominates its setting.

Continue the ascent via switchbacking road. Poison ivy scales many of the tree trunks. At a T-junction stay right; to the left lies the **Orchard Trail**. At a clearing at 0.6 mile, take a moment to admire nature's artwork. Here, wild grape literally cloaks the trees, shaping rounded, curious topiary-like forms. The roadway maintains a pleasant gradient.

At 0.8 mile, reach the high point (elevation 1,389 feet) and an overlook. View the lake some 400 feet below, the rounded crowns of the framing deciduous trees, the opposite wooded ridge, and distant folded ridges. Now descend to an unmarked junction at 1 mile. Go left for the loop, still on a cropped-grass woods road. To the right the road dead-ends.

Hike past a huge out-of-place sycamore. Uphill, the forest engages with ancient shade trees and twisted, woody grapevines. At 1.3 and 1.7 miles keep descending right to avoid the **Tiffany Ridge Trail**. Below lies Munnell Hollow.

At 1.75 miles tag Fox Feather Trail where it loops and proceed forward on a joint segment of trail. In 200 feet, bypass the **Iron Bridge Trail** as it heads right. Now above R.J. Duke Lake, view a cattail marsh at the mouth of Munnell Hollow. A heron standing far into the cloudy water may reveal how shallow this part of the reservoir is.

At the next junction, bear right for the unmarked lakeside route and a change of setting. On this easy walk, view the open water as well as fish, heron, kingfisher, and turtle. At the day use, follow a service road left to return to the parking area (2.4 miles).

54 Youghiogheny (The Yough) River Rail Trail

General description:	This mostly natural 27-mile rail trail hugs the exciting Youghiogheny River, between Confluence and Connellsville, passing through Ohiopyle. Another 43 miles extend the exploration north, and still it grows. Ultimately the rail-to-trail system will span 315 miles, linking Pittsburgh and Washington, D.C.
General location:	Between Confluence and Connellsville.
Special attractions:	Open and filtered Youghiogheny River overlooks, tributary waterfalls, picturesque cliffs, rhododendron, fall foliage, fishing, Ohiopyle Falls.
Length:	25.5 miles one-way between Connellsville and Ramcat Put-in.
Elevation:	Find a 500-foot elevation change.
Difficulty:	Easy to strenuous depending on length and allotted time.
Maps:	Forbes State Forest; Ohiopyle State Park brochure.
Special concerns:	Find bicycle rentals and amenities at Connellsville, Ohiopyle, and Confluence. Cyclists must yield to pedestrians and stay off all side trails. Mileposts numbered north from Confluence help travelers track progress; trail posts with initials identify river rapids. No swimming.
Season and hours:	Year-round, spring through fall for hiking. Daylight hours.
For information:	Ohiopyle State Park; The Yough River Trail Council.

Finding the trailhead: In Connellsville, locate trailhead parking and amenities at Yough River City Park (at the intersection of First and Third streets). In Ohiopyle, access the trail from Ferncliff Peninsula parking (at the north end of the Pennsylvania 381 bridge) or at Middle Yough Take-out, east of the visitor center at the north end of Ohiopyle. From Confluence, the trail heads north off PA 281, following the west bank downstream.

The hike: This rail trail pairs up with a premier whitewater for Pennsylvania and the eastern United States. Compressed cinders surface the 8-foot-wide trail, which travels between 20 and 100 feet above "the Yough." The river variously presents smooth straightaways, scenic bends, and churned pools with giant boulders. Much of the way, a leafy mosaic overlaces the trail. Openings allow for glimpses of the river's 1,700-foot-deep gorge.

On an upstream (north-to-south) tour, leave Yough River City Park in Connellsville, following the sidewalk or bike lane south along residential Third Street. The actual rail trail starts at a kiosk and mapbox, 0.5 mile. When touring the trail in this direction, use the numbered mileposts to

225

Youghiogheny (The Yough) River Rail Trail

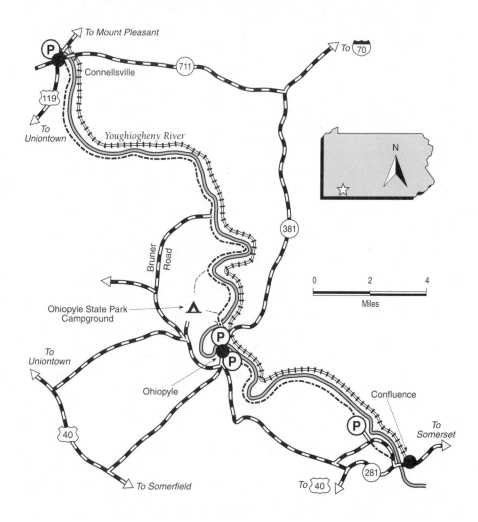

count down the distance to Confluence. The well-groomed trail invites carefree strolling, with long stretches of solitary travel away from the central bustle of Ohiopyle.

Initially the overhead cathedral is open, with trees and shrubs screening out views of the industrial river. Upon crossing a pair of railroad bridges, enter an outstanding, uninterrupted natural tour to Ohiopyle. Fractured, mossy cliffs engage, joined by a leafy umbrella of oak, maple, tulip poplar, sycamore, hickory, ash, box elder, and elm. Benches invite pause and spur trails branch to the river—a broad even band along this lower stretch.

Some 2.5 miles into the tour (between mileposts 25 and 24), discover a seasonally pretty 15-foot falls, its bold ledge, and rhododendron banks. At 5

Youghiogheny River, Ohiopyle State Park.

miles (milepost 22), pass a river-overlook bench. A wooded flat then spans between river and trail. An active railroad travels the opposite shore.

Slowly the trail grades higher. At 7.5 miles pass a private Baptist camp, keeping to the trail. Honeysuckle, trillium, chicory, coneflower, and Queen Anne's lace introduce sprinkles of color while tulip poplars dominate the pioneering young trees.

For the next 3 miles (between mileposts 19 and 16), open, sunny stretches mark travel, with the trail now 100 feet above the river. Prior to a landslide, a bench seat presents a fine river snapshot of an S-bend upstream. Post-rain tours find side-stream cascades in full glory. At 11 miles (milepost 16), cross lightly traveled Bruner Road which leads to a river take-out. Showy rhododendron next frames travel.

Ahead discover "river rapid country," where the Yough drops 200 feet over the next 7.5 miles. A louder river voice often paired with squeals of river-runners accompanies travel. Lettered posts signal a succession of rapids rumbling below the trail; pass Stairstep Rapid at 12 miles (milepost 15).

South of milepost 14 examine the cliff bedding for a coal seam, and shortly after, reach a trail post for the pink-blazed **Kentuck Trail**, which follows Sugar Run upstream. A 0.2-mile round-trip detour visits a 15-foot cascade on Sugar Run. The rail trail proceeds upstream, quickly coming to a signed junction for the **Jonathan and Kentuck trails**. Here a similar-length uphill detour finds a serial falls on Jonathan Run.

Pursuing the Yough upstream, pass the Bottle of Wine and the Dimple and Swimmer rapids. A section of blasted-rock follows. South of milepost 11, three trails journey right to explore Ohiopyle State Park. Then at 16.4 miles, High Bridge presents a grand river perspective, with up and down-stream views. Spectators commonly gather to watch the kayaks and rafts.

Hike through Ferncliff Peninsula Parking, and at the Borough of Ohiopyle cross the PA 381 bridge. There turn left (east) and hike past the visitor center to Middle Yough Take-out (17 miles/milepost 10) to continue the rail trail.

Or, hike south into town for food, drink, or a visit to Ohiopyle Falls, where the river drops 90 feet over a 1-mile distance. In 1754, this wild churn forced George Washington to abandon his plans for using the Yough to move troops and supplies in the capture of Fort Duquesne (Pittsburgh).

Closer to the river, the rail trail now bustles with the rent-a-bicycle crowd from Ohiopyle. Mowed shoulders open the corridor; better shade follows in another mile. A forested flat sometimes distances the trail from the river, but side paths branch to shore. Midway between mileposts 8 and 7, view another tributary cascade and gain an open river view. As the tree border to the river narrows, hikers are lured aside to watch rafters.

At 21 miles (milepost 6) find easy river access. Later, islands and bars of sycamore and silver maple punctuate the Youghiogheny River. At 24.8 miles (approaching milepost 2), a river spur leads to a large boulder slab for admiring the waterway. The river shows agitation here; this stretch of the Yough has both class I and II whitewater.

At 25.5 miles arrive at the Ramcat Put-in, with parking and pit toilets. To avoid road travel, end or turn back here. The bike trail proceeds out the parking access road, crosses a paved road, and passes fields and houses to again cross a road at 26.5 miles. At trail's end (27 miles), a sign points travelers left along a rural road to Confluence. Cross the bridge to enter town, 28 miles.

55 Ohiopyle State Park

OVERVIEW

Just north of the tri-state border of Pennsylvania, West Virginia, and Maryland, this 19,046-acre Pennsylvania state park cradles a 14-mile stretch of the impressive Youghiogheny River as it cuts through Laurel Highlands. The spectacular setting boasts both whitewater excitement and a variety of hikes. Besides serving as a gateway to the Laurel Highlands Hiking Trail and host to a fair stretch of the Youghiogheny River Rail Trail, this park offers foot trails that explore a unique natural area, visit river and tributary water-falls, and top rocky promontories to survey the 1,700-foot-deep gorge.

General description:	4 foot trails introduce the park from river to ridge.
General location:	At the borough of Ohiopyle.
Special attractions:	Youghiogheny River; Ferncliff Peninsula, a National Natural Landmark; Ohiopyle Falls; tree fossils; old-growth forest; rhododendron, laurel, and azalea blooms; scenic cliffs; fall foliage.
Length:	Ferncliff Trail, 2-mile loop; Great Gorge Trail, 4 miles round trip (or 2-mile shuttle); Baughman Trail, 5.5 miles round trip; Meadow Run Trail, 2-mile loop.
Elevation:	Ferncliff Trail, 100-foot elevation change; Great Gorge Trail, 200-foot elevation change; Baughman Trail, 1,000-foot elevation change; Meadow Run Trail, 200-foot elevation change.
Difficulty:	Ferncliff Trail, easy to moderate; Great Gorge Trail, easy; Meadow Run Trail, easy to moderate; Baughman Trail, moderate.
Maps:	State park brochure.
Special concerns:	There is no trail camping. Beware of poison ivy and exercise caution along the river rock. Parking can be chaotic during summer. Color-coded blazes guide hikers.
Season and hours:	Year-round, spring through fall for hiking. 8 a.m. to sunset.
For information:	Ohiopyle State Park.

Finding the trailhead: From the junction of U.S. Highways 119 and 40 in Uniontown, go east on U.S. 40 for 10.4 miles. At Chalk Hill, turn left (north) on State Route 2010/Chalk Hill Road for Ohiopyle State Park. Arrive at a multiple junction in 6.3 miles. Straight leads to the park's Kentuck Camp-ground in 1.5 miles; to the left, Holland Hill Road leads to the Old Mitchell Place; and to the right, Chalk Hill Road leads to Pennsylvania 381, Ohiopyle, and the trailheads. Enter Ohiopyle in 1.5 miles.

Ohiopyle State Park

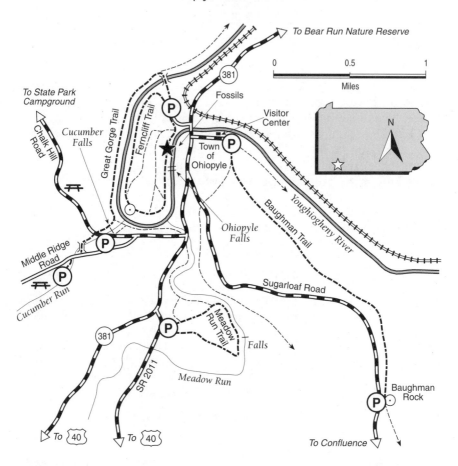

The hikes: Start both the **Ferncliff Trail** and the **Great Gorge Trail** from Ferncliff Peninsula Parking: In north Ohiopyle, turn west at the north end of the PA 381 bridge.

For **Ferncliff Trail**, take either the closed fire lane that leaves the entrance road or a footpath from the parking area and hike south to a kiosk. From there pass under the abandoned railroad bridge to find a plaque for the National Natural Landmark, which signals the loop.

Proceed forward along the river, passing amid tulip poplar, oak, and locust; side paths break away to the roiling river. At 0.2 mile reach a fossil site. Discover both scaly and stringy tree fossils; an interpretive sign helps with the identification. Look for more examples as you stroll the river bedrock.

The Ferncliff Trail travels the perimeter of Ferncliff Peninsula housed in a tight horseshoe bend of "the Yough." Black blazes indicate the way over the rock. At 0.4 mile, top a rocky jut that extends into the fury of Ohiopyle Falls for an unmatched front-row seat. Feel the energy, mist, and danger. Opposite the base of the falls, ascend right to enter woods. Here rhododendrons bombard the senses.

Along the peninsula rim, spurs lead to river views; stay well back from the edge. Signed interior trails branch to the right. Old-growth hemlock, white pine, tulip, hickory, oak, and maple generate a soothing backdrop. Where the trail descends at 1.25 miles, spy precarious rock overhangs and boxy boulders. The trail later rolls to tour a transitioning meadow-woods. Close the loop at the monument (1.9 miles), and turn left to end at 2 miles.

For the **Great Gorge Trail** follow the "bike trail" signs north from Ferncliff Peninsula Parking for the **Youghiogheny River Rail Trail** (See hike 54). Cross the railroad bridge for an exceptional overlook of the Yough, and then at 0.25 mile, turn left at the sign "to Great Gorge Trail." Meet the actual trail in another 200 feet and turn left (upstream). The trail contours the slope some 100 feet above the roaring river, but the thick woodland of the slope denies views.

A natural arbor enfolds the 5-foot-wide trail, with rhododendron growing toward the river. Unofficial trails branch in both directions. At 1.2 miles, **Meadow Run Trail** arrives on the left; a hike along it requires wading or rock hopping across Cucumber Run. Keep to the Great Gorge Trail.

At 1.4 miles, approach Chalk Hill Road. To add a view of Cucumber Falls, detour left across the old road bridge and descend the stairs for a fine look at this broad, 50- to 70-foot veil. Rhododendrons claim one wall of its rocky bowl.

At 1.5 miles, resume the Great Gorge Trail and pursue Cucumber Run upstream. After crossing Chalk Hill Road, admire the clear water of Cucumber Run as it sheets over bedrock, spills in cascades, and cuts small chasms.

With a footbridge crossing of the run, meet Middle Ridge Road, cross the road bridge, and continue upstream to Cucumber Run Picnic Area (2 miles). Along the final journey, stay toward the center of the mowed path to avoid poison ivy and thorny bramble. Return as you came.

For the **Baughman Trail** start at Middle Yough Take-out: South of the PA 381 bridge, turn east on Sheridan Street and drive past the visitor center to take-out parking. A sign marks the **Baughman and Sugarloaf trails**.

Head right at the sign and then bear left at the split to contour the slope above the rail trail. Red blazes soon point out a hard right uphill on a rocky footpath. At 0.2 mile, bear left following a woods road for a more moderate ascent. A full forest enfolds travel as sound of the river echoes uphill.

At 0.7 mile, a 100-foot spur to the left leads to a cliff jut and seasonal view. A second woods road now continues the ascent, and boulders add to the forest. The trail advances in pulses, with many of the blazes faded beyond recognition. On the ridge (1.9 miles) ascend along the same track, ignoring side roads that branch away. Where more sunlight penetrates, bramble and briar win footing. Grouse may flush from hiding.

Meadow Run Trail, Ohiopyle State Park.

Sounds from Sugarloaf Road signal the trail is closing in on Baughman Rock. At 2.75 miles, arrive between the rock and vista parking. Turn left to mount the natural rock incline for an open overlook of the bending Yough, its wooded canyon, The Flats, and Laurel Highlands. Oaks and maples frame the site; rhododendron seasonally add to views. When ready, backtrack to the trailhead.

To reach the **Meadow Run Trail**, 0.5 mile south of Ohiopyle on PA 381, bear southeast on SR 2011 for the park office. In 0.1 mile find trail parking on the left. Behind a park information sign at the foot of the grassy parking lot slope, follow the yellow-blazed trail that enters the woods to the right. Travel a mixed maple-oak woods, with an understory of blueberry, laurel, rhododendron, and azalea—a pretty, early summer showcase. Cross a tall-meadow clearing, finding tulip poplar and cucumber magnolia. In places, unruly grape shapes a bizarre menagerie of leafy shapes.

The trail contours and descends to follow a former road grade at 0.5 mile. Leave the grade, finding more laurel and rhododendron beneath a gray cliff with ominous overhangs. At 0.8 mile, the first of several short spurs branch to cascade overlooks. Pursue Meadow Run downstream.

The waterway can present a variety of impressions, depending on rainfall. Its hemlock corridor engages. The trail rolls, coming to the spur for Flat Rock—an aptly named feature at 1.5 miles, and the loop's return at 1.6 miles. The return follows the wide grade left uphill. Detour downstream a few strides to view Deep Hole.

The return trail draws out of the hemlock cool, passing amid beautiful big tulip, cucumber, and black cherry trees. Remnant rock walls add to the setting. Emerge at the unmarked path directly behind the park information sign (2 miles). The trail to the right leads to "the slides" for additional discovery.

56 Cowans Gap State Park

OVERVIEW

In the shadow of Tuscarora Mountain, this 1,085-acre state park offers lake, creek, and woodland recreation. Within the park's 10-mile trail system, find paths that challenge and relax. View the park from ridgetop and valley floor.

General description:	3 hikes present the park offering.
General location:	55 miles southwest of Harrisburg.
Special attractions:	Vistas, lake access for fishing and swimming, picturesque Little Aughwick Creek, flowering shrubs, fall foliage.
Length:	Knobsville Road Trail, 2 miles round trip; Lakeside Trail, 1.5-mile loop; Plessinger–Tuscarora Loop, 4-mile loop.
Elevation:	Knobsville Road Trail, 700-foot elevation change; Lakeside Trail, flat; Plessinger–Tuscarora Loop, 800-foot elevation change.
Difficulty:	Knobsville Road Trail, moderate; Lakeside Trail, easy; Plessinger–Tuscarora Loop, strenuous.
Maps:	State park brochure; Buchanan State Forest.
Special concerns:	No trailside camping within the park. Expect difficult, rocky travel on the Plessinger–Tuscarora Loop; on all trails, beware of poison ivy.
Season and hours:	State park: year-round, spring through fall for hiking.
For information:	Cowans Gap State Park.

Finding the trailhead: From the junction of U.S. Highways 522 and 30 (1 mile north of McConnellsburg), go east on U.S. 30 for 3.4 miles. At Tuscarora Summit, turn left on State Route 1005/Aughwick Road and go another 5.9 miles to find the park office on the left.

From Fort Loudon, go 4 miles north on Pennsylvania 75 and turn left on Richmond Road. Go 3 miles more and turn left on Aughwick Road to reach the park office in 0.2 mile.

The hikes: Start all of these hikes from parking lot 5: Reach it via the park road to camping area B, which passes west behind the park office. Lot 5 is the first parking area.

For **Knobsville Road Trail**, park at lot 5 and hike west on the park road, crossing the bridge over Little Aughwick Creek. Where the park road curves right for camping area B, proceed forward on gravel Knobsville Road past the group camping area to round a gate. Oak, maple, birch, gum, pine, and dogwood frame the closed fire lane; greenery hugs its sides. With a steady, even ascent, bypass grassy logging roads and twice cross a landslide that opens a tunnel view to Tuscarora Mountain.

Laurel and berry bushes add to the mix after 0.6 mile. Filtered views through the tree crowns build anticipation for the overlook. At 1 mile reach the vista platform for an open-aisle view. Spy Cowans Gap Lake, Tuscarora Mountain, the low-swinging U of Cowans Gap, and the farmlands and Kittatinny Mountain beyond. Return as you came.

Ideal for that morning exercise walk or for putting a cap on the day, the easy **Lakeside Trail** has multiple starting points. Locate a signed start west of parking lot 5, 150 feet prior to the Little Aughwick Creek bridge. Follow the yellow-blazed trail along the east shore of the narrow inlet cove, traveling counterclockwise through the spruce-shaded developed park, with its tables, rustic stone shelters, Brightville Interpretive Center, boat rental, and concession. The trail passes within 20 feet of shore and extends cross-lake

Cowans Gap State Park

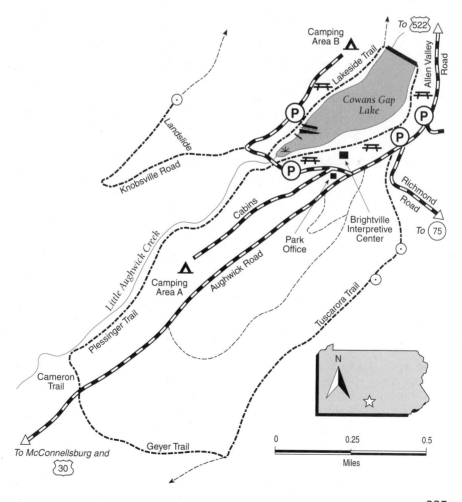

views at a wooded ridge. Manmade Cowans Gap Lake is an attractive, dark, shimmery host.

Hardwoods replace the spruce as the trail draws away from the developed park, now joined by the blue-blazed (formerly orange) **Tuscarora Trail**. At 0.75 mile, traverse the dam and spillway bridge. Admire the intricate stonework of the spillway, pierced by grasses and washed by a shallow stream. Upon crossing, stay left for the Lakeside Trail to round below camping area B. Tulip poplar, pine, and spruce shade travel.

Ample clues betray the presence of beaver: girdled and tumbled trees, pencil-point stumps, and a lodge (1.2 miles). Now cross-lake views present Tuscarora Mountain. Round past a boat launch and handicapped fishing platform, before crossing the road bridge over Little Aughwick Creek to close the loop at 1.5 miles.

Tied together by the **Cameron, Geyer, and Lakeside trails,** the **Plessinger–Tuscarora Loop** offers a superb, but often rugged hike, exploring much of the eastern half of the park. It tours the shores of Little Aughwick Creek and tops the ridge of Tuscarora Mountain.

Locate the signed and red-blazed **Plessinger Trail** as it heads upstream from the Little Aughwick Creek bridge west of parking area 5. Bending Little Aughwick Creek is a pretty, tree-draped, shallow water flowing over a rocky bed. The trail for the most part hugs its shore. Fern, azalea, and laurel color the understory; a mature leafy forest shades travel. Puddles may collect, and rocks and roots rise in the trailbed.

By 0.4 mile, the trail passes between camping area A and the creek. Watch closely now for blazes as the meandering path makes quick, subtle direction changes. Weirs and islands alter the creek's flow. Find hemlock, some large black gum, and knee- to waist-high laurel. At 1.1 mile reach a T-junction amid an attractive fern flat: To the right lies the now-closed Twin Springs Trail; go left on the unmarked **Cameron Trail** to continue the loop.

This grassy, woods road climbs steadily to Aughwick Road (1.3 miles), tracing the boundary between the state park and Buchanan State Forest. Across Aughwick Road, **Geyer Trail** advances the loop. Follow the white boundary blazes, avoiding an early turn to the right.

The trail streaks up the flank of Tuscarora Mountain, passing amid an oak-dominant mixed forest. As the old road tapers to foot trail, find rockier footing. After the trail has leveled out, meet the blue-blazed **Tuscarora Trail** and follow its footpath left (north); a woods road hosts the way south. More ankle-twisting travel occurs along the ridgetop. Snags, maple, and birch share ranks with the oaks.

A left spur at 2.2 miles offers a restricted view at the upper reaches of the ridge to the west. At 2.3 miles a rocky slope to the right opens a window to the east-northeast, overlooking the valley to Kittatinny Mountain. Ahead travel a picturesque realm of rocks and slabs, before reaching the finest view at 2.5 miles for a more open look east.

Clamber over the rocky ridge tip, dipping to Cowans Gap. Curled rock tripe lichen coats the rock, laurel abounds, and steep pitches mark travel.

Spy red eft, box turtle, and millipede as you watch your footing.

At 3.3 miles bear left on a woods road, paralleling Richmond Road into the developed park. Now pursue blue blazes through the park to meet the yellow-blazed **Lakeside Trail** (3.5 miles). Turn left and follow the shore of Cowans Gap Lake to the Little Aughwick Creek bridge and the loop's close, 4 miles.

57 Tuscarora Trail, Tuscarora Mountain South

General description:	This day-hike sampling of the long-distance Tuscarora Trail System (a bypass to the Appalachian Trail) travels atop the southern extent of Tuscarora Mountain, snaring limited views. The bypass spans from southern Pennsylvania through Maryland to Northern Virginia. This leg travels State Game Lands 124.
General location:	60 miles southwest of Harrisburg.
Special attractions:	Limited views, rock overhangs, solitude, wildlife sightings, fall foliage.
Length:	10.2 miles round trip.
Elevation:	Find a 300-foot elevation change.
Difficulty:	Moderate.
Maps:	Buchanan State Forest; Keystone Trails Association: Tuscarora Trail, Sections 7 and 8.
Special concerns:	No overnight camping on State Game land. Blue (formerly orange) blazes mark the trail. Heed postings for neighboring private land.
Season and hours:	Spring through fall.
For information:	Potomac Appalachian Trail Club.

Finding the trailhead: From the junction of U.S. Highway 522 and Pennsylvania 16 in McConnellsburg, go southeast on PA 16 East for 3.5 miles to find a broad turnout for parking on the right. The Tuscarora Trail crosses PA 16 0.1 mile farther south. When arriving from Cove Gap—the site of Buchanan's (President James Buchanan) Birthplace Historical Park, go 2 miles north on PA 16 to find the trail.

The hike: On the west side of PA 16 behind the road distance sign, follow the **Tuscarora Trail** south toward PA 456. With a quick burst of climb, the trail contours uphill at an angle. Pass amid a low-stature, tangled woods with meadowy floor, following a thin boot track. Cross a faint woods road and top the ridge. Here lichen-mottled rock slabs claim the crest. The rocks show an eastern incline and western ledge, presenting partial views west. The trail then rolls southbound.

Tuscarora Trail, Tuscarora Mountain South

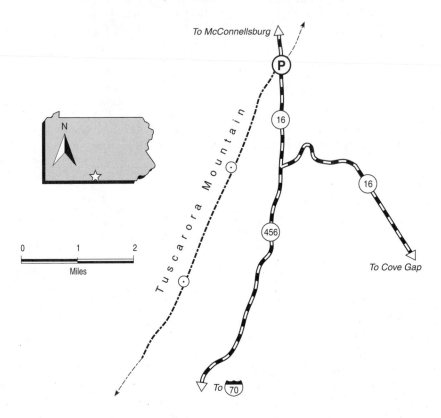

While the woods have a tangled character, it is not tangled in the classic sense. The disheveled appearance owes to the many bowed trunks, bent limbs, and suspended branches and tumbled trees that have yet to crash to the ground. Winds commonly wash over the summit invigorating leaves and travelers. Oaks are notably absent from the array of hickory, birch, maple, ash, and shad. Poison ivy makes a sporadic appearance.

At a mile, recent logging has torn apart the setting but opened views. Later the summit broadens. Enjoy encounters with deer, turkey, and box turtle. Muffled noise from PA 16 may sometimes be heard. Mostly (once out of the logging zone), the tour conveys an isolated, wild feeling.

Atop the next bump (1.6 miles), steal western glimpses. On tiptoe view the far end of the rural valley and the blue ridges disappearing in the distance. More visits to the rocky crest follow. Then at 2.1 miles, angle across an east-west running grassy woods road. By detouring right a few strides along the road, add another piece to the vista puzzle.

Pass patches of bramble and greenbrier. While well off the trail, these plants can grow with abandon. Where the ridge narrows add limited looks east and find rougher footing. Snags contribute to the skyline.

At scarcely more than 3 miles, the unmarked **Alice Trail** arrives on the left. After which, the Tuscarora Trail drifts onto the western flank to pass a trail register (3.1 miles). Rocky areas alternate with the earthen trail. At 4.3 miles, pass beneath the jumbles and overhangs of the rocky summit crest and return to the summit.

Between 4.6 and 5.1 miles, the tour affords eastern valley-ridge views, culminating with an east-west view at 5.1 miles to bring the described tour to a close. To the south Maryland beckons. Alternative ending sites to shorten the tour include the woods road at 2.1 miles, the register at 3.1 miles, or the rock crest at 4.3 miles.

58 Friendship Hill National Historic Site

OVERVIEW

On a bluff overlooking the Monongahela River sits the country manor of Albert Gallatin, a Swiss immigrant who played a key role in this nation's early adventure into democratic rule. He served as Secretary of the Treasury under Presidents Jefferson and Madison, and he secured funding for both the Louisiana Purchase in 1803 and the Lewis and Clark Expedition, 1804-1806. Lewis and Clark honored him when naming the 3 forks of the Missouri River: They are the Jefferson, Madison, and Gallatin rivers; all flow through Montana.

When Gallatin built this home at Friendship Hill in 1789, it overlooked the edge of the untried western frontier and what Gallatin hoped would be a corridor to prosperity. The Monongahela drains to the Ohio River—a springboard to points west, but the water route proved unfeasible. Instead, the National Road and later railroads carried the nation west.

Explore mansion and grounds, learn about Gallatin, and rediscover the growth of our nation. The Friendship Hill Trail System holds national recreation trail distinction.

General description:	An interpretive loop explores the grounds of the country estate. Link and side trails allow for varying or extending the tour.
General location:	12 miles southwest of Uniontown, Pennsylvania; 10 miles north of Morgantown, West Virginia.
Special attractions:	Guided or self-guided tours of the multi-era 35-room mansion, a holographic likeness of Albert Gallatin that speaks to visitors, a glen of old-growth trees, historic gravesites, waterfalls, a gazebo overlook of the Monongahela River, rhododendron and laurel.
Length:	Main Loop, 4-mile loop.

Elevation:	Find a 150-foot elevation change.
Difficulty:	Moderate.
Maps:	The Friendship Hill National Recreation Trail map.
Special concerns:	Carry water; do not drink from natural sources as surface water is highly acidic. Keep to the trails, stay back from the bluff rim, and be alert on the steep, slippery descent to the river. Do not collect or disturb natural features. Find the trail system color-coded and well-signed. Green indicates the Main Loop, red the side trails, and yellow the link trails.
Season and hours:	Daily year-round, except Christmas Day. 8:30 a.m. to 5 p.m. When the snow is sufficiently deep, cross-country skiing replaces hiking (Consult park map.)
For information:	Friendship Hill National Historic Site.

Finding the trailhead: From the junction of Pennsylvania highways 21 and 166 in north Masontown, go south on PA 166, reaching the park entrance on the right in 7.1 miles.

The hike: For the **Main Loop**, from the Gallatin House parking area, follow the broad, sidewinding concrete walk toward the mansion. Pass a wildflower garden and a sculpture portraying Gallatin, the surveyor. Like many of his day, he played multiple roles in life.

Fashioned of brick, frame, and stone, the restored Gallatin House greets visitors with quiet dignity. A stone well, towering shade trees, broad lawns, and sprawling white barn complete the image. Pass through the breezeway (0.2 mile) to find the entrance to the visitor center, which occupies the old stone kitchen. There gain information on house and trail.

Now follow signs for Sophia's Grave, proceeding south to the gazebo, which overlooks a bluff to the Monongahela River. Rhododendron and picturesque oaks add to the country setting; interpretive panels explain trail features.

Turn left at the gazebo and hike along the bluff's rim. Here, an abrupt conifer-deciduous slope plunges to the river. Soon find the first of the green-marked posts and an arrow pointing the way to Sophia's Grave.

Skirt the upper edge of a hayfield, seasonally dotted by rolled bales, before entering the old-growth glen of Sophia's Woods. A stone enclosure protects the grave; Sophia was Gallatin's first wife. The cathedral forest harkens to the woods of Gallatin's time.

The rush of Rhododendron Run now complements the harmonic notes of birds. At the upcoming clearing, overlook the shrubs to the right to glimpse a 15-foot, lacy waterfall as it races over a canted cliff. To the left lies a wildlife pond active with turtle, frog, and heron. Cross a footbridge over the outlet to resume on woods path. Poison ivy grows to the sides.

At each upcoming junction, stay the green trail. Cross a series of footbridges over the waters draining to Rhododendron Run. Beautiful big beech and scenic snags add to the woods character. The industrial noises rising from the Monongahela River would have delighted Gallatin, the entrepreneur. Pass from old-growth to mature second-growth forest, coming to a steep switchbacked descent to the river floodplain.

After the first switchback, view a falls on South Run. A series of cascades transforms this cataract into a ribbon of white racing water after a rainstorm. At the base of the bluff (1.1 miles), bear right on an old farm road. Silver maple, sycamore, and elm inhabit the floodplain. Cross a footbridge over lower Rhododendron Run and pause to admire its serial falls, cascades, and leafy canyon. A couple of huge boulders that tumbled from the bluff now redirect travel. Gather glimpses of the broad Monongahela River.

Drawing away from the river tanglewood, ascend past the **South and North cutoffs** (yellow-blazed at 1.9 and 2.1 miles respectively), both of which head right. The farm road extends a pleasant woods stroll, interrupted by a pipeline corridor and the crossing of Ice Pond Run. Beyond the trees to the left lies the Monongahela Railroad.

Keep left for the outer loop and at 2.5 miles, cross a footbridge over Dublin Run. In another 0.1 mile, the Main Loop bears right, as a spur heads straight to New Geneva—the community begun by Gallatin. A moderate ascent through a younger, tighter woods follows.

As the trail levels and older trees offer shade, look for Clare Cemetery on the left. A rustic stone wall rims this small cemetery housing the head and foot stones of Thomas Clare, who died in 1814. Clare owned the tract called "Dublin" that adjoined Gallatin's property and is now part of the park.

Gallatin House, Friendship Hill National Historic Site.

Friendship Hill National Historic Site

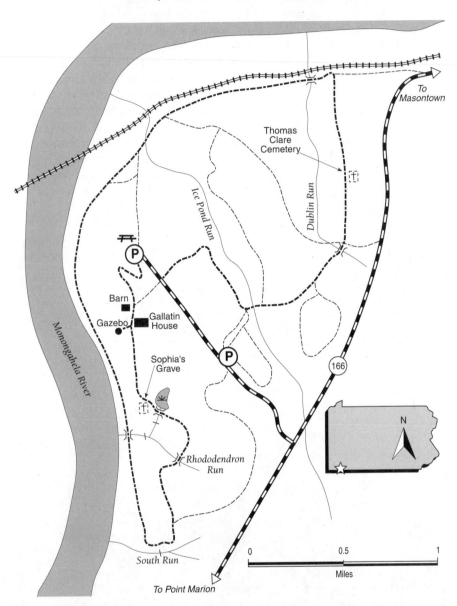

To Masontown

Thomas Clare Cemetery

Ice Pond Run

Dublin Run

Monongahela River

Barn

Gazebo

Gallatin House

Sophia's Grave

Rhododendron Run

South Run

To Point Marion

166

N

0   0.5   1

Miles

Resume along the wooded farm road, crossing the yellow-marked **School Spur** (3.1 miles), a second footbridge over Dublin Run, and a pipeline corridor with a red trail. Then continue forward past **North Meadow Loop** and cross a culvert for Ice Pond Run to reach the next junction: Bear right, still on farm road, for the full loop; the yellow trail to the left leads to parking.

At 3.5 miles, turn left off the farm road and follow a mowed swath at the edge of an open field. It recalls the agrarian past at Friendship Hill. Next cross the park road and pass between stone pillars to travel a gravel service road to the mansion (3.8 miles). Enjoy a second look or join a tour before returning via the concrete walk (4 miles).

59 Quebec Run Wild Area

OVERVIEW

In Fayette County, Pennsylvania, at the Pennsylvania–West Virginia border, this 4,765-acre forested area offers hikers a first-rate wilderness retreat. The wild area spans from the eastern slope of Chestnut Ridge to Big Sandy Creek. It is drained by Quebec, Tebolt, and Mill runs.

General description:	A lasso-shaped tour incorporates several named trails and visits some of the area's finest features.
General location:	12 miles south of Uniontown, Pennsylvania; 18 miles northeast of Morgantown, West Virginia.
Special attractions:	Clear water, trout-supporting streams; abundant rhododendron; areas of mountain laurel; mixed mesophytic forest (predominantly maple and tulip poplar), with oak highlands and hemlock flats; grist mill ruins; solitude.
Length:	Wild Area Hiking Tour, 8.7 miles round trip.
Elevation:	Travel between 1,550 feet along lower Mill Run and a high point of 2,200 feet at the Brocker-Hess trail junction.
Difficulty:	Moderate.
Maps:	Quebec Run Wild Area; Forbes State Forest (Maps are sometimes available at the trailhead.)
Special concerns:	Primitive backpack camping is allowed by permit only; contact the headquarters for a free permit. Do not disturb or collect natural features. During hunting season, wear bright colors. Blue blazes mark trails.
Season and hours:	Spring through fall for hiking.
For information:	Forbes State Forest.

Finding the trailhead: From the junction of U.S. Highway 40 and Pennsylvania 381 in Farmington, go south on PA 381 for 4.6 miles. In the village of Elliottsville, take a right turn off PA 381, followed by a left on State Route 2004. At the Y-junction in 1 mile, bear right on Quebec Road (a paved and gravel road). In another mile cross Mill Run to find the marked trailhead parking on the left.

The hike: For this 8.7-mile **Wild Area Hiking Tour**, head right on **Mill Run Trail**. The footpath rolls along the lower slope, tracking Mill Run downstream. Hornbeam, witch-hazel, and a few hawthorn fill out the leafy forest. Along creek flats, hemlock and rhododendron grow. Deer may cross paths with hikers.

Side tributaries thread to Mill Run; cross most via a simple step-over or atop rocks or limbs. At 0.9 mile, make an abrupt right turn to meet the **Miller Trail** in 100 feet. Bear left for Mill Run Trail and cross a larger side water that may require wading.

At 1.1 miles, reach the loop junction and bear left for a clockwise tour, still on the Mill Run Trail. The **Rankin Trail** on the right holds the return. Cross a wooden footbridge over Quebec Run and continue along the hemlock-deciduous flat to a footbridge over Mill Run (1.3 miles).

To add a visit to the grist mill ruins, one must detour across the bridge, ascend the steep eroded east bank, and hike downstream 0.1 mile to the ruins. View a foundation, a mill race, and woods growing in the middle of what was the mill. Moss, fern, and lichen decorate the stones.

Return to the bridge and resume the Mill Run Trail (1.5 miles). At the bridge, pause for an unobstructed look at the scenic waterway—one of the hallmark waters of the wild area. Now follow the west bank of Mill Run downstream.

The trail occasionally rolls up the drainage slope. Along side tributaries view low-growing laurel, fountains of fern, and skunk cabbage bogs. Bending Mill Run continues to enchant, until the trail climbs away at 2.5 miles. At a dip, the Mill Run Trail ends at **West Road** (now a hiker trail). Turn right on West Road to continue the loop.

Travel the recessed bed of leaves and grass for a steady, moderate ascent. At the junction with **Tebolt Trail** (2.8 miles), hikers have an option as these are parallel trails. For this loop (the shorter of the 2), stay West Road, proceeding forward on a nicely wooded passage. The trail goes unblazed here but the line of travel is clear, despite vegetation rising up in the grade and a scattering of logs.

At 3 miles, bear right on a more defined grassy lane for easy walking. Colorful mushrooms dot the woods floor. Other discoveries may include a dispersal of curled, leathery egg shells from a successful turtle nest, American chestnuts (once the dominant tree of the eastern forest), or a turkey.

Continue forward (west) on West Road, topping a small rise, before reaching Quebec Road at 3.8 miles. The loop resumes uphill to the left in 50 feet, with the **Brocker Trail** continuing westbound travel. To shorten the tour, descend along Quebec Road to Quebec Run bridge and the Rankin Trail junction and turn right.

Quebec Run Wild Area

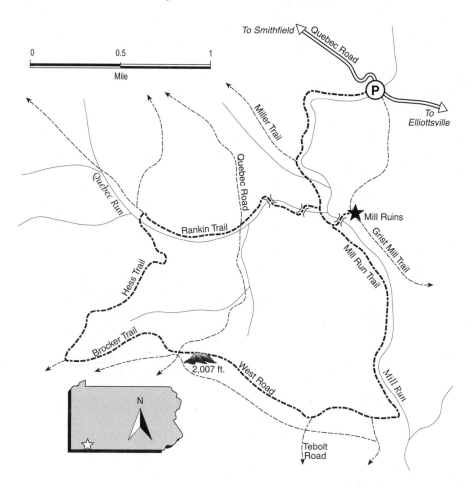

Brocker Trail gently rolls. Again, the path is vegetated and strewn with a few logs. Large patches of fern dress the oak forest, only to be replaced by rhododendron and laurel. Enjoy full shade from the leafed out maple and birch trees. At 4.7 miles reach an unsigned but blazed T-junction with the **Hess Trail** and turn right.

Before long, follow a contouring, woods road that crosses small headwaters; tulip poplars thrive here. By 5.7 miles descend. A rhododendron thicket announces Quebec Run. At 6.25 miles wade or rock-hop across the 10-foot-wide run to reach the north bank and **Rankin Trail**.

For the loop, turn right on the Rankin Trail to parallel Quebec Run downstream. Pass within sound, snaring occasional glimpses of the run. Mossy boulders add to a tour, and the rhododendron explodes.

At 7 miles cross Quebec Road and keep to the north bank. The trail briefly rolls uphill before crossing Quebec Run via a wooden footbridge. Meander downstream to cross back over the run (7.5 miles). At 7.6 miles close the loop at Mill Run Trail and hike left, retracing the first 1.1 miles to the trailhead.

60 Martin Hill Wild Area

OVERVIEW

Encompassing Martin Hill and the southern extent of Tussey Mountain, this 11,500-acre wild area beckons hikers with its natural wilds and remote adventure. Seldom-walked trails explore summit and flank. The featured Tussey Mountain hike travels closed Tussey Mountain/Wigfield Road for a carefree mountaintop tour. In winter the route doubles as a cross-country ski trail.

General description:	The selected hike traces the broad plateau of southern Tussey Mountain for a skyline tour but one lacking views.
General location:	40 miles southeast of Johnstown, Pennsylvania; 15 miles northeast of Cumberland, Maryland.
Special attractions:	An arid, low-stature mixed forest; thickets of laurel and berry bushes; wildlife sightings; quiet; fall foliage.
Length:	10 miles round trip.
Elevation:	Find a 350-foot elevation change between the trailhead and high point south of the Fetters Trail junction.
Difficulty:	Easy to moderate.
Maps:	Buchanon State Forest.
Special concerns:	Carry water. Tent camping is allowed; pitch camps 500 feet off Tussey Mountain/Wigfield Road and 500 feet from any public roadway. Secure permits at the forest office. Loop travelers be forewarned: the side trails that descend and contour the mountain flanks are overgrown and log-strewn. Mileage signs allow hikers to track progress. Rattlesnakes do dwell here, but ant mounds are more likely to cause trouble. Wear fluorescent orange during hunting seasons.
Season and hours:	Spring through fall for hiking.
For information:	Buchanon State Forest.

Finding the trailhead: From Bedford, go 2 miles east on U.S. Highway 30 and turn south on Pennsylvania 326. At Sweet Root Picnic Area in 14.2 miles, turn right on Black Valley Road/State Route 3007. In 0.8 mile, turn right on Beans Cove Road/S.R. 3005 and proceed another 1.9 miles to find

Martin Hill Wild Area

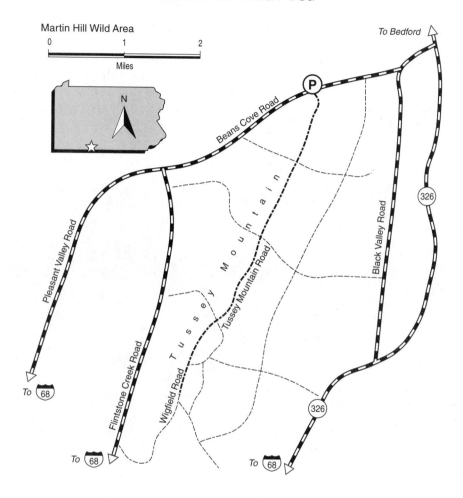

Martin Hill Wild Area

0   1   2

Miles

N

To Bedford

P

Beans Cove Road

Pleasant Valley Road

Tussey Mountain

Tussey Mountain Road

Black Valley Road

326

Flintstone Creek Road

Wigfield Road

To 68

To 68

To 68

326

326

parking for Martin Hill Snowmobile Trail on the right; closed Tussey Mountain Road on the left.

The hike: Round the gate to hike south on orange-blazed Tussey Mountain Road. Oak, sassafras, black gum, pine, maple, locust, and aspen shape the low-stature ridge forest. Deer, mourning dove, and itty-bitty, eye-annoying black bugs may accompany travel.

The old road allows for carefree walking. Delicate grasses pierce the gravel, and the incline is comfortable. Laurel, scrub oak, fern, berry bushes, and honeysuckle weave a tight understory thicket. When ripe, blueberries draw hikers aside. American chestnuts may be spied near the 1-mile sign.

At 1.25 miles cross **Fetters Trail**. The broad, mildly undulating ridge denies views. By 1.5 miles, the trail levels off and slowly descends. By 2 miles, thick grasses claim the road and oaks bring fuller shade for a relaxed country-lane appeal. Animals likewise use this travel artery. Sightings may include fox, turkey, bobcat, and perhaps a black bear.

At 2.4 miles, cross the **Johnson Trail** to continue the backbone tour. Then at 3.75 miles hike past the **Morris Trail** on the right and an orange-blazed trail on the left. Tussey Mountain again shows a wilder aspect. More maple and beech and a jungle of small-trunked trees add visual dimension.

Tussey Mountain Road becomes Wigfield Road at 4.5 miles. Proceed forward to the 5-mile sign—the chosen turnaround for the day hike. Southbound, the trail descends to Flintstone Creek Road off the western flank. Return as you came or go exploring.

Wild blueberries, Martin Hill Wild Area, Buchanon State Forest.

Hershey Dutch Region

This region of southeast Pennsylvania unites the valley and ridge province of the Appalachian Mountains and the verdant farm valleys of York, Lancaster, and Cumberland counties. Traverse the elongated arched ridges and become enmeshed in the old-world charm of Amish country. Discoveries vary from an intriguing "river of rocks" to the racing, cool-water excitement of Kellys Run. Visit a world-renowned outpost for the fall hawk watch and revisit the state's industrial past. At and around the Civil War battle site of Gettysburg, discover where a rich chapter in American history was played out. Throughout the region, mixed woods, rhododendron and laurel, and treasured valley and ridge vistas enhance travel.

61 Appalachian National Scenic Trail

General description:	This 2,155-mile national scenic trail from Maine to Georgia cuts across southeastern Pennsylvania between New Jersey and the Mason–Dixon Line at Maryland. The Appalachian Trail (AT) traverses ridges and dips through gaps, logging some of its most rugged miles within the state. The Pennsylvania leg takes the better part of a month to complete.
General location:	Between the village of Delaware Water Gap and Pen Mar Park in Maryland.
Special attractions:	Vistas, fall hawk migration, laurel and rhododendron, historic sites, fall foliage.
Length:	232.2 miles one-way.
Elevation:	Travel between a low of 300 feet at the Delaware River and highs in excess of 2,000 feet on South Mountain.
Difficulty:	Strenuous.
Maps:	The official Appalachian Trail guide and maps published by the Keystone Trails Association.
Special concerns:	Hikers need to work out the logistics for carrying and obtaining adequate food and supplies, plan what to do in case of an emergency, and arrange for transportation at trail's end. Expect rocky, difficult conditions. Be careful not to confuse the irregular white blazes that mark state forest and game land boundaries, with the white rectangles of the AT. Blue blazes indicate spurs to lookouts, springs, and high-

water bypasses. Always carry a supply of drinking water as ridgetop sources can be dry. Be alert for snakes.

Normally off-limits to all camping, the state game lands along the AT do allow camping for thru-trail hikers. Pitch sites within 200 feet of the AT and 500 feet from any water. Stays are limited to 1 night per site and no open fires during times of fire hazard.

Season and hours: Spring through fall.
For information: Appalachian Trail Conference.

Finding the trailhead: The AT crosses numerous Pennsylvania state routes, traverses Michaux State Forest, and passes through several named parks. Pennsylvania thru-state hikers will find the northernmost access at the Interstate 80 bridge at the village of Delaware Water Gap. Find the southernmost access at Pen Mar Park: At Rouzerville turn southeast off Pennsylvania 16 onto Pen Mar Road and follow it to the park at the Maryland state border.

The hike: The first national scenic trail in the United States, the AT salutes the mountain wilds of 14 eastern states. Conceived in the early 1920s, this hiker filament rolls atop the ancient Appalachia Mountains, dipping to cross the important eastern river valleys. Most of the AT greenway has received permanent public protection; some 4,000 volunteers along with 200 public agencies maintain and oversee the trail.

Open to foot travel only, the AT advances primarily via footpath and woods road, with some sections on developed roads. As the protected greenway itself can be narrow, keep to the trail to avoid straying onto private land.

While some 28 Pennsylvania shelters lie along or just off the trail, a tent remains standard equipment. Pitch camps in established sites to minimize environmental harm. At Pine Grove Furnace State Park, an American Youth Hostel offers overnight accommodations.

On a north-south journey through Pennsylvania, discover 3 distinct tour sections: the ridge province, valley flatland, and southeastern forest. The ridge province spans more than 150 miles. Travel is atop the state's signature long, flat ridges with dips through gaps. The valley flatland serves as the bridge; much of the passage here is alongside farms, pastures, hedgerows, and small towns. Forest travel appropriately enough signs off the tour for Penn's Woods.

Southbound, the AT climbs from the Delaware River past Winona Cliffs to top Mount Minsi (elevation 1,480 feet). It then follows the ridge of Kittatinny Mountain southwest, gathering occasional views. The most impressive one comes at Wolf Rocks (8.8 miles). Find the trail rolling and rocky. In order to cross Wind Gap (15.3 miles), the AT dips 300 feet.

Blue Mountain travel ahead can be quite dry, so be sure to carry a good supply of water. The ridge holds but modest changes in grade and forest habitat. Find chestnut oaks common, with gum, sassafras, laurel, and maple.

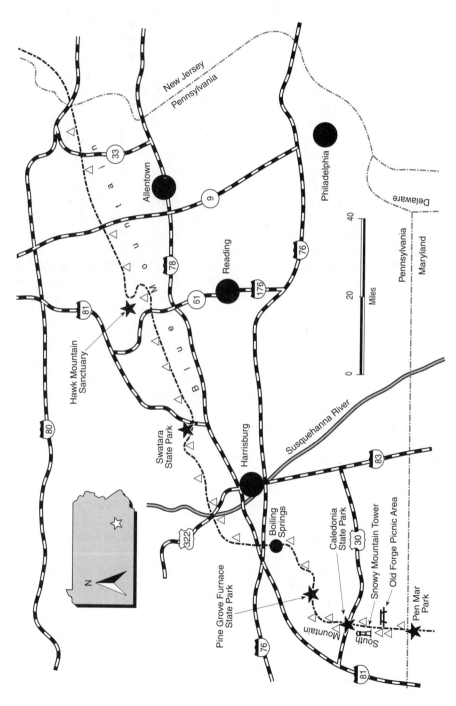

Four named views occur over the next 20 miles. A steep descent to Lehigh River then interrupts the reverie. Cross PA 873 at 35.9 miles.

From Lehigh Gap again climb 1,000 vertical feet to resume Blue Mountain travel, with occasional views. At 45 miles claim Bake Oven Knob (elevation 1,560 feet) for a 180-degree southern perspective; the site is also famous for its autumn hawk watches. At 46.8 miles, Bear Rocks extend a full 360-degree valley and ridge panorama. Where the eastern slope steepens gain dramatic cliffs. At 50.3 miles, cross Blue Mountain Summit on PA 309 (elevation 1,360 feet).

Still Blue Mountain hosts the tour. At Tri-county Corner (55.8 miles) gain another sweeping vista. At 60.7 miles, the AT turns east off the ridge; straight leads to the private Hawk Mountain Sanctuary—the best site in the nation from which to watch the migration of predatory birds. For hikers who take this worthwhile detour, be sure to pay the entry fee at the museum. The sanctuary's trails visit overlooks and an unusual river of rocks (See hike 62).

Keeping to the AT, follow Blue Mountain as it takes an odd curve. Amid the woods, keen-eyed travelers may detect barren flats that hint at former charcoal hearths. The AT again plunges and climbs 1,000 vertical feet to reach the Pinnacle (elevation 1,635 feet), with its spectacular cliffs and views at 68.4 miles. Pulpit Rock (elevation 1,582 feet) likewise rewards with vistas. Below it, discover a pair of caves and sheer cliffs. More hearths preface the AT's arrival at Windsor Furnace, 72.7 miles. The AT then drops 800 vertical feet for the crossing of PA 61 at Port Clinton (78.7 miles).

Blue Mountain trends southwest and with it the AT. Find the trail more rocky in places. Auburn Lookout (81.4 miles) offers a natural view. Cross PA 183 at 93.7 miles. At 97.6 miles, a 0.4-mile spur leads to Shikellamy Lookout, and at 99.9 miles, a side-trail loop that includes a 500 stone step journey to the Round Head viewpoint.

PA Highways 501 and 645 mark off distance before Swatara Gap signals the next major plunge. It is where the AT crosses under I-81 (at 113.6 miles) and meets and briefly follows PA 443. The trail remains reasonably flat for 4 miles then climbs to traverse Second Mountain. At Rausch Gap Village, discover a cemetery, foundations, and other clues to the one-time industrial community. An old stage road then advances the tour for 7 miles along Sharp Mountain.

At 124.2 miles, the AT passes through the ruins of Yellow Springs Village, where a blue side trail journeys to the site of a stone tower and old mine adit. Again travel stage road. At mile 127 stone hop across Rattling Run, and soon after, reach Stony Mountain. The next descent leads to the PA 325 crossing in Clarks Valley.

The AT next climbs to and travels atop Peters Mountain, until a 1,000-foot vertical descent leads to Susquehanna River (147.7 miles). Ring up a number of views, including a valley overlook from Shikellimy Rocks.

Cross the river at Clarks Ferry Bridge for a 3-mile stretch on paved road; watch for blazes. With a steep ascent, top Cove Mountain and reach Hawk Rock, 151.1 miles. Rocks nag at the ankles as the trail remains atop the

Backpacking the Appalachian Trail, Buchanon State Forest.

mountain for some 7 miles. Descend to PA 850 and climb up and over Little and Blue mountains to leave the ridge province at 162.4 miles.

Valley flatland follows, with much of the area along the trail now private. Enjoy rural settings as you cross farm roads. Where the trail passes south through the village of Boiling Springs (174.6 miles), find the Mid-Atlantic Regional Office for the Appalachian Trail Conference. In another 1.5 miles, the AT leaves the Cumberland Valley for a rolling tour across forested mountains and hills to PA 94 (183.4 miles).

Michaux State Forest is now the host. Laurel and blueberry bushes abound as the AT ascends Trents Hill (185.6 miles), only to descend to the PA 34 crossing in another mile. Where the trail descends Piney Mountain, pass a spur to Pole Steeple View.

At Pine Grove Furnace State Park (194 miles), hikers find historic buildings, a store, and overnight hostel. A walking tour introduces the iron works of Pine Grove Furnace and the village it supported. Cross PA 233 for more forest travel. Along the broad summit of South Mountain, expect to cross a series of state forest roads. Five shelters serve thru-hikers along this AT stretch.

Caledonia State Park greets hikers where the trail next dips. Here enjoy a wondrous array of rhododendron along the East Branch Conococheague Creek and the old millrace. Cross U.S. 30 at 214 miles, and ascend Rocky Mountain.

Still enjoy woods of oak, maple, sassafras, tulip poplar, and black gum. Groves of hemlock vary the tour's look. In 4 miles, the AT turns off Rocky Mountain to climb Snowy Mountain. There a short side trail leads to a fire tower for views (221.2 miles). Chimney Rocks in another 2 miles again serve up views.

Descend to pass through Old Forge Picnic Area (224.8 miles), where Antietam Shelters can be found amid beautiful big trees, laurel, and rhododendron. Rock outcrops, rich forest, and multistory vegetation frame the path. PA 16 marks off travel at 229.3 miles. The trail then rolls up and over Mount Dunlop to the hiker bridge across Falls Creek (231.6 miles). Hikers bid farewell to Pennsylvania, hello to Maryland at Pen Mar Park, 232.2 miles.

Given that spatial constraints necessarily limit the detail of this description, thru-trail and day hikers should contact the Keystone Trails Association or Appalachian Trail Conference for official maps and detailed guides. Or consult your local library, bookstore, or backpacker/outfitter store.

62 Hawk Mountain Sanctuary

OVERVIEW

Astraddle Kittatinny Ridge in eastern Pennsylvania, this 2,380-acre, private nonprofit sanctuary has been proclaimed the best site in the nation for watching the fall migration of predatory birds. Between mid-August and mid-December, an average of 20,000 eagles, ospreys, hawks, and falcons ride the winds south. The spectacle draws visitors from around the world. Superb vistas, seasonal rhododendron and laurel blooms, an unusual periglacial boulder field, and museum and art gallery further recommend a visit to Hawk Mountain Sanctuary.

General description:	A series of short trails explore the sanctuary and offer access to the Appalachian Trail. Two hikes of varying difficulty may be toured individually or joined together to view skyline, woods, and a white flow of rocks.
General location:	20 miles north of Reading.
Special attractions:	Ridge and valley vistas, fall migration of raptors, spring migration of warblers, site of a gravity railroad, native wildflower/habitat garden, museum/gallery.
Length:	Lookout Trail, 1.75 miles round trip, including spurs; River of Rocks Trail, 4-mile loop (4.7 miles round trip from visitor center); the combined tour, 5.75 miles.
Elevation:	Lookout Trail, 200-foot elevation change; River of Rocks Trail, 700-foot elevation change.
Difficulty:	Lookout Trail, moderate; River of Rocks Trail, strenuous.
Maps:	Trail Guide Hawk Mountain.
Special concerns:	An admission fee is charged; pay at the trail gateway or visitor center. No pets, radios, bicycles, horses, smoking, camping, fires, or alcoholic beverages, and no collecting or disturbing natural features. Hike at your own risk; boots are recommended. Visitation peaks in October, with a shuttle operating to ease traffic and parking congestion. Midweek visits offer greater tranquility. Binoculars are available for rent, and trails are color-coded.
Season and hours:	Year-round. Trails: dawn to dusk; Visitor Center: 9 a.m. to 5 p.m. (open 8 a.m. during fall migration, September 1 through November 30), closed Thanksgiving, Christmas, and New Year's days.
For information:	Hawk Mountain Sanctuary Association.

Finding the trailhead: From Interstate 78/U.S. Highway 22 west of Hamburg, take exit 9, go north on Pennsylvania 61 for 4.4 miles, and turn right (east) on PA 895 at a sign for Hawk Mountain. In 2.5 miles at Drehersville, go east on State Route 2018/Hawk Mountain Road for 1.9 miles; the parking entrance is on the right.

The hikes: Begin hikes at the information pavilion, where daily bird counts are posted. Follow the path indicated "to Lookouts and Sanctuary Trails." The attractive brick walk travels past the National Natural Landmark monument and gives way to a woods lane framed by black gum, oak, birch, maple, laurel, and sassafras.

Cross Hawk Mountain Road, pass through the gateway entry station, and ascend. At 0.2 mile reach South Lookout, where interpretive boards depict the various predatory birds in flight. The natural rock crest presents an open view of the forested ridges, the River of Rocks directly below, and the serene rural valley beyond. To the east spy 3 named ridge features: Hemlock Heights, Owl's Head, and the Pinnacle.

From South Lookout, the **Lookout Trail** (orange blazed) heads left for North Lookout; the **River of Rocks Trail** (red) heads right. Take the Lookout Trail first, quickly locating Appalachian Overlook—a rocky jumble with comparable views of the area skyline and migration path. Chestnut oaks favor the ridge, as do berry bushes and laurel. Bench seats invite pause. As

South Lookout, Hawk Mountain Sanctuary.

Hawk Mountain Sanctuary

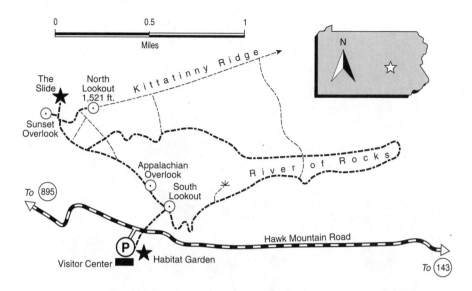

the Lookout Trail advances, short spurs continue to branch right to unnamed vantages for viewing Hawk Mountain.

At 0.3 mile the orange-blazed **Escarpment Trail** heads right for an alternative route to North Lookout or a potential loop return. Continue forward on the Lookout Trail, which narrows with rocks piercing the trailbed. At 0.5 mile, hike past the northern terminus of the River of Rocks Trail and then the **Express Trail**, which heads right for yet another approach to North Lookout.

Log-reinforced and natural stone steps take the Lookout Trail to an area of hemlocks and a T-junction (0.6 mile): To the left discover a forked path which leads to The Slide (straight ahead) and Sunset Overlook (to the left, via a short difficult rock scramble). To the right, the Lookout Trail travels the Hall of the Mountain King to North Lookout (elevation 1,521 feet). Together, the spurs and Lookout Trail unravel the history for this part of the sanctuary.

Excavated sands from here were used in construction and in the production of glassware. The hiked trail traces the old Drehersville cart road; the Slide records where a gravity-run railroad traveled the steep north flank in the 1890s; and the Hall is where the sand was collected and loaded onto cars. Ironically, prior to 1934, hunters would stand at the Slide and shoot raptors as they migrated past.

Reach North Lookout at 1 mile, after taking both round-trip spurs. The site holds a grand 200-degree panoramic view with a fine vantage of Hawk Mountain/Kittatinny Ridge along which thermals rise to carry the raptors

Hawk sculpture, Hawk Mountain Sanctuary.

south. View the ridge backbone, valley quilt, and several time-worn plateaus of the Appalachian Mountains.

For hikers interested in extending the tour, the **Skyline Trail** continues east from North Lookout along Kittatinny Ridge to East Rocks and the **Appalachian Trail**. On return to the visitor center, hikers may choose to tour either the Escarpment or Express trail (look for the orange blazes veering left as you descend from North Lookout) or add a tour of the River of Rocks Trail. A direct return to the center ends the hike at 1.75 miles.

For a clockwise tour of the 4-mile **River of Rocks Trail**, start at the 0.5-mile junction on the Lookout Trail. The wooded River of Rocks Trail ascends east amid a tremendous show of rhododendron and laurel, crosses the Escarpment Trail, and begins its rugged descent. Exercise care amid the rocks.

In 0.5 mile, blazes point hikers left to the first of a pair of junctions with the yellow-blazed **Golden Eagle Trail**, which climbs to the Skyline Trail. Stay the red blazes. Huckleberry joins the laurel, and grouse fright upon approach. Pockets and channels of rock punctuate the meandering descent.

At 1.3 miles, pass an island of rhododendron and a gurgling spring beneath the boulder rubble to travel at the outskirts of the River of Rocks. This long, broad stream of glaring white rock against rock and rock upon rock defies plant growth. Continue "downstream" through the rimming woods.

At 2 miles, reach the second junction with the Golden Eagle Trail. By turning right on it and passing through a gap in the rocky stream, hikers may shorten the loop. Again, keep to the River of Rocks Trail. The cathedral woods of tulip poplar, maple, birch, and oak hosts easier walking.

At the wide foot of the river, gain intriguing views upstream of the "great white way." Rocks again challenge footing on the uphill return. Be alert for the few sprigs of poison ivy. At 2.9 miles, the trail bears right on an old woods road being joined by the river cut-across of the Golden Eagle Trail. Pursue the red blazes still ascending.

Rhododendron shapes a pretty passage where the trail crosses a small drainage at 3.5 miles. On the opposite shore lies a junction. Here an orange spur journeys left to the sanctuary shelters (not for public use); the River of Rocks Trail angles uphill; and a second orange spur descends right to White Oak Swamp (a wetland meadow) in 0.1 mile. Keep to the red-blazed trail for a sometimes steep, switchbacking ascent. Arrive at South Lookout at 4 miles and turn left to return to parking.

63 Colonial Denning State Park

OVERVIEW

This 273-acre wooded park occupies Doubling Gap, created where Blue Mountain makes an S-shaped bend. Doubling Gap Run threads through the park, with manmade 3.5-acre Doubling Gap Lake serving as the recreational centerpiece. Short hiking trails explore the park and link up with the greater area trail system. From the park, access the 105-mile Tuscarora Trail atop Blue Mountain.

General description:	2 hikes present the park offering: an easy interpretive trail along the lake/run floodplain (Doubling Gap Nature Trail) and a moderately taxing trail that climbs to a natural ledge atop Blue Mountain for a Cumberland Valley view (Flat Rock Trail).
General location:	30 miles west of Harrisburg.
Special attractions:	Cumberland Valley view, swimming and fishing, mountain laurel and spring wildflowers, fall foliage.
Length:	Doubling Gap Nature Trail, 1.4 miles round trip; Flat Rock Trail, 4.4 miles round-trip.
Elevation:	Doubling Gap Nature Trail, 60-foot elevation change; Flat Rock Trail, 1,200-foot elevation change.
Difficulty:	Doubling Gap Nature Trail, easy; Flat Rock Trail, moderate to strenuous.
Maps:	State park brochure; the flier titled "Hiking and Nature Trails: Colonel Denning State Park and the Surrounding Tuscarora State Forest;" Keystone Trails Association's Tuscarora Trail Map, Sections 1 through 4.
Special concerns:	No trail camping within the state park; camp only within the designated park campground.
Season and hours:	Year-round, Nature Trail: 8 a.m. to sunset; Flat Rock Trail: 24 hours.
For information:	Colonel Denning State Park.

Finding the trailhead: At the junction of Pennsylvania Highways 850 and 233 in Landisburg, go south on PA 233 for 7.5 miles to reach the park entrance on the left. Or go 8 miles north from Newville on PA 233 and turn right.

The hikes: Start **Doubling Gap Nature Trail** on the west shore of Doubling Gap Lake at the dam. If parked at the beach, traverse the dam and spillway bridge to descend the handicapped-access ramp to a fishing dock and start of the interpretive trail, which is not wheelchair accessible.

The small open water of Doubling Gap Lake is half rimmed by woods, half by the dam and developed beach. Edge the lake in the shade of maple,

Colonel Denning State Park

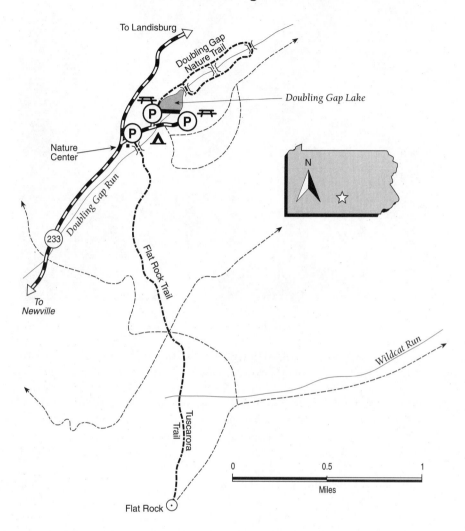

oak, birch, hickory, and white pine. Poison ivy grows amid the forest wildflowers.

Cross a footbridge over a tiny inlet and avoid a secondary path to shore. At 0.2 mile reach the loop junction, and bear left for a clockwise tour. Some hemlocks add to the forest. Interpretive plaques introduce the stream habitat. As the trail ascends the drainage slope, travel amid big white pine and pass a bench seat from which to glimpse the shimmery thread of Doubling Gap Run and surrender to the forest quiet.

Proceed forward across the next tributary bridge; a cut-across heads right. Mayapple and hepatica may be spied near the bridge. Travel a spatially open woods with walnut, locust, and ash growing above a meadowy floor.

Flat Rock, Tuscarora State Forest.

Back on the floodplain, follow gurgling Doubling Gap Run downstream to a footbridge at 0.75 mile. Cardinal flower decorate the stream. Mink, deer, and woodpecker may be spied. Cross to hike the east shore downstream. Soon the cut-across trail arrives via a bridge on the right; continue forward. Where the woods grow soggy, jack-in-the-pulpit flourish.

At 1 mile, cross a footbridge over a side tributary and travel the hemlock-hardwood flat to cross back over Doubling Gap Run and close the loop (1.2 miles). Turn left and retrace the first 0.2 mile of the hike.

At the park nature center near the Nature Program Pavilion and outdoor amphitheater, cross the footbridge over Doubling Gap Run to begin **Flat Rock Trail**. Ascend wood-braced earthen steps veering away from the campground to travel a hemlock plateau and later oak-hardwood forest. Gum, maple, and tulip poplar rise amid the oaks. Witch hazel, striped maple, and berry bushes weave a midstory. Red blazes mark the wide forest path.

At 0.4 mile, follow a narrow woods road uphill to the left for a steep climb to the springhouse ruins. Birch, nettle, and jewelweed grow along the road, hinting at the former purpose of these standing structures. If downfalls have not been cleared from the travel artery ahead, take the bypass that streaks uphill from the ruins.

By 0.7 mile enter the laurel belt of the slope; a few azalea grow trailside. The trail grows rugged, rocky, and steep before topping Blue Mountain at the Wagon Wheel (1 mile). The journey to Flat Rock resumes via the blue-blazed (formerly orange-blazed) **Tuscarora Trail** straight ahead.

Radiating outward from the Wagon Wheel, the Tuscarora Trail also branches right, with the yellow-blazed **Woodburn Trail** soon branching off of it to the left. Angling back to the left at the hub is the **Warner Trail**, and at a diagonal left is the **Lehman Trail**. Signs help sort out travel options.

Proceed forward on the Tuscarora Trail, wide and earthen, for a slow descent through mixed forest. Muddy pockets precede the grouped-limb crossing of the headwaters of Wildcat Run. The trail then rolls uphill before making a mild descent to the vista ledge (2.2 miles); the Tuscarora Trail veers left on narrow footpath just prior to the ledge.

The natural rock perch presents one of the finest views in the state, looking out over Cumberland Valley as it sprawls south. Ridges rise up blue in the hazy sunlight. Sparkling communities, silos, and barns and textured fields contribute to the farm-woods tapestry. Enjoy a full 180-degree view, with the ragged limbs of snags adding to looks west. Return as you came.

64 Middle Creek Wildlife Management Area

OVERVIEW

In northern Lancaster County this 6,254-acre wildlife management area (WMA) offers picnicking, fishing, hunting, wildlife watching, and nature study. Nine miles of trail traverse the site's varied habitats, which include hardwood forest, conifer plantation, cultivated and non-cultivated fields, wetland, scrub, and creek and lake impoundment shores. Explore ridgetop and valley floor. Extended by the Coleman Estate/Furnace Hills tract, the WMA contributes to a vast contiguous open space preserving unbroken forest and a vital wildlife corridor between Lancaster and Lebanon counties.

General description:	The selected 4 short hikes present much of the WMA's varied terrain and wildlife. Altogether 8 hikes are possible, including a tour of the Horseshoe Trail, part of a 134-mile hiking trail link between Valley Forge and the Appalachian Trail.
General location:	18 miles southwest of Reading.
Special attractions:	400-acre Middle Creek Impoundment; vistas; bird watching, with resident Canada geese, eagles seen nearly daily in summer and fall, and migrant snow geese and tundra swans in winter/early spring; laurel and wildflowers.
Length:	Conservation Trail, 1.5-mile loop; Willow Point Trail, 0.8 mile round-trip; Millstone Trail, 1.1-mile loop; Middle Creek Trail, 2.5 miles round trip.

Elevation: Conservation Trail, 100-foot elevation change; Willow Point Trail, flat; Millstone Trail, 300-foot elevation change; Middle Creek Trail, 50-foot elevation change.

Difficulty: Millstone Trail, moderate; all others, easy.

Maps: State Game Lands 46; Middle Creek Wildlife Management Area map and self-guided tour brochures (available at visitor center).

Special concerns: Become acquainted with the rules governing fishing, hunting, and propagation area closures. Poison ivy grows most everywhere. No feeding the waterfowl, collecting, or picnicking outside of the designated areas.

Season and hours: Year-round, daylight hours. Visitor Center: Tuesday through Saturday 8 a.m. to 4 p.m., with Sunday hours noon to 4 p.m. March 1 through November 30 only.

For information: Middle Creek Wildlife Management Area.

Finding the trailhead: From Ephrata, go 4.3 miles west on U.S. Highway 322 to Clay and turn right on State Route 1035/North Clay Road at a sign for the WMA. In 1.1 miles at Hopeland, turn right on SR 1026/Hopeland Road, and in another 0.6 mile turn left on Kleinfeltersville Road. Go 3 miles more and turn left on Museum Road for the visitor center.

From Pennsylvania 897 in Kleinfeltersville, travel 2.3 miles south on Kleinfeltersville Road to Museum Road.

The hikes: Off the northernmost parking area for the visitor center, start the **Conservation Trail** where a sign indicates "hiker path." An interpretive brochure pairs to the tour. Hike the mowed path up the open slope between fields. Geese sound their presence; their harsh notes mingle with the melodies of songbirds. Some 280 bird species have been identified within the WMA. Watch for yellow triangle markers with black tips pointing the direction of travel.

From the tour's vista, admire the vast, shallow lake impoundment, its island, and framing ridge before entering a woodland of oak and tulip poplar. A chaos of greenery claims the understory. The trail nudges or traverses wildlife management habitats explained by the brochure.

Wildflowers spangle the fields while wild berry, grape, and rose compose the hedgerows. At 0.4 mile, bear left at the fork to follow footpath and earthen lane and cross a wetland boardwalk. Skunk cabbages seasonally lend a pungent aroma. Summer rains bring mud.

Cross a small drainage to reach the foot of a grassy slope. Bear right and skirt Sunfish Pond with its lei of pond lilies; sumac and wild rose hinder views. Tag Museum Road at 1.4 miles, turn left, and hike past the visitor center to close the loop, 1.5 miles.

Locate the marked parking and trailhead for **Willow Point Trail** by driving 0.8 mile north on Kleinfeltersville Road from its intersection with Mu-

Middle Creek Wildlife Management Area

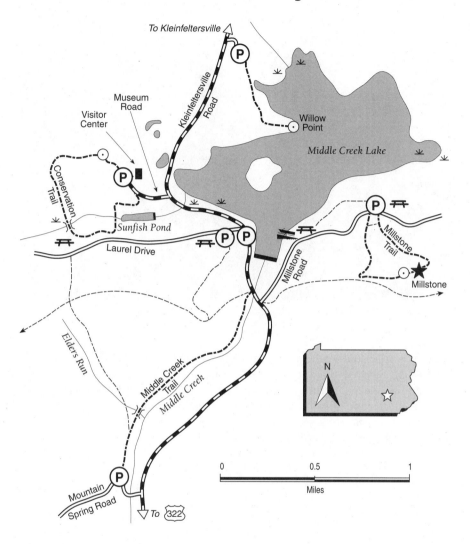

seum Road. Follow the path that leaves the corner of the parking area to edge a field of clover and Queen Anne's lace; a couple of big chestnut trees preside trailside. Where the path bears right, overlook a cultivated field grazed by geese; yellow songbirds decorate the strangled woods off to the left. Keep an eye skyward to view circling bald eagles or a passing heron.

At Willow Point (0.4 mile) sits a bird-watching bench/table. From it admire the open shallow lake, the large central island, and folded wooded ridges. Deer may be spied across the way. Return as you came.

For the **Millstone Trail**, take Millstone Road east off Kleinfeltersville

Middle Creek Lake, Middle Creek Wildlife Management Area.

Road, 0.8 mile south of the Museum Road intersection. Go 0.7 mile east to White Oak Picnic Area and the trail's start.

The hike shares its initial 200 feet with the 15-station **Braille Trail**; follow the guide rope uphill. At the double-strike peach blaze, pursue the Millstone Trail up the rock-studded forest path for a moderate ascent. Maple, beech, birch, oak, and tulip poplar weave a full overhead umbrella, with laurel, sassafras, and berry bushes amid the understory. Lichen and pebble conglomerates mark the trailbed rock. Atop the slope, a large millstone rests amid the rock rubble (0.4 mile). In bygone years, a millstone quarry occupied the crest.

Pass a scenic multi-trunked oak to reach Valley View at 0.5 mile. Peer across a slope of young trees to Middle Creek Impoundment, a smaller pond beyond, a mosaic of fields and woods, and distant ridges. A hewn-log seat welcomes pause.

From the viewpoint, turn left into woods, still pursing the peach blazes for a slow and then moderate descent on a wide trailbed. Come out at Millstone Road at 1 mile and turn right to return to White Oak Picnic Area, 1.1 miles.

For **Middle Creek Trail**, park at the dam and walk 0.1 mile south on Kleinfeltersville Road to find this blue-blazed trail as it heads west into forest via boardwalk. The yellow-blazed **Horseshoe Trail** heads uphill to its right. Tulip poplar and beech are well represented. Mayapple, fern, and hog peanut color the forest floor.

Stroll an abandoned trolley line, paralleling Middle Creek downstream. The creek flows smooth and slow but becomes more riffling downstream. A 50- to 100-foot-wide wooded buffer often separates trail from creek. Find a few tumbled trees to duck or step over. A congestion of young trees, shrubs, and wildflowers claims a utility corridor at 0.4 mile. Shortly after, private property occupies the opposite shore.

Trunks of yellow birch and a lazy creek bend at 0.8 mile add to a tour. A low bluff hosts the trail. Where a corduroy spans a drainage, look for salamanders. At 1.1 miles cross the Elders Run footbridge; it utilizes masonry from the trolley-line bridge. At the road fork at 1.25 miles, hikers may turn around; hike the **Elders Run Trail**, which heads right; or take the path straight ahead to dirt Mountain Spring Road (1.4 miles) for a shuttle-hike option.

65 Nolde Forest Environmental Education Center

OVERVIEW

At this 665-acre environmental education center (EEC), a series of trails help educators and students learn about natural habitats and develop an environmental ethic. When purchased in the early 1900s by hosiery baron Jacob Nolde, the property consisted of reverting farm fields, meadows, and brush, with a single white pine that inspired Nolde to grow a forest. Under his direction conifers were planted and the forest reborn. The center office now occupies the tudor-style Nolde Mansion and an interpretive trail explores its grounds. Admire the mansion's stonework, slate roof, stained-glass windows, turrets, and balconies.

General description:	3 hikes introduce the EEC offering.
General location:	3 miles south of Reading.
Special attractions:	Mature conifer-hardwood forests, turtle pond, mansion and sawmill, wildlife sightings.
Length:	Chestnut Trail-Middle Road Loop, 1.75-mile loop, including spur to Painted Turtle Pond; Watershed Trail, 2.2 miles round-trip; Boulevard Trail, 3 miles round-trip.
Elevation:	Chestnut Trail-Middle Road Loop, 200-foot elevation change; Watershed Trail, 400-foot elevation change; Boulevard Trail, 500-foot elevation change.
Difficulty:	All, easy to moderate.
Maps:	State Park brochure.
Special concerns:	Keep to the trails and keep pets leashed or leave them

at home. Take precautions for ticks. Park only in designated parking areas, not on roadways. No picnicking or overnight use of the park, no swimming, and no disturbing of natural features. Despite this being an EEC, trailhead and junction signs are few, so carry a park map at all times.

Season and hours: Year-round. Trails and the Sawmill and North Pond parking areas: sunrise to sunset; mansion area parking: 8 a.m. to 4 p.m. only.

For information: Nolde Forest Environmental Education Center.

Finding the trailhead: From Pennsylvania 625/New Holland Road 3 miles north of Knauers, 2 miles south of Kenhorst (a suburb of Reading), turn west on Main Entrance Road for the mansion and Chestnut Trail-Middle Road Loop. From the main entrance, go 0.8 mile north on PA 625 for Sawmill Parking Area and the start of the other two trails.

The hikes: For the **Chestnut Trail–Middle Road Loop**, look for the sunken grade of the **Chestnut Trail** heading southwest off the Main Entrance Road opposite a hydrant just prior to the entrance to Mansion Parking. Plantation forest rises to the right, a mixed conifer-hardwood forest spreads left. Cicadas sometimes lend voice to the woods. Proceed forward past the **Oak Trail** to enjoy cathedral oaks and tulip poplars and later planted spruce.

At an unmarked junction at 0.2 mile, descend left 0.1 mile to visit Painted Turtle Pond. Mats of duckweed top this tiny manmade pond. View turtles on the sunning platforms, newts, and frogs. While tranquil in appearance, road noise does carry to the site.

Return to the 0.2-mile junction (0.4 mile), and turn left to resume the Chestnut Trail. Pass **Buck Hollow Trail**, which heads left, to reach a T-junction with **Kissinger Road** (a fire road). Turn left for the chosen loop and a mild ascent. Spiny conifer snags rise amid the forest, while a crash in the treetops and litter of debris may betray a raccoon or red squirrel. Insects can reduce the maple leaves to lace.

At 0.8 mile, encounter the first junction marker at a 4-way intersection with the **Owl Trail**; keep to the fire road. In another 0.1 mile, find a picnic area and toilets at a junction of the Owl Trail and Kissinger and Middle roads. Bear right on **Middle Road**, also a fire road, to return to the mansion area. Woody grape vines entangle the woods.

Tag the tour's high point and pass in and out of conifer plantations. Again hike past the Owl Trail, remaining on the 2-track Middle Road. An orderly aisle of red pine shapes an eye-pleasing arrow-straight passage, as needles soften the lane. Descend past a water tank and massive tulip poplar.

At 1.5 miles turn left on Kissinger Road, only to take a quick right off of it. At 1.7 miles bear left, avoiding the Oak Trail, to cross the **Laurel Trail** and emerge near Mansion Parking. Turn right to close the loop (1.75 miles).

The **Watershed and Boulevard trails** share a common start at Sawmill Parking. Cross Angelica Creek either on closed **Forester Road** or ascend

Nolde Forest Environmental Education Center

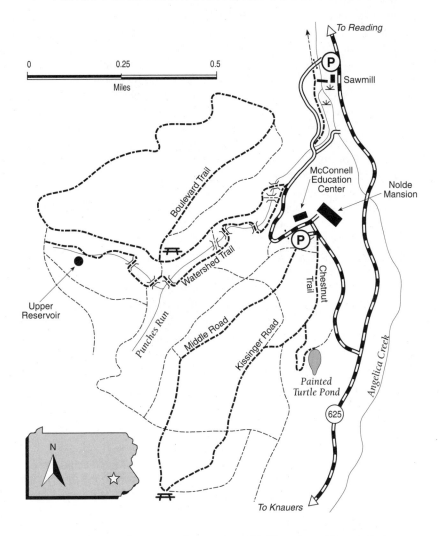

the stairs and cross by way of the sawmill diversion. Turn left (upstream). Soon Punches Run, which flows into Angelica Creek, takes the baton. Again road noise can intrude on the charm of the creekside tour. View both natural and manmade cascades.

Cross a footbridge over Punches Run and pass a teaching station to arrive at the junction of Mansion and Forester roads (0.25 mile). Bear right on **Mansion Road** (now open to hiking only) and hike upstream. Hemlocks, rhododendrons, and a variety of ferns lend to the road's atmosphere.

As the road surface changes to pavement find another teaching station and junction. Leave Mansion Road, coming to the parting of the ways (0.4 mile): Bear left on a cinder footpath for the **Watershed Trail**; to the right lies the **Boulevard Trail** (a gravel fire lane).

The Watershed Trail meanders upstream along Punches Run and its right headwater fork, crisscrossing the waterways several times on footbridges. Large beech trees, small bogs of skunk cabbage, hemlocks, and an array of colorful rainy-year mushrooms add to the tour.

At 0.75 mile, the trail meets **Cabin Hollow Road**. Bear left to cross the road bridge and resume the upstream hike along the headwater fork. To the right lies Boulevard Trail and restrooms. Hike past the concrete tank of Upper Reservoir to the **Spruce Trail**; it marks the end of the **Watershed Trail** at 1.1 miles. Retrace your steps or go exploring.

From the 0.4-mile junction, the **Boulevard Trail** travels a parallel route upstream, overlooking sparkling Punches Run and the Watershed Trail. Find an easy to moderate ascent through similar cathedral forest with big beech trees. At 0.7 mile Cabin Hollow Road arrives on the left; bear right on the Boulevard Trail, quickly coming to the loop junction with tables and toilets nearby. Go left for a clockwise tour.

The fire road again overlooks the waterway and Watershed Trail, before switchbacking up slope. At 1.1 miles, bear right as the Spruce Trail arrives on the left. Find the tour's high point amid a mature forest of tulip poplar, oak, walnut, and ash. Beyond a grove of spruce the descent increases.

At 1.8 miles, the Boulevard Trail curves right past a rock outcrop 40 paces off the trail. While the jumble of rocks extends no views, it does offer a pleasing site to surrender to the woods quiet. Close the loop at 2.25 miles and retrace the first 0.75 mile to the trailhead.

66 Mill Creek Trail

General description:	In the eastern portion of French Creek State Park, this relaxing woodland stroll only briefly meets Mill Creek, but it offers a chance to shake off the cobwebs of society and perhaps discover those in nature. It also offers hikers an opportunity to extend the tour with a visit to the historic iron-making community recreated at Hopewell Furnace National Historic Site (NHS).
General location:	15 miles southeast of Reading.
Special attractions:	Mixed woods, wildlife sightings, charcoal hearths, access to Hopewell Furnace NHS.
Length:	Mill Creek Trail, 5.8 miles round trip; Lenape Extension, 4.4 miles round trip; Self-guided Historic Site Trail, 0.75 mile round trip. Combined tour, 10.95 miles round trip.

Elevation:	Mill Creek Trail, 500-foot elevation change; Lenape Extension, 300-foot elevation change. Self-guided Historic Site Trail, less than 100-foot elevation change.
Difficulty:	Mill Creek Trail and Lenape Extension, moderate; Self-guided Historic Site Trail, easy.
Maps:	French Creek State Park map; Hopewell Furnace Official Map and Guide.
Special concerns:	When adding a visit to Hopewell Furnace National Historic Site, pay admission fee at the visitor center. Keep to the marked, color-coded trails; carry a map and water. No overnight camping, fires, or hunting within the national park; no camping within the state park, except at established campgrounds. Beware of bees.
Season and hours:	Spring through fall for hiking, daylight hours. NHS: 9 a.m. to 5 p.m. daily, except Thanksgiving, Christmas, and New Year's days.
For information:	French Creek State Park; Hopewell Furnace National Historic Site.

Finding the trailhead: From the junction of Pennsylvania Highways 10 and 23 in Morgantown (reached off Interstate 76), go east on PA 23 for 5.4 miles and turn north on PA 345. Stay on PA 345 for 4.8 miles to reach Shed Road. The trail heads east off Shed Road near the junction. Gravel roadside parking accommodates up to 20 vehicles.

The hike: Hike east off Shed Road to enter an oak woods intermixed with maple, birch, tulip poplar, and gum. Find a dual blazing: red stripe on white for the **Mill Creek Trail**; green for the **Lenape Trail**. A few azalea, fern, and chestnut saplings grow in the understory. Travel a woods road with a dirt and cobble bed for a mild ascent. At 0.3 mile, the Lenape Trail splits to the right to enter the NHS; keep to the Mill Creek Trail.

Bigger trees now punctuate the forest, as the trail edges National Park Service lands. Deer, skunk, and woodpecker may be spied. A powerline corridor briefly interrupts the woods at 0.5 mile. In this gentle terrain, the trail shows only a hint of incline before coming to the loop junction (0.9 mile).

Continue straight for a counterclockwise tour. Logs strew the forest floor, as a moderate descent follows. Mid-summer visitors may hear a parent bird noisily urging its offspring from the nest. At the insistence of squirrels, acorns rain from the oaks.

At 1.5 miles, the red-blazed **Raccoon Trail** shares the way for about 200 feet, arriving on the right and departing on the left. At 1.75 miles, bear left to avoid a spur to the **Buzzards Trail**. Again ascend amid beech trees, some marred by carvings. As the area was previously harvested to fuel the iron furnace at Hopewell, keen-eyed hikers may detect rounded clearings that betray former charcoal hearths.

The trail rolls to cross a seasonal rocky drainage. On the following ascent, discover mountain laurel. At 2.5 miles, a woods road advances the trail with a descent. At 3.1 miles, be alert as the trail angles back to the left, leaving the road. Cross picturesque Mill Creek via rocks and gravel. The clear-flowing stream engages with humped-back rocks that frame and redirect its flow. Upon crossing, bear right, cross a side drainage, and resume the woods stroll.

At 4 miles the trail swings right, as a red stripe on blue trail heads straight. Ascend to an unmarked spur that branches right to Millers Point—an outcrop knoll for admiring the forest setting. The blazed Mill Creek Trail then tops a rise to tour the broad oak-clad plateau to close the loop, 4.9 miles. Retrace the first 0.9 mile to end at 5.8 miles. Or, add the **Lenape Extension** by turning left at 5.5 miles.

The extension offers a similar woods tour on a slowly descending, wide earthen trail. The green blazes occur at a broader interval. Hike past a post indicating a charcoal hearth and gain noise from PA 345. In 0.9 mile (6.4 miles), the trail swings left to descend log-braced earthen steps past a tiny springhouse.

Beyond a footbridge lies the Y-junction with the Raccoon Trail. Follow the green and red dual blaze to the right along a wetland drainage that supports tall azalea. Cross a rotting footbridge to reach a woods road at an old picnic shelter (7 miles). Bear right to round a gate and exit onto Baptism–Hopewell Road.

Hopewell Furnace National Historic Site.

Mill Creek Trail

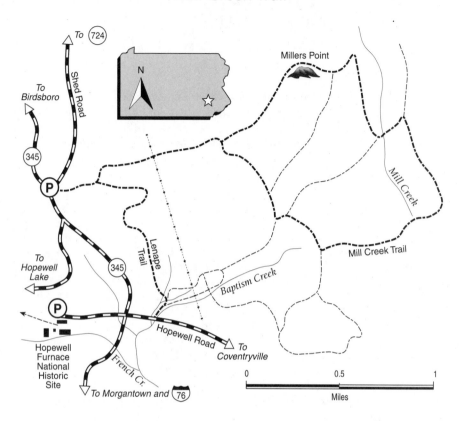

To reach the NHS, turn right, hike along the road for 0.2 mile, cross PA 345, and follow the park entrance road to Hopewell Furnace visitor center (7.7 miles). At the center, hikers may pay fees to tour the museum and walk the village streets.

A 0.75-mile self-guiding tour introduces the village; living history days bring the picturesque community to life. Discover restored structures and learn about the iron-making era. The history of the furnace dates to 1772. Return via the Lenape Trail to Shed Road Trailhead for a 10.95-mile tour.

67 Kings Gap Environmental Education Center

OVERVIEW

This 1,443-acre environmental education center (EEC) on South Mountain in Cumberland County encompasses a variety of habitats through which students and educators learn about nature. The 15 miles of trail that web the park traverse rocky ridgetop, hardwood forest, stream and pond habitats, and conifer plantation. A hilltop mansion houses the center office; its garden and grounds offer yet another microcosm to explore.

General description:	3 areas make up the EEC: the Mansion, Pond, and Plantation areas. The 7 selected hikes introduce each of the 3.
General location:	25 miles southwest of Harrisburg.
Special attractions:	Vistas, mixed forests, ant mounds, charcoal hearths, wildlife sightings.
Length:	Rock Scree-Ridge Loop, 2 miles round trip; Woodland Ecology Trail, 0.6 mile round trip; Scenic Vista Trail, 2 miles round trip; White Oak Trail, 0.3-mile loop; Watershed Trail, 2 miles round trip; Whispering Pines Interpretive Trail, 0.25-mile loop; Pine Plantation Trail, 0.6-mile loop.
Elevation:	Rock Scree-Ridge Loop, 150-foot elevation change; Woodland Ecology Trail, 50-foot elevation change; Scenic Vista Trail, 300-foot elevation change; White Oak Trail, minimal elevation change; Watershed Trail, 100-foot elevation change; Whispering Pines Interpretive Trail and Pine Plantation Trail, minimal elevation change.
Difficulty:	Rock Scree–Ridge Loop, Scenic Vista Trail, and Watershed Trail, moderate. All others, easy.
Maps:	EEC brochure (generally available at parking areas and at park office).
Special concerns:	Carry water. Beware of poison ivy and beware of poisonous snakes. Be alert along the stonework of the mansion gardens where snakes commonly seek out rodents. Keep to trails, keep pets leashed, and no collecting. Color-coded blazes and junction signs aid travelers.
Season and hours:	Year-round, 8 a.m. to sunset for trails. Office: 8 a.m. to 4 p.m. weekdays.
For information:	Kings Gap Environmental Education and Training Center.

Kings Gap Environmental Education Center

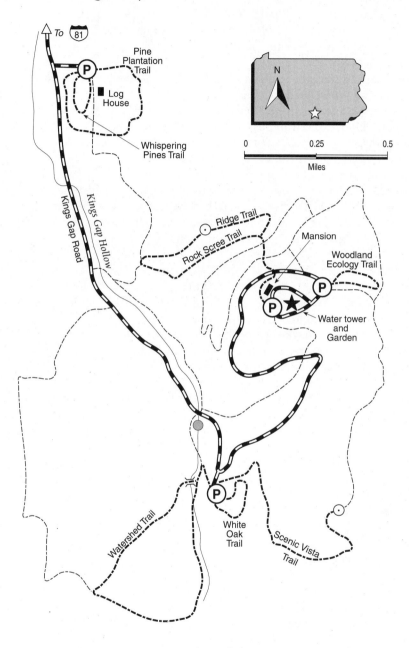

Finding the trailhead: From Interstate 81, take exit 11 and go south on PA 233 for 2.4 miles. Turn left on Pine Road, go 2.2 miles, and turn right to enter the EEC on Kings Gap Road. Find Pine Plantation Area Parking at 0.25 mile, Pond Area Parking at 2 miles, Woodland Ecology Trail Parking at 3.5 miles, and Mansion Area Parking at 3.8 miles.

The hikes: Representing the trails of the *Mansion Area* are the **Rock Scree–Ridge Loop** and **Woodland Ecology Trail**.

Start the **Rock Scree–Ridge Loop** at the Mansion Parking Area. From the information kiosk and trail post, proceed downhill. As the trail contours the slope below the mansion, turn left on the red-blazed **Rock Scree Trail**, descending log-braced steps to cross the park road at 0.1 mile.

A predominantly chestnut oak forest enfolds the trail. A few mountain laurel dot seasonal color to a tour. Pass a teaching station and twice cross the green-blazed **Forest Heritage Trail**, before reaching the loop junction at 0.4 mile. Head left, still on the Rock Scree Trail. The loop will conclude via the purple-blazed **Ridge Trail** straight ahead.

Black gum and maple now join the oaks. Enjoy tranquil strolling with filtered lighting, insect chirrs, and snaps betraying the movement of wildlife. Alongside the trail, study a logic-defying gum tree with hollow base and vibrant canopy. Where the trail travels the foot of a bouldery forest slope, take a pair of switchbacks at 0.7 mile.

White scree patches mark the uphill slope as hikers approach the 1-mile junction. Here abandon travel of the Rock Scree Trail, which continues to Pine Plantation. Instead, turn right on the Ridge Trail to ascend the ridge backbone. Tree-filtered glimpses foreshadow the scenic view to come. As the ridge gains a bouldery top, the trail briefly dips to the upper reaches of the south flank.

At 1.4 miles is the overlook where a broad gap amid the oaks presents a look north at Cumberland Valley—a patterned quilt of cropland, field, and forest, where vultures ride the thermals. Follow purple blazes away from the post to arc right for an easy descent to close the loop (1.6 miles). Retrace the first 0.4 mile.

The **Woodland Ecology Trail** (purple-blazed) starts at the parking area below the mansion just prior to the divided traffic-flow. Reach the loop junction in 100 feet; interpretive plaques introduce the natural history. Travel amid a chestnut oak, black gum, and pitch pine woods with a berry understory.

Kings Gap was repeatedly harvested to produce charcoal to fuel the Cumberland Furnace in Huntsdale (1794 to 1854). Depleted soils account for the lack of abundant vegetation. The forest's many multiple trunks owe to the trees' start from stumps. Midway, the ecology trail kisses the yellow-blazed **Maple Hollow Trail**. Enjoy a pleasant 0.6-mile woods stroll.

Three trails represent the *Pond Area* offering: **Scenic Vista Trail**, **White Oak Trail**, and the **Watershed Trail**.

Start the orange-blazed **Scenic Vista Trail** opposite the kiosk at Pond

Area Parking. Ascend amid an oak-berry woodland. Hike past a group of picnic tables and skirt the paved **White Oak Trail** for a steady contouring ascent. Gum, tulip poplar, maple, pitch pine, sassafras, and snags fill out the forest.

Pass a teaching station and at 0.2 mile, ascend a woods road to the right. The climb intensifies at 0.4 mile, but the woods provide a relaxing setting as lone-standing, twisted mountain laurels dot the terrain.

At a junction post at 0.75 mile, bear left to return to foot trail and traverse a barren circular site that has the telltale look of a charcoal hearth. The trail then rolls atop the hill to the vista (1 mile). Here an arc of three benches extends a northwestern look, with pitch pines partitioning the view. Admire the rural valley, Kings Gap Hollow, and distant Blue Mountain. Through ridge sags spy more rural landscapes. Return as you came or continue the hike to the Mansion Area.

The paved, all-ability **White Oak Trail** starts at the paved parking pad reserved for disabled visitors. Bear left at the initial junction for a clockwise tour. Both Braille and large print interpretive panels introduce basic concepts of natural history. Tour similar oak, gum, maple, and pine forest. Pass a hearth site before closing the loop (0.3 mile).

The purple-blazed **Watershed Trail** starts at the Pond Area kiosk. Follow a pebble-surfaced access trail past a teaching station to a woods road (0.1 mile). Turn left on the woods road; to the right leads to the pond.

Trees shade the passage. In 200 feet, reach the loop junction and cross a

Farmland view, Kings Gap Environmental Education Center.

footbridge over Kings Gap Hollow for a counterclockwise tour. Kings Gap Hollow is a pretty trickling stream that measures but a couple of feet wide; the summer sun can steal the stream altogether. Pass another teaching station and keep right to avoid a pair of cut-across trails that shorten the loop.

The Watershed Trail then drifts away from the hollow, passing amid an oak-pine habitat with high- and low-bush blueberry, elegant ferns, and small azalea. Where it travels the valley bottom, find more maple and gum. Colorless Indian-pipe pierces the woods floor.

At a wayside at 0.4 mile, learn about the Allegheny mound-building ants that influence the terrain ahead. These red-and-black ants can kill young trees within a 50-foot radius of their mound, but they cannot battle moss. Hike 0.2 mile past the panel to discover an active mound on the right. Most of the ones that follow have been abandoned, reclaimed by moss and pioneer plants. The mounds measure 2 to 4 feet in diameter and stand up to 18 inches high.

Where the purple blazes indicate a swing left at 0.75 mile, the **Boundary Trail** (green) branches away to the right. The Watershed Trail then rolls up and over a small rise to again turn left at 1.1 miles. A few rocks rise in the foot trail as it follows Kings Gap Hollow downstream. In places, sphagnum moss and skunk cabbage win footholds.

At 1.5 miles cross a side spring and then the main hollow stream. Keep right as a cut-across merges on the left. At 1.7 miles, proceed forward to avoid the second cut-across and a spur to the right that leads back to the parking lot. Close the loop, 1.8 miles; end the hike just shy of 2 miles.

Two trails travel the *Pine Plantation Area*: **Whispering Pines Interpretive Trail** and **Pine Plantation Trail**.

Start the paved **Whispering Pines Interpretive Trail** off the designated wheelchair-accessible parking site. Bear right at the restroom to reach the loop junction. Interpretive panels in Braille and large print introduce the area; exercise caution where panels instruct you to investigate by feel as poison ivy has a way of intruding. The plantation's uniform rows address hikers.

Along the tour, hikers learn that the 42-acre plantation was once a farm. On the old farmhouse foundation sits a relocated cabin that dates to the 1850s; walnut trees shade the lawn. Conclude the tour amid white pines and tamarack.

The **Pine Plantation Trail** (orange-blazed) swings a broader loop, exploring the same plantation; begin at the teaching station. Follow a mowed path to the right, passing amid the tamarack and pine. The trail alternately shows a cushiony bed of needles or one of vegetation. Shrub-filled breaks occur between plots. Here find wild rose, grape, brier, poison ivy, and wildflowers. The chaos of shrubs contrasts the orderly tree rows. An interlude with a doe and fawn may add to a tour. Midway, cross the red-blazed **Rock Scree Trail**. Tag the end of the Rock Scree Trail to close the loop (0.6 mile).

68 Caledonia State Park

OVERVIEW

This 1,130-acre South Mountain state park has a 12-mile system of nature, hiking, and history trails. Rediscover the era of charcoal hearths and iron furnaces, and touch a page from Civil War history. Along the East Branch Conococheague Creek, explore a wondrous rhododendron realm. The Appalachian Trail threads through the park on its 2,000-mile odyssey.

General description:	3 hikes introduce the park's natural and historical features.
General location:	40 miles southwest of Harrisburg.
Special attractions:	A superb rhododendron showcase (one of the best in the state), iron furnace, millraces, Thaddeus Stevens' blacksmith shop, mountain laurel, fall foliage.
Length:	Whispering Pine Nature Trail, 0.4-mile loop; Thaddeus Stevens Historical Trail–Charcoal Hearth Trail Loop, 3.1-mile loop; Ramble Trail, 2.6 miles round trip.
Elevation:	Whispering Pine Nature Trail, minimal elevation change; Thaddeus Stevens Historical Trail–Charcoal Hearth Trail Loop, 600-foot elevation change; Ramble Trail, 100-foot elevation change.
Difficulty:	Whispering Pine Nature Trail, easy; Thaddeus Stevens Historical Trail–Charcoal Hearth Trail Loop, moderate to strenuous; Ramble Trail, moderate.
Maps:	State park, Caledonia Trails, and Whispering Pine Nature Trail brochures; Thaddeus Stevens Historical Trail guidebook.
Special concerns:	Keep to the trails; no trail camping. In the floodplain some footbridges may be washed out.
Season and hours:	Year-round; daylight hours for hiking.
For information:	Caledonia State Park.

Finding the trailhead: The park is at the intersection of U.S. Highway 30 and Pennsylvania Highway 233. Locate the Furnace Parking Area off PA 233 at the northeast corner of the intersection. For the park office and Whispering Pine Nature Trail, go 0.1 mile north on PA 233 from U.S. 30 and turn left (west).

The hikes: Whispering Pine Nature Trail begins west of the park office and east of a large day-use parking area. Pick up an interpretive brochure at the park office. Start at the trail shelter and follow numbered posts and white blazes to tour the braided floodplain of Conococheague Creek. Enjoy an enchanting realm of big white pines, eastern hemlocks, tulip poplars, and rhododendron bushes. The brochure walks visitors through the process of tree identification. Pass a tumbled colossus, and admire the site's rhododendron, which grow 18 feet high. The radial leaves of the rhododendron dazzle year-round. Conclude the loop at 0.4 mile.

Start the other two hikes from Furnace Parking Area. A guidebook (available at the park office) introduces features of the **Thaddeus Stevens Historical Trail**; look for furnace symbols along the way.

For the **Thaddeus Stevens Historical Trail–Charcoal Hearth Trail Loop**, hike the paved path that ascends to the left of Caledonia Iron Furnace (Site 3 on the tour. Find the first two features across PA 233.) Set back in the slope of Graeffenburg Hill, the furnace was built in 1837 by Thaddeus Stevens, a prominent abolitionist. Due to Stevens' political bent, on June 26, 1863, Confederate General Jubal A. Early ordered the destruction of this furnace works community

At the end of the pavement, bear left for site 4, the former location of a waterwheel. Overlook the attractive rockwork of the millrace stream. At the footbridge is the loop junction; cross to pursue the historical trail upstream along the west levee. Hemlock, pine, oak, and gum offer shade. The highway drone is inescapable at the start.

At 0.2 mile cross back over the race to ascend a hemlock-darkened slope for a rolling, contouring hike. At 0.4 mile is a junction. Here the historical trail descends to cross PA 233 to reach the millrace reservoir (visible from the junction). For the loop, follow the yellow blazes of the **Charcoal Hearth Trail**. It remains along the foot of the slope amid hemlock forest; avoid a spur to the group camp area.

By 0.9 mile, ascend via wagon road. Where more light penetrates, discover laurel. A count down of the numbered charcoal hearths starts at site 5—a good introduction for untrained eyes. This cleared and leveled site once held a smoldering wood pile that produced charcoal to fuel the area's iron furnace. Ascend into hardwood forest and bountiful laurel. At 1.4 miles, the trail switchbacks around hearth 1.

Top Graeffenburg Hill (elevation 1,522 feet) and begin a sleepy meandering descent. Lichens adorn the tree trunks and hemlocks return to the mix. By 2.3 miles the descent steepens; beware of roots and loose gravels. Round above the millrace to close the loop at the bridge, 3 miles; descend the fragment of pavement to end in another 200 feet.

For **Ramble Trail**, hike west across PA 233 from Furnace Parking, cross a footbridge over Rocky Mountain Creek, and traverse lawn to meet a gravel lane. To the left is the Blacksmith Shop, a white-painted brick-and-stone building with a bell tower. Turn right for the yellow-blazed Ramble Trail.

The lane edges lawn and shade trees—former pastures that served as a field hospital during the Battle of Gettysburg. Pass the pool area and Trail Center log cabin. At 0.3 mile (near Pine Shelter), find the loop junction at a bridge over East Branch Conococheague Creek.

Forgo crossing, instead hike downstream along the south shore. Initially the white blazes of the **Appalachian Trail** join the yellow ones of the Ramble.

Caledonia State Park

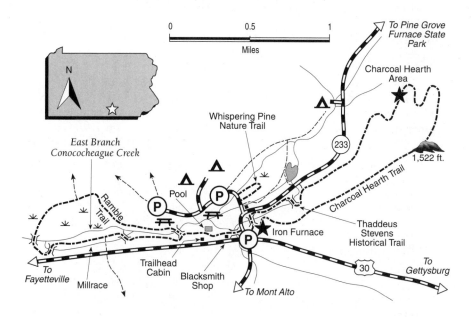

The creek flows swift with small cascades; effusive rhododendron lines its bank. The wide earthen trail likewise tours a rhododendron jungle with grand old hemlocks. Bear right at the fork at 0.4-mile as an island divides Conococheague Creek. While U.S. 30 hums above, it cannot detract from the stage.

At 0.6 mile cross a footbridge over a diversion to hike the levee of Old Rolling Mill race. Then at 0.7 mile proceed forward as the AT heads left over a millrace bridge to cross U.S. 30. As the floodplain narrows, overlook both race and creek. At 1.1 miles cross a stone bridge and view the moss-colored stone walls from the old mill complex. The tour now swings right to traverse the floodplain.

Upon meeting the first creek flow, hike upstream a few feet to reach a footbridge (1.2 miles). Cross and pass a designated carving post intended to deter vandalism of trees and property. Two more footbridges span the divided creek waters. Beyond them, hike the soggy, root-snarled floodplain. The wonderland of hemlock and rhododendron helps one dismiss the occasional misstep. Big oak, tulip poplar, and pines are other trail signatures.

Meander the floodplain to travel a wide gravel lane at 2.1 miles, still crossing side drainages to eventually gain a creek overlook. Hike past Pine Shelter and a bench-swing that overlooks Conococheague Creek at 2.3 miles. Then close the loop by crossing the bridge. Retrace the gravel road east across the park, veering off it prior to the Blacksmith Shop to cross PA 233. End at Furnace Parking, 2.6 miles.

69 Kellys Run Natural Area

OVERVIEW

In Lancaster and York counties, the Pennsylvania Power and Light Company manages 5,000 acres bordering the lower Susquehanna River/Lake Aldred shores as part of the Holtwood hydroelectric project. Within the vast conservation/recreation area, a 7.5-mile national recreation trail network explores the wilds of Kellys Run Natural Area, located on the southeast shore. Discover the scenic glen of Kellys Run, with its cliffs, cascades, and rhododendron, and overlook Lake Aldred from 500 feet above at the Pinnacle.

General description:	This hike consists of a loop tour of Kellys Run Trail and a detour along the Conestoga Trail to Pinnacle Overlook.
General location:	15 miles south of Lancaster.
Special attractions:	The scenic glen of Kellys Run, Lake Aldred overlooks, schist cliffs and overhangs, rhododendron and laurel, wildlife sightings, fall foliage.
Length:	Kellys Run Trail, 4-mile loop; Conestoga Trail to Pinnacle Overlook, 2-mile, round-trip spur.
Elevation:	Travel between 200 feet near the mouth of Kellys Run to 705 feet at Pinnacle Overlook.
Difficulty:	Strenuous.
Maps:	Kellys Run–Pinnacle Trail System map and Trails for Hiking or Walking at Lake Aldred (seasonally available at Holtwood Recreation Area).
Special concerns:	No trail camping. Be careful fording and scrambling over the slippery rocks of Kellys Run, and avoid during high water. Wear bright colors during hunting season.
Season and hours:	Spring through fall, 8 a.m. to sunset.
For information:	Pennsylvania Power and Light Company, Holtwood Land Management Office.

Finding the trailhead: From Interstate 83 at York, take exit 6E and go south on Pennsylvania 74/Queen Street. Go 21.1 miles south on PA 74 and turn east on PA 372/Holtwood Road to cross the Susquehanna River below Holtwood Dam. In 1.8 miles turn left (north) on River Road. In another 0.4 mile, turn left on Old Holtwood Road to find the entrance to Holtwood Recreation Area on the right in 0.3 mile.

The hike: Enter the woods at the foot of the grassy slope below Pavilion 1. Find a dual blaze: Blue indicates **Kellys Run Trail**; orange, the **Conestoga Trail**. The shared, wide earthen trail passes through a full woods of tulip

Kellys Run Natural Area

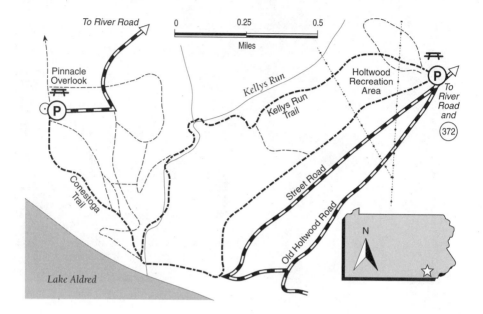

poplar, maple, sassafras, and spruce. Woody vines and poison ivy entangle the trees.

In 100 feet find the first of two junctions with the yellow-blazed **Oliver Patton Trail**; stay with the dual blue-orange blaze. Twice the trail crosses utility corridors. As it rolls to higher ground, chestnut oaks and laurels make an appearance. When Kellys Run sounds below, find early showings of rhododendron.

After crossing a small tributary meet the red-blazed **Loop Trail** (0.8 mile), and descend toward the rush of Kellys Run. Slabs of wavy-patterned schist rise up in and along the trail. Approaching the run, find mature forest and an unruly explosion of rhododendron. On a downstream tour, view the alternating riffles, sheets, and cascades as Kellys Run squeezes through pinched rock channels and forms deep pools.

An imposing overhang looms 60 feet above the trail as hikers come upon the 1st bridgeless crossing. Ford the main run and cross a nearly equal-sized side run. Near a couple of larger pools linked by cascades at 1.2 miles, a blazed fork indicates low- and high-water travel options.

Find the trail extremely rugged amid the steep-sided canyon. At 1.4 mile pass the white-blazed **Pinnacle Trail** that ascends to the right. The Kellys Run Trail then rolls back downhill to a gorgelike setting with overhangs and cliffs and exciting pinched waters. Rhododendron caps the rocks. Hemlock, maple, tulip poplar, and birch bring shade. Be careful of the canted, wet rock surfaces and loose gravel.

At 1.5 miles and 1.6 miles, blazes on the rock indicate crossings of Kellys

Kellys Run, Kellys Run Trail System.

Run. The trail then ascends to travel a narrow terrace overlooking the run's cascading plummet to the Susquehanna River. At 1.75 miles, the orange-blazed Conestoga Trail ascends north to Pinnacle Overlook via the rock steps to the right while Kellys Run Trail continues forward to an abandoned road in 100 feet for the loop's return.

Turn right to add Lake Aldred overlooks. Ascend and scramble over a rocky point. Cracks in the sharp-edged slabs provide toe-holds. At 1.9 miles ascend via an old woods road. Oak, maple, and gum now compose the ridge woods. In 0.1 mile veer left on a footpath to emerge at a pipeline clearcut with views south of Holtwood Power Plant and Norman Wood Bridge.

At a post in the pipeline corridor, again veer left on a woods path. Greenbrier sometimes snatches at passersby. The trail contours to a Virginia pine-dressed rock promontory for an open look across the reservoir. Vultures or a V of passing geese may grace the sky.

At the next outcrop set, views become more restricted.

At 2.25 miles, the orange-blazed route ascends right to meet and follow a wagon road left. Travel is shared with a yellow-blazed trail. The reservoir is now mostly a glare beyond the trees. At a wagon road junction, follow the route that curves and ascends right; avoid the wagon road to the left.

Cardinals adorn the branches as the trail emerges at a gate at the southwest corner of Pinnacle Overlook, 2.75 miles. Find open and shaded benches, tables, and a board identifying reservoir features. April through October, piped water and restrooms benefit travelers. Scan the open water of 2,400-

acre Lake Aldred, Reed and Duncan Islands (both formerly inhabited by Indians), and the canyon's low, rounded wooded ridges. In the afternoon, vultures pass at eye-level as they circle on the thermals. In September-October watch for migrating birds of prey.

Backtrack the Conestoga Trail, descending to Kellys Run Trail (3.75 miles), and turn right to complete the counterclockwise loop. Reach the abandoned road and turn left to cross its bridge over Kellys Run for a farewell view. A slow ascent follows. Tour open woods of locust, sumac, and elm. At 4.25 miles, pass under a gate and approach a city street, only to veer away left.

Round a second gate and continue the loop's return. The wide, cropped-grass trail offers carefree strolling while benches welcome hikers to pause. Wild grape and thorny vegetation thrive. After the trail flattens, look for it to turn left, passing at the edge of a field. While some blazes are masked the trail offers the only logical course of travel.

Next turn right on a sun-drenched mowed path, sometimes enlivened by turkeys. At 5.2 miles return to the viney forest, proceeding forward past the red Loop Trail. Cross a pair of powerline corridors to enter the far west end of Holtwood Recreation Area. Traverse the park to close the loop near Pavilion 1, 6 miles.

Philadelphia Region

The southeastern corner of the state, around Philadelphia, holds surprising natural wealth. Even within the metropolitan area itself, discover a prized old-growth canyon realm—Wissahickon Creek Gorge. Totally insulated from the sights and sounds of the city, this gorge would be the pride of any community. Elsewhere in the region, wetlands, fields, and thickets vary travel. When history-tracking, discover the home and grounds of John James Audubon. Or walk the towpath of the Delaware Canal, revisit Washington's crossing of the Delaware, and unravel the tale of the early industrial-commercial era.

70 Delaware Canal National Heritage Trail

General description:	The 60-mile Delaware Canal represents the most intact canal of the early and mid 19th century, with many of its operational features still in place. The parallel towpath today is recognized as a National Heritage Trail.
General location:	Along the Delaware River between Easton and Bristol.
Special attractions:	River and canal views; Washington's Crossing; historic locks, aqueducts, and lockkeeper houses; pedestrian bridge to the New Jersey shore and Delaware and Raritan Canal; historic buildings that date to the 1700s.
Length:	41.1 miles one-way, Easton to Washington's Crossing.
Elevation:	Find less than 200 feet of elevation change.
Difficulty:	Varies depending on length and allotted time.
Maps:	Delaware Canal State Park brochure.
Special concerns:	Carry sunscreen and drinking water. Find some amenities at bordering parks. Farm markets, town stores and eateries, country inns, and campgrounds ease thru-trail travel. Washington Crossing State Historic Park (SHP) is a fee site. Respect private lands that border the route.
Season and hours:	Year-round. Washington Crossing SHP Visitor Center: 9 a.m. to 5 p.m. Tuesday through Saturday; noon to 5 p.m. Sunday.
For information:	Delaware Canal State Park.

Finding the trailhead: The northern terminus is located in Easton south of the Lehigh River off Pennsylvania 611 at Hugh Moore Historical Park (site of the old Canal Museum). In Bristol, locate the canal towpath between PA 13 and Bristol Pike as it passes through Grundy Municipal Park. Washington Crossing SHP is reached off PA 32 at Taylorsville.

The hike: At Easton, cross the walkway to overlook the thick wooden gates of Lock 24 and hike the east levee south. The towpath is mowed on a weekly schedule. To the north is Lehigh Canal and additional discovery.

Interpretive panels introduce the Delaware Canal (1831 to 1932) and the lifestyle it supported. The towpath greenway traverses farmland, residential and industrial areas, and charming towns of history. Wetland sometimes claims the canal; elsewhere the water allows for canoeing. Parallel roadways provide access and some intrusion, but the natural corridor usually wins out.

Delaware Canal National Heritage Trail

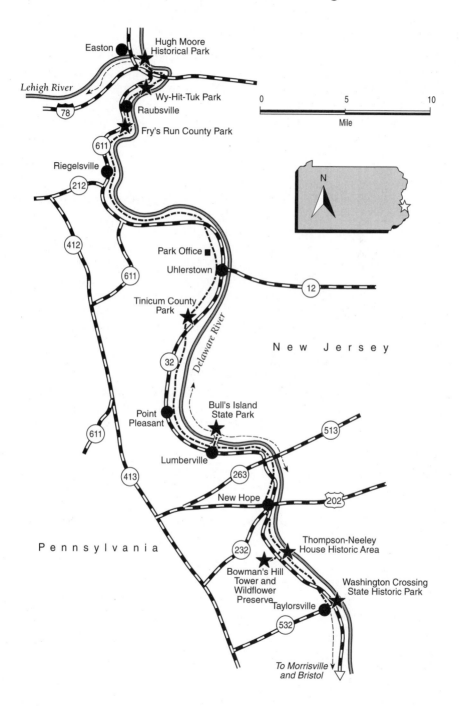

Easton

Hugh Moore Historical Park

Lehigh River

Wy-Hit-Tuk Park

Raubsville

78

Fry's Run County Park

611

Riegelsville

212

412

611

Park Office

Uhlerstown

12

Tinicum County Park

32

Delaware River

New Jersey

Point Pleasant

Bull's Island State Park

513

611

Lumberville

263

413

New Hope

202

Pennsylvania

232

Thompson-Neeley House Historic Area

Bowman's Hill Tower and Wildflower Preserve

Taylorsville

Washington Crossing State Historic Park

532

To Morrisville and Bristol

N

0   5   10
Mile

While tracking the canal's history, hikers also discover the beauty of the Delaware River without ever manning an oar.

Night-heron and kingfisher lend to waterway views while sycamore, maple, cottonwood, box elder, ash, elm, and locust bring shade to the levee. Poison ivy appears now and then.

Gradually PA 611 drifts away from the canal and towpath. At 2.2 miles footbridges span the canal to Wy-Hit-Tuck County Park, with its tree-shaded lawns, tables, restrooms, and a 5-site canoe camp. When crossing to the county park, heed the no pets rule.

The canal's cloudy water reflects the leafy shore. Additional panels introduce the role of the canal in the transport of coal to the Eastern Seaboard. Muskrat, rabbit, and hummingbird grow the list of wildlife sightings. At 4 miles, more bridges span the canal. With no roadside parking along PA 611, these bridges serve local access only.

The towpath continues to offer views of the broad Delaware River. Before long, spy a toothed-gear raised gate and spillway. As the tour loses its tree border to the west, roads and communities become a part of the tour.

At 5.2 miles travel through Raubsville, with much of the town situated between the canal and river. Hikers pass at the back doors of private residences; keep to the trail. From the town, pass Locks 22 and 23, a lockkeeper's house, and a west bank picnic area—part of the Theodore Roosevelt Recreation and Conservation Area.

The canal footbridge at 6.8 miles accesses Fry's Run County Park. It also offers a look at Kleinhan's Aqueduct 10; although rebuilt, it has the original rockwork bottom. The open corridor ahead offers 0.5 mile of unobstructed river views. Farmfields and woodlands obscure PA 611.

At Riegelsville (8.6 miles) discover canal-era inns and eateries still in operation. Where the towpath passes under the Delaware Road bridge, hikers may venture into town. Again the trail parallels PA 611 and river views depart. At Lock 21 (9.7 miles), a sportsman's access and launch offers the next shuttle opportunity.

Farm country travel follows. While picturesque, the openness of the trail can make for hot travel. Where the towpath next crosses under a road bridge, a farm market invites hikers aside with tastes of the season. Farther south an attractive stone house and stone-and-frame barn greet travelers. PA 32 now parallels the canalway.

Where the trail journeys past Indian Rock Inn (13.1 miles), study the cliff for the image of an Indian head. South of intermittent Falls Creek, the towpath and PA 32 cross. At Upper Black Eddy (15.9 miles), find the trail distanced from the highway and river. Black Eddy was a popular fishing spot for President Grover Cleveland. Past the state park office, enjoy a more isolated section of travel. At Uhlerstown (19 miles), view a 1832-built covered bridge, Lock 18, and well-kept private structures recalling the era.

At 21.2 miles, take a midway break where the towpath travels the western edge of Tinicum Buck County Park. Find shaded picnic tables, toilets, and a campground just a few strides from the trail. To get water, hike east

Lock, Delaware Canal State Park.

into the park. The restored Erwin Stover House and a classic bank barn may draw travelers 0.3 mile aside to see them.

Again find the river and canal paired where Marshall Island divides the river flow. During low water, spy stepped rocks that shape the river's Tumble Falls. Enjoy partial shade and discover more remnants from the canal's past. Historic homes at the village of Point Pleasant (26.1 miles) add to the charm of the tour. Next pass Lock 13, with its heavy hinged gates, crank box, and stonework.

In Lumberville (28 miles), find access to a general store and pedestrian bridge over the Delaware River. At Lock 12, depart the canal to travel the 0.25-mile river span to Bull's Island New Jersey State Park, where camping is available.

Forgoing the detour, remain on the towpath as it traverses agricultural land. Communities, most of them scenic and historic, appear with regularity. At New Hope, the canalway and PA 32 again cross, and hikers may encounter mule-pulled barges; locate the barge concession at the south end of town.

At 37.1 miles, enter the Bowman's Hill Section of Washington Crossing SHP. By crossing the bridges and hiking west, visit the 18th-century Thompson-Neeley homesite, where tours are given. Bowman's Hill rises to the west; from it, Washington's men monitored the British troop movements.

As the towpath proceeds south through the park, discover an arc of rocks and a flag toward the river—the nation's first unknown soldiers plot. It honors the soldiers who died December 25, 1776. Ringing the flag are 13 polished stones representing the 13 colonies.

Southbound the route again crosses PA 32 at Jericho Creek, which marks the northeast corner of William Penn's land purchase of July 1682. The national heritage trail then edges the field above the David Library of the American Revolution to emerge at PA 532 at Taylorsville.

Hike the road east to the McConkey's Ferry Area of Washington Crossing SHP (41.1 miles). There find a visitor center, historical tours and artifacts, and a monument commemorating Washington's crossing of the Delaware River, on Christmas night 1776. For thru-trail hikers, this area signals an ideal ending as the national heritage trail grows increasingly industrial with few amenities.

71 Tohickon Valley Trail

General description:	This hike tours the north canyon wall of Tohickon Creek, passing through Tohickon Valley Park and the High Rocks Area of Ralph Stover State Park. Find overviews and limited access to bending Tohickon Creek—host for the tour.
General location:	25 miles northeast of Philadelphia.
Special attractions:	Tohickon Creek overlooks and access, High Rocks cliffs and viewpoints, wildlife sightings, forest wildflowers, fall foliage.
Length:	7.3 miles round trip, with opportunity to shorten.
Elevation:	Find a 200-foot elevation change.
Difficulty:	Moderate.
Maps:	Ralph Stover State Park brochure.
Special concerns:	Keep back from the High Rocks rim. No trail camping.
Season and hours:	Spring through fall. Tohickon Valley Park and High Rocks Area both close at sunset.
For information:	Buck County Department of Parks and Recreation; Ralph Stover State Park.

Finding the trailhead: From Point Pleasant, cross the Tohickon Creek bridge and go north on Pennsylvania 32. In 0.1 mile, bear left on Cafferty Hill Road and continue 1.1 miles to Tohickon Valley (Buck County) Park on the left. Go 0.1 mile farther for Deer Wood Campground. Both offer trail access.

The hike: When starting from Tohickon Valley Park, hike the paved road to Doe Run Cabins; it lies to the right of the main parking area. Descend 0.2 mile to where the cabin road bends left and step over a cable barrier on the right to ascend a gravel trail. Dogwood, hickory, maple, tulip, oak, and ash weave the overhead cathedral. Downhill hear the rush of Tohickon Creek, uphill view a stone wall.

At 0.3 mile bear left for this upstream tour, now following a red circle on white blaze. To the right lies Deer Wood Campground (Campers, locate the cable-barred trail off the entrance road as you arrive at the campground.)

The trail skirts the campground plateau, passing a rusted auto frame. Virginia creeper and poison ivy scale the tree trunks. View the shimmery ribbon of Tohickon Creek and discover challenging side trails that plunge to its shore. After the ascent resumes, look for the blazed route to angle right at 0.7 mile; a well-traveled but unmarked trail proceeds forward.

Stay the blazed trail to round the head of a rocky, intermittent drainage, still contouring the upper reaches of the slope. At the next drainage, gain a better perspective on the steep-walled canyon. Dark rocks jut from the lower slope. Their tilt seemingly defies gravity.

Along the rim, pass through a breach in a scenic stone wall. Mayapple, jack-in-the-pulpit, and geranium lend seasonal color. As the blazed trail descends a slight ridge at 1.4 miles, the unmarked trail returns on the left. Proceed forward for more rolling rim travel. Hemlocks enrich shade.

Across the small drainage at 2 miles, enter the High Rocks Area and temporarily lose blazes. Secondary paths descend to the rocks, but avoid the rocks unless you are a credentialed climber. A wire-mesh fence lines the cliff rim. At 2.2 miles, arrive at the first of the named vistas—Doan's Overlook. From here, view a horseshoe bend on Tohickon Creek and win a cliff perspective.

Cedars amid the rock herald Cedar Overlook, which is next. At an unnamed vista feel your heartbeat quicken as you overlook a plummeting red cliff. At 2.3 miles reach Balcony Overlook for more ledge and overhang views. Deep in the wooded canyon sparkles tea-colored Tohickon Creek. Argillite Overlook (2.4 miles) marks the final named view. It also signals a likely turnaround spot to shorten the hike.

For the full tour, remain along the rim, ignoring the spur at 2.5 miles that branches right to Tory Road Parking—a popular access for climbers and mountain bikers. Maintain the same travel line. A fence still deters hikers from the jutting rock. Before long, white blazes guide the way through mixed woods to paved Stover Park Road (2.8 miles).

Cross the road and re-enter woods, coming to a trail fork: The path to the right travels the rim of the north canyon slope while the path to the left descends to Tohickon Creek. Together they offer loop travel, but neither is blazed.

Tohickon Creek, Tohickon Park.

Tohickon Valley Trail

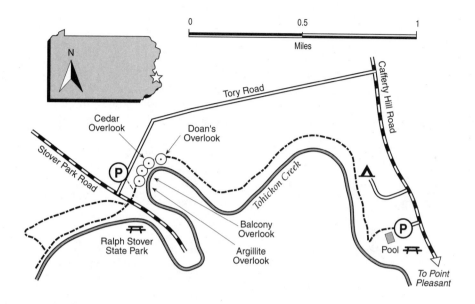

Travel the tree-shaded rim, continuing the upstream journey. A steep slope drops away to the creek. Off to the right view a cedar woods. The primary trail hugs the rim; avoid secondary paths that branch away. Cross a seasonally dry drainage and the upper end of a rock wall to enter a meadow.

Now pass between wooded slope and meadow rise. The chest-deep grasses and wildflowers often host bluebird and seclude deer. The rock wall at 3.5 miles marks a junction. Descend left, crossing the wall, to reach the creek trail (3.7 miles). To the left lies the close of the loop. Detour right 0.1 mile to enjoy a sycamore-shaded gravel bar on the creek. Night creatures harvest shellfish at the bar; by day insects enliven the canopy.

Resume the loop at 3.9 miles, traveling the wooded creek flat downstream; beware of poison ivy. Beech, ash, and dogwood join maple and oak; worms churn the soil. The trail narrows as it passes through a small meadow to contour the foot of the wooded slope. Overlook Tohickon Creek—attractive, riffling, and often channeling a welcomed breeze. Pass a fragment of rock wall at a drainage and angle uphill away from the creek. Close the loop at 4.5 miles and retrace the hike's first 2.8 miles.

72 Mill Grove–Audubon Wildlife Sanctuary

OVERVIEW

At this Montgomery County historic site, visit Mill Grove the first American home of John James Audubon (1803 to 1806) and stroll the varied habitats of its 175-acre grounds. Despite the intrusive sights and sounds of urban society, this nature sanctuary captures the aura of a bygone era. The ivy-clad fieldstone farmhouse (now a museum) sits on a rise above Perkiomen Creek; fields and woods sprawl from its doorstep, hosting a surprising variety of wildlife. Indoors discover the artwork of Audubon and a mural-tribute to Audubon by George M. Harding. Outdoors discover the terrain and habitat that inspired young Audubon in his nature pursuits and devotion to wildlife art.

General description:	A series of short, color-coded nature trails explore the grounds of Mill Grove, a National Historic Landmark. Two hikes present much of the area and its history.
General location:	15 miles northwest of the heart of Philadelphia.
Special attractions:	Mill Grove—home to John James Audubon, built in 1762 and site of an early-day grist mill, lumber mill, and lead mine; Audubon's works, including the double-elephant folio *The Birds of America* (1826-1839); mixed woods; wildflower fields; some 175 species of bird; Perkiomen Creek.
Length:	Wildflower and Lucy trails Hike, 1.7 miles round trip; Audubon and Coppermine trails Hike, 1.3 miles round trip.
Elevation:	Find a maximum 100-foot elevation change.
Difficulty:	Both hikes, easy to moderate.
Maps:	The Audubon Wildlife Sanctuary Trail Map (available at kiosk).
Special concerns:	Keep to the trails. No pets, no collecting or disturbing of natural features, no picnicking, and no bicycles. While the trails are short, a confusion of junctions confront travelers; carry a map to sort out options. Watch for poison ivy and beware of drainage dips and burrows.
Season and hours:	Year-round. Mill Grove Museum: 10 a.m. to 4 p.m., Tuesday through Saturday; 1 p.m. to 4 p.m. on Sunday. Grounds: 7 a.m. to dusk, Tuesday through Sunday. The entire site is closed on Mondays; on Thanksgiving, Christmas, New Year's, and Easter days; and on July 4.
For information:	Mill Grove–Audubon Wildlife Sanctuary.

Mill Grove–Audubon Wildlife Sanctuary

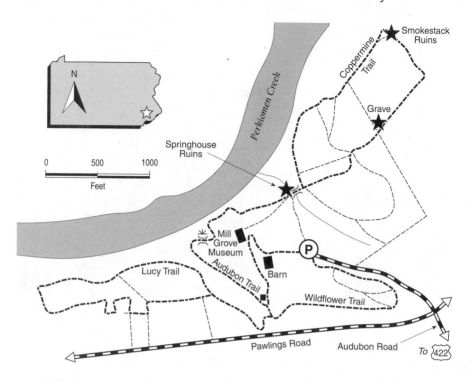

Finding the trailhead: From U.S. Highway 422 in Audubon (north of the Schuylkill River bridge), take the Pennsylvania 363 exit, go north for 0.3 mile, and turn left (west) on Audubon Road. Follow Audubon Road for 1.1 miles and cross Pawlings Road to reach the entrance of Mill Grove. Find parking in another 0.4 mile.

The hikes: For the **Wildflower and Lucy trails Hike**, pass through the wooden gates to the left of the information kiosk. In a few strides, bear left past the chemical toilets to travel at the edge of a lawn for a horseshoe-shaped tour of the **Wildflower Trail** (red blazes). Rabbits and woodchucks scurry about in morning.

In 150 feet find a travel option: Either hike the outer trail alongside the hedge and mature shade trees of Mill Grove's entryway, staying left at all junctions. Or, travel a passage amid the tanglewood of box elder, sycamore, walnut, and wild grape. Where the interior trail forks, take either path and bear right upon meeting the outer red trail.

Where the paths come together, find an unruly wildflower field to the left, a tangle of grape, rose, dogwood, and sumac to the right. Songbirds enliven both field and woods. At 0.4 mile, end the Wildflower Trail at a road to a cottage.

Garter snake, Mill Grove–Audubon Wildlife Sanctuary.

To add a tour of the **Lucy Trail** (white blazes), cross the paved lane and ascend the steps to travel a deep woods of elm, oak, birch, cherry, box elder, and tulip poplar. Jack-in-the-pulpit and vines contribute interest, as do accents of dogwood and sassafras.

The Lucy Trail is a network of loop options and dead-end spurs. Find the first junction in 0.2 mile (0.6 mile on the combined tour) and proceed forward on a lane with ankle-deep vegetation. At 0.7 mile, turn right for the long loop. Then at 0.9 mile, bear left to continue the loop; the spur straight ahead quickly ends at an old beech tree, 3 feet in diameter.

At a field, again bear left for the loop. Shoulder- to head-high wildflowers draw attention as hikers follow a mowed path at the edge of the woods. At the 4-way junction ahead, turn left for a tanglewood passage to the next field. On arrival at that field, go left, only to bear right in a few strides to follow a wide mowed swath at the field's edge.

At 1.25 miles, turn left into woods to close the loop (1.3 miles). Turn right to return to the paved lane near the cottage at 1.5 miles. For the most direct return, hike toward the cottage and bear right at the road fork. The lane comes out at the museum/parking area, 1.7 miles.

For the **Audubon and Coppermine trails Hike**, pass through the gate to hike the paved lane toward the fieldstone house (museum) and scenic stone barn. This is the **Audubon Trail** (yellow blazes).

Bear left to round below the barn recessed in the hill and hike past a couple of massive old sycamores. An attractive rail fence lines the walk, adding to the charm of the tour. While the present-day site has the look of a country gentleman's estate, when Audubon stayed here it was a working farm with a lead mine.

At 0.2 mile, arrive at the cottage and road junction. Bear right to hike a private lane past the cottage. Jewelweed and joe-pyeweed grow amid the slope tangle. At 0.3 mile turn right and descend toward a small pond and Perkiomen Creek where it is broadened by a dam. Bear right to cross an arched stone bridge. Cattails overtake the tiny manmade pond. Eyes trace the long sweep of the lawn uphill to the stately manor. Now travel the edge of the lawn, overlooking Perkiomen Creek.

The quiet, cloudy water serves up crisp reflections. Silver maple, sycamore, and pinoak grow along its banks. Watch for herons or a passing flock of geese. Butterflies decorate the estate grounds.

Hike past a set of stairs descending to the creek and bear left prior to the stone bank of the terraced lawn. The stone wall/bank was a device to deter animals from browsing on the manor garden and lawn. Up to this point, navigation of the estate has been primarily between features and not blazes.

A blazed woods lane now advances travel. Proceed forward as a pair of spurs branch right to the museum and parking lot, respectively. At 0.5 mile, a bench seat overlooks the roofless, deep stone springhouse recessed in the slope.

At the bridge is a 4-way junction. Go left for the Audubon Trail and proceed forward at the yellow-blazed fork in just a few paces. Hemlocks now rise amid the hardwoods. Gain filtered looks at Perkiomen Creek and hike up the hill. Steps advance the ascent to the rim; avoid trails branching right.

Keep to the rim, with the blue blazes of the **Coppermine Trail** replacing the yellow ones of the Audubon Trail at 0.7 mile. In 200 feet bear left, overlooking the steep wooded slope to the creek, and pass a cluster of beech trees marred by initials. Ignore a path that descends to the creek. At 0.8 mile, either blue fork will serve travelers as they again meet at the stone smokestack from the old copper smelter. Hints of the mine are lost to nature. Copper was discovered here in 1830, long after Audubon had quit the property.

Follow the blue trail as it rounds past the stack to tour a wide woods lane. At a T-junction, stay right; to the left lies a gate leaving the sanctuary. A few brambles bow into the lane. A harmless snake, the rare noisy arrival of cicadas, or squirrels leaping through the canopy may divert attention. At 1 mile, a rail fence encloses the unmarked grave of a miner along with a picturesque shade tree. Proceed forward at each of the next three junctions for the simplest return. By the end, yellow will again be the guiding color.

Find a pleasant woods stroll coming to a T-junction (1.2 miles); go left to reach the bridge and springhouse. Retrace the tour to the parking lot and museum spurs. Turn left on the first spur to end at the parking lot, 1.3 miles.

73 Pennypack Wilderness

OVERVIEW

Pennypack Wilderness is a nonprofit trust project consisting of an expanding natural area for protecting and restoring habitat throughout the central Pennypack Creek watershed. The preserve's fields, forests, and streams represent a vestige of what was. Management's effort to return the land to its native plant species represents what can be. The specialness of the area and its mission to be wild won it recognition as a national urban wildlife sanctuary. A network of short trails explores the site.

General description:	A perimeter circuit introduces the habitats at Pennypack Center and serves as a launch pad to the other named trails. A hike/bike trail traverses the wilderness along Pennypack Creek.
General location:	In Huntingdon Valley, 15 miles northeast of Philadelphia.
Special attractions:	Bird watching, with 150 bird species identified within the wilderness; pretty Pennypack Creek and its historic bridges; wetlands; wildflowers; fall foliage.
Length:	Perimeter Loop, 0.7-mile loop; Hike/Bike Trail, 3-miles one-way. (Both consist of several named trails.)
Elevation:	Trails show minimal elevation change.
Difficulty:	Both, easy.
Maps:	Pennypack Trails Map (available at center).
Special concerns:	No pets or bicycles are allowed within Pennypack Center. However, they are permitted on the Hike/Bike Trail; keep pets leashed. Practice wilderness ethics: keep to the trails, leave no trace, and do not disturb plants or animals. Beware of ticks.
Season and hours:	Year-round, 9 a.m. to 5 p.m. Monday through Friday; 10 a.m. to 3 p.m. Saturday; and 1 p.m. to 5 p.m. Sunday.
For information:	Pennypack Ecological Restoration Trust.

Finding the trailhead: From Interstate 276 in the north metro area, take exit 27 (Willow Grove) and go south on Pennsylvania 611 for 1.9 miles. Turn east on PA 63/Moreland Road, go 0.6 mile, and turn left on Edge Hill Road. Stay on it, crossing Terwood Road, to reach the center in 1.3 miles.

The hikes: The **Perimeter Loop** travels 3 adjoining trails. Clockwise, they are: Wood's Edge, Pond, and Crabapple Meadow. From the junction post at the northwest corner of visitor parking, follow the **Wood's Edge Trail** parallel to Edge Hill Road; the **Evergreen Trail** branches right. Young planted

Pennypack Wilderness

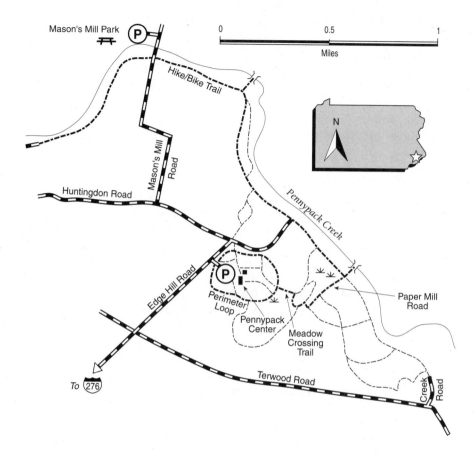

pine and mixed hardwoods frame the cushiony woods lane. Dogwood, sassafras, ash, maple, gum, and oak fashion an intriguing mosaic, especially pretty in fall. Poison ivy abounds.

At the 4-way junction in 0.1 mile, cedar-lined **Old Lane** heads right; the **Mitchell Trail** heads left across Huntingdon Road to Pennypack Creek and the **Hike/Bike Trail**; and the Perimeter Loop proceeds forward. Insects enliven the canopy, challenging the occasional plane roar. Beyond the **Dogwood Trail**, continue to skirt woods that grow the roster of tree species. Where the trail travels along a tangled hedgerow, scan field, woods, and wooded rise.

Reach a bench seat at the **Meadow Crossing Trail** junction (0.3 mile). This mowed path heads left to meet both the **Rosebush and Paper Mill Road trails** that, in turn, access the **Hike/Bike Trail**. From the bench, view woods, vine thicket, and open fields. Chance sightings include rabbit, fox, butterfly, a Cooper's hawk, and Baltimore oriole.

Bear right to continue the loop via the **Pond Trail**. Pass the **Goldenrod Trail** in a matter of strides. The next right leads to the Visitor Center; keep left for the Perimeter Loop, soon coming to the center's willow-ringed, duck-weed-colored pond. The adjacent experimental wetland is designed to cleanse the pond's waters. Skirt a springhouse and pass an unmarked trail on the left. This unmarked trail threads through the newly acquired Raytharn Farm, a 160-acre preserve for meadow-nesting songbirds. On the farm trail discover two spectacular vistas before meeting the south end of the Hike/Bike Trail.

Amid conifers, the **Pine Straw Trail** to the Visitor Center heads right as **Crabapple Meadow Trail** takes charge of the Perimeter Loop. Deer or wild turkey surprise as the trail edges shoulder-high vegetation and grape-tangled woods. A few crabapple trees support the trail's name. Close the loop near the entrance gate, 0.7 mile.

With virtually no public parking at the terminus streets to the **Hike/Bike Trail**, access it via the **Mitchell or Meadow Crossing trails** from **Perimeter Loop** or from Mason's Mill Park (Follow Edge Hill Road north past the entrance to Pennypack Wilderness, turn left on Huntingdon Road, and then right on Mason's Mill Road. Cross the bridge over Pennypack Creek to reach this neighborhood park on the left). Three trails also make up the linear route: **Creek Road**, **Pennypack Creek Trail**, and **Pennypack Parkway**.

For this hike, follow the Perimeter Loop clockwise for 0.3 mile and turn left on Meadow Crossing Trail—a wide mowed swath that divides 2 meadows. Pass into Overlook Woods to reach a trail junction: The path to the right leads to **Paper Mill Road**; left is the **Rosebush Trail**. Either path leads to the Hike/Bike Trail. From the junction, secure a view of an area replanted with native trees, shrubs, and fern.

For this tour, turn right, soon reaching Paper Mill Road (open to foot traffic only), and turn left to descend to the creek. Hike past the **Management Trail**, which journeys right exploring an oak-beech woods, and meet the Hike/Bike Trail at the abandoned, partially paved Creek Road at 0.6 mile.

Here hikers may opt for a 0.5-mile walk downstream or 2.5-mile hike upstream. Both extend tranquil, mostly shaded tours, with views of the bending 20-foot-wide Pennypack Creek. They also offer options to vary the return. Cross over the bikeway to view Pennypack Creek and its floodplain from a restored 1817-built stone bridge. A duck or kingfisher may animate the scene. Sycamores dress the shore.

For the long tour, hike upstream (a left upon first meeting the Hike/Bike Trail; a right upon returning from the bridge). Frogs sound from a wildlife pond and wetland to the hiker's left. Where the Hike/Bike Trail next overlooks the creek, the Rosebush Trail arrives on the left.

At 1.1 miles (mileage includes 0.6 mile from trailhead), round a gate to skirt an area of large stone residences; respect private property. Follow the roadway that hugs the creek upstream to re-enter the wilderness at the next

Forest trail, Pennypack Wilderness Park.

gate (1.25 miles). Tulip poplar, beech, gum, maple, dogwood, and rhododendron clad the abutting slope.

The Mitchell Trail arrives on the left at 1.3 miles; keep to the Hike/Bike Trail (Creek Road). Skunk cabbages dot the creekside woods. Spurs to the right access **Webb Walk**—a short side loop that passes closer to Pennypack Creek. Big sycamores add to travel near a private church property (1.5 miles).

Look for the footpath of Pennypack Creek Trail to veer left, just prior to the 2nd historic stone bridge (circa 1840). Hikers may wish to detour onto the bridge for a creek view as the trail now pulls away from Pennypack Creek. On the foot trail, tour wild meadow, a vine tangle, and mixed woods to Mason's Mill Road (2.2 miles).

Cross the road and round the gate to resume the upstream tour on Pennypack Parkway, a quiet gravel lane. Travel amid a cathedral woods of ash, maple, beech, oak, and tulip poplar. After a long absence, Pennypack Creek bends back toward the trail (2.8 miles). Small drainages thread the woods, bringing with them jewelweed and skunk cabbage. Impressive big-diameter trees grace the area, with beech trees favoring shore. At 3.1 miles, a gate signals the end of the creek tour. Retrace steps for a 6.2-mile round trip.

74 Wissahickon Creek Gorge, Fairmount Park

OVERVIEW

In northwestern Philadelphia, 8,700-acre Fairmount Park enfolds the spectacular setting and outdoor recreation along 7 miles of Wissahickon Creek Gorge. Despite its city location, the park is a remarkable island—wild and free from the intrusion of city skylines and traffic sounds. Cathedral forest, broad-flowing Wissahickon Creek, scenic outcrops, historic stone bridges, ruins that date to the 1700s, and a battle site from the American Revolution contribute interest to touring. Hikers, cyclists, joggers, and equestrians explore an exciting network of trails.

General description:	Forbidden Road (closed to vehicles) and an interlocking network of color-coded trails invite a variety of round-trip, shuttle, and loop tours. The featured 2 loops utilize Forbidden Road and the Orange Trail, touring the banks of Wissahickon Creek.
General location:	In northwestern Philadelphia amid the neighborhoods of Chestnut Hill, Mount Airy, Germantown, East Falls, Roxborough, Manayunk, and Lafayette Hill.
Special attractions:	Ancient hardwood forest, Wissahickon Creek and its side drainages, rhododendron and wildflowers, fall foliage, wilderness solitude.
Length:	Southern Loop, 5.7-mile loop, including a round-trip spur to Germantown Battle Site; Northern Loop, 5.5-mile loop, including a round-trip spur to the Tree House Visitor Center and Andorra Nature Center.
Elevation:	The trails show only a 100-foot elevation change.
Difficulty:	Both, moderate (Forbidden Road portions, easy).
Maps:	Map of the Wissahickon Valley, for purchase at the Tree House or at book, bike, and outdoor stores in park vicinity.
Special concerns:	No swimming, camping, or alcohol. Keep pets leashed; beware of poison ivy off the trail. Cyclists and joggers must yield to pedestrians; all must yield to horseback riders. Forbidden Road is regularly patrolled. Find toilet facilities at Valley Green and Andorra Nature Center. Mileage posts along Forbidden Road mark off 0.5-mile increments.
Season and hours:	Year-round, daylight hours.
For information:	Fairmount Park Commission.

Wissahickon Creek Gorge, Fairmount Park

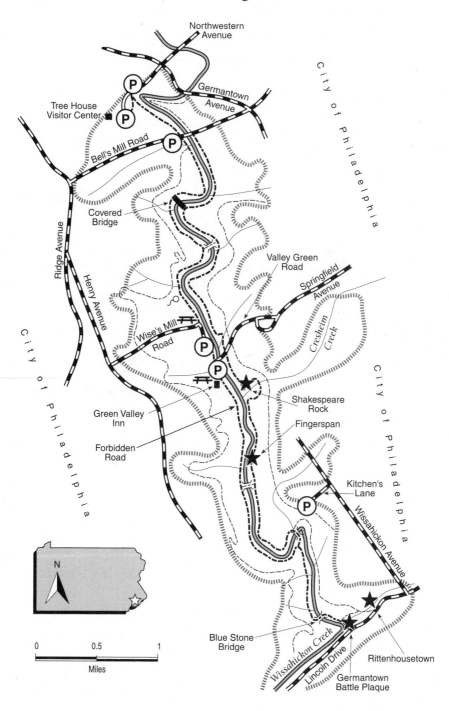

Finding the trailhead: Germantown Road parallels the park's eastern border; Henry Avenue the western border. Find primary trail parking at Valley Green: From Germantown Road in Chestnut Hill, go west on Springfield Avenue and Valley Green Road. From Henry Avenue in Roxborough, go east on Wise's Mill Road. Also find sizable parking areas off Bell's Mill Road and Northwestern Avenue, both to the north, and at Kitchen's Lane to the southeast.

The hike: Start both hikes at the Valley Green Trailhead. For the **Southern Loop**, pick up the **Orange Trail** at the Valley Green Road bridge and turn south to hike the east bank downstream. Pigeons and ducks animate air and water while a kingfisher brings a wilder note to the scene. Shading the canyon are maple, locust, box elder, and birch, along with massive beech and tulip poplar, witch-hazel, and the occasional rhododendron.

The wide, rolling foot trail contours the lower canyon slope, fluctuating between 15 and 50 feet above Wissahickon Creek. Graffiti mars the stage at 0.4 mile near Shakespeare Rock, so named for a plaque bearing a quote from *Two Gentlemen of Verona*; otherwise, the natural merit of the tour is 1st-rate. Framed by folded metamorphic rock, neighboring Devils Pool is an engaging dark shimmery basin fed by an attractive cascade.

Pass beneath an abandoned stone arch bridge well overhead and descend to cross Cresheim Creek via rocks. On the opposite shore bear right, cross back under the stone arch bridge, and resume downstream travel along Wissahickon Creek. Pass the three-story stone house of the Valley Green Canoe Club and a small dam washed by a 3-foot cascade. Cross a dead-end street and ascend steps. Here spy an old stonework wall that recalls a structure from early-day Philadelphia. Small sandy beaches or rocky overlooks may call hikers to shore.

The "Fingerspan" next marks off travel. Nearly 60 feet long with an arched roof 9 feet high, this metal grate walkway spans a steep slope and skirts cliff. Still the mature forest engages. At 1.3 miles hike past the **Green Trail**, which crosses a double-arch stone bridge to **Forbidden Road** for a chance to shorten the loop. At the trail junction, Wissahickon Creek measures 100 feet across and is shadowed by big sycamores.

Continue downstream along the east shore. Outcrops can shape the slope and prescribe travel. Along the creek at 2 miles, find a monument denoting a 1723 baptismal site. Cross a picturesque side creek and at 2.1 miles cross to the west shore of Wissahickon Creek and Forbidden Road. The Orange Trail continues south but requires road travel to make a loop.

Upon crossing, a side trip south (left) on Forbidden Road leads to 1896-built Blue Stone Bridge in 0.6 mile and the plaque denoting the 1777 Germantown Battle site in 0.9 mile. From the battle site, hikers may extend this side trip into history by taking the path journeying east to Rittenhousetown. Established in 1690, Rittenhousetown was the site of the first paper mill in the United States. The earliest building on the grounds dates to 1707.

Wissahickon Creek, Fairmont Park.

Opting for a 1.8-mile, round-trip visit to the Germantown Battle plaque, resume the loop at 3.9 miles. The gravel lane of Forbidden Road travels the west bank for a new perspective on canyon and creek. Forbidden Road itself dates back to 1823.

Ascend past an old lookout shelter, keeping to Forbidden Road. A rail fence and attractive stonework add to the tour's charm, as do many big trees. Spy another ruins recessed in the hillside. At Valley Green, pass a historic inn that still serves lunches and dinner to close the loop at 5.7 miles.

For the **Northern Loop** from Valley Green Inn, follow **Forbidden Road** north (upstream) along the west bank. Hikers share the way with cyclists and joggers. For a brief stretch, travel the access road to Valley Green's Westside Parking. Carefree travel resumes at 0.2 mile.

Stroll past a creek flat with tables, benches, and a fitness trail. Forest tranquility envelopes the hike while a small dam launches a 5-foot cascade across the breadth of the creek. Wissahickon Creek Gorge boasts some of the finest big tulip poplars in the state. A night heron may preside along shore or cardinals adorn a branch. Benches suggest a pause to take in the scenery.

At the foot of an eroded rock slope at 0.6 mile, pass a public spring that was dedicated in 1854. After the arrival of a stepped side-creek at 0.8 mile, more sunlight rains through the leafy cathedral. Come upon a shelter above the creek and the first bridge link to the **Orange Trail** for shortening the tour; keep to Forbidden Road.

At 1.3 miles, view a restored 1737 covered bridge with solid sides and picket-cut entry eaves. Again, keep to the west shore. A parklike greenway separates trail and creek, and enormous sycamores draw attention.

At Bell's Mill Road (2.1 miles), find a corner picnic area and trail option. Hikers may continue north via the crosswalk another 0.6 mile to Andorra Nature Center and the Tree House Visitor Center, where a system of nature trails, trail information, and chemical toilets are available. Or, for the loop alone, turn right and cross the road bridge.

The described tour includes the 1.2-mile, round-trip spur to Andorra Nature Center. Upon return to Bell's Mill Road, cross the road bridge and follow the east bank downstream at 3.3 miles. Multiple colors blaze the start; follow the orange blazes.

The wide trail rolls along some 30 feet above shore. At 3.6 miles, sentinel tulip poplars dazzle with diameters in excess of 4 feet. Cross a concrete bridge over a large side creek and bear right. Younger trees briefly clad the slope.

Keep to the east shore, hiking past the covered bridge for a second time. The trail proceeds forward to round an abandoned stone structure and tour a grassy bench. Back amid woods, dark rock outcrops bring visual interest. At 4.3 miles, descend the steps through a picturesque stone archway and cross a stone bridge over a cascading side-creek to resume southbound travel on the Orange Trail. Hikers wishing to avoid an upcoming rocky area on the Orange Trail should instead cross to Forbidden Road and backtrack the hike's start.

Where the Orange Trail again bears right at 4.5 miles, find more rhododendron and the addition of hemlocks. When conditions are wet, be especially cautious scrambling over the rock outcrops. Cross a pair of side creeks and bear right to cross Wissahickon Creek on the Valley Green Road bridge. Conclude the hike at 5.5 miles.

75 John Heinz National Wildlife Refuge at Tinicum

OVERVIEW

This 1,200-acre national wildlife refuge (NWR) protects the largest remaining freshwater tidal marsh in the state of Pennsylvania. The drone of Interstate 95, the roar from Philadelphia International Airport, and an encroaching industrial skyline, all demonstrate how close the state came to losing this vital piece of natural history. Besides the tidal marsh, the refuge encompasses a 145-acre impoundment pond, braided creeks, non-tidal marsh, old fields, and woods. Together, they provide critical nesting and resting habitat for birds and other wildlife. A network of trails invites hikers to explore. Tidal influenced Darby Creek hosts a 4.5-mile canoe trail only navigable between the 2 hours preceding and 2 hours following high tide.

General description:	Hikers travel service road, boardwalk, and foot trail, exploring the refuge and visiting observation decks and blinds. Carry binoculars and guidebooks.
General location:	10 miles southwest of the heart of Philadelphia.
Special attractions:	Freshwater marsh and estuarine stream habitats, bird and other wildlife sightings, wildflowers and aquatic plants (Check the refuge calendar of "Phenological Events" to see what wildlife is arriving or nesting and what plants should be in bloom.)
Length:	8.2 miles for a barbell-shaped tour. Shorter hike options exist.
Elevation:	Terrain and trails are virtually flat.
Difficulty:	Easy to moderate.
Maps:	Refuge trail map.
Special concerns:	Carry drinking water. Keep to trails and keep pets leashed. No swimming, hunting, collecting, or fires. Anglers, please note the fish in Darby Creek are contaminated.
Season and hours:	Year-round, 8 a.m. to sunset. Visitor Center: 9 a.m. to 4 p.m.
For information:	John Heinz National Wildlife Refuge at Tinicum.

Finding the trailhead: From the junction of Bartram Avenue and 84th Street, north of I-95 and Philadelphia International Airport, go northwest on 84th Street for 0.7 mile and turn left on Lindbergh Boulevard. Go 0.2 mile and turn right on 86th Street to enter the refuge via gravel road.

The hikes: From the parking area at the end of the refuge road past the small information station, take the gated service road straight ahead toward the observation tower. The hike's return will be via the service road on the left. To the right, find a dock and the canoe access to slow-moving Darby Creek.

The service road passes between Darby Creek and the large open marsh of the impoundment pond. Box elder, silver maple, willow, and locust partially frame travel; poison ivy thrives at the shoulder. Benches welcome wildlife viewing while a few interpretive signs introduce the refuge inhabitants. At 0.2 mile, stairs descend left to a boardwalk that spans the marsh.

Detour left along the boardwalk to a central viewing platform (0.3 mile) for up close viewing of the duckweed, yellow pond lily, and arrowhead. Search for turtles, frogs, snakes, and fish. Darting swallows, red-winged blackbirds, wading egrets, and colorful dragonflies may add to a visit. For a 0.5-mile loop, continue across the boardwalk to the east shore of the impoundment where a foot trail returns north.

For the full refuge tour, turn back at the viewing bench, and resume travel south along the impoundment's west shore. Areas of phragmites (plumed reeds), purple loosestrife, and cattail vary the texture of the refuge landscape. While the city backdrop is loud, the natural attractions win over travelers and the service roads allow for carefree strolling.

At 0.8 mile reach a bi-level observation tower for open-water looks. Keen-eyed travelers may spy turtle snouts barely breaking the water's surface. Small islands dot the south end of the impoundment. At 1.4 miles, follow a spur to the right to a wildlife viewing blind that overlooks a richly textured open tidal marsh. Observe tern, cormorant, heron, geese, and gulls.

Marsh observation platform, John Heinz National Wildlife Refuge at Tinicum.

John Heinz National Wildlife Refuge at Tinicum

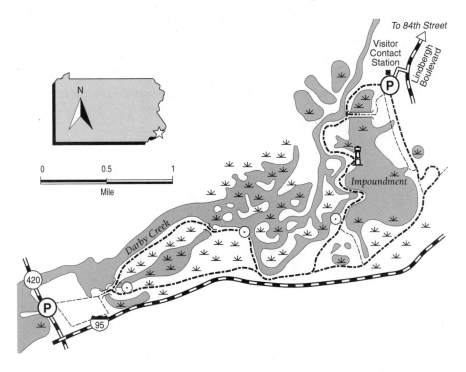

Resume the service road tour; ignoring a foot trail that branches left. Travel now is on 2-track through wildflower grassland. Reach a T-junction (1.8 miles), and turn right to explore the western refuge. A left completes the impoundment loop for a 3.8-mile hike.

Noisy I-95 companions westbound travel through an edge community of woods and field. At 2.25 miles bear right on foot trail to the next blind. A jungle growth of vegetation pinches the trail, but the path remains good. Fox or rabbit may be spied while a bench seat offers looks across the marsh to the Philadelphia city skyline. At 2.4 miles is the wildlife blind.

The barbell-shaped tour continues west past the blind, still on a vegetation-squeezed footpath. View open water, textured marsh, a sea of phragmites, and perhaps an egret flying low in the distance. A few silver maple and willow lend partial shade to the dike. At a bridge crossing at 2.9 miles, enjoy unobstructed looks at an open water channel. Rustles betray wildlife, and a muskrat may part the water.

By 3.5 miles look for the trail to clear and widen for easier walking. The wetland landscape undergoes change. At 4.1 miles, cross a tiered bridge over a second channel, coming to a junction. Bear left for the barbell-shaped tour; the right leads to a parking area on PA 420.

Ahead the trail bends left to parallel I-95 east back across the refuge.

Find the next observation blind on the left; it overlooks open water and a pond-lily marsh. Past the blind stretches shadeless travel. At 4.9 miles and 5.7 miles, pass through gates. Scattered nesting platforms and boxes facilitate nature.

At 5.75 miles proceed forward to close the west-end loop. Then at 6.2 miles (the 1.8-mile junction), proceed forward to complete the impoundment loop. Gradually trees return, bringing partial shade to the service road. Remain on the service road to return along the wooded east shore of the impoundment pond. Avoid foot trails that branch left. A few wetland views sign off the tour, which ends at 8.2 miles.

APPENDIX A—HIKER'S CHECKLIST

Not every item on this checklist will be needed for every trip, so customize the list based on your needs and comforts, the duration of the outing, weather, and the unexpected. Use this list as an organizing tool for planning, packing, and minimizing oversights. Feel free to pencil in items that you find critical to a successful trip.

Ten Essentials

- [ ] extra food
- [ ] extra clothing
- [ ] sunglasses
- [ ] knife
- [ ] firestarter
- [ ] matches in waterproof container
- [ ] first-aid kit and manual
- [ ] flashlight
- [ ] map(s) for the trail
- [ ] compass

Clothing

- [ ] lightweight underwear
- [ ] longjohns
- [ ] under socks
- [ ] wool boot socks
- [ ] long pants
- [ ] shorts
- [ ] long-sleeved shirt
- [ ] T-shirts
- [ ] wool sweater or shirt
- [ ] wool hat and gloves
- [ ] visor or cap
- [ ] raingear
- [ ] warm coat or parka
- [ ] belt
- [ ] bandanna
- [ ] swimsuit or trunks
- [ ] hiking boots
- [ ] sneakers or camp shoes

Personal Items

- [ ] contacts or eyeglasses
- [ ] comb
- [ ] toothpaste and brush
- [ ] biodegradable soap/towelettes
- [ ] towel
- [ ] nail clipper and tweezers
- [ ] facial tissue or handkerchief
- [ ] toilet paper and trowel
- [ ] sunscreen and lip balm
- [ ] insect repellent
- [ ] wallet and keys
- [ ] emergency medical information
- [ ] watch

Gear

- [ ] water bottles
- [ ] pack(s)
- [ ] tent, with required poles and pegs
- [ ] ground cloth
- [ ] sleeping bag and foam pad
- [ ] stove and fuel
- [ ] pots and eating utensils
- [ ] can opener
- [ ] rope
- [ ] stuff bags
- [ ] large trash bags for emergency shelter for self or gear
- [ ] plastic bags for trash
- [ ] zip-locked bags for foodstuffs
- [ ] aluminum foil

Food

- [ ] 3 meals, plus snacks for each day
- [ ] extra food for delays
- [ ] salt/pepper
- [ ] vegetable oil
- [ ] drink mixes

Health & Safety Items

- [ ] medications
- [ ] emergency blanket
- [ ] water pump or purification tablets
- [ ] whistle
- [ ] pencil and paper
- [ ] picture wire for emergency repairs

Miscellaneous

- [ ] mosquito netting
- [ ] binoculars
- [ ] camera and film
- [ ] guidebooks
- [ ] identification books
- [ ] fishing gear and valid license

APPENDIX B—FURTHER READING

Appalachian Hiker II by Ed Garvey. Appalachian Books.

Appalachian Trail Guide to Pennsylvania, Ninth Edition edited by Maurice J. Forrester, Jr. Keystone Trails Association.

Backpacking One Step at a Time, Fourth Edition by Harvey Manning. Random House.

The Basic Essentials of Map and Compass by Cliff Jacobson. ICS Books.

Be Expert with Map and Compass by Bjorn Kjellstrom. Charles Scribner's Sons.

A Child's Introduction to the Outdoors by David Richey. Pagurian Press Limited.

The Complete Walker III by Colin Fletcher. Alfred A. Knopf.

A Field Guide to the Birds by Roger Tory Peterson. Houghton Mifflin Co.

Fifty Hikes in Central Pennsylvania by Tom Thwaites. Backcountry Publications.

Fifty Hikes in Eastern Pennsylvania by Carolyn Hoffman. Backcountry Publications.

Fifty Hikes in Western Pennsylvania by Tom Thwaites. Backcountry Publications.

Finding Your Way in the Outdoors by Robert L. Mooers, Jr. E.P. Hutton Co., Inc.

A Guide to Field Identification: Wildflowers of North America by Frank D. Venning. Golden Press.

Guide to the National Wildlife Refuges by Laura and William Riley. Collier Books.

Guide to The Susquehannock Trail System, Second Edition by Chuck Dillon. Pine Creek Press, Publisher.

Mountaineering First Aid, Third Edition by Martha J. Lentz, Steven C. Macdonald, and Jan D. Carline. The Mountaineers.

Mountaineering Medicine by Fred T. Darvill. Wilderness Press.

Pennsylvania Hiking Trails, Eleventh Edition-1993. Keystone Trails Association.

The Shrub Identification Book by George W.D. Symonds. William Morrow and Company.

Travel Light Handbook by Judy Keene. Contemporary Books.

Wild Country Companion: The Ultimate Guide to No-trace Outdoor Recreation and Wilderness Safety by Will Harmon. Falcon Publishing Co., Inc.

Wilderness Basics: The Complete Handbook for Hikers and Backpackers, Second Edition by the San Diego Chapter of the Sierra Club. The Mountaineers.

APPENDIX C—WHERE TO FIND MAPS

For trail maps produced by the managing agencies, contact the information source indicated in the trail summary. The complete address and phone number for each source is listed in Appendix D.

For copies of United States Geological Survey topographic quadrangles (USGS quads), check at libraries, at most backpacking and mountaineering stores, or at specialty maps and publications stores. Study the Pennsylvania state index to identify the name of the quad(s) that cover the area of interest. Or, contact the United States Geological Survey Map Distribution Center, Box 25286 Federal Center, Building 41, Denver, CO 80225; ask for the Pennsylvania index and price list.

To obtain a variety of state maps and books on the state's geology and natural history, contact the Pennsylvania State Book Store, Department of General Services, 1825 Stanley Drive, Harrisburg, PA 17103; 717-787-5109.

The Keystone Trails Association (KTA) monitors government action and proposals that relate to or impact trails or the sport of hiking. The organization publishes a number of maps and guides and helps coordinate trail maintenance and hiking club activities throughout the state.

For information on becoming a member or for ordering the Keystone Trails Association maps or books, including the most current edition of Pennsylvania Hiking Trails, contact Keystone Trails Association, P.O. Box 251, Cogan Station, PA 17728-0251.

APPENDIX D—LAND MANAGEMENT LISTINGS

Allegheny National Forest
P.O. Box 847
222 Liberty Street
Warren, PA 16365
814-723-5150

Appalachian Trail Conference
P.O. Box 807
Washington and Storer
College Place
Harpers Ferry, WV 25425
304-535-6331. For orders only,
dial toll free: 1-888-ATSTORE.

Bald Eagle State Forest
District Headquarters
P.O. Box 147
Laurelton, PA 17835-0147
717-524-4373 or 717-922-3344

Beechwood Farms Nature Reserve
614 Dorseyville Road
Pittsburgh, PA 15238
412-963-6100

Bradford Ranger District
Allegheny National Forest
Star Route 1, Box 88
Bradford, PA 16701
814-362-4613

Buchanon State Forest
District Headquarters
R.R. 2, Box 3
McConnellsburg, PA 17233
717-485-3148

Buck County Department of
Parks and Recreation
901 East Bridgetown Pike
Langhorne, PA 19047
215-757-0571

Caledonia State Park
40 Rocky Mountain Road
Fayetteville, PA 17222
717-352-2161

Colonel Denning State Park
1599 Doubling Gap Road
Newville, PA 17241
717-776-5272

Cook Forest State Park
P.O. Box 120 (River Road)
Cooksburg, PA 16217
814-744-8407

Cowans Gap State Park
H.C. 17266
Fort Loudon, PA 17224-9801
717-485-3948

Delaware Canal State Park
Box 615 A
R.R. 1
Upper Black Eddy, PA 18972
610-982-5560

Delaware State Forest
District Headquarters
HC 1, Box 95A
Swiftwater, PA 18370-9723
717-895-4000

Delaware Water Gap National
Recreation Area
Bushkill, PA 18324
717-588-2451

Drake Well Museum
R.D. 3
Titusville, PA 16354
814-827-2797

Elk State Forest
District Headquarters
P.O. Box 327
Emporium, PA 15834
814-486-3353

Erie National Wildlife Refuge
11296 Wood Duck Lane
Guys Mills, PA 16327
814-789-3585

Fairmount Park Commission
Memorial Hall
West Park
P.O. Box 21601
Philadelphia, PA 19131-0901
215-685-0000

Forbes State Forest
District Office
P.O. Box 519
Laughlintown, PA 15655
412-238-9533

French Creek State Park
843 Park Road
Elverson, PA 19520
610-582-9680

Friendship Hill
National Historic Site
R.D. 1, Box 149-A
Point Marion, PA 15474
412-725-9190

Gallitzin State Forest
District Headquarters
155 Hillcrest Drive
P.O. Box 506
Ebensburg, PA 15931
814-472-1862

Hawk Mountain
Sanctuary Association
1700 Hawk Mountain Road
Kempton, PA 19529-9449
610-756-6961
www.hawkmountain.org

Hopewell Furnace
National Historic Site
2 Mark Bird Lane
Elverson, PA 19520
610-582-8773

Jennings Environmental
Education Center
2951 Prospect Road
Slippery Rock, PA 16057-8701
412-794-6011

John Heinz National Wildlife
Refuge at Tinicum
Refuge Headquarters
Scott Plaza II
Suite 104
Philadelphia, PA 19113
610-521-0662

Keystone Trails Association
P.O. Box 251
Cogan Station, PA 17728

Kings Gap Environmental
Education and Training Center
500 Kings Gap Road
Carlisle, PA 17013
717-486-5031

Lackawanna State Forest
District Headquarters
401 Samters Building
101 Penn Avenue
Scranton, PA 18503
717-963-4561

Lake Wallenpaupack
Pennsylvania Power and Light
Company
P.O. Box 122
Hawley, PA 18428-0122
717-226-3702

Laurel Ridge State Park
R.D. 3, Box 246
Rockwood, PA 15557
412-455-3744

Lehigh Gorge State Park
c/o Hickory Run State Park
R.R. 1, Box 81
White Haven, PA 18661
717-427-5000

Linn Run/Laurel
Mountain Complex
P.O. Box 50
Rector, PA 15677-0030
412-238-6623

Little Pine State Park
HC 63, Box 100
Waterville, PA 17776-9705
717-753-6000

Marienville Ranger District
Allegheny National Forest
HC 2, Box 130
Marienville, PA 16239
814-927-6628

McConnell's Mill State Park
R.R. 2, Box 16
Portersville, PA 16051-9401
412-368-8091 or 368-8811

Mid State Trail Association
P.O. Box 167
Boalsburg, PA 16827

Middle Creek Wildlife
Management Area
P.O. Box 110
Kleinfeltersville, PA 17039
717-733-1512

Mill Grove–Audubon
Wildlife Sanctuary
Audubon and Pawlings Roads
P.O. Box 7125
Audubon, PA 19407
610-666-5593

Montour Preserve
R.R. 1, Box 292
Turbotville, PA 17772-9500
717-437-3131

Nolde Forest Environmental
Education Center
2910 New Holland Road
Reading PA 19607
610-775-1411

Northcentral Region Headquarters
Pennsylvania Game Commission
P.O. Box 5038
Jersey Shore, PA 17740
717-398-4774
1-800-422-7551

Ohiopyle State Park
P.O. Box 105
Ohiopyle, PA 15470-0105
412-329-8591

Oil Creek State Park
R.R. 1, Box 207
Oil City, PA 16301-9733
814-676-5915

Oil Creek State Park Bike Rentals
814-677-4684

Oil Creek and Titusville Railroad
P.O. Box 68
Oil City, PA 16301
814-676-1733

Pennsylvania Power
and Light Company
Holtwood Land Management
Office
9 New Village Road
Holtwood, PA 17532
717-284-2278

Pennypack Ecological
Restoration Trust
2955 Edge Hill Road
Huntingdon Valley, PA 19006-5099
215-657-0830

Pine Creek Outfitters
R.R. 4, Box 130B
Wellsboro, PA 16901
717-724-3003

Pocono Environmental
Education Center (PEEC)
R.D. 2, Box 1010
Dingmans Ferry, PA 18328-9614

Potomac Appalachian Trail Club
118 Park Street SE
Vienna, VA 22180
703-242-0315

Potter County Recreation Inc.
P.O. Box 245
Coudersport, PA 16915
814-435-2290

Presque Isle State Park
Department of Conservation and
Natural Resources
P.O. Box 8510
Erie, PA 16505-0510
814-833-7424

Promised Land State Park
R.R. 1, Box 96
Greentown, PA 18426
717-676-3428

Raccoon Creek State Park
3000 State Route 18
Hookstown, PA 15050
park office: 412-899-2200
nature center: 412-899-3611

Rails-to-Trails of
Blair County
Inc.
P.O. Box 592
Hollidaysburg, PA 16648-0592

Ralph Stover State Park
6011 State Park Road
Pipersville, PA 18947

Raystown Lake
U.S. Army Corps of Engineers
R.R. 1, Box 222
Hesston, PA 16647
814-658-3405

Ricketts Glen State Park
R.R. 2, Box 130
Benton, PA 17814-8900

717-477-5675

Rothrock State Forest
District Headquarters
Rothrock Lane
P.O. Box 403
Huntingdon, PA 16652
814-643-2340

Ryerson Station State Park
R.D. 1, Box 77
Wind Ridge, PA 15380
412-428-4254

S.B. Elliott State Park
c/o Parker Dam State Park
R.D. 1, Box 165
Penfield, PA 15849-9799
814-765-0630

Seneca Highlands Association
Drawer G
10 East Warren Road
Custer City, PA 16725
814-624-7802

Shenango Conservancy
94 E. Shenango Street
Sharpsville, PA 16150

Shenango Lake Resource Manager
2442 Kelly Road
Hermitage, PA 16150
412-962-4384

Shenango Outing Club
P.O. Box 244
Greenville, PA 16125

Sizerville State Park
R.R. 1, Box 238-A
Emporium, PA 15834-9608
814-486-5605

Snyders–Middleswarth State Park
c/o Reeds Gap State Park
R.D. 1, Box 276-A
Milroy, PA 17063
717-667-3622

Sproul State Forest
District Headquarters
HCR 62, Box 90
Renovo, PA 17764
717-923-6011

Stone Valley Recreation Area
The Pennsylvania State University
108 Business Services Building
University Park, PA 16802-1002
814-863-0762
http://www.psu.edu/Stone_Valley

Susquehanna Riverlands
R.R. 1, Box 1797
Berwick, PA 18603
717-542-2306

Susquehannock State Forest
District Headquarters
P.O. Box 673
Coudersport, PA 16915
814-274-8474

The Susquehannock Trail Club
P.O. Box 643
Coudersport, PA 16915

Tiadaghton State Forest
District Headquarters
423 E. Central Avenue
South Williamsport, PA 17701
717-327-3450

Tioga State Forest
District Headquarters
P.O. Box 94
Route 287 S.
Wellsboro, PA 16901
717-724-2868

Tuscarora State Forest
District Headquarters
R.D. 1, Box 42-A
Blain, PA 17006
717-536-3191

U.S. Army Corps of Engineers
Tioga–Hammond Lakes
R.R. 1, Box 65
Tioga, PA 16946-9733
717-835-5281

Worlds End State Park
P.O. Box 62
Forksville, PA 18616-0062
717-924-3287

Wyoming State Forest
District Headquarters
P.O. Box 439
Bloomsburg, PA 17815
717-387-4255

The Yough River Trail Council
P.O. Box 988
Connellsville, PA 15425
412-628-5500

About the Authors

Over the past seventeen years, the Ostertags, Rhonda (a writer) and George (a photographer), have collaborated on two eastern hiking guidebooks and five western outdoor guidebooks; sold hundreds of articles on topics of nature, travel, and outdoor recreation; and participated in environmental impact studies. They have once again pointed their boots east, with *Hiking Pennsylvania*.

After hiking more than 2,500 miles of trail within Penn's Woods, the couple knows the state of Pennsylvania and speaks from first-hand knowledge of the trail. Other titles by this team include *Hiking New York* (1996) and *Hiking Southern New England* (1997), both with Falcon, and *California State Parks: A Complete Recreation Guide* (1995) and *100 Hikes in Oregon* (1992) with The Mountaineers, Seattle, Washington.

Index

S

S. B. Elliott State Park, 87-91, *89*
Salmon Creek Loop, 71, 73, *73,* 74-75
Sand Mountain Fire Tower, 163
Sawmill Trail, 196
Scenic Vista Trail, 274, *275,* 276-77
School Spur, 243
Scrub Oak Trail, 108
Seldom Seen Trail, 73, *73,* 74
Self-guided Historic Site Trail, 270-71, 273
Self-guided Interpretive Trail, 14
Semans Trail, *63,* 66
Seneca Division, 20
Seneca Falls, 103
Seneca Trail, 79, *81,* 82-83
Shaver's Creek Environmental Center, 193
Shaver's Creek Trail, *194,* 196
Shaver's Creek-Wood's Route Loop, 193, *194,*
  196
Shawnee Falls, 103
Sheldon Reynolds Falls, 102
Shenango Reservoir, 29
Shenango Trail, 30, *31,* 32, 33
Shenango Trail System, 29-33, *31*
Shuman Point Natural Area Hiking Trail,
  97-99, *98*
Sidewalk Trail, 14, 15, *17,* 18-19
Silver Thread Falls, 116
Sinnemahoning Creek, 56
  Bennett Branch of, 87
Sizerville Nature Trail, 54-56, *55*
Sizerville State Park, 54-56, *55*
Skyline Trail, 259
Slippery Rock Gorge Trail, 174, *175,* 176-77
Smiths Knob, **150**
  Loyalsock Trail to, 148-50, *149*
Snowy Mountain, 254
Somerset-Westmoreland County Line
  Monument (1923), 213
Songbird Sojourn Interpretive Trail, 75, 78
South Cutoff, 241
South Fork Trail, 89, 91
South Loop (Allegheny National Forest
  Region), 76-78, *77*
South Loop (Pocono Mountains Region), 124,
  126
South Mountain, 254, 274, 279
Southern Loop, 302, 304
Spice Bush Short-cut, 126, 127
Spring Hollow Walk, 188, *189,* 189-90
Spruce Trail, 270
Stahl Cemetery, 222, **223**
Steel Hollow Trail, *63,* 67
Stevens, Thaddeus, 280

Stone Valley Recreation Area, 193-97, *194*
Stony Mountain, 252
Sugar Lake Division, 20
Sugarloaf Knob, 211
Sugarloaf Trail, 231
Sunrise-Scenic Gorge Trail, 120, *121,* 123-24
Susquehanna River, 252
Susquehanna Riverlands, 124-28, *125*
Susquehannock Trail, 4
Susquehannock Trail Club, 58
Susquehannock Trail System, 57-61, *59*

T

Tall Timbers Trail, 165-67, *166*
Tatman Run Recreation Area, 204, 207
Tebolt Trail, 244
Telephone Trail, 200
Terrace Mountain Trail, 204-8, *206*
Thaddeus Stevens Historical Trail, 280, *281*
Thaddeus Stevens Historical Trail-Charcoal
  Hearth Trail Loop, 279, 280, *281*
Theodore Roosevelt Recreation and
  Conservation Area, 288
Thick Mountain Trail, 166
Thompson-Neeley homesite, 290
Three Mitten Trail, 221, *222,* 223
Thunder Swamp Trail System, 111
Tiadaghton Primitive Camp, 70
Tiffany Ridge Trail, 224
Tinicum Buck County Park, 288
Toddler's Trail, 190
Tohickon Creek, 291, *292,* 293
Tohickon Valley Trail, 291-93, *293*
Towpath Trail, 32, 124, *125,* 127
Tracy Ridge Campground, 35
Tracy Ridge Trail, 34, *35,* 35-36
Tracy Ridge-Johnnycake Loop, 34-37, *35*
Travis Trail, 185
Tree House Visitor Center, 302, 306
Trents Hill, 254
Trough Creek State Park, 204, *206*
Tsuga Nature Trail, 20, 23-24
Tumbling Waters Trail, 120, *121,* 122
Tunnel Trail, 167-70, *169*
Turkey Path, 68
Tuscarora Falls, 103
Tuscarora Mountain, 234, 235, 236
  South, 237-39
Tuscarora Trail, 4, 192, 234, *235,* 236,
  237-39, *238,* 260, 262-63
Tuscarora Trail System, 237
Tussey Mountain, 195, 196, 246
Two Ponds Trail, 120, *121,* 122
Two Ponds-Tumbling Waters Trail, 120, *121*